D0153352

THE DICTIONARY OF CONTEMPORARY POLITICS OF SOUTH AMERICA

THE DICTIONARY OF CONTEMPORARY POLITICS OF SOUTH AMERICA

Phil Gunson, Andrew Thompson, and Greg Chamberlain

Macmillan Publishing Company
New York

First American edition published in 1989 by
Macmillan Publishing Company,
A Division of Macmillan, Inc.

Macmillan Publishing Company
866 Third Avenue, New York, NY 10022

First published in Great Britain by Routledge,
A Division of Routledge, Chapman and Hall Ltd.

Library of Congress Catalog Card No.: 88-27185

Printed in Great Britain

printing number
1 2 3 4 5 6 7 8 9 10

Library of Congress Cataloging-in-Publication Data

Gunson, Phil.
The dictionary of contemporary politics of South America.
Bibliography: p.
1. South America—Politics and government—20th century—Dictionaries. I. Thompson, Andrew, 1953– II. Chamberlain, Greg. III. Title.
JL1851.A25G86 1989 980'.03'03 88-27185
ISBN 0–02–913145–6

Contents

List of maps vii
Introduction ix
Dictionary of Contemporary Politics of South America 1
List of entries by country 309

List of maps

South America	xii
Antarctica	12
Argentina	16
Bolivia	35
Brazil	43
Chile	57
Colombia	67
Ecuador	101
Guyana	136
Paraguay	210
Peru	225
Suriname	275
Uruguay	291
Venezuela	299

Introduction

Anyone compiling a guide to a whole continent's worth of shifting political sands becomes accustomed to a number of standard responses. Among the most common is, 'But it'll all be out of date two weeks after you've finished!' It is of course true that by the time you pick this book off the shelf the political landscape of all the countries described will have changed, whether subtly or dramatically. Alliances will have been broken and new ones forged. Leaders will have been ousted or voted from office, and some may even be dead. In some cases, the consensus wisdom of the pundits may have been turned on its head. To a hi-tech generation increasingly accustomed to 'real-time' information, 'contemporary politics' may simply be yesterday's news. So what is the purpose of trying to capture it in print before it can be safely filed away as history?

To pose this question is to realise that there is no easy distinction between the contemporary and the historical. All history, and especially that of our own century, is open to constant reinterpretation, either in the light of new evidence or simply according to the scholarship and prejudices of the age. And the *perception* of past events plays a critical role in shaping our view of the present. Shorn of its historical context, the contemporary scene is a bewildering mass of raw data upon which the ill-informed (or worse, the cynical manipulator of opinions) can superimpose a convenient pattern. An uprising born of centuries of injustice, to take one example, can so easily appear the product of a foreign conspiracy when commentators look no further than a superficially peaceful yesterday.

In compiling this volume, the authors have therefore chosen to go beyond the immediate past and pick out some of the themes, events and personalities of preceding decades. The reader will find not just an entry on Peronism as a contemporary phenomenon but one on the late General Perón. The chaos of present-day Colombia is illuminated by entries on the 'violencia' of the 1940s and 1950s; while the astonishing political longevity of President Alfredo Stroessner is traced to the little-known Paraguayan civil war of 1947.

As journalists we are well aware that information is not value-free, and that even the process of selecting seemingly incontrovertible 'facts' involves interpretation. But while not altogether eschewing the expression of opinion, we have sought as far as possible to identify it as such, and to reflect genuine controversies where these exist.

The decision as to what to leave out is always the most difficult one, and most readers are bound to find themselves occasionally cursing the omission of just that entry which would have resolved the question of the moment. Our main criterion – given the inevitable pressure on space – has always been the likely frequency with which a particular entry would be consulted. On the whole we have opted for fewer, longer entries rather than a greater number of short ones, on the grounds that the former are likely to be more useful.

The comparative length of entries is a rough guide to the importance we feel the subject merits, although in some cases it simply reflects the organisation of the material. While some items which might have had their own entries are grouped together, in other cases an important entry has been cut to avoid duplication. The system of cross-referencing and single-line entries should eliminate the need for guesswork on the reader's part.

There was a time, not so long ago, when ignorance about Latin America was almost flaunted by politicians in the northern hemisphere. Before the 1982 South Atlantic war a British minister in charge of relations with the region could shamelessly admit to almost total ignorance of its politics. Before armed conflict broke out in Central America, even a globetrotter like Henry Kissinger was noted for his dismissive attitude to anything south of the Mexican border. When the first Sandinista government delegation arrived in the Soviet Union, officials were said to be unsure whether they spoke Spanish or Portuguese. Nowadays the political and economic importance of the region is more widely recognised, but it would be idle to pretend that ignorance and prejudice have been vanquished. One book can do little to change that, but it can at least provide a start for those genuinely concerned to see beyond the clichés.

The authors would like to acknowledge the generous assistance given by a number of specialists in the region who suggested changes in particular entries. They include Jon Barnes, Sue Branford, John Crabtree, James Dunkerley, Hugo Martinez Viademonte, Jan Rocha, James Painter, María Costa Pinto, Luis Nin Estevez. We would also like to thank the staff of the Latin America Bureau in London, and in particular Raquel Caravia, for their guidance in finding useful sources. Any errors are, of course, our own responsibility.

London, July 1988

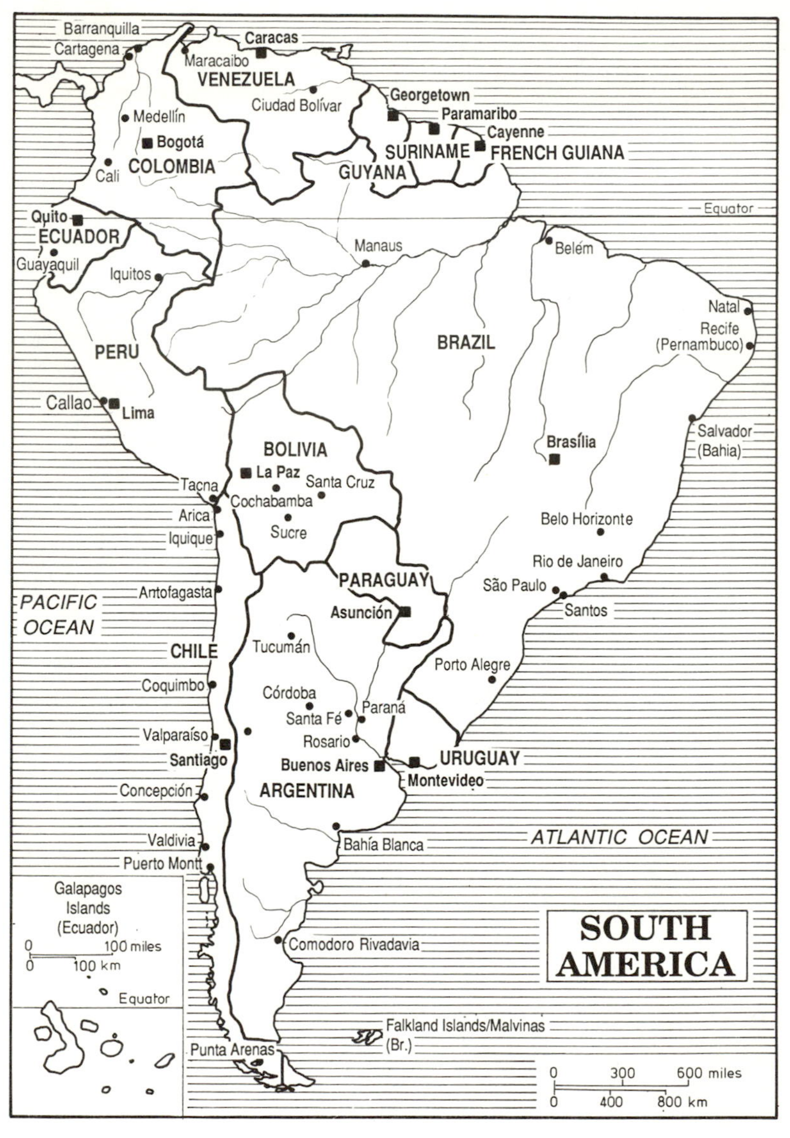
Barranquilla
Cartagena
Caracas
Maracaibo
VENEZUELA
Ciudad Bolívar
Georgetown
Paramaribo
Cayenne
Medellín
Bogotá
COLOMBIA
Cali
SURINAME
FRENCH GUIANA
GUYANA
Equator
Quito
ECUADOR
Guayaquil
Iquitos
Manaus
Belém
Natal
Recife
(Pernambuco)
PERU
BRAZIL
Callao
Lima
Salvador
(Bahia)
Brasília
BOLIVIA
La Paz
Santa Cruz
Tacna
Cochabamba
Arica
Sucre
Iquique
Belo Horizonte
Rio de Janeiro
São Paulo
Santos
Antofagasta
PARAGUAY
Asunción
PACIFIC
OCEAN
CHILE
Tucumán
Porto Alegre
Coquimbo
Córdoba
Paraná
Santa Fé
Valparaíso
Rosario
Santiago
Buenos Aires
URUGUAY
Montevideo
Concepción
ARGENTINA
ATLANTIC OCEAN
Valdivia
Bahía Blanca
Puerto Montt
Galapagos
Islands
(Ecuador)
0
100 miles
0
100 km
Equator
SOUTH
AMERICA
Comodoro Rivadavia
Falkland Islands/Malvinas
(Br.)
Punta Arenas
0
300
600 miles
0
400
800 km

Abadía Rey, Adelaida: see **Workers' Self-Defence Movement**.

Abadía Rey, Héctor Fabio: see **Workers' Self-Defence Movement**.

abertura

The Portuguese word for 'opening', *abertura* was used by the Brazilian President Gen. João Figueiredo after he came to power in 1979 to signify the opening out or widening of the closed political system under military rule. Although *abertura* ultimately led to the ending of military rule – Figueiredo was the fifth and last military president after the 1964 coup – it was an uneven and at times contradictory process. The government concentrated its efforts on maintaining control of and manipulating the liberalisation. The 1979 political amnesty, for example, was designed not only to seek conciliation, but also to protect the military from eventual human rights charges and sow dissension in the ranks of the opposition by permitting the return of exiles likely to set up competing parties. Likewise, the political reforms of the same year ended the two-party system, in a move designed to fragment anti-government forces. When it looked as if the opposition – even when split among various groupings – might win, Gen. Figueiredo cancelled municipal elections in November 1980. The main PMDB opposition made important gains in November 1982 in the state and congressional elections, and under the pressure of an economic and foreign debt crisis, strikes, and growing popular mobilisations, Gen. Figueiredo accepted the need for a return to civilian rule. But even then he refused to cede the demands of the *diretas já* campaign, invoking special powers in 1984 to frustrate the attempt to modify the constitution to allow direct elections for his successor.
See also **amnesty (Brazil 1979); Brazilian Democratic Movement Party; *diretas já*; Figueiredo**.

ACHA (Chilean Anti-communist Alliance): see **death squad**.

Action for National Liberation (*Acão Libertadora Nacional*/ALN)

A Brazilian guerrilla organisation set up by Carlos Marighela in the late 1960s. Marighela and other dissident members of the Communist Party (PCB) attended a conference of the Latin American Solidarity Organisation (OLAS) in Cuba in 1967, without party authorisation. They returned convinced of the need to launch an armed struggle against the military regime. The group broke with the PCB and issued a manifesto

stating that 'our main activity is not building a political party, but unleashing revolutionary activity . . . guerrilla activity is itself the command of the revolution . . . the revolutionary's duty is to make revolution'. The ALN began military activities from early 1968. It provided military support in September 1969 for the kidnapping of US ambassador Burke Elbrick (carried out by MR–8) and kidnapped the Swiss ambassador in December 1970. Marighela was killed by the police in November 1969 and his successor, Joaquim Cámara Ferreira, was killed in October 1970. The ALN was one of the larger guerrilla groups active in 1968–71, but like the others it was unable to survive the counter-insurgency onslaught by the security forces.
See also **Brazilian Communist Party; Guerrilla movements** (Brazil); **Marighela; MR–8**.

AD: see **Democratic Action**.

Adams, John Quincy: see **Monroe doctrine**.

adhesionistas: see **Brazilian Democratic Movement**.

Advanced Democracy *(Democracia Avanzada)*: see **Communist Party of Uruguay**.

AFL-CIO: see **American Institute for Free Labor Development**.

Agency for International Development (AID): see **American Institute for Free Labor Development**.

Agrarian Labour Party: see **Frei Montalva, Eduardo**.

Aguirre Cerda, Pedro: see **Popular Front**.

ALADI: see **Latin American Integration Association**.

Albuja, Gen. Manuel: see **Vargas Pazzos rebellion**.

Albuquerque Lima, Gen. Alfonso: see **Authoritarian Nationalists**.

Alende, Oscar: see **Intransigent Party (PI); Radical Party** (Argentina).

Alessandri Palma, Arturo: see **Alessandri Rodríguez; Ibáñez del Campo**.

Alessandri Rodríguez, Jorge
1896–1986. President of Chile 1958–64. Born in Santiago, son of ex-president Arturo Alessandri Palma ('the Lion of Tarapacá') (1920–4 and 1932–8). Attended the School of Engineering, from which he graduated in 1919, obtaining a faculty position. Congressional deputy 1926–30. President of a paper and cardboard manufacturing company in Puente Alto. Minister of finance (1947) under President Gabriel González Videla. Senator 1956–8. Elected president 1958, with the backing of the Conservative Party (PC) and the Liberal Party (PL), together with the 'Doctrinaire' faction of the Radical Party (PR) and other minority parties of the centre in a coalition called the Alliance of Popular Parties and

Forces (dissolved after the election). Alessandri defeated the left's Salvador Allende by only 33,000 votes. In government he attempted, with partial success, to combat inflation by stabilising wages and prices, but severe inflation followed the 1960 earthquake; the peso was devalued and a new currency, the escudo, introduced. A mild agrarian reform law was passed in 1962. He was chosen as presidential candidate of the National Party (PN) in 1970, this time losing by a narrow margin to Salvador Allende, due to the conservative vote being split between the PN and the Christian Democrats, whom the former saw as too radical. He withdrew from politics after the election and was not an enthusiastic supporter of the Pinochet regime, installed after the 1973 coup against Allende, although in 1976 he agreed to participate in Gen. Pinochet's Council of State.
See also **National Party** (Chile).

Alfaro, Gen. Eloy: see **Alfaro Lives!**

Alfaro Lives! (*Alfaro Vive!*)
(aka *Alfaro Vive, Carajo!*, sometimes loosely translated as 'Alfaro Lives, Dammit!', and as the Eloy Alfaro Popular Armed Forces). An Ecuadorean guerrilla organisation, founded in the 1970s but not militarily active until 1984. Named after the author of Ecuador's nineteenth-century Liberal reform, Gen. Eloy Alfaro (president 1895–1901 and 1905–12). Alfaro was a profoundly anti-clerical mestizo leader who dominated Ecuadorean politics until his death in 1912. The Liberals instituted freedom of religion, curbs on Church power, and economic reforms. Alfaro was imprisoned during a brief Conservative resurgence in 1911 and murdered by a mob in 1912. *Alfaro Vive* is thought to have under 1,000 members. It has strong links with Colombian and Peruvian guerrillas (M–19 and *Túpac Amaru*), with whom it formed the America Battalion in 1985/86. Four M–19 members were reported to have been among those who died in a gunbattle in Guayaquil in 1985 when troops sought to rescue an Ecuadorean banker kidnapped by *Alfaro Vive*.

The organisation claims to be left wing (but non-Marxist) nationalist, and to identify with the parties of the Democratic Left (ID) in Congress. Its aims include the nationalisation of foreign oil investments, banks and foreign trade. In May 1986 it said it would end armed actions if the government resolved the country's economic problems and strengthened democracy. The Febres government claimed that members had received training in Nicaragua and Libya. The AV leadership says no links exist with the *Montoneras Patria Libre*, the other Ecuadorean guerrilla group, whom it accuses of 'adventurism'. Top leader Arturo Jarrín ('Ricardo') was killed in a gunbattle in October 1986, bringing deaths of key members to three in 10 months.
See also **America Battalion; Free Nation Montoneras**.

Alfonsín, Dr Raúl
b. 1926. An Argentine Radical Party (UCR) politician and lawyer who was elected president in 1983 after the collapse of the Process of National

Reorganisation (PRN) military regime. Born in Chascomús, province of Buenos Aires, he graduated from the Universidad Nacional de La Plata as a lawyer. He joined the UCR in 1944. Elected a Chascomús municipal councillor in 1950, he went on to sit on the Buenos Aires province legislature in 1952. Alfonsín was imprisoned briefly by the Peronist government in 1953. He was elected to the Chamber of Deputies in 1963, and retained this position until the military coup in 1966. In the same year Alfonsín founded the Renovation and Change Movement (*Movimiento de Renovación y Cambio*), which emerged as a left of centre tendency within the UCR, initially in a minority. He stood unsuccessfully for the UCR presidential nomination in 1973. In that year's elections he was again chosen to sit in the Chamber of Deputies and remained a member until the military coup in 1976.

During the ensuing Process of National Reorganisation regime, Alfonsín spoke out against human rights violations. He became president of the Permanent Assembly of Human Rights. He was also one of the few politicians publicly critical of the decision by the administration of Gen. Leopoldo Galtieri to occupy the Falklands/Malvinas islands by force in April 1982. In December 1982 he forged an internal UCR alliance between his Renovation and Change Movement and the 'Córdoba line' branch of the party; this allowed him to obtain both the nomination and the presidency of the party. An intensely fought political campaign, together with his image as a man committed to respecting civil rights, are credited for his victory over the Peronist candidate, Dr Italo Lúder, in the elections held on 30 October 1983. During and after the campaign Alfonsín argued that his objective was to end the half-century-old cycle of militarism and political instability in the country, creating a modern democracy. After taking office on 10 December 1983, he announced the state prosecution of nine former members of military juntas (including three former presidents) on charges ranging from murder through to the disappearance of political opponents. Sentences were delivered in December 1985, and included life imprisonment for two of the accused. Dr Alfonsín also replaced many senior officers. But after a military uprising in April 1987 he was forced to make concessions to army demands for an end to the human rights trials, by introducing legislation on 'due obedience'.

In June 1985, after inflation had grown to an annual rate of 1,200%, Alfonsín introduced the Austral austerity programme, and created a new currency of the same name. The programme succeeded in bringing inflation down below 100% in 1986, but thereafter it began increasing again. In 1986, he proposed a plan to move the federal capital from Buenos Aires to the town of Viedma in Patagonia, as part of a package of constitutional reforms to overcome the over-centralisation of the economic and political system. But after the UCR lost its congressional majority in the September 1987 elections, Alfonsín was forced to drop most of these reforms.

See also **Austral: due obedience; Radical Party** (Argentina).

Allamand, Andrés: see **Party of National Renovation**.

Allende Gossens, Dr Salvador

1908–73. President of Chile 1970–3. Born in Valparaíso, the son of a lawyer. Medical degree from the University of Chile School of Medicine (1926–32). His involvement in politics as a student led to his expulsion from the university, but after the overthrow of President Carlos Ibañez (aided by street demonstrations in which Allende took part) he completed his degree. He was a house doctor at a Valparaíso hospital during the short-lived Socialist Republic of Marmaduke Grove (1932), to whom he was related by marriage. Arrested and tried after its fall, but acquitted after five trials, Allende was to be imprisoned twice and exiled once in his life for political activities. A founder member of the Chilean Socialist Party (PS) in 1933, he was elected deputy for Quillotín and Valparaíso in 1937. In 1938 he was the Valparaíso organiser of the presidential campaign of Popular Front candidate Pedro Aguirre Cerda, and the following year he became minister of health in Aguirre's government. During his tenure he introduced health insurance and accident compensation for workers and special benefits for working mothers and their children.

Elected senator for different areas of the country four times (1945–70), he was also vice-president of the senate for five years and its president for two (1968–9). From 1943 he was secretary general of the PS. On three successive occasions he was an unsuccessful candidate for the presidency of Chile: in 1952 (6% of the vote), 1958 (29%) and 1964 (39%). In 1955 he became president of the National Front of the People left-wing coalition, but he was elected president of the republic in 1970 as the candidate of the broad left Popular Unity (UP) coalition. He had to be confirmed in office by Congress due to his lack of an overall majority. Before taking office, Allende declared his main objectives to be: the recuperation (nationalisation) of basic resources; radical agrarian reform; nationalisation of banks and credit; and import and export control.

As president he introduced far-reaching economic and social reforms, including the nationalisation of the banks and of strategic resources such as the copper mines, as well as extensive agrarian reform, though he was hampered by the opposition majority in Congress. UP increased its share of the vote during his presidency, but political polarisation became extreme, with the left (both within and outside UP) accusing the government of dragging its feet, while the right organised to overthrow it amid spurious accusations of unconstitutional behaviour. Aided by the US government and US corporations (including ITT and the copper companies), the armed forces staged a successful coup on 11 September 1973. Allende died during the attack on the presidential palace (La Moneda).

See also **Pinochet Ugarte; Popular Unity; Socialist Party of Chile**.

Alliance for Progress

A US-sponsored economic and social development programme for Latin America launched by President John F. Kennedy. The *Alianza para el*

Progreso was largely conceived as a response to the revolutionary threat posed by Fidel Castro's victory in Cuba. Pressure was to be exerted on the continent's conservative elites to grant reforms, to reduce the appeal of revolutionary movements. As proposed by Kennedy, the Alliance was a re-working and broadening of an idea launched by President Juscelino Kubitschek of Brazil in 1958 under the title of 'Operation Pan America'. In a speech to Latin American diplomats on 13 March 1961, Kennedy called on the people of America 'to join in a new alliance for progress . . . a vast cooperative effort, unparalleled in magnitude and nobility of purpose, to satisfy the basic needs of the American people for home, work, and land, health and schools'. The programme's targets included achieving a minimum of six year's schooling for all children, a literacy campaign, the eradication of malaria, a boost to house-building, and provision of drinking water to half the population.

Members of the Interamerican Economic and Social Council (IA-ECOSOC) of the OAS, with the exception of Cuba, signed the Declaration of the Peoples of America and the Charter of Punta del Este on 17 August 1961, which brought the Alliance into being. The declaration bound the signatories to take 'immediate and concrete actions to secure a better life, under freedom and democracy, for the present and future generations'. Total external funds deemed necessary for the ten-year programme were US$20bn, of which half was to come from the US as low-interest, long-term loans. To qualify for Alliance for Progress aid, countries had to submit long-range development plans for the approval of a panel of experts. The Alliance stressed land tax reforms as essential for a better distribution of income. Although there was progress in some of the areas identified by the Alliance – including annual economic growth above the targeted 2.5% per capita in some years, by the late 1960s much of the impetus had been lost. The more conservative governments were unwilling to pursue even mild land reform measures sought by the programme, and the local economies remained dependent on developments in international commodity markets.

Alliance of Popular Parties and Forces: see **Alessandri Rodríguez**.

Alliance of the Nationalist Left: see **Democratic and Popular Union**.

Almeyda, Clodomiro: see **Socialist Party of Chile**.

Almeyda, Dr Manuel: see **Popular Democratic Movement**.

Alsogaray, Alvaro: see **Union of the Democratic Centre**.

Altamirano, Carlos: see **Socialist Party of Chile (PSCh)**.

Alva Orlandini, Javier: see **Belaúnde Terry**.

Alvarez, Gen. Gregorio

b. 1925. President of Uruguay 1981–5. A Uruguayan army officer closely involved with the 1973 military coup, he reached the rank of general in February 1971, at the height of the counter-insurgency campaign against the MLN-Tupamaros. In September 1971 he was appointed head of ESMACO, the newly created joint general staff, designed to coordinate military and police counter-insurgency operations. In February 1973 when the military forced a reluctant President Bordaberry to accept the creation of COSENA, the national security council with special powers, Alvarez was appointed its new permanent secretary. From there he moved to become commander of the 4th military region in 1974–8, a period in which his units gained notoriety for the torture of political prisoners. In 1978 he became army commander, ascending to the rank of lieutenant general. He retired early in 1979, but retained influence through a significant number of active service officers who remained *goyistas* (after his nickname, 'Goyo' Alvarez).

Occasionally credited with 'Peronist' leanings, Gen. Alvarez was known as the most ambitious of his fellow officers, wanting to break with the system of collective military leadership to establish his own pre-eminence. His appointment to the presidency in September 1981 – the first and only officer in the military regime to hold that office, previously restricted to civilian figureheads – seemed to indicate that his chance had come. But other officers were wary of allowing him to emerge as a strongman; and Alvarez faced growing popular dissatisfaction with the regime. He had taken office after the regime's defeat in the 1980 constitutional referendum, and at a time of deepening economic difficulties. So rather than prolonging his rule, Gen. Alvarez found himself presiding over negotiations to end the *Proceso* and allow elections. Following the elections in November 1984, Gen. Alvarez stepped down on 15 February 1985, two weeks before the inauguration of Julio Sanguinetti. Alvarez was forced to step down early because the incoming civilian president refused to accept his presence at the inauguration ceremony.

See also ***autogolpe*, *Club Naval* Pact, *Proceso***.

Alvarez Plata, Federico: see **Revolutionary Nationalist Movement**.

Alvear, Marcelo T. de: see **Radical Party** (Argentina); **Yrigoyen**.

Amazonas, João: see **Communist Party of Brazil**.

Amazon Pact

An eight-nation treaty regulating the development and protection of the Amazon basin region, signed on 3 July 1978 by Bolivia, Brazil, Colombia, Ecuador, Guyana, Peru, Suriname, and Venezuela. The treaty proclaims the freedom of river navigation, and the need to ensure the rational use of water, and recognises the right to exploit the Amazon for national economic development provided it is not harmful to other signatories. Other articles cover the promotion of tourism, the need for cooperation in scientific research, and for improvements in health, transport, and communications infrastructure. The Amazon Cooperation Council, composed of diplomats from each member state, meets annually to oversee the implementation of the treaty. Every two years there are meetings at foreign minister level.

a

America Batallion (*Batallón America*)
A left-wing 'guerrilla international' founded in late 1985/early 1986, which operates in the southwestern Colombian departments of Valle and Cauca. The prime mover was the 19 April Movement (M–19) of Colombia, and combatants are mostly Colombian, though they are also said to include Salvadoreans, Nicaraguans, Panamanians, Ecuadoreans, Bolivians, Peruvians, and Venezuelans. Formally affiliated are the Alfaro Lives group (Ecuador) and the Túpac Amaru Revolutionary Movement (MRTA) of Peru.
See also **Alfaro Lives!; M–19; Túpac Amaru Revolutionary Movement**.

American Anti-communist Alliance (AAA) (Colombia): see **death squad**.

American Institute for Free Labor Development (AIFLD)
Founded in 1962 by the US government, right-wing trade union leaders and private corporations, with the aim of fostering anti-communist unions in the Americas, largely in response to the Cuban revolution. The bulk of its finance (over 95%) comes from the US Agency for International Development (AID), though the initial idea came from George Meany, the then head of the US labour federation AFL-CIO. Companies such as Shell, United Fruit and W.R. Grace provide donations. The institute is a non-profit corporation, with a board originally comprising union officials and corporate executives, but now only the former. Its stated aim is 'the development of the democratic trade union movement in Latin America and the Caribbean'. It trains union members and others, many through a three-month course at its training centres in Virginia and Maryland. It also carries out other social projects, including housing schemes, but according to former Central Intelligence Agency employees it works closely with the CIA, as well as with ORIT, the western hemisphere affiliate of the International Confederation of Free Trade Unions (ICFTU), and has helped form or re-establish over 1,000 unions since 1976. AIFLD has been accused of involvement in the overthrow of Cheddi Jagan (Guyana, 1964), Salvador Allende (Chile, 1973) and João Goulart (Brazil, 1964).
See also **ORIT**.

American Popular Revolutionary Alliance (APRA): see **APRA**.

amnesty (Brazil, 1979)
The amnesty law introduced in 1979 had been promised by Gen. João Figueiredo, who took office as president in March of that year, as part of the process of liberalisation known as *abertura*. In the event it fell far short of the full, general, and unrestricted amnesty sought by the opposition. Those favoured by the amnesty included people convicted of political offences, but excluding kidnapping, robbery, or acts of violence against persons. The law allowed, at least in theory, for the reinstatement of public employees and military personnel removed under previous institutional acts, but in practice such reinstatement was conditional on the existence of vacancies and the approval of the relevant authorities

on a case-by-case basis. Clauses in the law also protected members of the security services from prosecution on charges of human rights violations, and provided for the issuing of 'declarations of absence' as a tacit recognition that the 'disappeared' were dead as far as the law was concerned. The legislation also allowed for the return of political exiles. In this matter the government was largely motivated by the desire to split the opposition – the move came in tandem with political reforms ending the two-party system.
See also ***abertura***; **Figueiredo**.

amnesty (Uruguay, 1985, 1986)
On the restoration of constitutional rule in March 1985, the newly-installed Uruguayan Congress voted an amnesty for all those imprisoned for political reasons during the military regime. Those charged with murder and acts of violence – mainly members of the MLN-Tupamaros guerrillas – benefited from a reduction in sentences, with the result that all were released from jail. But the legislation specifically excluded members of the security services from the scope of the amnesty; with the transition to democracy they therefore became liable for prosecution on charges of violating human rights during the dictatorship. As the possibility of military officers being committed for trial loomed closer in the second half of 1986, the armed forces began to exert increasing pressure for the amnesty to be extended to security personnel. Army chiefs warned that they would deliberately put themselves in contempt (*desacato*) by ordering their subordinates to ignore writs to appear in court to face charges. President Julio Sanguinetti favoured the extension of the amnesty to the military, and after a long political crisis the government finally got the appropriate amnesty bill through the Chamber of Deputies in December 1986, only hours before the first army officer, a lieutenant colonel, had been due to appear before a civilian court to face human rights charges. The Broad Front left-wing coalition and other parties then began to campaign for the repeal of the legislation, seeking to force a referendum on the issue. By November 1987 leaders of the repeal campaign were claiming they had more than the 550,000 signatures (representing one-quarter of the total electorate) needed under the constitution to force a referendum.
See also ***Proceso***; **Sanguinetti**.

Amodio Pérez, Héctor: see **National Liberation Movement-Tupamaros**.

Amurrio, Casiano: see **Revolutionary Party of the National Left.**

ANAPO (Popular National Alliance/*Alianza Nacional Popular*)
A Colombian party, founded in 1960 as a political vehicle for former dictator (1953–7) Gen. Gustavo Rojas Pinilla, but not formally registered as a party until 1971. Prior to this, its candidates generally stood on either Liberal (PL) or Conservative (PC) party lists, as required under the terms of the National Front, which it opposed. Initially, most of its support came from the Conservative bloc, to which Rojas Pinilla himself belonged

– a novelty in a country where radical movements had tended to emerge from the PL. Its platform was nationalist and reformist, neutral in international affairs, and with strong similarities to the Peronist movement in Argentina. It did not rule out the use of force to bring Rojas to power. Among its aims was the nationalisation of the major banks.

By 1970 it had become the strongest opposition group, winning 72 out of 210 seats in that year, and in the presidential election Rojas Pinilla came close to victory. Misael Pastrana, the National Front candidate, was declared the winner only after a lengthy recount under state-of-siege regulations. He was declared to have won 40% to Rojas' 38%. ANAPO alleged fraud, and the M–19 guerrillas, who sprang originally from the ranks of the party, took their name from the date of the election, 19 April. By 1974, however, ANAPO had passed its peak. Under Rojas' daughter, María Eugenia Rojas de Moreno Díaz, it moved sharply rightwards, producing an estrangement with M–19. It won only 15 of 199 seats in the 1974 elections, while María Eugenia Rojas, the first woman presidential candidate in Colombian history, took 10% of the vote. The death of Rojas himself in 1975 was a further blow, and the 1978 electoral alliance between ANAPO, the National Opposition Union (UNO) and the Independent Liberal Movement (MLI) failed to make an impact.
See also **M–19; National Front; Rojas Pinilla**.

Anaya, Adm. Jorge: see **South Atlantic War**.

Ancón, Treaty of: see ***salida al mar***.

Andean Pact (*Pacto Andino*)
An economic integration treaty (the Cartagena Agreement), signed in December 1970 in Bogotá, Colombia, by Bolivia, Chile, Colombia, Ecuador, and Peru, established the Andean Common Market within the Latin American Free Trade Association (LAFTA, now ALADI). Venezuela became a member in 1973. The agreement stressed central planning at the regional level rather than free trade. Its provisions included: a common external tariff structure and the abolition of intraregional tariffs; control over transnational companies (e.g. insistence on reinvestment in the sub-region of profits from foreign investment); preferential treatment for Ecuador and Bolivia on grounds of lesser development; a joint or parallel production programme, encouraging specialisation within the sub-region; import substitution and the elimination of inefficiencies.

The political body governing the Pact is the *Comisión Mixta* (Joint Commission), headquartered in Lima, which consists of a plenipotentiary from each country and meets three times a year. The three-member Council (*Junta del Acuerdo de Cartagena*), supported by the consulting committee of experts, ensures the implementation of agreements. Council members, appointed for a three-year term, act unanimously and do not represent their country. Other organs include the Andean Development Corporation (*Corporación Andina de Fomento*). Progress has been marred by quarrels over implementation of the principles and by economic difficulties. Chile withdrew in 1976 after the military junta's liberal economic policies came into serious conflict with the Pact (as amended by the Lima Protocol), and in 1980 Bolivia boycotted meetings. From 1982 onwards, Venezuela, Colombia, Bolivia, and Ecuador all took measures to restrict imports from the region. Neither trade liberalisation nor policy harmonisation targets were met, and by 1984 intra-regional trade had fallen back to 3.1% of the members' total external trade, compared with 3.9% in 1980. The Febres Cordero government in Ecuador threatened withdrawal in 1985, mainly over the issue of restrictions on foreign investment (Decision 24), and a feeling on the part of most members that the initial goals were over-ambitious led to a far-reaching revision of the agreement in 1987.

The 'Modifying Protocol' of 12 May 1987, which had taken four years to negotiate, eliminated Decision 24, allowing members total freedom to determine their foreign investment regime; it abandoned the common external tariff and customs union goals, along with sectoral development programmes for industry; and it accepted the principle of bilateral, as opposed to multilateral agreements. Some observers concluded that the Pact was effectively dead.

See also **Latin American Integration Association**.

Angeloz, Eduardo César

b. 1931. An Argentine politician chosen as the Radical Party's presidential candidate for the 1989 elections. Born in Córdoba province, Angeloz worked in a car sales company, and became a provincial and then federal senator for the Radicals. In 1983 his *línea Córdoba* faction of the party supported the nomination of Dr Raúl Alfonsín who went on to defeat the Peronist candidate; in those polls Angeloz was elected governor of Córdoba. In the September 1987 provincial and legislative elections, which were otherwise disastrous for the Radicals, Angeloz was re-elected as governor. This success earned him Alfonsín's support for the succession, and in July 1988 Angeloz won party primaries for the presidential nomination with 88% of the vote. Considered to be on the centre-right of the party, Angeloz promised to continue the government's privatisation programme, cut back state spending, and boost exports. Despite seeking better foreign-debt payment terms, he was widely seen as a supporter of financial orthodoxy.

See also **Alfonsín; Menem; Radical Party** (Argentina).

Antarctic Treaty

Argentina and Chile from Latin America were original signatories of the Antarctic Treaty in 1959, along with Australia, Belgium, Britain, France, Japan, New Zealand, Norway, USSR, USA, and South Africa. Brazil was one of a number of later signatories. The treaty covers the entire area south of latitude 60° S, where all forms of nuclear experiment are banned. The use of the continent for military purposes is also prohibited and the objective of international cooperation in peaceful scientific research is affirmed. Pre-existing sovereignty claims are held in suspense: Article 4 states that 'nothing taking place while the present treaty is in

a

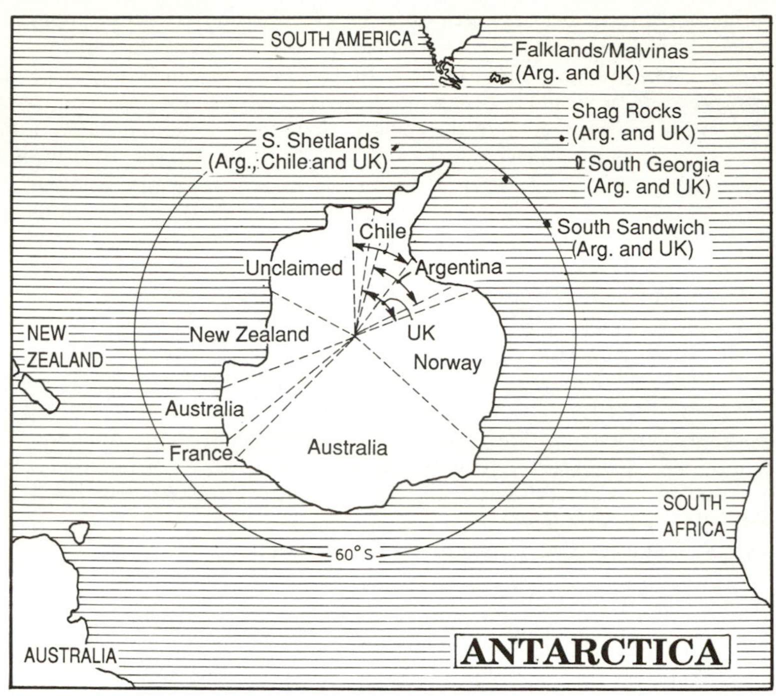

force shall constitute a basis for asserting, supporting, or denying a claim to territorial sovereignty'. Both Argentina and Chile have made overlapping claims, and both of these are in conflict with a claim by Britain. Argentina claims a triangle of territory with its base on latitude 60° S, its limits on longitudes 25° and 74° W, and its apex on the South Pole. The Chilean claim also has its apex on the South Pole and its base on latitude 60° S, but its limits are longitude 53° and 90° W. The British claim, of similar triangular shape, lies between longitude 20° and 80° W. The Soviet Union and the United States have made no claims of their own, and refused to recognise anyone else's.

Both Chile and Argentina, like other countries (among them Australia, France, Japan, New Zealand, Poland, South Africa, USSR, Britain, and the USA) maintain a network of scientific bases in the area. Despite the disclaimers of Article 4 of the treaty, both countries have continued to carry out acts designed to affirm sovereignty claims. These have ranged from holding a cabinet meeting in the Antarctic (Chile) through to issuing postage stamps, marking the claimed areas as part of national territory on official maps, and having a pregnant woman give birth in the Antarctic (Argentina). While making no territorial claims as such, both Peru and

Brazil have expressed increasing interest in the Antarctic and have organised scientific expeditions.

In total the Antarctic has an area of 13.9 million square kms; the land mass is shrouded by some 11.5 million cubic kms of ice, representing 70% of the world's store of fresh water. Deposits of iron ore and coal discovered on the mainland have so far proved too small for commercial exploitation, but vast areas remain unexplored. Uranium, copper, molybdenum, and platinum have been found in small quantities. Recoverable oil and gas reserves are thought to be 10 billion barrels, but no detailed seismic studies have been carried out so far. Awareness of the continent's living resources has been increasing, with attention concentrating on fin fish and krill.

Anti-communist Front For National Defence (FADN): see **Conservative Party** (Ecuador).

Anti-imperialist Revolutionary Front (FRA) (Bolivia): see **Movement of the Revolutionary Left** (Bolivia).

Anti-marxist Group (GRAPA) (Chile): see **death squad**.

Aponte, Guillermo: see **Socialist Party** (Bolivia).

APRA (aka **Peruvian Aprista Party**) (*Partido Aprista Peruano*/PAP) Founded in 1930 as the Peruvian branch of the American Popular Revolutionary Alliance (APRA, f. 1924) by Víctor Raúl Haya de la Torre. It began as a populist, nationalist movement and evolved into a conservative party during the 1950s and 1960s; but with the election of Alán García as general secretary in 1982 it acquired a social democratic bias. Its traditional base is among the northern middle and working class, but it has also developed strength in urban labour and some business backing. After 1945 it controlled the Confederation of Peruvian Workers, but today the CTP (though fairly insignificant) has more autonomy. Lima and the south have traditionally been hostile, but in November 1986 Jorge del Castillo became the first APRA mayor of Lima. Although anti-communist, it was strongly influenced by the Russian and Mexican revolutions. It was pro-indigenous and anti-US, stressing unity between students and workers, land reform and a united Latin America. Economically it was protectionist and favoured state control.

From 1931 to 1956 the party was subjected to persistent persecution and it was either illegal or barred from elections for the period 1933–45. This helped forge it into a verticalist, authoritarian party in which Haya tolerated no rivals to his leadership. In 1945 it formed a National Front coalition with Social Christians and others, and Social Christian lawyer José Luís Bustamante y Rivera was elected with 45% of the vote. APRA was legalised as the *Partido Popular*, but although it obtained three cabinet posts in recognition of its parliamentary majority, relations with the government turned sour. In 1947 it withdrew from the cabinet and in 1948 an abortive revolt was blamed on APRA militants. A military dictatorship followed, and the party did not regain its legal status until

1956, after it had given support to the right-wing Peruvian Democratic Movement (MDP) and backed an old enemy, Manuel Prado, member of a powerful banking family. As president, Prado sponsored the reactivation of APRA in 1957, and from then until 1962 it opted for coexistence (*convivencia*) with the right, losing much influence with its traditional followers. In 1960 pro-Cuban dissidents formed APRA-Rebelde. In 1962 Haya just failed to obtain the 33% of the vote needed to become president, and, although he withdrew his candidacy, the military intervened to forestall his election by Congress. In 1963 he was defeated by a coalition of the Popular Action (AP) party and the Christian Democrats (PDC). By allying itself with the Odriístas in parliament, however, APRA blocked legislation and used the legislature to channel funds to local areas and win greater electoral strength.

During the 1968–80 military regime the party was broadly supportive of the government. In 1978 it won the most seats in the constituent assembly elections (in which AP did not stand), but it was defeated in the 1980 general elections under Armando Villanueva (leader, 1979–82) and underwent a split, with a faction leaving to form the Hayista Base Movement (MBH) under former APRA leader Andrés Tównsend. Alan García (party president from 1985) won the 1985 election convincingly, and the party took 107 of the 180 seats in the lower house. Its stated aims were: to ensure an adequate food supply; to promote rural development; to create 4 million jobs in 15 years; to reduce the fiscal deficit to zero within three; to curb state expenditure (especially on the military) and raise taxes to 20% of GDP; to resist IMF pressure; and to restructure the police force and bring human rights violators to justice.

Economically it is split between a heterodox and a more orthodox wing. In the November 1986 municipal elections it took control of eight major cities, three of which had been run by the United Left (IU). APRA is an associate member of the Socialist International.
See also **Democratic Convergence; García Pérez; Haya de la Torre**.

Aramburu, Gen. Pedro Eugenio

1903–70. President of Argentina in 1955–8, who was kidnapped and killed by left-wing guerrillas in 1970. In the early 1950s, Aramburu figured prominently in military conspiracies against the regime of Gen. Juan Domingo Perón. Considered the original leader of the movement which led to the successful September 1955 coup (the 'Liberating Revolution'), Aramburu was nevertheless caught unawares by the timing of the uprising and by the success of Gen. Lonardi's forces in Córdoba. As a result it was Lonardi who assumed the presidency on 23 September 1955, while Aramburu became head of army General Staff. Yet Lonardi's brand of nationalism and his flirtation with neo-Peronism rapidly alienated sectors of military opinion, and Aramburu (backed by the *gorila* faction) was installed in his place on 13 November 1955. Aramburu inaugurated a second, more radically anti-Peronist, stage of the *Revolución Libertadora*, marked by the systematic persecution of supporters of the 1946–55 regime. His decision to execute by firing squad 27 military and civilian leaders of the failed 8/9 June 1956 pro-Peronist uprising was often cited as an important precedent in the subsequent cycle of pro- and anti-Peronist violence.

During his term in office Aramburu called elections to a constituent assembly (28 July 1957) from which Peronists were excluded. General elections, from which the Peronists were again excluded, were held on 23 February 1958. They were won by Arturo Frondizi of the Intransigent Radical Party (UCRI), with Peronist support. In subsequent years Aramburu remained an influential figure, mediating in successive military crises, and standing unsuccessfully as presidential candidate for UDELPA (*Unión del Pueblo Argentino*) in May 1963. He was kidnapped by Montoneros guerrillas on 29 May 1970; news that he had been 'executed' was released on 17 July 1970. The guerrillas' action was attributed both to revenge for his anti-Peronist role and to a desire to eliminate him as a possible political option for the regime.
See also **Liberating Revolution; Montoneros**.

Arango, Jorge: see **Workers' Self-Defence Movement**.

Arañíbar Quiroga, Antonio: see **Revolutionary Party of the Nationalist Left.**

Arboleda, Pedro León: see **Communist Party of Colombia–Marxist-Leninist**.

Arce Gomez, Col. Luís: see **Movement of the Revolutionary Left** (Bolivia).

ARENA: see **National Renovating Alliance**.

Arenas, Jacobo: see **Revolutionary Armed Forces of Colombia**.

ARGENTINA, Republic of

Capital: Buenos Aires
Independence: (from Spain) 1816
Area: 2,766,656 sq km
Population (1987): 31.14m (85.3% urban)
Pop. growth rate (1970–86): 1.6%
Pop. density: 11.21/sq km
Infant mortality (1980–5): 36 per thousand
Life expectancy at birth (1980–5): 69.7
Literacy (1982): 94.2%
GDP per capita (1987e): US$2,745
Foreign debt per capita (1987e): US$1,658
Main exports (1985): basic grains (36%), cattle and meat (5%), leather and wool (7%)

Political system

Constitution: 1853. *Head of state/government*: President Raúl Alfonsín (Radical Party/UCR) (1983–), elected to take over from Gen. Reynaldo Bignone, the last of a series of military presidents during the 1976–83

a

BOLIVIA
PARAGUAY
Salta
San Miguel
de Tucumán
Corrientes
BRAZIL
Santa Fé
Córdoba
URUGUAY
Mendoza
Rosario
BUENOS
AIRES
La Plata
CHILE
Mar del
Plata
Bahía Blanca
ARGENTINA
Comodoro Rivadavia
Falkland/ Malvinas
Islands
(Conflict with UK)
Río Galegos
Tierra del Fuego
Beagle Channel
(Dispute with Chile)
0 100 200 300 400 500 miles
0 200 400 600 800 km

Process of National Reorganisation regime. The president is chosen every six years by an electoral college of 600 directly-elected members. Consecutive re-election is forbidden, and the president must be a Roman Catholic. Legislative power is vested in Congress, composed of a 254-strong Chamber of Deputies and a 46-strong Senate. One half of the Chamber of Deputies is elected every two years, for a four-year term in office. Senators are appointed for nine-year terms by the provincial legislatures; one third of the Senate is renewed every three years.

Political organisations

Parties (seats in Senate/Chamber of Deputies following 6 September 1987 congressional elections): Radical Party/UCR (18/117); Justicialist (Peronist) Party/PJ (21/105); Union of the Democratic Centre/UCD (-/7); Intransigent Party/PI (-/5); Autonomist Liberal Pact/PAL (2/4); Christian Democratic Party/PDC (-/3); Progressive Democratic Party/PDP (-/2); Popular Neuquino Movement/MPN (2/2); Renovation Party of Salta/PRS (-/2); Movement of Integration and Development/MID (1/1); Bloquista Party (San Juan)/PB (2/1); Democratic Party (Mendoza)/PD (-/1); Socialist Unity/US (-/1); Provincial Rio Negrino Party/PRN (-/1); White Flag/BB (-/1); Provincial Action/AP (-/1); Popular Jujeño Movement/MPJ (-/1).

The following parties have no congressional representation: Federal Alliance/AF; Popular Left Front/FIP; Movement Towards Socialism/MAS; Communist Party/PCA; Workers' Party/PO; Popular Christian Party/PPC; Democratic Socialist Party/PSD; Popular Socialist Party/PSP.

Main labour organisation: General Confederation of Labour/CGT.
Main employers' organisation: Argentine Industrial Union/UIA.

Argentine Anti-communist Alliance (AAA): see **death squad**.

Argentine Communist Party (*Partido Comunista Argentino*/PCA)
Active in the country since 1918, the PCA originally emerged as a Marxist faction of the the Socialist Party. In the 1920s and 1930s it built up a significant presence within the trade union movement and obtained a few congressional seats. Together with the Socialists and others, the PCA controlled the leadership of the General Confederation of Labour (CGT). But the party's influence in the labour movement fell drastically as a result of the rise of Peronism in the early-to-mid 1940s. Colonel Perón rapidly unionised workers in the new expanding industries, in areas previously disregarded by the PCA. The party also suffered because it was unwilling to back radical action in areas such as the meat-packing plants, discouraged by the Soviet Union because disruption might hinder the flow of supplies to the Allies in the Second World War. In the 1946 election the PCA joined with Radicals, Socialists and Conservatives in the Democratic Union (*Union Democrática*) to oppose Perón. It described Perón's movement as 'nazi-fascist'. Peronism's success in building up a mass working class following in the 1946–76 period effectively reduced

a

the PCA to a party of intellectuals with only a tenuous presence in the working class.

The party was banned after the 1966 coup, but regained its legal status after the 1976 military takeover. During most of the 1976–83 regime its policy was one of 'critical support' for what it described as the moderate tendency within the regime. This line was maintained despite the fact that many PCA militants were among the victims of the dirty war. The party's stance was linked to the good relations established between the military and the Soviet Union; Argentina had refused to join the US grain embargo against the Soviet Union, and the Moscow government in turn refused to condemn the military's human rights record. In the 1983 elections the PCA reversed a long standing policy by supporting the Peronist presidential candidate and trying to work in the labour movement alongside the Peronist unions. Although the party at various points expressed theoretical support for revolutionary armed struggle, it remained committed in practice to an essentially electoral existence.
See also **dirty war; Peronism**.

Argentine Revolution (*Revolución Argentina*)

The name taken by the 1966–73 military regime which came to power in the 28 June 1966 coup against the civilian government of Dr Arturo Illia. Gen. Juan Carlos Onganía, the regime's first president, had planned the takeover with precision: it has been called Argentina's first 'scientific coup', complete with preparatory work in the national media to create a climate favourable to military intervention. Onganía's advisers were in the main drawn from right-wing Catholic circles, with a deeply corporatist ideology. Unlike previous military interventions, which saw themselves as transitional, the Argentine Revolution foresaw an extended period of de facto rule. Gen. Onganía introduced liberal economic policies. Politically the regime was repressive, intervening in university affairs and stepping up censorship.

By 1969 there were growing signs of rebellion: the appearance of the first guerrilla movements, student and trade union protests, the *Cordobazo*, all helped wear down Onganía's authority. On 8 June 1970, angered by his lack of a clear political programme, the three members of the military junta deposed Gen. Onganía. They chose as his successor the virtually unknown Gen. Roberto Lévingston, who lasted only 10 months in office before he too was replaced on 26 March 1971 by Gen. Alejandro Lanusse, who retained both his positions as junta member and army commander. Lanusse set about organising a 'great national accord' (*Gran Acuerdo Nacional* – GAN) which was to permit an orderly withdrawal of the armed forces to barracks and new elections – there was even talk of a candidate mutually acceptable to officers and civilians. But the regime moved towards the elections in a disorderly fashion, under growing pressure, including a series of bombings and kidnappings by the guerrillas.

In November 1972 Gen. Juan Perón returned to the country for the first time in 18 years, although he was not allowed to stand in the March

1973 elections. The victorious Peronist candidate, Héctor Cámpora, took office on 25 May 1973. At the inaugural ceremony Gen. Lanusse and other outgoing members of the *Revolución Argentina* were insulted by the crowds to the chant of 'se van, se van, y nunca volverán' ('they're going, they're going, and they'll never return').
See also ***Cordobazo*; Lanusse; Onganía**.

Arismendi, Rodney: see **Communist Party of Uruguay**.

Armed Forces of Popular Resistance: see **Movement of the Revolutionary Left** (Chile).

Armed Revolutionary Movement (MAR): see **guerrilla movements** (Brazil).

Army–Peasant Pact (*Pacto Militar–Campesino*): see **Bánzer Suárez**.

Army–Union Pact (*Pacto militar–sindical*)
An army–trade union pact was denounced by the Argentine Radical Party (UCR) presidential candidate, Raúl Alfonsín, in the 1983 election campaign. While the existence of the pact was strongly denied by both parties, and documentary proof was never produced, the suspicion of some kind of understanding between army officers and right-wing Peronist trade unionists such as Lorenzo Miguel of the UOM was widespread. Some analysts believe that the pact – real or suspected – helped swing the electorate in Alfonsín's favour in the 30 October 1983 elections. Most unions had remained under government control during the military regime, and in 1983 they were being handed back to 'normalising committees' of union leaders. Under the terms of the alleged pact, the army would ensure that the union factions aligned with Miguel received a majority on the 'normalising committees' for key unions, in return for Miguel using his influence under any future Peronist administration to prevent human rights trials of military officers.
See also **General Confederation of Labour; Miguel.**

Arns, Cardinal Paulo Evaristo: see **Radical Church** (Brazil).

Arron, Henck
b. 1936, Paramaribo. Premier of Suriname 1973–80 and 1988– . Arron obtained a degree in international banking in the Netherlands and worked with the Amsterdamse Bank before returning to Suriname. There he joined the Vervuurts Bank and became managing director of the Volkskredietsbank in 1963. He joined the National Party of Suriname (NPS) in 1961 and was elected to parliament in 1963. In 1970, on the death of Johan Pengel, he became chairman of the NPS. Arron led the National Party Coalition to victory in the 1973 general election, becoming premier and (until 1977) finance minister. From 1977 to 1980 he served as foreign minister. He led the country to independence from the Netherlands in November 1975 and with a reshuffled coalition won re-election in 1977. He had announced fresh elections for February 1980, but his government was overthrown by the army a few days before the vote. Arron was jailed

for several months in 1980–1, but resumed the leadership of the NPS when the army lifted the ban on political activity in November 1985. After the NPS won 14 seats in the November 1987 general elections, he was elected vice-president of the republic by the national assembly in January 1988 and named prime minister of a coalition government the same month.
See also **Bouterse; National Party of Suriname**.

Arroyo del Rio, Carlos: see **Conservative Party** (Ecuador); **Velasco Ibarra**.

Arze, José Antonio: see **Party of the Revolutionary Left**.

Astiz, Lt Alfredo: see **South Atlantic War**.

Austral
In June 1985 President Raúl Alfonsín of Argentina announced a drastic anti-inflationary programme. Its main features were a price and wage freeze, action to cut the state deficit, and the creation of a new currency. The old currency, the Peso Argentino, was replaced by a new unit, the Austral (conversion was at one Austral for 10,000 Pesos Argentinos). The new policy, which lasted with various adjustments for the following two years, was generically known as the 'Austral programme'. It was the first of what were to be known as 'heterodox' economic adjustment policies, such as those followed by President García in Peru after 1985 and the Cruzado programme in Brazil (early 1986). One of its novel features was the attempt to break inflationary expectations and to attack what was described as 'inertial' inflation. In Argentina the Austral programme was initially highly successful, bringing down the annual rate of inflation from over 1,000% to under 100%. In late 1986 and throughout 1987, however, the rate of price increases went back up into three digits.
See also **Alfonsín; Cruzado**.

autenticos: see **Brazilian Democratic Movement**.

Authentic Peronist Party: see **Montoneros**.

Authentic Radical Liberal Party (*Partido Liberal Radical Auténtico*/PLRA) (Paraguay)
Set up in 1978 after a series of factional quarrels within the Liberal tradition, the PLRA is in the anti-Stroessner camp, boycotting elections under existing regulations, and calling for democratisation, the ending of the state of siege, and respect for human rights. The PLRA was one of the four signatories of the National Accord (*Acuerdo Nacional*) opposition pact in 1979; it is not legally recognised as a party. Domingo Laíno, one of the PLRA's most prominent leaders, was systematically persecuted from the party's creation until his expulsion from the country in December 1982. Laíno was arrested on charges of subversion on 7 July 1978 after he had testified against the regime before the OAS; he was released on 8 August 1978. He was arrested again in 1979 and 1980. He was deported after making statements said to be insulting to the memory

of former Nicaraguan dictator Anastasio Somoza (who was killed in Asunción in 1980). Laíno made a number of attempts to return to the country, but was repeatedly turned back on entry before finally being allowed in in 1987. Other PLRA leaders such as Juan Manuel Benítez and Abdón Saguier also suffered arrest; in 1984 Pablo Martínez, a peasant organiser for the party, died in police custody.
See also **Laíno; Liberals** (Paraguay); **Stroessner**.

Authentic Revolutionary Nationalist Movement (MNR-A): see **Guevara Arze**.

Authentic Revolutionary Party (PRA): see **Guevara Arze**.

Authoritarian Nationalists

A description sometimes used for a tendency within the 1964–85 military regime in Brazil which favoured both tight political controls and a nationalist policy on foreign investment, together with some domestic reforms. This current of military thinking began to emerge in opposition to Marshal Castello Branco and Gen. Costa e Silva, the first two military presidents, who were judged to have gone too far in subordinating the economic development model to the interests of foreign capital. Gen. Alfonso Albuquerque Lima, who as interior minister supported the draconian Institutional Act 5 of December 1968, was a representative of this group. He stressed the need for a better distribution of the fruits of economic growth, both geographically, to favour the backward areas such as the north-east and the Amazon, and in terms of social classes, to favour the poorer groups in society. These concerns had led him to clash with the civilian technocrats in charge of economic policy in the first years of the regime. His slogan was *integrar para não entregar* ('integrate so as not to hand over'), the implication being that Brazil was in danger of being handed over to foreign interests. He also called for land reform, an issue which was otherwise taboo under military rule. In the succession crisis of September/October 1969 the military high command imposed their own candidate, Gen. Garrastazu Medici, a political hard-liner committed to maintaining continuing authoritarian controls. Unlike Albuquerque Lima, he wanted to use the controls to preserve existing, pro-foreign capital economic policy.

autogolpe

The Uruguayan military coup of 27 June 1973 was frequently described as an *autogolpe* (a coup against oneself) because on paper at least it was the incumbent president, Juan María Bordaberry, who suspended constitutional government, closing parliament and banning opposition parties. In reality, the coup was part of a longer and more complex process (sometimes referred to as the 'slow coup') in which power shifted decisively into the hands of the armed forces. Bordaberry had emerged as the victor of the controversial November 1971 elections, taking office in March 1972. The legitimacy of his government was severely questioned by the Blanco Party – which maintained it had been the victim of electoral fraud – and the leftist Broad Front (*Frente Amplio*) coalition. At the

a

same time the *fuerzas conjuntas* – the armed forces and police – were given a free hand in counter-insurgency operations against the Tupamaros guerrillas. In April–May 1972, as a result of armed clashes and internal betrayal, the guerrillas suffered a crushing military defeat. Fresh from these successes, officers were keen to expand their powers, and initiate an attack on traditional politicians, having obtained evidence of corruption from imprisoned guerrillas.

The military's new interventionism came to a head in the crisis of February 1973, known as 'bitter February', in which the service chiefs presented Bordaberry with an ultimatum. The president was forced to sign an agreement at the Boisso Lanza air force base, accepting the creation of a military-dominated national security council (known as COSENA) with veto powers over his administration, as well as other demands. From then on he was effectively a political prisoner of the armed forces. Between February and June 1973 Bordaberry aligned himself with his new military masters in preparation for the final offensive against their common enemy – the opposition in parliament and the trade unions. The 27 June measures to close parliament, ban opposition parties, close down the National Workers' Convention (CNT) labour federation, and arrest opposition figures were jointly agreed by Bordaberry and the military. The CNT organised a general strike in opposition to the coup, but after two weeks the stoppage proved impossible to maintain. Bordaberry had defeated his enemies, but remained president only on the sufferance of the armed forces; indeed, he was abruptly removed from office on 12 June 1976 after a disagreement with the military leaders, and replaced by another figurehead civilian.
See also **Bordaberry; *Proceso***.

Avengers of the Martyrs Commando (COVEMA) (Chile): see **death squad**.

Aylwin, Patricio: see **Christian Democrat Party** (Chile).

Azules and *Colorados*

The names given to rival Argentine military factions involved in a violent struggle for dominance in 1962–3. The *Azules* considered themselves more professional, and with a greater commitment to constitutional government. The *Colorados* were a continuation of the *gorila* tradition, marked by extreme anti-Peronism and a belief in the military's right to dictate terms to civilian administrations. Tensions between the two groups rose when the armed forces deposed the administration of Dr Arturo Frondizi in March 1962, with many *Colorados* arguing for military rule. The *Azules* were nevertheless able to ensure that the presidency went to José María Guido (the provisional president of the Senate), conserving at least the outward forms of constitutionality. In April 1962 *Colorado* officers forced Guido to declare provincial elections (held earlier that year) void; this provoked a rebellion of *Azul* officers. Their tanks moved out of the Campo de Mayo garrison and advanced on *Colorado* positions in Buenos Aires. The crisis was resolved by negotiations in which *Azul* officers obtained key positions, but had to accept the annulment of the provincial elections.

In August after a rebellion by Gen. Federico Toranzo Montero, *Colorado* officers began recovering their positions in the military heirarchy. President Guido was quickly surrounded by *Colorado* appointees. The *Azul* group, in which cavalry commander Gen. Juan Carlos Onganía was emerging as a leader, carefully planned its counter-attack. When demands for the removal of top *Colorado* officers were rejected, the Campo de Mayo garrison rebelled on 20 September. *Azul* units moved out on the attack, but the fighting did not go beyond skirmishes, with the *Colorados* generally on the defensive. *Azul* units seized radio stations to broadcast their communiqués; the most famous was Nr 150 from Campo de Mayo, which pledged the rebels' support for elections, professionalism, and the subordination of the military to the civilain authorities. The crisis ended with a complete victory for the *Azules*. The government called elections for 1963 and *Azul* leaders began planning a multi-party coalition, the National and Popular Front, which was to include the Peronists. But the Front was hit by political disagreements and the second thoughts of *Azul* officers, who remained essentially anti-Peronist, though less so than their *Colorado* rivals.

Taking advantage of these difficulties, the *Colorados* launched a new rebellion on 2 April 1963. The centre of the uprising was Punta Indio naval base, quickly besieged by the 8th Armoured Cavalry regiment from Magdalena, which had earlier suffered bombardment by naval aviation. Fighting was more intense on this occasion, with casualties reported at over 15 dead and 50 wounded. Again the *Azules* obtained a military victory, but to do so had to make political concessions to obtain air force support. As a result the government adopted a more clearly anti-Peronist line, banning all electoral candidates who had expressed support for the 'escaped tyrant'. The victorious *Azules* appeared to be adopting the *Colorado* platform. The Front's presidential candidate was barred from standing. With the Peronists excluded, the 7 July 1963 elections were won by Dr Arturo Illia of the People's Radical Party (UCRP) with 26% of the vote.

See also **Onganía; *gorilas*; Argentine Revolution**.

Baca Carbo, Raúl: see **Roldós Aguilera**.

Bahia Group: see **Marighela**.

Balbín, Dr Ricardo: see **Radical Party** (Argentina).

Baldomir, Gen. Alfredo: see **Terra**.

Bánzer Suárez, Gen. Hugo
b. 1926. President of Bolivia 1971–8. Born in Santa Cruz, the grandson of German immigrants and the son of a senior commander in the Chaco War. Educated at the Army College (Colegio Militar del Ejército), La Paz. Promoted rapidly under the post-1952 MNR revolutionary government, Bánzer undertook further training at the School of the Americas, Panama Canal Zone (1955) and the Armoured Cavalry School, Ft Hood, Texas (1960). He was commander of the 4th Cavalry Regiment in the 1960s and a colonel at the age of 35. His army speciality was logistics. He served as minister of education under President Barrientos until 1967, when he was sent as military attaché to Washington DC. From 1969 to 1970 he was director of the Army College.

He seized power in a military coup against the government of Gen. Juan José Torres in August 1971, governing initially under the terms of a pact (the Nationalist Popular Front/FPN) with the Revolutionary National Movement (MNR) and the Bolivian Socialist Falange (FSB). With his so-called '*autogolpe*' (or internal coup) of November 1974 he formed an exclusively military regime, which became notorious for its brutal repression of all opposition. Trade unions and independent political activity were suppressed. In one incident, the so-called 'massacre of the valley', between 80 and 200 peasants protesting at price rises were killed by the army in January 1974. This effectively destroyed the credibility of the pact between the military and the peasants originally forged in the 1960s by Gen. René Barrientos, even though it was formally renewed thereafter at annual intervals by official peasant leaders. The economy was opened up to foreign investors and Bánzer received warm support from the US and Brazilian governments and the Santa Cruz business community. There was a brief economic boom, followed by declining growth rates and rising inflation.

After seven years of de facto rule (Bolivia's longest presidency in over a century), he bowed to internal and US pressure to call elections in July

1978, putting up Gen. Juan Pereda as official candidate for the presidency. Fraud in favour of Pereda led to popular calls for the annulment of the result, and Bánzer distanced himself from his candidate, who then staged a coup, ousting Bánzer on 21 July 1978. Bánzer then formed the Nationalist Democratic Alliance (ADN) as his vehicle for the 1979 elections, and came third in both 1979 and 1980, with 15–17% of the vote. After briefly backing the military regime which seized power in 1980, the ADN withdrew its support, and Bánzer was exiled in May 1981, accused of a coup plot. In the 1985 presidential elections, he topped the poll, with almost 29%, but Congress gave the presidency to Víctor Paz Estenssoro, who had come second. Bánzer and the ADN subsequently forged a 'Pact for Democracy' with Paz, though without formal participation in government.

See also **Nationalist Democratic Alliance**.

banzerato

The term applied to the seven-year de facto rule of Gen. Hugo Bánzer Suárez in Bolivia.

See also **Bánzer Suárez**.

Barco Vargas, Jorge: see **Barco Vargas**.

Barco Vargas, Virgilio

b. 1921. President of Colombia 1986– . Born in the northeastern city of Cúcuta, a member of a powerful family which derived most of its income from one of Colombia's first oil developments, the Barco concession. Trained in engineering and economics in the USA; obtained a doctorate in economics from the Massachussets Institute of Technology. Liberal Party (PL) member of the chamber of deputies 1949–51 and of the senate 1958–66. Minister of public works 1958–61. Ambassador to the UK (1961–2) and twice to the USA. Minister of agriculture 1963–4. Mayor of Bogotá 1966–9. World Bank executive director (IBRD/IFC) and IDA from 1969.

Considered a 'centrist technocrat', and a skilful administrator, Barco was elected president in 1986 on promises of an end to guerrilla violence, firmer control over the military, an end to human rights abuses and job creation out of coffee, coal, and oil wealth. In his inaugural speech he pledged efforts to resolve the border dispute with Venezuela (which flared up again in 1987), to reform the state of siege law and to 'eradicate absolute poverty'. However, his US-style tax reform widened the gap between rich and poor. He has a reputation for personal honesty, but his brother Jorge was involved in a number of government scandals in the 1970s. Unemployment stood at 13–15% when Barco took office in August 1986, but healthy growth projections suggested he would have more room for manoeuvre in economic policy. (Nonetheless, unemployment was up to 18% by the end of 1986, and the president announced a major, 15-month plan to combat it.) He stresses private investment, especially in agriculture, and fiscal austerity.

The biggest winning margin in Colombian history (59% of the vote on

b

an unusually high 60% turnout) over right-wing Conservative Alvaro Gómez Hurtado, plus a substantial congressional majority, enabled him to put an end to the vestiges of the National Front system, under which opposition figures were given cabinet seats. However, some expected him to be dominated by his close ally, former president Julio César Turbay Ayala, the boss of the PL 'machine'. He does not share the enthusiasm of his predecessor, Belisario Betancur, for the Contadora peace process in Central America (of which Betancur was the architect), nor the latter's distaste for the International Monetary Fund. He is closer to the US than Betancur. He surprised some critics early in his presidency by stating a wish to consolidate the peace process with the country's guerrillas, though the truce ceased to hold over large areas of the country and Barco refused talks unless the guerrillas laid down their arms. Doubt was cast on his ability to deliver the structural reform integral to the process when after a few months agriculture minister José Fernando Botero resigned and was replaced by Luis Guillermo Parra Durán, a representative of the major landowners. Barco continued the campaign against drug trafficking with renewed vigour after the murder by traffickers of a prominent newspaper editor, Guillermo Cano, and later of Attorney-general Carlos Mauro Hoyos, introducing further emergency powers under which major figures such as Carlos Léhder of the Medellín cartel were extradited to the US. In June 1987, however, the Supreme Court found the extradition treaty unconstitutional.

As violence of all kinds escalated, the PL lost popularity, despite a buoyant economy. It fared poorly in the country's first direct mayoral elections in 1988, and Barco was accused of a lack of leadership.
See also **Liberal Party** (Colombia).

Barrantes, Alfonso: see **United Left** (Peru).

Barrientos, Gen. René: see **Bánzer Suárez; Christian Democrat Party** (Bolivia); **Revolutionary Nationalist Movement**.

Barrios, Gonzalo: see **People's Electoral Movement;** ***trienio***.

Barroso, Gustavo: see **Integralism**.

Báteman Cayón, Jaime: see **M–19**.

Batlle y Ordóñez, José: see ***batllismo***.

batllismo

The reformist political doctrine which has dominated Uruguay's Colorado party and the country for most of the twentieth century. It is named after José Batlle y Ordóñez (1856–1929), who in his two presidencies (1903–7 and 1911–15) oversaw a period of rapid economic growth, income redistribution, and far-reaching reforms which laid the foundations for a welfare state. State banks were created and public sector monopolies in the insurance, electricity, and telegraph sectors were set up; the eight-hour day was introduced in 1915; and there were new taxes on wealth and on absentee landownership. *Batllismo* was essentially a multi-class alliance, supported by sectors of the middle and working classes. But while the redistribution of income to urban areas was substantial, it was achieved without a frontal challenge to the interests of the landowners, as Batlle was in office at a time of exceptionally favourable international economic conditions.

Batlle's initial reformist impetus became ossified after his death; there were disagreements over the collegiate executive and a conservative reaction set in. The share-out of patronage through the *coparticipación* system and the creation of a clientilist network were some of the less positive aspects of *batllismo* in practice. Critics of *batllismo* on the left point out that when export prices slumped in the 1930s the movement was unable to prevent the coup d'etat by Gabriel Terra, backed by the landowners. Batllista rule was re-established in the 1940s, particularly during the presidency of the founder of the movement's nephew, Luis Batlle Berres, in 1947–51 – another period of growth associated with favourable international economic conditions. But the movement was unable to reverse Uruguay's economic stagnation in the 1950s and 1960s, which contributed to the advent of the 1973–85 military dictatorship. By the late 1960s and early 1970s Colorado presidents such as Jorge Pacheco Areco and Juan María Bordaberry, while paying lip-service to Batlle's ideals, led right-wing administrations. Yet under the 1973–85 military dictatorship a new generation of younger Colorados emerged, pledging a return to the movement's roots. The Colorados returned to power in 1985 under the presidency of Julio María Sanguinetti.

See also **Colorado Party** (Uruguay)**; Collegiate Executive; *coparticipación*; Sanguinetti**.

Beagle Channel dispute

A long-running territorial conflict between Argentina and Chile, which brought them to the brink of war in 1902 and in 1978, but which was finally settled in 1985. The channel, running along the southern coast of Tierra del Fuego just above an archipelago of small islands leading down to Cape Horn, was named after the British ship HMS *Beagle* which first navigated it in 1830. Tension over ownership rose at the turn of the century and seemed likely to lead to war in 1902. An arbitration decision by the British Crown helped settle limits in Patagonia and Tierra del Fuego; but the ruling was not specific about the small islands in the Beagle Channel. These were occupied by Chile but claimed by Argentina.

In 1971, with reports that the area could be rich in oil deposits stimulating interest, both countries again agreed to British arbitration. It was decided that because of Britain and Argentina's separate dispute over the Falklands/Malvinas, the actual ruling would be sought from the judges on the International Court of Justice at The Hague and Britain would simply endorse their findings. The judges ruled in May 1977, awarding the disputed Picton, Lennox, and Nueva islands, together with much of the channel waters, to Chile. The Argentine military junta rejected the decision and said it refused to recognise it as binding. Against a background of growing tension, including troop movements and the arrest of each other's nationals on spying charges, there were unsuccessful attempts to resolve the matter by bilateral negotiations. Plans were made in Argentina to take the islands by force, but the invasion was called off at the last moment in December 1978 when the Vatican stepped in offering its services as a mediator. The Vatican's first peace proposals were made in 1980; they were not public but were presumed to be favourable to Chile. The Chilean government accepted them immediately but Argentina played for time, asking for 'clarifications' and refusing either to accept or to reject them formally. It was not until after Argentina's defeat in the 1982 South Atlantic War with Britain, and the subsequent collapse of military rule, that progress was made. The civilian government of President Raúl Alfonsín finally agreed to a revised Vatican peace plan in 1984–5. Under its terms Chile's right to the islands was recognised, but its claim to offshore waters east of Cape Horn was met only in part. See also **South Atlantic War**.

Bedoya Reyes, Luis: see **Christian Democrat Party** (Peru); **Democratic Convergence**.

Bedregal, Guillermo: see **Revolutionary Nationalist Movement**.

Belaúnde Terry, Fernando

b. 1912. President of Peru 1963–8 and 1980–5. Born in Lima. Educated at the University of Texas (architecture degree 1935). Member of Congress 1945–8. Dean of the architecture faculty, National Engineering University, 1955–60. An unsuccessful candidate for the presidency in 1956, Belaúnde founded the Popular Action (AP) party in 1957 out of the electoral machine he had created the previous year. He was narrowly defeated for the presidency in 1962, but after the intervention of the armed forces, was finally elected in the following year. His objective was modernisation through major public works projects and a moderate programme of reforms (especially agrarian reform), but he was frustrated by opposition in Congress (dominated by the opposition APRA party) and among conservative business groups.

Overthrown in a military coup by Gen. Velasco Alvarado on 3 October 1968, he lived in the USA until allowed to return in 1976. During this period he was visiting professor of urban planning at Georgetown, Harvard, Columbia, and George Washington universities. In an impressive political comeback, Belaúnde won the presidency on the AP ticket again in 1980, when the armed forces withdrew to the barracks. His congressional majority was assured by an alliance with the Popular Christian Party (PPC). After an initial honeymoon period, however, his second term saw a catastrophic decline in his party's fortunes, brought on by a combination of economic mismanagement and increasing repression, the latter prompted in part by the growth of the Shining Path guerrilla movement. Foreign policy was dominated by the search for a 'special relationship' with the US, interrupted only by Peru's backing for Argentina in the 1982 Falklands/Malvinas war. The developmentalist policies which Belaúnde himself still favoured clashed with the neo-

classical theories of his economic team, known as 'The Dynamo', who resisted the taxation of business which would have paid for infrastructural works. Instead, these were financed by heavy foreign borrowing and the printing of money, at a time when Latin America was experiencing the first impact of the debt crisis. Real incomes fell as unemployment grew, and a series of natural disasters exacerbated the problem. Fierce rivalries between Prime Minister Manuel Ulloa and second Vice president and Senate leader Javier Alva Orlandini plagued AP from 1980 onwards. Alva began openly criticising the government's economic policies as part of his own bid for the presidential nomination. Belaúnde himself proposed an electoral alliance with the Popular Christian Party (PPC) for 1985, though without success. Constitutionally, he could not stand for re-election, but his government was the first since 1912 to complete an elected term of office and hand over to an elected successor.
See also **Dynamo, The; Popular Action; Velasco Alvarado**.

***Belgrano, ARA*:** see **South Atlantic War**.

Beltrán Prieto, Luis: see **People's Electoral Movement**.

Benidorm, Pact of: see **Gómez, Laureano**.

Benítez, Juan Manuel: see **Authentic Radical Liberal Party (PLRA)**.

Bertrand, Léon

b. 1951. One of French Guiana's two deputies in the French parliament, mayor of St Laurent de Maroni, the second largest town, and leader of the Guianese branch of the Gaullist Rally for the Republic (RPR). Born in St Laurent. A science teacher and estate agent, Bertrand was elected to Guiana's General Council in 1982 and to the Regional Council in 1985. He has been mayor of St Laurent since 1983. He was elected a deputy in 1988 after beating the incumbent, Paulin Bruné, also an RPR member.

Betancourt, Rómulo

1908–81. Founding member of Venezuela's *Acción Democratica* (AD) who was provisional president in 1945–8 and president in 1959–64. Generally considered one of the architects of Venezuela's post–1958 democratic stability. Born in Guatire, Miranda, he attended the Liceo Caracas where one of his teachers was the novelist, later to become AD president, Rómulo Gallegos. A member of the 'Generation of 1928', Betancourt was involved in the student protests that year against the dictatorial rule of Gen. Juan Vicente Gómez, for which he was briefly imprisoned. On his release he took part in the abortive 28 April rebellion, escaping afterwards to Colombia. From exile there and in the Dominican Republic, Curaçāo, Trinidad, and Costa Rica, he was involved in various unsuccessful efforts to overthrow Gómez. He joined the Communist Party in Costa Rica in 1930, a decision he was later to describe as 'a youthful attack of smallpox that left me immune to the disease'.

Returning to Venezuela after the death of Gómez in 1936, he was involved in leftist groups such as *Organización Revolucionaria Venezolana* (ORVE). Despite a 1937 deportation order he managed to stay in the country in hiding until captured in 1939 and sent into a new exile, this time in Chile and Argentina. In 1940 he published *Problemas Venezolanos* concentrating on the problems of the oil industry and economic development, the first of many books he was to write. Back in Venezuela in 1941, he founded AD, which in alliance with young army officers led the October 1945 coup which inaugurated the period known as the *trienio*. As head of the seven-man ruling junta and provisional president, Betancourt brought in social and economic reforms, including higher taxes for the rich and the 50/50 formula for splitting oil profits with the foreign companies. During his rule there were elections for a constituent assembly, followed by the first direct presidential elections in Venezuelan history – in both AD obtained a landslide victory. But the new president, Betancourt's onetime teacher Rómulo Gallegos, was deposed by a military coup in November 1948 which initiated a period of persecution of the party and led to the consolidation of the dictatorship of Gen. Marcos Pérez Jiménez. Betancourt was again forced into a long exile, in New York, Cuba, Costa Rica, and Puerto Rico.

Following the January 1958 revolution he returned to the country and signed the *Punto Fijo* agreement with the Social Christian Party (COPEI) and the Democratic Republican Union (URD) in an attempt to guarantee a stable democracy. Betancourt ran as the AD candidate in the December 1958 elections, winning with 49.9% of the vote. After taking office in February 1959, however, he came into increasing conflict with radicals and nationalists, many in his own party, who were dismayed at his anti-communist and pro-US line. The URD withdrew from the coalition government in November 1960 protesting at Betancourt's attacks on the revolutionary government in Cuba. Domestically, he attacked the Communist Party (PCV) and the Movement of the Revolutionary Left (MIR) (which had broken away from AD), closing newspapers, arresting political opponents, and creating a new police force, DIGEPOL, which was frequently charged with maltreatment of political detainees. In response, his government was challenged by a long and bitter guerrilla insurgency; it was also buffeted by right- and left-wing military rebellions. But despite this AD was able to build up its influence in both the trade union movement and poor urban areas at the expense of the left. It was also able to introduce some reforms and lay the basis for economic growth; it was in 1960 that Venezuela became one of the five founding members of OPEC. These successes were reflected in the December 1963 elections, when despite guerrilla efforts to boycott the polls, over 90% of the electorate turned out. After standing down from the presidency Betancourt remained a senator, acting as elder statesman and adviser to subsequent AD administrations. He died in New York in 1981.
See also **Betancourt doctrine; Democratic Action; guerrilla insurgency** (Venezuela); ***Punto Fijo; trienio***.

Betancourt doctrine

A foreign policy principle upheld by Venezuela during the 1959–64 government of President Rómulo Betancourt, according to which democratic countries in the hemisphere should refuse diplomatic recognition to dictatorships. Betancourt outlined the doctrine at the 2nd Congress of the Inter-American Association for Democracy and Freedom in April 1960. It was the duty of democratic governments to isolate dictatorships of both the left and the right, and to place former dictators on trial for their crimes. During his term in office, Venezuela concentrated its criticism on Cuba and the Dominican Republic. The long enmity between Betancourt and Rafael Trujillo of the Dominican Republic came to a head on 24 June 1960 when an assassin hired by Trujillo almost succeeded in killing Betancourt. The Venezuelan president obtained OAS support for sanctions against the Dominican Republic. In the case of Cuba, Betancourt accused Fidel Castro of supporting the Venezuelan guerrillas.

In November 1961 Venezuela broke diplomatic relations with Cuba, the following January it supported the resolution to expel Cuba from the OAS, and in November 1963, following interception of a Cuban arms shipment, it asked the OAS to impose sanctions against Havana. But Venezuelan efforts to rally other hemispheric nations into a collective withdrawal of diplomatic recognition from de facto regimes in Paraguay, Haiti, Argentina, Guatemala, the Dominican Republic, and Peru, were a failure. The Betancourt doctrine did not survive the advent of a COPEI government and was not reactivated by later AD administrations.
See also **Organisation of American States**.

Betancur Alvarez, Diego: see **Independent and Revolutionary Workers' Movement**.

Betancur Cuartas, Belisario

b. 1923. President of Colombia 1982–6. Born in Amagá, Antioquia, into an extremely poor family; 16 of 21 brothers and sisters died as children. Secondary education at a seminary, from which he was expelled for 'lack of vocation'. As a student at the Universidad Pontífica Bolivariana, Betancur had to sleep rough for the first two years before obtaining a scholarship. He switched from architecture to law, eventually going into politics and journalism. As a youth he belonged to an extreme right-wing movement, but he later joined the Conservative Party (PC, now PSC). In 1946 he was elected a deputy and in 1950 he was appointed to the constituent assembly by President Laureano Gómez. He was prominent in the opposition to dictator Gen. Rojas Pinilla (1953–7), for which he was several times jailed, and supported the National Front agreement between the PC and the Liberals (PL). On three occasions (1962, 1970, and 1978) he stood unsuccessfully for president on the PC ticket.

The de facto leader of the progressive wing of the PC, Betancur was finally elected in 1982 thanks to the split in the PL vote. Domestically he sought peace with the country's many guerrilla movements (despite opposition from the powerful military establishment) and an end to corruption and to military repression; while internationally he adopted an activist foreign policy (including the formation of the Contadora peace process for Central America, attempts to form a regional debt cartel, and rapprochement with Cuba) which conflicted in many respects with that of the US. In 1982 he took Colombia into the Non-Aligned Movement. Betancur also confronted the powerful drugs barons, supporting the extradition treaty with the US, a policy which led to the murder of justice minister Rodrigo Lara Bonilla in 1984. In November 1982 an amnesty was declared for guerrilla combatants and around 2,000 accepted. In 1984 Betancur succeeded in signing peace agreements with the three main armed organisations, the FARC, the M–19, and the EPL, though others rejected the truce. As well as amnesty, the government offered political and social reform if the guerrillas would disarm and reincorporate themselves into civilian politics. The plan included agrarian reform, the direct election of mayors and guarantees of equality for political parties other than the PL and the PC, which had shared power for a quarter of a century under the National Front system. The election of mayors was expected to work heavily against the PC, which had benefited from a 50/50 split with the PL despite the latter's overwhelmingly greater support in the towns. The incorporation of the guerrillas into civilian politics in time for the 1986 elections was not achieved, partly due to delays in the reform programme and partly to deliberate wrecking by the armed forces and dissident guerrilla factions. The government also refused to lift the state of siege imposed after Lara Bonilla's murder. However, the FARC and its ally the Communist Party (PCC) did set up the Patriotic Union (UP) which successfully campaigned for Congress and polled well in the presidential elections.

Betancur's personal standing declined substantially during his period in office, due mainly to his lack of success in consolidating the peace process, to the increase in crime, and to unemployment which topped 15%, the highest official figure in Colombian history. In other respects Betancur handed his successor an improving economy, with reduced budget deficits and economic growth around 4%. The Palace of Justice siege of December 1985, in which the president's refusal to negotiate with the M–19 led to the deaths of almost 100 people, marked the effective end of his attempt to defy the armed forces over internal security and cost him much of his remaining support. After the siege, Betancur declared all-out war on the M–19, but, to the surprise of many, the fragile peace process survived into the presidency of Virgilio Barco. In May 1987 the attorney general began investigations into allegations of corruption against Betancur and his former defence minister, Gen. Vega Uribe, in relation to contracts for the Málaga naval base.
See also **Social Conservative Party**.

Bignone, Gen. Reynaldo: see **Process of National Reorganisation**.

Bitar, Jaco: see **Workers' Party**.

Blancas, Carlos: see **Christian Democrat Party** (Peru).

Blanco, Hugo

b. 1933. Trotskyist political leader in Peru. Born in Cuzco, the son of a mestizo lawyer. Educated at the University of Buenos Aires (agronomy). Probably Latin America's best-known Trotskyist, Blanco spent much time among the Quechua indians as a teenager. He joined the Trotskyist movement in Argentina and acquired trade union experience working as a meat-packer. On his return to Lima he was involved in preparing a hostile reception for the then US vice-president Richard Nixon, and, in danger of arrest, returned to Cuzco to organise the peasantry. In 1961 he co-organised the short-lived Revolutionary Left Front (FIR), of which the biggest member organisation was Revolutionary Workers' Party (POR), Peruvian section of the Fourth International. The Front's activities were confined to bank robberies, and bitter internal wrangling brought its demise in 1962. Blanco was arrested in 1963 after narrowly escaping summary execution and held in solitary confinement for three years, despite a general strike called immediately after his capture.

At his trial in 1967 the prosecution asked for the death penalty, but an international outcry prevented his execution and he was sentenced to 25 years imprisonment on El Frontón island, off Callao. He was freed under an amnesty decreed by the Velasco Alvarado government in December 1970, but prevented from travelling to Cuzco. In September 1971 he was arrested again and deported to Mexico after calling for the release of all political prisoners. He is currently spokesperson for the Revolutionary Workers' Party (PRT), the Peruvian representative of the Fourth International, founded in 1978. In the 1980 elections he was one of three PRT leaders elected to the Chamber of Deputies, though his membership of the lower house was subsequently suspended and he spent most of the Belaúnde presidency abroad. Since 1985 he has worked closely with one of the member parties of the United Left (IU).
See also **Trotskyism**.

Blanco Party (*Partido Nacional*)

One of the two traditional parties which have dominated Uruguayan politics in the twentieth century. The Blancos earned their name from the white flag used by the Conservative side in the 1836–8 civil war, although the grouping is now formally known as the *Partido Nacional* (National Party). During the nineteenth-century civil wars the party was controlled by landowning interests. The rural poor made up the irregular Blanco armies which fought the Montevideo elites. The Blancos had a succession of *caudillo* leaders, the most famous of whom was Aparicio Saravia. After the defeat of the last major Blanco uprising led by Saravia in 1904, the party concentrated on electoral politics, developing its strength in the rural constituencies. While it regularly won control of these, it failed to win nationally until 1958. That year also saw the introduction of the collegiate executive; the Blancos obtained six of the nine seats available, retaining their majority after the 1962 elections. In 1966, however, the Colorados won again – and at the same time the single-person executive was re-established.

The party contains many different internal tendencies, ranging from conservative movements such as *herrerismo* through to more reformist groupings such as *Por la Patria*. In the 1971 elections Wilson Ferreira Aldunate of *Por la Patria* won the most votes, but he narrowly lost to

Juan María Bordaberry of the Colorados under the *ley de lemas* vote aggregation system. After the 1973 coup Ferreira Aldunate was forced to leave the country into exile and other reformist Blancos were persecuted inside Uruguay. Hector Gutiérrez Ruiz, the former president of the Chamber of Deputies, was kidnapped and murdered in Argentina. Despite military hopes that the more conservative sectors of the party would re-establish control, in the 1982 internal elections *Por la Patria* and its ally *Movimiento de Rocha* established a dominant position on the party's executive committee, known as the *Directorio*.

In mid-1985, challenging the military ban on him, Ferreira Aldunate sailed into Montevideo on a chartered ship. He was arrested on arrival and kept in prison until after the November elections. The party refused to accept the military's decision to exclude its main leader from the presidential race, and for that reason did not sign the *Club Naval* accords with the armed forces. The Blancos did field a substitute candidate, Alberto Zumarán, who campaigned on the promise of calling new elections at a later date without political exclusions. Although defeated by the Colorados in the presidential race, the Blancos, together with the *Frente Amplio*, controlled between them a majority in congress.
See also **Collegiate Executive; *Club Naval* Pact; Ferreira Aldunate; *Ley de Lemas*.**

Boff, Leonardo: see **liberation theology**.

Bogotazo

A wave of riots in the Colombian capital, Bogotá, sparked by the assassination on 9 April 1948 of the populist Liberal leader Jorge Eliécer Gaitán, in which much of the centre of the city was sacked. The worst of the rioting was quelled after two days, but the events are frequently cited as the catalyst for the years of violent civil strife, known as '*la violencia*', which followed. The only immediate political consequence was the formation of a new coalition government comprising Conservatives and Liberals.
See also **Gaitán; Liberal Party** (Colombia); ***violencia, la***.

Boisso Lanza agreement: see **Bordaberry**.

Bolívar Simón: see **Organisation of American States**.

BOLIVIA, Republic of

Administrative capital/largest city: La Paz
Legal/judicial capital: Sucre.
Independence: (from Spain) 1825
First constitution: 1826
Area: 1,098,581 sq km
Population (1987): 6.73m (49.6% urban)
Pop. growth rate (1980–5): 2.7%
Pop. density: 6.13/sq km
Infant mortality (1980–5): 124.4 per thousand
Life expectancy at birth (1985): 50.7
Literacy (1985): 63.2%

GDP per capita (1986e): US$926
Foreign debt per capita (1987e): US$718
Main (legal) exports (1985): natural gas (55%); tin (28%)

Political system

Head of state/government: Víctor Paz Estenssoro (MNR-H) (1985–); elected to succeed Hernán Siles Zuazo (MNR-I) (1982–5). The president is elected for a four-year term and may not be re-elected. In the case of the president's death or failure to take office, the vice president becomes interim head of state. Congress consists of a 27-member Senate (three for each of the nine provinces) and a 130-member Chamber of Deputies. Senators and deputies are also elected for four-year terms. All those over 21 (including illiterates since the 1952 revolution) and all married persons over 18 are obliged to vote. Proportional representation is in use. The last general elections were in July 1985.

Political organisations

Parties (seats at last election): Revolutionary Nationalist Movement ('Historic' wing)/MNR-H (59); Nationalist Democratic Alliance/ADN (51); Movement of the Revolutionary Left/MIR (16); Left-MNR/MNR-

I (8); MNR-9 April Revolutionary Vanguard/MNR-VR (6); Socialist Party-1/PS-1-Marcelo Quiroga (5); United People Front/FPU (comprising Communist Party of Bolivia/PCB and MIR dissidents) (4); Bolivian Socialist Falange/FSB (3); Christian Democrat Party/PDC (3); Tupaj Katari Revolutionary Movement/MRTK (2); Nationalist Centre/CEN; Left FSB/FSBI; Revolutionary Left Front/FRI; Mandate for Action and National Unity/MAN; Revolutionary Agrarian Movement of the Bolivian Peasantry/MARC; National Left Movement/MIN; MNR-Julio wing; MNR of the People/MNRP; Democratic Left Offensive/OID; Revolutionary Unity Organisation/OUR; Marxist-Leninist Communist Party of Bolivia/PCMLB; Party of the National Revolution/PRN; Authentic Revolutionary Party/PRA; Revolutionary Party of the National Left–Gueiler/PRING; Revolutionary Party of the Nationalist Left/PRIN; Social Democrat Party/PSD; Bolivian Union Party/PUB; Party of the Republican Socialist Union/PUSR; Workers' Vanguard Party/PVO.

Main labour organisations: Central Organisation of Bolivian Workers/COB; Mineworkers' Union Federation/FSTMB; Union Confederation of Rural Workers of Bolivia/CSUTCB; Oil Workers' Union Federation/FSTPB. *Main employers' organisations*: Confederation of Private Businessmen of Bolivia/CEPB; National Exporters' Chamber; National Chamber of Commerce; National Association of Mine-owners/ANMM.

Bolivian Communist Party (*Partido Comunista de Bolivia*/PCB) Founded in 1950 after youth sections under José Pereira split away from the Party of the Revolutionary Left (PIR) over the latter's (1946–52) alliance with the political right. The leaders of the new party were students and teachers, but developed support among urban workers and miners. The PCB was critically supportive of the 1952 revolutionary regime of the MNR, calling for a broad-based 'national liberation front' rather than rule by one party, but eventually went into open opposition. It won 1.5% of the vote in 1956 with the support of the PIR and 1% in 1960 when standing alone.

In 1964 it opted for abstention in protest at the re-selection of the MNR's Víctor Paz Estenssoro. After the Barrientos coup of that year the PCB initially joined other parties and the trade union confederation COB in a 'Revolutionary Committee of the People' which backed the military regime. It put up its own candidates (under the title of the National Liberation Front/FLIN) in the July 1966 elections rather than joining the united left front: neither won any seats. The party split in March 1965 into pro-Moscow and pro-Peking wings, each of which 'expelled' the other.

The pro-Chinese faction became the PCB–Marxist-Leninist, which gained some organised strength among the peasantry, but whose main base has always been among the miners. The PCB–ML advocated armed revolution, but became involved in electoral politics, participating in the 1978 Left Revolutionary Front with Juan Lechín's PRIN and the Trotskyist POR. In 1979 it lost some popularity by backing the conservative

Víctor Paz of the MNR-H. In 1980 it backed the candidacy of Lechín himself until he withdrew in favour of Siles.

The pro-Moscow PCB agreed in 1967 to assist 'Che' Guevara with his plan to infiltrate into Argentina, but disapproved of his decision to set up a guerrilla '*foco*' in Bolivia. Individual members did collaborate, but the PCB expelled some of its youth section who were involved with the ELN. It also made clear that its own strategy had not changed. With the PCB–ML and the Trotskyist POR, it was banned by Barrientos in 1967. After Gen. Torres' 1970 coup it argued in favour of participation in government, though this did not come about. It took part in the short-lived Popular Assembly (described as 'an organ of popular power') in 1971 with other parties of the left.

For the 1978/79/80 elections the PCB renewed its alliance with Hernán Siles Zuazo, forming part of his Popular Democratic Union (UDP) coalition, though it was not legalised until he was finally allowed to take power in 1982. Thereafter it held two key cabinet posts, labour and mining, and effectively controlled the state mining corporation, Comibol, as well as leading the labour movement. However, in September 1984 its members were ousted from leadership of the union confederation COB, and in December it withdrew from the cabinet in some disarray. The leadership was purged, with Simón Reyes taking over from Jorge Kolle Cueto. For the 1985 elections the PCB joined the United People Front (FPU), but failed to obtain any seats. In July 1985 it suffered a serious split: five of its top leaders were expelled for 'divisionism' in a pre-emptive move by general secretary Simón Reyes; and the bulk of the youth wing, plus the Cochabamba district organisation, left the party. Short of mass support, the party nonetheless still has strong representation in the miners' federation (FSTMB) leadership. Reyes became executive secretary of the COB in 1987.
See also **COB; National Liberation Army** (Bolivia).

Bolivian governments post-Bánzer

Between the overthrow of Gen. Hugo Bánzer in July 1978 and the accession of the elected government of Hernán Siles Zuazo in October 1982, Bolivia had eight presidents, none of whom had won an election. Gen. Juan Pereda Asbun, the 'official candidate' in 1978 who seized power when his election fraud failed, was forced by internal and international (including US) pressure to announce fresh elections in which he would not stand. He refused, however, to hold them before 1980. In November 1978 he was in turn overthrown by younger officers anxious for an orderly return to the barracks. His replacement was army commander Gen. David Padilla Arancibia, who immediately scheduled elections for July 1979. Padilla and the so-called '*movimiento generacional*', while clearly anti-communist, took steps to neutralise the right. Bánzer himself, who had been threatening a coup against Pereda, was retired from the army and sent as ambassador to Argentina.

In a much cleaner election, Siles Zuazo won a plurality but did not command the necessary majority in Congress to ensure election. Wálter

Guevara Arze, president of the senate, was chosen to head an interim administration, pending fresh elections in 1980. However, on 1 November 1979, Col. Alberto Natusch Busch staged a coup, stating that the Guevara government was too weak to remain in power. The powerful trade union confederation, the COB, declared a general strike and Natusch was immediately isolated. In the street battles and government repression which followed, at least 200 people died and 125 disappeared. The US cut off relations and suspended aid, and Natusch's government gained no support internationally. It was forced out within days, replaced this time by a government headed by Bolivia's first woman president, the head of the lower house, Lidia Gueiler Tejada. Despite the constant threat of a coup, which intensified after the appointment as army commander of Gueiler's cousin, Gen. Luís García Meza Tejada, the elections went ahead on 29 June 1980, and Siles won a more convincing victory. But less than three weeks later, García Meza seized power, declaring his intention to stay in power for 20 years. Thirty people were killed in the coup, including Socialist leader Marcelo Quiroga Santa Cruz. Support for the move had come from the Argentine military government and the cocaine mafia, both of which helped fund the García Meza regime. The US broke off relations and declared an economic boycott, and the new junta was widely condemned internationally for its extreme brutality and criminality. Among the right-wing extremists of foreign origin who worked for its intelligence services was Nazi war criminal Klaus Barbie, who had been living in Bolivia since 1951 and was later expelled by the Siles government to stand trial in France. Despite its outlaw status, however, the junta succeeded in remaining in power for a year.

In August 1981 García Meza was overthrown, and power passed into the hands of another, more unstable junta, which eventually appointed army commander Gen. Celso Torrelio Villa as president. He announced elections for 1983 and won a restoration of relations with the US, but he was in turn replaced, in July 1982, by Gen. Guido Vildoso Calderón. The armed forces were too divided and discredited to hold power in the face of popular mobilisation, and Siles Zuazo formally took office in October 1982.

Bolivian Revolutionary Workers' Party (PRTB): see **National Liberation Army** (Bolivia).

Bolivian Socialist Falange (*Falange Socialista Boliviana*/FSB)
An overtly fascist, right-wing nationalist party, founded in Chile in 1937 after the Chaco War by Bolivian students who modelled it on the Spanish Falange. Their leader was Oscar Unzaga de la Vega. In 1951 the FSB won 11% of the vote in a general election. After the MNR-led coup of 1952 it became the principal right-wing opposition, claiming to represent authentically Catholic policies. It organised many abortive uprisings against the government, as well as participating in elections. The most serious uprising was in April 1959, when the Falange held part of La Paz for six hours. Among the 50 deaths was that of Unzaga, said by the

government to have committed suicide. After his death the party reduced its armed activity and sought stronger links with nascent Christian democrat forces, as well as representing the regional interests of the south-eastern province of Santa Cruz. After the closure of Congress in 1969 internal divisions widened, leading to the formation of the Left FSB (FSBI) in 1970.

The FSBI opposed the 1971 Bánzer coup and suffered repression during the *banzerato*. In December 1971, with the National Left Movement (MNI) and the Túpaj Catari Peasant Movement (MCTC), it formed the National Left Front (FIN). The strains continued, despite the FSB's participation for the first time in government as a member of the Popular Nationalist Front under Gen. Bánzer from 1971 to 1974 (when its leader, Dr Mario Gutiérrez, became foreign minister). In 1978 and 1979 its forces were divided, and in the latter year it won only nine seats out of 144. In 1980, former health minister and Santa Cruz politician Carlos Valverde Barbery, who had taken control of the party, became its presidential candidate, winning 5% of the vote. The party divided into two factions, under Gutiérrez (since deceased) and Gastón Moreira Ostría respectively, who parted company in 1974 over the latter's support for the military. It has been supplanted by Bánzer's Nationalist Democratic Action (ADN), which attracted many FSB dissidents, and in response it has moved (at least rhetorically) to the left, opposing the ADN–MNR pact. FSB support is restricted mainly to the urban bourgeoisie and the small business sector. In 1985 it won only three seats in Congress.
See also **Bánzer Suárez**.

Bonifaz, Neptali: see **Conservative Party** (Ecuador).

Bordaberry, Juan María

b. 1928. President of Uruguay, 1972–6. A onetime Blanco who changed parties to join the Colorados, Bordaberry was born into a land-owning family. He served as agriculture minister under the administration of Jorge Pacheco Areco. In the November 1971 elections he stood as the *continuista* candidate, winning narrowly amid allegations of electoral fraud. During his term in office civil liberties were further restricted and the armed forces were given greater powers in the counter-insurgency campaign against the MLN-Tupamaros guerrillas. The military chiefs established virtual veto powers over the president in February 1973, after a confrontation in which Bordaberry was forced to sign the Boisso Lanza agreement (establishing among other things a military-dominated National Security Council, COSENA). Bordaberry and the armed forces were nevertheless able to unite in June 1973 when the president ordered the closure of Congress and took dictatorial powers in the so-called *autogolpe*. Bordaberry continued in office until 1976 when the military refused to accept his extreme right-wing constitutional proposals and replaced him with a more malleable civilian figurehead.
See also ***autogolpe; Proceso***.

b

border dispute (*Peru/Ecuador*)

The frontier between Ecuador and Peru remained undefined after the break-up of the Republic of Gran Colombia in 1830, and for more than 100 years relations between the two countries gradually worsened as a result of the dispute. In 1941 Peru invaded southern Ecuador at two points (allegedly in self-defence), seizing large areas of Amazonian territory from the much weaker Ecuadorean army. An armistice was arranged by Argentina, Brazil, and the US, after which Peru was awarded the bulk of the territory in dispute, amounting to some 55% of total Ecuadorean land area, under the Rio de Janeiro Protocol of 1942. The Protocol was repudiated in 1960 by Ecuador, which argues that it was imposed by force and that the discovery of a previously unknown river makes its principles impossible to follow. Border demarcation stopped as a result, and 78 kilometres remains unmarked. The guarantor powers ruled that the Ecuadorean repudiation was illegal. Much of the oil discovered in Ecuador since the 1960s has been found close to the disputed territory, a factor which helped create further tension. In January/February 1981 armed clashes again took place along the 1942 border, but the intervention of the four guarantor countries (the fourth being Chile) prevented a full-scale war. Most official Ecuadorean documents bear the slogan 'Ecuador has been, is and shall be an Amazonian country'. On his inauguration in 1988, President Borja of Ecuador reiterated his country's desire for negotiations with Peru. This led to the early departure of the Peruvian delegation, which President García had declined to join at the inauguration because of the dispute.

Borja Cevallos, Rodrigo

b. 1935. President of Ecuador 1988– . A professor of law and former member of the Radical Liberal Party (PLR), social democrat Rodrigo Borja founded his own party, the Democratic Left (ID) in 1970. He stood for the presidency in 1978, when he came fourth, and again in 1984, when he was narrowly defeated by León Febres Cordero. In 1988 he defeated Abdalá Bucaram of the Roldosista Party (PRE) by 46% to 41% in the run-off. A coalition with the Christian Democrats (*Democracia Popular*/DP) assured him of a congressional majority, and he included one DP member in his cabinet. Borja signalled a clear break with the overtly pro-US foreign policy of right-winger Febres Cordero. He immediately restored relations with Nicaragua and announced his intention of strengthening links with the Non-Aligned Movement, as well as seeking membership of the Group of Eight (the Contadora and Lima Groups). Among those present at his inauguration were Presidents Daniel Ortega of Nicaragua and Fidel Castro of Cuba. Borja said the 'social debt' must be paid before the country's US$10bn foreign debt, but was expected to be pragmatic in renegotiating the latter, while seeking greater Latin American unity on the issue. He denied any nationalisation plans and said his intention was to stimulate production by increasing consumer spending and granting tax incentives to industry and agriculture. He also promised stricter exchange and interest rate controls. An emergency

economic plan, including a 35% devaluation and the doubling of fuel prices, brought immediate street protests.
See also **Democratic Left**.

Born brothers: see **Montoneros**.

Bosnegers: see **Jungle Commando/Suriname National Liberation Army**.

Bossa Nova: see **Sarney**.

Botero, José Fernando: see **Barco Vargas**.

b

Bouterse, Col. Desi

b. 1945. Ruler of Suriname 1980–8. After attending business school in Paramaribo, Bouterse went to the Netherlands in 1968 and joined the Dutch army. In 1974 he served with NATO forces in West Germany, later returning to Suriname to become an army sports instructor. In 1978 he became chairman of the soldiers' newly-formed trade union, and on 25 February 1980 was a leading member of the group of leftist officers which seized power from the civilian government of premier Henck Arron after complaining about poor conditions. He emerged as head of the military government in August 1980 after a power struggle with radicals. He then drew closer to Cuba, Grenada and later Libya, and brought two small Marxist parties into the government. But his political isolation, at home and abroad, became acute after the execution in his presence of 15 opposition figures in December 1982. The Netherlands cut off all aid in protest.

Shock at the 1983 US invasion of Grenada made him back away from the left and economic pressure obliged him to agree to the return of the old political parties in 1985. He was also under pressure from foreign-backed rebels in eastern Suriname. He handed power back to the old parties in 1988 after parliamentary elections in November 1987, but he and the army remained very powerful. Bouterse sponsored the creation of the National Democratic Party in July 1987, but the party won only three seats in the November poll.
See also **Jungle Commando**.

Bravo, Douglas

b. 1933. A Venezuelan left-wing activist and prominent guerrilla leader in the 1960s and 1970s, Bravo was born in the small town of Cabure in Falcón state. He founded a Communist Party (PCV) youth group in his home town in 1946. After entering Maracaibo University in 1953, he dedicated himself to political activism. He had backed the 1950 oil workers' strike and a 1952 student strike, and was imprisoned briefly on both occasions. He was involved in the planning of the 1958 revolution against Gen. Marcos Pérez Jiménez. He emerged after the fall of the dictatorship as a leader of the militant wing of the PCV political committee, who encouraged the party to back armed struggle against the government of Rómulo Betancourt. Bravo was one of the first to take to the hills to organise fighters. Although captured and imprisoned late in 1961, he managed to escape in March 1962; in the same year he formed the José Leonardo Chirinos Front in his home state of Falcón, which established a rural guerrilla *foco* along the lines of those which had recently succeeded in Cuba. The Front was named after the leader of a slave revolt in the area in 1795.

Bravo later became a key leader in the National Liberation Front/National Liberation Armed Forces (FLN/FALN) guerrilla organisation. In 1965/66, as the PCV began moving away from armed struggle, Bravo led the FLN/FALN away from the party, insisting on the need to keep on fighting. In 1967, despite being supported by Fidel Castro, Bravo was expelled from the PCV. Most guerrillas stopped fighting under the terms of an amnesty offered by the COPEI government after 1969, but it was not until September 1979 that Bravo agreed to accept an amnesty, setting up a new group, the Party of the Venezuelan Revolution (PRV) in the early 1980s.
See also: **FLN/FALN;** ***foquismo*****; guerrilla insurgency** (Venezuela)**; Venezuelan Communist Party.**

BRAZIL, Federative Republic of

Capital: Brasilia
Independence (from Portugal) 1822
Area: 8,411,965 sq km
Population (1987) 141.45m (72.2% urban)
Pop. growth rate (1980–5): 2.3%
Pop. density: 15.9/sq km
Infant mortality (1980–5): 70.7 per thousand
Life expectancy at birth (1980): 60.1
Literacy (1980): 68.7%
GDP per capita (1987e): US$2,428
Foreign debt per capita (1987e): US$857
Principal export commodities (% of total 1985 exports): coffee (10.2%); soya (9.9%); transport equipment (9%); iron ore (7%); meat products (3.3%)

Political system

Constitution: 1969, as amended in April 1977, December 1978, January 1979. In November 1986 a Constituent Assembly was elected, empowered to draft an entirely new constitution, the country's eighth. *President*: José Sarney (PMDB) (1985–); chosen in indirect elections to succeed Gen. João Figueiredo (military regime). Congress voted in 1985 to re-establish direct presidential elections. Although the presidential term under the amended 1969 constitution was set at six years, the Constituent Assembly was expected to reduce it to four. The Senate has 72 members, three elected for each state and three for the Federal District. Senators have eight-year terms in office. Alternately one third and two thirds of the senate seats come up for re-election every four years. The number of members of the Chamber of Deputies is proportional to population, with each state electing not less than eight and not more than 60. There were

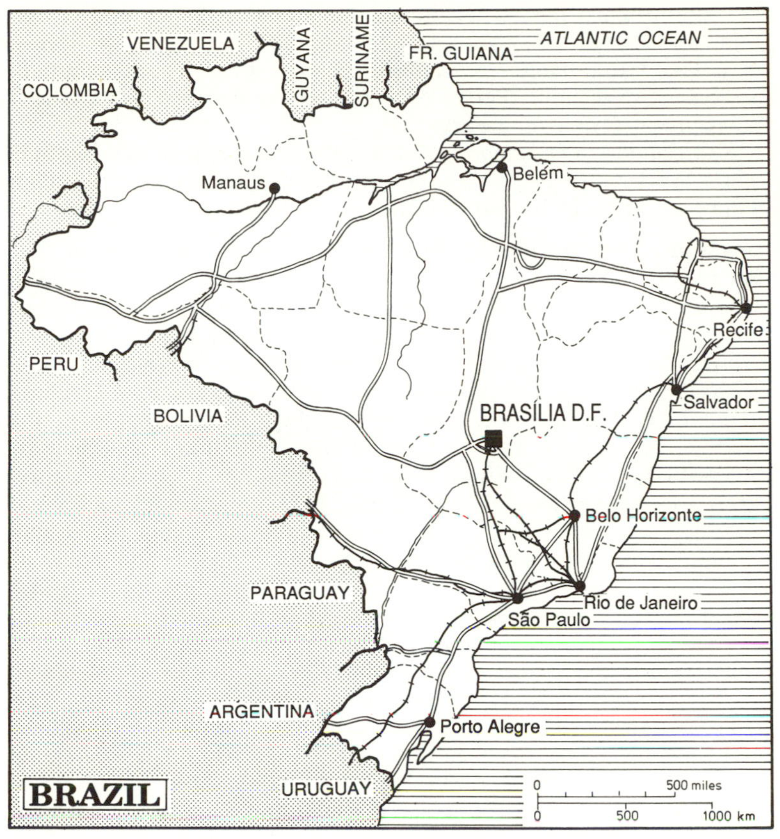

487 deputies elected in November 1986. Each is elected for a four-year term.

Political organisations

Parties (seats in Senate/Chamber of Deputies): Brazilian Democratic Movement Party/PMDB (45/261); Liberal Front Party/PFL (15/116); Democratic Social Party/PDS (5/32); Democratic Trabalhista Party/PDT (2/24); Christian Democratic Party/PDC (1/5); Liberal Party/PL (1/6); Brazilian Municipalist Party (1/-); Brazilian Socialist Party/PSB (1/1); Brazilian Trabalhista Party/PTB (1/18); Workers' Party/PT (-/16); Brazilian Communist Party/PCB (-/3); Communist Party of Brazil/PCdoB (-/5)

The following parties have no congressional representation: Party of the Brazilian People/PPB; Municipalist Communitarian Party/PMC; Humanist Party/PH; Social Christian Party/PSC; Trabalhista National Party/PTN; Nationalist Party/PN; Renovating Trabalhista Party/PTN; Brazilian Liberal Party/PLB; Agrarian Socialist and Renovating

Trabalhista Party/Pasart; National Communitarian Party/PCN; New Republic Party/PNR; National Mobilisation Party/PMN; Socialist Party/PS; Reforming Trabalhista Party/PRT; Youth Party/PJ; Nationalist Democratic Party/PND; Progressive Renovating Party/PRP; Independent Democratic Party/PDI.

Main labour organisations: General Confederation of Labour/CGT; Single Workers' Centre/CUT. *Main employers' organisations*: São Paulo State Federation of Industry/FIESP.

b

Brazilian Communist Party (*Partido Comunista Brasileiro*/PCB)
Founded in 1922, the party began organising a General Labour Confederation in the late 1920s. In 1935 it received an important boost when it was joined by the *tenente* leader and hero of the Long March, Luis Carlos Prestes. In the same year the PCB launched the National Liberating Alliance (*Aliança Nacional Libertadora*/ANL), an attempt at creating a Popular Front in line with Comintern policy. Prestes rose rapidly to become party leader. The ANL was anti-imperialist and anti-capitalist, but its main emphasis was on a common front against fascism. In July 1935, coinciding with a change in Comintern policy, Prestes issued a more radical manifesto, calling a general strike; the government of President Getulio Vargas responded by banning the ANL. Prestes and other militants were involved in encouraging the military uprisings of 23–27 November 1935 in army barracks in Rio de Janeiro, Recife, and Natal, in what has been described as the first armed communist uprising in Latin America. But the rebellion was easily suppressed, and was followed by mass arrests of PCB and ANL members, including Prestes.

The party was banned during the *Estado Nôvo* until 1945, when it took part in the elections, gaining 10% of the vote. The PCB was banned again in 1947–60, and during the 1964–85 military regime. Under the post-1964 military regime it operated clandestinely, publishing the newspaper *Voz Operaria* sporadically. Party members were persecuted and imprisoned, particularly in 1975/76. Prestes and other leaders returned from exile under the terms of the 1979 amnesty; *Voz Operaria* resumed regular publication in 1980. In the November 1982 congressional elections the PCB gave unofficial support to opposition parties such as the Brazilian Democratic Movement (PMDB) and the Workers' Party (PT). The entire Central Committee was arrested, and later released, during the Party Congress in December 1982. A new PCB Congress in January 1984 confirmed a 'Eurocommunist' policy of seeking a nationalist/democratic government, and expelled the veteran Prestes, who continued to argue the case for a revolutionary administration. The party supported the Democratic Alliance candidate, Tancredo Neves, in the 1984/85 election campaign.
See also **Communist Party of Brazil; Long March; Prestes**.

Brazilian Democratic Movement (*Movimento Democrático Brasileiro*/MDB)
The only permitted opposition party in Brazil under military rule in the 1965–79 period. After the political reforms of 1979, which introduced a

multi-party system, it changed its name to PMDB. the MDB came into being after Institutional Act 2 of 1965 abolished the existing groupings. The MDB bloc in congress was made up of deputies and senators who, in the main, had previously been in the Trabalhista Party (PTB). The party gradually built up considerable strength in urban areas where opposition to military rule spread. But it struggled under many disadvantages such as an electoral system heavily weighted in favour of the ruling party, and the far-reaching central government controls on all opposition activity. In the three months after the introduction of Institutional Act 5 in December 1968, for example, almost 40% of the MDB deputies were removed from congress (*cassados*) by presidential order.

The party made important gains in congressional elections in November 1974. Both the more right-wing internal tendency known as the *adhesionistas* and the leftist *autenticos* sought to make maximum use of the political liberalisation under the administration of Gen. Ernesto Geisel, known as the period of *distensão*. But political controls were again re-introduced when it looked as if the MDB might win the 1978 elections. In 1979 the new administration of Gen. João Figuereido introduced political reforms which led to the formation of the PMDB.

See also **Brazilian Democratic Movement Party; National Renovating Alliance**.

Brazilian Democratic Movement Party (*Partido Movimento Democrático Brasileiro*/PMDB)

The party came into existence as a result of the 1979 political reforms, which dissolved its predecessor, the MDB, and allowed the emergence of a multi-party system. Most centrist MDB congressmen joined the PMDB. The party did well in the 1982 congressional elections, taking 200 seats in the chamber of deputies and 21 in the senate. It also obtained nine out of 23 governorships. In 1984 the PMDB emerged as the driving force in the campaign for an end to military rule and direct presidential elections. Although the *diretas já* campaign failed to obtain the desired direct elections, it cemented the Democratic Alliance with the Liberal Front Party (PFL) which successfully backed the presidential candidacy of Tancredo Neves. In January 1985 Neves was elected along with José Sarney as vice-president. Although he was much more closely aligned with the PFL, Sarney had to join the PMDB, as the constitution required the presidential and vice-presidential candidates on each ticket to belong to the same party. As a result of the president-elect's fatal illness it was Sarney who became president. The PMDB's influence on the government was exerted mainly through its veteran president, Ulysses Guimarães.

In the November 1986 state and congressional elections the PMDB enjoyed a landslide victory, winning an outright majority in both houses of congress and taking 22 out of 23 state governorships. The party traditionally accommodated a wide variety of opinion, ranging from moderate conservatives through to the left, and this heterogeneity if anything increased when it came to power, with many previous supporters of the military regime joining its ranks. Despite this, the PMDB's real

electoral identity was based on its opposition during the long years of military rule, its commitment to social reforms, and its economic nationalism.
See also ***diretas já***; **Liberal Front Party; Sarney**.

Brazilian Economic Miracle

A period of rapid economic growth under the post-1964 military regime, which lasted from the late 1960s to the early 1970s. Economic policy immediately after the military coup was under the control of planning minister Roberto Campos, who pursued an anti-inflationary stabilisation programme. But after 1967, largely under the control of finance minister Antônio Delfim Netto, the emphasis was on growth. The period most often referred to as that of the 'economic miracle' is 1967–73, characterised by annual GDP expansion of around 10%, and the emergence of Brazil as an important exporter of manufactured goods. At the same time, however, the distribution of income in the country became more unequal and in some areas of the country the poor became worse off in absolute terms. To a considerable extent this was a logical result of an economic policy which gave growth a higher priority than distribution, which stressed prestige development projects and which ruled out land reform. The period of rapid growth was also associated with authoritarian central control and widespread repression of the opposition to the regime. For these reasons the real nature of the 'economic miracle' is still subject to intense debate.
See also **Castello Branco; Costa e Silva**.

Brazilian Expeditionary Force (FEB)

A Brazilian military force which fought with the Allied armies in Italy towards the end of the Second World War. The FEB had important political effects within Brazil itself. In the short term, the identification with the Allies and the defeat of fascism brought pressure to bear on President Getulio Vargas to dismantle the authoritarian *Estado Nôvo* and call elections in 1945. It also influenced the military officers who, fearful that Vargas would manipulate the elections, forced him to resign in October 1945. In the longer term the FEB was a formative experience for many young officers who were later to come to the fore. They included Humberto Castello Branco, the first post-1964 military president. Castello Branco and other FEB veterans formed an identifiable strand of political thinking within the military. They believed that Brazil could profit from a close relationship with the United States, were distrustful of excessive nationalism and anything that smacked of Mussolini-style corporatism, and held a rather abstract belief in the virtues of democracy, although they were prepared to put democracy to one side in favour of what they saw as the more pressing needs of national security and development. This strand of thought is often contrasted with the hard-line military groups which were both more authoritarian and in some senses more nationalist.
See also **Authoritarian Nationalists; Castello Branco; *Estado Nôvo*; Superior War School; Vargas**.

Brazilian Integralist Action (AIB): see **Integralism**.

Briones, Carlos: see **Socialist Party of Chile**.

British Guiana: see **GUYANA, Republic of**.

Brizola, Leonel de Moura

b. 1922 A Brazilian centre-left politician in the *trabalhista* tradition, Brizola played an important political role in the early 1960s as governor of his home state of Rio Grande do Sul. From this vantage point he provided substantial but always critical support for president João Goulart (who was also his brother-in-law). To the left of the president on a number of issues, Brizola frequently criticised Goulart's more conciliatory stance in relation to US capital in the country. In October 1962 Brizola was elected deputy for the Trabalhista Party (PTB) in Guanabara. As right-wing pressure against Goulart's reform programme increased, Brizola called for a radicalisation of government policy. In particular he wanted more decisive action on the land reform issue. In the March/April 1964 military coup, despite calling briefly for armed resistance, Brizola had to accept defeat and exile, with the new regime stripping him of all political rights. It was only 15 years later in 1979 that Brizola was able to return to Brazil. He immediately set up the *Partido Democratico Trabalhista* (PDT); as its leader he campaigned for and won the governorship of Rio de Janeiro in 1982. In office he embarked on a large school-building programme, although his traditional conservative opponents accused him of populist excesses and corruption. Brizola suffered a blow in November 1986 when the PDT candidate to succeed him in the governorship was beaten by the PMDB. But despite this set-back, Brizola was still seen in late 1987 as a future presidential contender.
See also ***Trabalhismo*; Goulart; Democratic Trabalhista Party**.

Broad Colombian Movement (MAC): see **Communist Party of Colombia**.

Broad Front (*Frente Ampla*): see **Lacerda**.

Broad Front (*Frente Amplio*)

A left-wing coalition formed in Uruguay in March 1971 to fight the general elections that year, and which went on to become the country's third major political organisation, after the two traditional parties. A total of 17 political groups originally came together in the alliance, of which the most important were: the Communist, Socialist, and Christian Democratic parties; dissident tendencies from the traditional parties such as *Lista 99* from the Colorados (later to take the name Party for the Government of the People) and the group around senator Enrique Erro from the Blancos; and others such as the 26th March Movement (sympathetic to MLN-Tupamaros) as well as various tiny Trotskyist groups. In the 1971 elections the Frente's presidential candidate was retired Gen. Líber Seregni, who polled over 18%, an historically high result for any left-wing candidate in Uruguay. The party's platform included a promise of land reform, nationalisations in the banking sector, and state control of the export trade.

Following the 1973 military coup, the *Frente*, along with many of its member parties was declared illegal. Gen. Seregni was imprisoned, remaining in jail for most of the 1973–85 period. Hundreds of other members of the coalition were also imprisoned or forced into exile and some lost their lives as a result of political repression and torture. Among them was Zelmar Michelini, a former senator and leader of *Lista 99* who was kidnapped and killed in Argentina. At the end of the military regime the *Frente* was legalised, in August 1984, to enable it to participate in the elections four months later. Party leaders had taken part in negotiations with the military leadership, and were signatories of the so-called '*Club Naval* Pact' which allowed the elections to go ahead. Gen. Seregni was banned from standing, however, and his place was taken by Juan José Crottogini, who came third with 20% of the vote. The party came close to winning control of the municipality of Montevideo, losing to the Colorados by only a small proportion of votes.
See also ***Club Naval* Pact; *Proceso*; Seregni**.

Broad Left Front (*Frente Amplio de Izquierda*/FADI)
An Ecuadorean political alliance of the left, founded in 1977, whose members include the Communist Party (PCE), the Ecuadorean Revolutionary Socialist Party (PSRE) and the Revolutionary Movement of the Christian Left (MRIC). Two smaller groups, the Second Independence Movement (MSI) and the People's Committee (*Comité del Pueblo*) left in 1980 to form the Ecuadorean Popular Revolutionary Union (URPE). In 1984 the FADI joined the newly-formed opposition coalition, the Progressive Front, having won two congressional seats. These grew to three in the mid-term elections of 1986, when FADI leader René Mauge (also general secretary of the Communist Party, PCE) was elected to Congress. In the same year it proposed the presidential candidacy of Gen. Frank Vargas Pazzos, and it withdrew in May 1987 from a proposed alliance of the left in opposition to the alternative candidacy of Jaime Hurtado of the maoist Popular Democratic Movement (MDP). It won two seats in the 1988 elections.
See also **Progressive Front; Vargas Pazzos rebellion**.

Bruné, Paulin: see **Bertrand, Léon** (French Guiana).

Brunswijk, Ronnie: see **Jungle Commando/Suriname National Liberation Army**.

Bucaram, Abdalá: see **Bucaram, Assad**.

Bucaram, Averroes: see **Bucaram, Assad**.

Bucaram, Assad
d. 1981. Ecuadorean populist leader; elected mayor of Guayaquil in 1962 and 1967; president of the Concentration of Popular Forces (CFP) party; and three times congressional deputy for Guayas province. The son of a Lebanese immigrant, he had no formal education but became a wealthy

businessman, and for many years the most influential politician of the *Costa* (coastal) region. He had broad popular support, but was opposed by the traditional Guayaquil oligarchy. Bucaram backed the Democratic Left Front (FID) coalition in the 1968 elections.

From 1970 to 1972 he was in exile, after being deported to Panama by the Velasco Ibarra regime. He was an outspoken opponent of the 1972–9 military government, and was jailed and again briefly exiled for his views. Banned by the military government from standing in the 1978/79 presidential elections, on the ostensible grounds of his foreign parentage, he was replaced by his niece's husband, Jaime Roldós Aguilera, who subsequently split with Bucaram when he (Roldós) moved towards left social democracy. Bucaram was elected as a deputy for the CFP and became chairman of Congress, but he died in May 1981. His son Averroes Bucaram also became a leader of the CFP and was elected president of Congress in August 1985, with the support of the pro-government majority. Assad's nephew (and Averroes' cousin), Abdalá Bucaram, police chief and later mayor of Guayaquil, fled the country in 1985 after being charged with offences against state security for questioning the military's share of the budget in a press interview in New York. He had previously been sentenced to four days in jail for alleging that police bullets had killed a kidnap victim during a rescue attempt. Abdalá, leader of the Roldosista Party (PRE), stood for president in 1988, losing in the run-off to Rodrigo Borja. Despite a congressional amnesty, charges of embezzlement against him remained outstanding and he fled once more to Panama after the elections.

See also **Concentration of Popular Forces; Roldós Aguilera**.

búfalo

A Peruvian term for a member of the APRA party's gang of thugs, organised to threaten and attack political opponents, even within Congress itself, and maintain discipline in party ranks. Alan García, who became general secretary of APRA in October 1982, moved to curb the activities of the '*búfalos*' as part of a campaign to clean up the party image.

See also **APRA**.

Buiskool, J. A. E.: see **National Party of Suriname**.

Bukovsky, Vladimir: see **Corvalán Lepe**.

Burnham, Forbes

1923–85. Prime minister of Guyana 1964–80, president 1980–5. Born in Kitty, British Guiana. A former lawyer, Forbes Burnham helped Cheddi Jagan found the People's Progressive Party (PPP) in 1950 and became its first chairman. Elected to the House of Assembly in 1953, he was minister of education in Jagan's short-lived left-wing government, removed in that year by the British colonial authorities. Backed by anti-communist officials in Britain and the US, he split with Jagan in 1955 and in 1957 founded the People's National Congress (PNC) party, which he led until his death. Though tainted by his collaboration with the foreign countries which enabled him to replace Jagan in 1964, at first in coalition with the small, right-wing United Force (UF) party, he steered a leftist and nationalist course soon after independence in 1966 and throughout the 1970s. He nationalised the country's key bauxite and sugar industries, striking an energetic figure in Third World forums, forging close ties with communist countries and leading a movement for Anglo-Caribbean unity.

b

In 1974 he declared the paramountcy of the PNC over the state and in 1978 organised a referendum which gave increased powers to the president, a post he then assumed in 1980 after a general election denounced at home and abroad as rigged. His reputation had earlier been tarnished by the murder of Guyanese leftist leader and historian Walter Rodney in Georgetown in June 1980, which many accused him of planning.
See also **People's National Congress; Rodney**.

Busch, Lt Col. Germán: see **Revolutionary Nationalist Movement**.

Bush Negroes: see **Jungle Commando/Suriname National Liberation Army**.

Bustamante y Rivera, José Luis: see **APRA**.

C

Caballero, Gen. Bernardino: see **Colorado Party** (Paraguay).

cabecitas negras*:** see ***descamisados.

Cabot Lodge, Henry: see **Monroe doctrine**.

cacique

A term widespread in hispanophone Latin America, said to be of Haitian or Cuban indian origin, and originally meaning an indian chief. It is used throughout the region to refer to a political boss (hence '*caciquismo*' – a political system based on the boss figure).
See also ***caudillo, caudillismo***.

Cafiero, Antonio: see **Peronism**.

Caldera, Rafael

b.1916. A leading Venezuelan Christian Democrat, co-founder of the COPEI party and president in 1969–74. Born in San Felipe, Yarucuy, Caldera went to the Jesuit Colegio San Ignacio de Loyola, from where he graduated with a baccalaureate in philosophy and letters in 1931. As a student at the Central University he became active in Catholic and anti-communist circles. In 1932–4 he was secretary of the central council of the Venezuelan Catholic Youth Organisation, later attending a meeting in Rome of Iberoamerican University Catholic Action (*Acción Católica Iberoamericana Universitaria*), where he befriended Eduardo Frei, a future Christian Democrat leader and president in Chile.

In 1936 Caldera founded the National Student Union (*Unión Nacional Estudiantil*/UNE), which described its philosophy as being based on 'Christian social principles'. Graduating in 1939 in law and political science, Caldera was elected deputy for Yarucuy state in 1941–4. After the 1945 coup which inaugurated the *trienio* of military and Democratic Action (AD) rule, Caldera accepted appointment as attorney general. He resigned in 1946, however, founding the Social Christian COPEI party and leading it in the campaign for the constituent assembly elections, at the end of which he was elected one of the party's 19 representatives in the assembly. He stood as a presidential candidate in the December 1947 elections, taking second place with 22% of the vote. Caldera initially welcomed the 1948 military coup against AD president Rómulo Gallegos, continuing to represent his party in Congress (while AD was banned).

But after Col. Marcos Pérez Jiménez came to the fore within the government and established dictatorial control in 1952, Caldera moved into opposition.

He was arrested various times by the regime; in August 1957, in the run-up to a referendum organised to prolong Pérez Jiménez' rule, Caldera was imprisoned for four months, and was then sent into exile. In New York he held talks with AD and Democratic Republican Union (URD) leaders which, after the January 1958 overthrow of Pérez Jiménez, led to the *Punto Fijo* agreement between the three parties, designed to guarantee the stability of the new democracy. Caldera stood in the December 1958 presidential elections, coming third with 17% of the vote. Under the terms of the *Punto Fijo* agreement, however, COPEI was represented at cabinet level in the new AD government. Caldera again contested the presidential elections as COPEI's candidate in December 1963, coming second with 20% of the vote. He criticised government repression of student demonstrations in 1964; in August 1965, as president of the Christian Democrat Organisation of America, he criticised US intervention in the Dominican Republic.

In the December 1968 elections, on his fourth attempt, Caldera was victorious, with 29% of the vote; COPEI had benefited from a division in AD. Caldera took office in March 1969; he legalised the Communist Party (PCV), which had been banned in 1962, and offered a pacification programme to the various guerrilla movements which were still active. In March 1973 the government legalised the Movement of the Revolutionary Left (MIR), which had decided to end its military campaign and return to electoral politics. Generally speaking, Caldera placed a higher priority on social justice during his presidency than on the rigid anti-communism his background might suggest. In foreign policy too he established diplomatic relations with the Soviet Union and took a more independent stance in relation to the United States, asserting Venezuelan influence in the Caribbean. In 1973 Venezuela joined the Andean Pact common market.

See also **Christian Democracy; COPEI**.

Calderón, Cecilia: see **Radical Alfarist Front**.

Calderón Muñoz, Abdón: see **military governments (Ecuador/1961–79); Radical Alfarist Front**.

Calvi, Roberto: see ***Propaganda Due***.

Calvo, Oscar William: see **People's Liberation Army**.

Cámara, Dom Helder: see **Integralism; Radical Church** (Brazil).

Cámpora, Héctor José

1909–80. Peronist politician who was elected president of Argentina in 1973 but stood down in the same year to make way for General Juan Perón. In 1946 he was elected to the federal Chamber of Deputies as a member of the Independent Party, but rapidly joined the ruling Peronists. He was appointed a member of the Superior Council of the Peronist movement in 1947 and was elected president of the Chamber of Deputies in 1948, a position which he retained until 1953. After the 1955 military coup, Cámpora was imprisoned in southern Argentina; but in March 1957 he was among a group of prisoners who managed to escape to Chile. He returned to Argentina in 1960. In November 1971 Cámpora was appointed Perón's personal representative inside Argentina. In December 1972 Perón, who was barred from standing himself, nominated Cámpora as the Justicialist Liberation Front (FREJULI) presidential candidate.

In the 11 March 1973 polls, Cámpora won with 49.6% of the vote on the slogan of 'Cámpora in government, Perón in power'. On taking office he decreed an immediate amnesty for all left-wing political prisoners (in the main members of the guerrilla groups which had been fighting against the military government) and re-established diplomatic relations with Cuba. He also sought and obtained a 'social pact' between business and labour. Cámpora's administration was on the left of the Peronist spectrum, both influenced and pressured by groups like the Montoneros. The tensions within the movement came out into the open on Perón's return on 20 June 1973, when Peronist right-wingers opened fire at Ezeiza airport on the Montoneros and other groups. The death toll was never clearly established, but according to some estimates was over 100. Under pressure from the right, Cámpora resigned the presidency on 13 July 1973, to make way for Perón to stand in new elections. He had been in office for seven weeks.

After the 24 March 1976 military coup, Cámpora sought asylum in the Mexican embassy in Buenos Aires. The military government refused to issue a safe-conduct pass to allow him to travel to Mexico, so he was forced to live as a refugee in the embassy for several years. He was finally allowed to leave shortly before his death in 1980.

See also **Justicialist Liberation Front; Montoneros; Peronism**.

Campos, Roberto: see **Brazilian Economic Miracle**.

Cano, Guillermo: see **Barco Vargas**.

Caracas, Jaime: see **Revolutionary Armed Forces of Colombia.**

Cartagena Agreement: see **Andean Pact**.

Cartagena, Junta del Acuerdo de: see **Andean Pact**.

Casaldáliga, Dom Pedro: see **Radical Church** (Brazil).

cassações

Orders for the removal of political rights (from Portuguese *cassar*, 'to hunt down') imposed by the 1964–85 military regime in Brazil, as established under the terms of the Institutional Acts, usually for a period of ten years. Prominent civilian politicians were *cassados* immediately after the 1964 coup, and the list was continually enlarged as the military rulers became successively more repressive in the late 1960s and early 1970s. The mechanism was used to cancel the mandates of federal, state, and municipal legislative members. The *cassações* provided a useful way of

terminating the public activities of troublesome members of the opposition; they also served as an additional instrument to bolster the ARENA majority in Congress at the expense of the MDB, since when a deputy or senator was *cassado*, his or her seat remained empty.
See also **Brazilian Democratic Movement; Institutional Acts** (Brazil); **National Renovating Alliance**.

Cassemiro, Dimas Antônio: see **guerrilla movements** (Brazil).

Castello Branco, Gen. Humberto de Alençar

C

1900–67. Leader of the 1964 military coup in Brazil and president, 1964–7. Born in Mecejana, Ceará. As a lieutenant colonel in the army, he took part in a training course in Fort Leavenworth in the US in 1943, prior to accompanying the Brazilian Expeditionary Force (FEB) in the European front during the Second World War. During the administration of João Goulart he was appointed head of the Second Army, then head of Army General Staff. Within the increasingly pro-coup officer corps he was considered a moderate. On 21 March 1964, as head of Army General Staff, he sent a circular to all units accusing President João Goulart of seeking to impose a revolutionary regime in the country – a sign to all those who did not already know that he was now firmly in the putschist camp. Following the 31 March 1964 coup and the proclamation of Institutional Act Number 1, by which Goulart was deposed and the armed forces took executive power, Castello Branco was promoted to the rank of field marshal (*mariscal*) and formally selected as president.

During his period in office many hundreds of citizens lost their political rights and the government established rigid controls on society. Diplomatic relations with Cuba were severed. Castello Branco also launched a series of administrative reforms, including the creation of the Central Bank and the National Housing Bank. In October 1965 Institutional Act 2 renewed and extended the government's exceptional powers, established indirect presidential elections, and abolished the existing political parties. Castello Branco also introduced the National Security law. He died in an air crash on 18 July 1968, shortly after stepping down from the presidency.
See also **Brazilian Economic Miracle; Brazilian Expeditionary Force; Coup of 1964** (Brazil); **Costa e Silva.**

Castillo, Jorge del: see **APRA**.

Castillo, Ramón: see **Infamous Decade**.

Castor, Elie

b. 1943, Cayenne. One of French Guiana's two deputies in the French parliament and mayor of Sinnamary. A former teacher and policeman, Castor became a parliamentary deputy for the Guianese Socialist Party (PSG) in 1981. He was elected president of Guiana's General Council in 1985.

Castro, Gen. Cipriano: see **Gómez, Gen. Juan Vicente**.

Castro, Fidel: see **Betancourt doctrine** (Venezuela); **Bravo, Douglas; Guevara de la Serna**.

Castro León, Col. Jesús María: see **Revolution of 1958** (Venezuela).

caudillo, caudillismo

'*Caudillo*' means 'leader' in various senses, including 'chieftain' or 'military leader', but in Latin America its most common usage is as a rough equivalent of 'political boss'. The *caudillo* is the man to whom (typically) a rural dweller owes his allegiance, and for whose choice of candidate he will be required to vote at election time. In return, the boss is expected to dispense political favours, including jobs. '*Caudillismo*' is a pejorative term for the political structure based on this system, which, though less influential than before, remains an important factor in many parts of the region. It is often held to be at the root of the failure of constitutional regimes. Its origins lie in the system of 'debt peonage' and the company store, which appeared in the seventeenth century as a replacement for slavery. In the past, the worker would have been required to fight on behalf of his boss. The post-independence era has been referred to as the 'age of the *caudillos*'.

C

Causa R: see ***Nueva Alternativa***.

CEB: see **liberation theology**.

CELAM II: see **Medellín**.

Central American Workers' Confederation (CCT): see **CLAT**.

***Central Unica de Trabajadores* (CUT) (Chile):** see **Communist Party of Chile (PCCh)**.

Chaco War

A prolonged military conflict between Bolivia and Paraguay in 1932–5 in which an estimated 100,000 people died and 250,000 were injured. The two countries went to war over the Chaco Boreal, a large area consisting mainly of deserts and swamps, ownership of which had been disputed since independence from Spain. Paraguay had maintained a token presence in the largely uninhabited area, but the issue was brought to a head by the (mistaken) belief that it contained large oil deposits. Bolivia also sought possession to establish a route by river through to the Atlantic (as the country had lost its Pacific coastline in the War of the Pacific with Chile in the 1870s). There had been border clashes in 1927; full-scale war broke out in 1932. Bolivia had a larger and better equipped army, but many of the indian soldiers from the Andes were ill-accustomed to the terrain and the Paraguayan troops were able to inflict some important defeats on their opponents. In fact the war rapidly depleted the energies and resources of both countries, with many soldiers dying from rampant illnesses as well as from the fighting itself.

A truce was declared in 1935 after both countries had mortgaged their economies in an attempt to keep their respective war efforts going. A

peace treaty in 1938 gave Paraguay about 75% of the disputed territory, while Bolivia was guaranteed use of a Paraguayan port and navigation rights through rivers to reach the Atlantic. The war had profound effects on both countries, setting back economic development and fostering political instability as well as exacerbating xenophobic tendencies.
See also ***Febreristas***.

Chandisingh, Ranji: see **People's National Congress**.

Chapultepec, Act of: see **Rio Treaty**.

***'Charro Negro'*:** see **Marquetalia**.

Charry Rincón, Fernando: see **Marquetalia**.

Chaves, Aureliano: see ***diretas já***.

Chaves, Juan Ramón: see **Colorado Party** (Paraguay).

Chávez, Dr Federico: see **Colorado Party** (Paraguay)**; Stroessner**.

Chicago Boys

A term used to describe the monetarist economists who took charge of policy under a series of military regimes in the 1970s. Many had graduated from the University of Chicago, where they had been pupils of Milton Friedman, the main exponent of the theory that money supply levels determine the rate of inflation. In office, they sought to apply 'shock measures' designed to remove all impediments to the free working of the markets and concentrating on cutting state spending and reducing protective tariffs. These policies were associated with rapid falls in real wages and employment, in a climate of political repression. One of the first Chicago graduates in charge of policy was Fernando Leniz, appointed economy minister by the Chilean military junta after the September 1973 coup. The term 'Chicago Boys' was later applied more loosely to ministers who graduated from other US universities and who were not pure monetarists, such as José Martínez de Hoz in Argentina and Alejandro Végh Villegas in Uruguay.
See also **Martínez de Hoz**.

CHILE, Republic of

Capital: Santiago
Independence (from Spain): 1818
Area: 756,629 sq km
Population (1987): 12.54m (83% urban)
Pop. growth rate (1970–86): 1.7%
Pop. density: 16.57/sq km
Infant mortality (1980–5): 23.7 per thousand
Life expectancy at birth (1980–5): 71
Literacy (1982): 91.7%
GDP per capita (1986e): US$2,306
Foreign debt per capita (1986e): US$1,639

CHILE
PERU
BOLIVIA
PARAGUAY
ARGENTINA
Arica
Iquique
Loa River
Antofagasta
PACIFIC
OCEAN
Copiapó River
Viña del Mar
Valparaiso
SANTIAGO
Concepción
Chillán
Temuco
Valdivia
Osorno
Puerto Montt
ATLANTIC
OCEAN
0 1 km
Sala y
Gomez I.
0 5 km
Easter Island
(Isla de Pascua)
Punta Arenas
Beagle Channel
0 100 200 300 400 500 miles
0 500 km

C

Main exports (1986): copper (41.9%); fruit (12%); seafood (10%); timber and products (9.7%)

Political system

Constitution: approved by controversial plebiscite in 1980 (permanent provisions were due to come into effect in 1988/89, prior to which many basic rights were suspended). *Head of state/government*: Gen. Augusto Pinochet Ugarte (1973–); seized power in a coup d'etat on 11 September 1973 from the elected left-wing Popular Unity (UP) government of Dr Salvador Allende. Pinochet was proclaimed president in December 1974, but only inaugurated in 1981. *Junta members*: Gen. Humberto Gordon (army); Gen. Fernando Matthei (air force); Adm. José Toribio Merino (navy); Gen. Rodolfo Stange (carabineros). Legislative functions are performed by the junta, assisted by four legislative commissions. The de facto regime planned to hold a plebiscite on 5 October 1988 on the question of Gen. Pinochet's continued rule. A simple majority would suffice to give him power until 1997, prior to which an election involving a choice of candidates was scheduled. If a majority was not forthcoming, Pinochet would rule for a further year before calling a fresh presidential election in which more than one candidate would be permitted. Under the permanent constitutional provisions, political parties with programmes based on 'class struggle' and those deemed to be 'harmful to the family' will not be permitted. Presidential elections will be every eight years, with no re-election permitted (this clause is suspended for the 1988 elections). The president will be permitted to declare a state of emergency for up to 20 days. There will be a two-chamber legislature, which the president will be permitted to dissolve once during his term. The upper chamber will comprise 26 elected and nine appointed members, who will serve for eight years, while the lower will comprise 130 deputies elected for a four-year term. All former presidents will become senators-for-life.

Political organisations

All party activity was banned in September 1973, although it continued in clandestine and semi-clandestine forms. A new party law was passed in 1984 and promulgated in January 1987. Under it, non-Marxist parties collecting affiliations from at least 0.5% of the electorate in eight or more of the country's 13 regions (including Santiago), or in three adjacent regions, are permitted to apply for registration.

Existing groups include: Christian Democrat Party/PDC; Communist Party/PCCh; Socialist Party/PS (split into a number of factions); National Party/PN; Radical Party/PR; United Popular Action Party /MAPU (split into at least two factions); National Renovation Party/PARENA (an alliance between the National Union/UN, the Independent Democratic Union/UDI, and the National Labour Front/FNT); Christian Left/IC; Liberal Party (or Movement); Humanist Party; National Action Movement/MAN; National Advance; Party of the Republican Right/PDR; Popular Socialist Union/USOPO; Radical Union; Radical

Democracy; Republican Right/DR; Social Christian Movement/MSC; Social Democrat Party/PSD. The Party for Democracy (*Partido por la Democracia*) was set up specifically to campaign for a 'no' vote in the plebiscite. Various armed opposition groups are active, of which the most important are the Manuel Rodríguez Patriotic Front/FPMR and the Revolutionary Left Movement/MIR (two factions).

Labour confederations have mostly been banned. The most important (affiliation in brackets) are: the National Trade Union Coordinating Body/CNS; the Christian Democrat Federation of Workers/FTDC; the Democratic Central Organisation of Workers/CDT (ORIT); and the National Workers' Command/CNT (ICFTU). *Main employers' organisations*: the Manufacturers' Association (*Sociedad de Fomento Fabril*)/SOFOFA; the Confederation of Production and Trade/CPC; the National Agricultural Association SNA; and the Confederation of Business Associations and Federations of Farmers of Chile/CAGFAC.

Chilean Anti-communist Alliance (ACHA): see **death squad**.

Chirinos, José Leonardo: see **Bravo**.

cholo

A disrespectful South American term for an indian who adopts the dress, customs, and language of the dominant (*mestizo*) culture for purposes of social advancement.

Chonchol, Jacques: see **Christian Left; MAPU**.

Christian Democracy *(Democracia Cristiana/DC)*

A political movement which arrived in Latin America from western Europe in the 1940s and 1950s, inspired by the examples of Italy and Germany and based essentially on the social doctrines of the Catholic church. The bulk of these dated from the nineteenth century, although after World War II the emphasis on corporativism which had led to support for fascism was eliminated. Christian Democratic parties stress the ideas embodied in the social encyclicals of Popes Leo XIII and John XXIII (including improved social conditions for the poor); the development of traditional values, such as those of the family; and opposition to the 'materialism' of both Marxism and consumer capitalism.

The period from 1960 to 1968 saw the growth of multi-class, reformist Christian Democrat parties throughout Latin America, led by the government of Eduardo Frei in Chile (1964–70), the first of its kind to be elected in the region. This coincided with the post-Cuban revolution, 'Alliance for Progress' period in US policy, with which many of the DC parties' aims were closely aligned. These included land reform and other social transformations intended to forestall 'other Cubas' by meeting minimum needs within an essentially capitalist framework, while supporting the values of family, church, and property. The Christian Democrats saw themselves as a 'third way' between capitalism and Communism, but the drift to the right of their leaderships led in many countries to the expulsion or withdrawal of radical/youth sectors and the formation of new, generally smaller parties of the 'Christian left' variety, many of which were willing to accommodate the 'atheistic materialism' of the Marxist left. The growth of 'liberation theology' in the region went hand-in-hand with this new movement. Splits also occurred on the right, most notably in Peru with the formation in 1976 of the Popular Christian Party (PPC). By 1973 the Chilean DC was ready to lend support to the military coup against the elected, left-wing government of Allende, while in Uruguay two years earlier its sister party had become a founding member of the left-wing Broad Front (*Frente Amplio*) coalition, working alongside communists and socialists. The second most important country in South America for Christian Democracy has been Venezuela, where the Social Christian COPEI party won the 1968 and 1978 general elections.

The regional body representing Christian Democracy is the Christian Democrat Organisation of America (*Organización Democristiana de América*), while the labour movement is headed by the Latin American Workers' Centre (CLAT). The West German Konrad Adenauer Foundation has poured large amounts of money into Latin American Christian Democracy, as have various agencies of the US government which in general perceives it as an ally.

See also **Alliance for Progress; Christian Democrat parties; CLAT; COPEI; liberation theology**.

Christian Democrat Organisation of America: see **Christian Democracy**.

Christian Democrat Party (Bolivia) (*Partido Demócrata Cristiano*/PDC)

Founded in 1954 by Remo di Natale as the Social Christian Party (PSC), the PDC took its present name in 1964. It professes a mainstream Christian Democrat philosophy, involving a 'third way' between capitalism and Communism, and was always a minor force, despite attempts by its university-based leaders to win converts in the trade union movement. It boycotted the 1966 elections, but accepted the labour ministry under Gen. Barrientos in 1967, withdrawing after his government sent troops to attack miners. The PDC youth later split off to form the Revolutionary PDC (PDCR), which became the Movement of the Revolutionary Left (MIR). PDC leader Benjamín Miguel was deported in 1974 for his opposition to the Bánzer government.

In 1979 the PDC joined a coalition with the Historic MNR (MNR [H]). In 1980 Miguel was running mate to Luis Adolfo Siles Salinas, whose Democratic Revolutionary Front–New Alternative (FDRNA) electoral coalition (of which the PDC was the mainstay) fared poorly. In 1983, President Siles Zuazo gave the PDC a cabinet post. Presidential candidate Luis Ossio won only 1.5% of the vote in 1985, while the party took three congressional seats. Now effectively moribund, it has unofficially ceased to operate as the PDC.

See also **Movement of the Revolutionary Left** (Bolivia).

Christian Democrat Party (Chile) (*Partido Demócrata Cristiano*/PDC)
Founded in June 1957 after the merger of the National Falange with the majority faction of the Social Christian Conservative Party (PCSC – dissolved that year). PDC candidate for the presidency in 1958 was Eduardo Frei, who came third out of four, but from 1961 until the suppression of parties by the government of Gen. Pinochet, the PDC was the largest single party in parliament, and Frei was president of Chile from 1964 to 1970. The PDC built up rural unions (illegal until it came to power) and developed a strong base among the peasantry. Its campaign slogan in 1964 was 'Revolution in Liberty'. The main elements of its programme were: the '*chilenización*' (but not nationalisation) of the largely foreign-owned mines (the country's main source of wealth); agrarian reform and legalisation of rural unions; and progressive tax reforms. Because of the threat posed by the left's candidate, Salvador Allende, Frei won the grudging support of the Liberal (PL) and Conservative (PC) parties for his candidacy and obtained a majority of the popular vote.

In 1965 the PDC took a majority of seats in the lower house; the first time for 100 years that this had been achieved. Its agrarian reform placed an 80-hectare ceiling on properties immune to redistribution. A major school building programme and expansion of teacher training was another achievement. The urban unions, however, which were pushing for reform of the labour code, fell further under the control of left-wing parties. Towards the end of Frei's term the PDC was split into factions. The left wanted an alliance with the Socialists (PS) and Communists (PCCh) in the 1970 elections, and split off in 1969 to form the Unified Popular Action Movement (MAPU). The so-called 'third force' (or *terceristas*), who had sought to mediate between factions later gave birth to the Christian Left (IC) party, and both these new groups joined the Popular Unity (UP) left-wing coalition in government (1970–3). The PDC presidential candidate, Radomiro Tómic (a *tercerista*) was on the left of the party and his stance helped push many voters into support for the right-wing National Party (PN). The PDC (which had lost popularity in part due to failure to deliver on reform promises and partly because of inflation and increased taxation of the middle classes) came third, and agreed to support UP leader Allende in return for an agreement on constitutional guarantees. After attempts at agreement on a government programme with the UP, the PDC went into open opposition, joining the PN and other parties in mid-term electoral alliances as well as seeking to block key government policies and ensuring the impeachment of many government ministers. During this period it received covert funding from the US Central Intelligence Agency.

The party welcomed the 1973 Pinochet coup, which it had helped bring about, partly by forcing a constitutional crisis and calling on the armed forces to restore constitutional order. However, after a few months the bulk of PDC members began to oppose the military government. It retained a working infrastructure despite the ban on all parties: by 1987 it held a majority on the governing bodies of many professional groups

and was dominant in the student movement, while PDC-led unions predominated in key sectors of the economy, including oil, banking, and the power industry. Its influence among business groups was limited by suspicions over its reformist tendencies and its equivocal stance towards the PCCh. Some PDC leaders were exiled for their opposition to the government. The PDC was a founder member of the *Multipartidaria* and Democratic Alliance opposition fronts but despite tactical collaboration with the Communist-led MDP alliance has sought to weaken the PCCh, its nearest rival in terms of size. It backed the 1985 multi-party 'National Agreement on a Return to Full Democracy' but has indicated a willingness to accept the 1980 constitution, despite the wishes of a large minority in the party. After electing right-wing Patricio Aylwin as party president in 1987, it moved immediately to register under the restrictive party law introduced earlier in the year. The PDC campaigned for a vote against Pinochet in the October 1988 plebiscite, but it declined to join the other 15 opposition parties in rejecting impunity for the regime over human rights abuses.
See also **Christian Democracy; Democratic Alliance; Frei Montalva**.

Christian Democrat Party (Paraguay) (*Partido Demócrata Cristiano*/PDC)
Set up in 1960 as the *Movimiento Social Demócrata Cristiano* (MSDC) before taking its current name in 1965, the PDC has opposed the regime of Gen. Alfredo Stroessner, calling for the lifting of the state of siege, the release of all political prisoners, and the return of the exiles. The PDC is generally centrist in orientation, calling for democratisation and economic development on the basis of private ownership and free enterprise. It has been refused legal recognition on the grounds that it has called for electoral boycotts. In the early 1970s it suffered from intense factional in-fighting. In 1971 three successive party conventions were held in an attempt to resolve a leadership dispute. In 1973 two rival party presidents and parallel party organisations came into being; the issue was resolved in favour of Luis Alfonso Resck in 1975.

In 1979 the PDC was one of the four signatories of the National Accord opposition agreement. The party has an estimated membership of around 40,000. It is run by a national committee appointed by the national convention, and it has separate sections for youth, labour, and women. Resck was arrested and deported from the country in July 1981 on charges of subversion.
See also **National Accord; Stroessner**.

Christian Democrat Party (Peru) (*Partido Demócrata Cristiano*/PDC)
Founded in 1955 by Héctor Cornejo Chávez in Arequipa, inspired by the encyclicals *Rerum Novarum* and *Quadragesimo Ano*. Mildly reformist, while stressing the right to private property and free enterprise. In 1956 the party won 13 seats in the lower house and four in the upper. In 1963–6 it was the junior partner in government with the Popular Action (AP) party. It split in two in 1966 when its right wing under Luis

Bedoya Reyes founded the Popular Christian Party (PPC). The left wing, still under Cornejo Chávez, backed the reformist military regime of Gen. Velasco Alvarado (1968–75) but was rejected by his successor, Gen. Morales Bermúdez. The PPC became a much more powerful force, and after gaining only two seats in 1978 constituent assembly, the PDC won none at all in the 1980 congressional elections, whereupon Cornejo Chávez retired from politics. The party's current president is Carlos Blancas, who entered Alan García's government as minister of labour and became justice minister after the Lurigancho massacre.
See also **Popular Christian Party**.

Christian Democrat Social Movement (MSDC): see **Christian Democrat Party** (Paraguay).

Christian Left (Chile) (*Izquierda Cristiana*/IC)
Originally an offshoot of the *tercerista* (third way) faction of the Chilean Christian Democrat Party (PDC), the Christian Left broke away in 1971 after the PDC formed an electoral pact with the right-wing National Party (PN) in opposition to the ruling Popular Unity (UP) coalition. It took 20% of the PDC youth section and 13% of main party members (including half a dozen deputies) with it and joined the UP government in the same year. Some leading members of another breakaway party, the Unified Popular Action Party (MAPU), later joined the IC. They included Jacques Chonchol who served as a minister under President Salvador Allende. The party's limited strength was mainly in the shanty towns (*poblaciones*) and among the Christian base communities. It withdrew from the government in November 1972 after Allende gave cabinet posts to military officers. With all other parties the IC was banned by the Pinochet military government after the 1973 overthrow of Allende. It joined the opposition Socialist Bloc on its formation in September 1983, but remained close to the Communist-led Popular Democratic Movement (MDP). The IC's attitude to the August 1985 National Agreement on Transition to a Full Democracy was equivocal, as was that of the MDP, although party leader Luis Maira did sign the Agreement. It favours the formation of a united party of the left, and joined the United Left coalition launched in June 1987.
See also **Christian Democrat Party; National Agreement on a Transition to Full Democracy; Popular Democratic Movement; Popular Unity; Socialist Bloc; United Left**.

Christian Left (IC) (Ecuador): see **Hurtado Larrea, Dr Osvaldo**.

Clark Memorandum: see **Monroe doctrine**.

CLAT/*Central Latinoamericana de Trabajadores* (Central Organisation of Latin American Workers)
The western hemisphere regional body of the World Confederation of Labour (WCL, formerly the International Federation of Christian Trade Unions (IFCTU)). Founded in 1954 as the Latin American Confederation of Christian Trade Unionists (CLASC), it took its present name in 1971.

CLAT is an anti-communist organisation, but generally perceived as being more critical of right-wing dictatorships than its pro-US counterpart, ORIT. Although formally autonomous it has very strong links with the Christian Democrat parties of Latin America, and in particular the Venezuelan party COPEI. In 1968 it signed an agreement with the pro-Moscow regional body, CPUSTAL, to promote unity in the Latin American labour movement, and it has several times issued strong criticisms of US-style capitalism and business unions.

It is heavily involved with rural labour and the promotion of moderate agrarian reform, and to this end created the Latin American Peasant Federation (FCL). The CLAT Congress meets every four years (most recently in Rio de Janeiro in 1985). The Council meets annually, and a 23-member executive committee meets every six months. Sub-regional bodies include the Central American Workers' Confederation (CCT). Thirty-four national and 18 regional organisations in the Americas are members of CLAT, which is headquartered in Caracas. It claims to represent 10.5m workers in 35 countries and territories.
See also **Christian Democracy; CPUSTAL; ORIT**.

Clayton-Bulwer Treaty: see **Monroe doctrine**.

Club Naval Pact

A controversial agreement reached in Uruguay on 3 August 1984, between the outgoing military regime and some of the country's main political parties, which confirmed the call to general elections on 25 November 1984 and the transition to civilian rule. Signatories of the agreement included the Colorado, Broad Front (*Frente Amplio*), and *Unión Cívica* parties. The Blancos refused to participate in protest at the arrest of their main leader, Wilson Ferreira Aldunate, and the regime's refusal to let him stand as a candidate. The *Frente Amplio*'s main leader, Gen. Líber Seregni, was also banned from standing, but the party nevertheless took part in the talks.

The agreement reached was embodied in Institutional Act 19, which (i) confirmed the elections and the date for the transfer of power; (ii) provided for the establishment of a National Defence Council, on which the three service chiefs would be represented, to advise the future government; (iii) established that military courts could only be used to try civilians during a state of siege, which in turn would only be declared after parliamentary approval; and (iv) stipulated that future commanders-in-chief of the three services would be chosen by the elected president from a short-list drawn up by the services themselves. These provisions were a watered-down version of the constitutional changes that the armed forces had long been seeking, to give them virtual veto powers over an elected government. Institutional Act 19 also provided for their eventual incorporation into the Constitution, after a referendum scheduled (but never in fact held) for November 1985.

The *Club Naval* Pact remained a subject of party-political controversy long after it was signed. The parties which participated justified the agreement by saying it was a necessary concession to the military to

guarantee that the elections would be held. The Blancos insisted that the Pact gave too much away, allowing the armed forces an unwarranted political role in future. They also accused the other parties of going along with an arrangement which unfairly excluded their main electoral rival, Wilson Ferreira Aldunate.
See also **Ferreira Aldunate; *Proceso*; referendum of 1980** (Uruguay).

COB/*Central Obrera Boliviana*
The main trade union organisation in Bolivia, founded in April 1952 after the revolution led by the Revolutionary Nationalist Movement (MNR). The COB has never been affiliated to any international body, but has close links with the World Federation of Trade Unions (WFTU) and its Latin American wing, CPUSTAL. It has from the beginning been the strongest challenger to the power of the army, although it was weakened in the mid-1980s by the collapse of the mining industry, its most important base. Almost all national unions are affiliated, but its leading force has always been the mineworkers' federation (FSTMB) under general secretary (until 1986) Juan Lechín, who was executive secretary of the COB from its foundation until 1987.

Its initial demands, set out in its May Day manifesto of 1952, included the nationalisation of the mines under workers' control, universal suffrage, an agrarian revolution led by the peasant unions, and the replacement of the army with worker/peasant militias. Several COB leaders took part in the first revolutionary government, which partially implemented some of these reforms. By its second Congress in 1957, the COB had serious differences with the government, and the four 'workers' ministers' resigned. This was the beginning of the end for the COB–MNR alliance, which was finished off by the conservative policies of the Paz Estenssoro government in the early 1960s. Both the MNR and the COB split, with pro-government sectors forming the 'COB for Revolutionary Unity' (COBUR), which was soon dissolved. Under Barrientos, trade union rights were suspended and hundreds lost their lives in a COB-led general strike in 1965.

The COB was the scene of many heated debates between the Communists (PCB) and their Trotskyist and other rivals. Its heterogeneous make-up was reflected, for instance, in the 1970 '*Tesis política*' which called both for a multi-class alliance and for permanent revolution under workers' control. The COB played a leading role in the Popular Assembly of 1971, which tried to push the reformist government of Gen. J. J. Torres further to the left. It called for arms to defend the Torres government, but they were not supplied. The COB and other unions were banned in 1974 under the Bánzer military dictatorship, and the COB was unable to hold a congress between 1970 and 1979. When it did so it reaffirmed its independence from political movements, disappointing Hernán Siles Zuazo's Democratic and Popular Union (UDP) coalition which had hoped to be aligned with the COB.

In November 1979 the COB called a general strike in response to a coup by Col. Alberto Natusch: the miners held firm even after the strike was lifted by the COB leaders, and Natusch was forced out after 16 days. In the same year, the Trade Union Confederation of Bolivian Rural Workers (CSUTCB) was formed. This linked up with the COB, marking a new phase in the worker–peasant alliance. When Gen. García Meza seized power in 1980, the COB's leaders were arrested and its headquarters bulldozed. Conflict between the organisation and the elected governments of Siles Zuazo and Paz Estenssoro was almost constant. Both were considered to have betrayed the working class. Further attempts were made to split the COB by promoting an alternative, the General Confederation of Bolivian Workers (CGTB). Weakened by internal disputes and the crisis in the mines, the COB postponed half a dozen times its 7th Congress, which finally took place in July 1987. See also **Lechín Oquendo; Revolutionary Nationalist Movement**.

C

COLINA (Commando of National Liberation): see **guerrilla movements** (Brazil).

Collegiate Executive

A constitutional innovation introduced in Uruguay in 1952–66, whereby instead of a president, executive power was held by a National Council of Government made up of nine members. The idea had for long been championed by José Batlle y Ordóñez, the Colorado Party leader who held office early in the century (1903–7 and 1907–11), who in turn had been inspired by the Swiss constitutional model. The desirability of a collegiate executive had been the subject of intense controversy for decades. It was finally written into the 1952 Constitution. The first National Council of Government took office on 1 March 1952, and new Councils were elected in 1955, 1959, and 1963. Typically, the winning party in elections was given six of the nine seats with the remaining three going to the runner-up. In the 1966 elections, however, the electorate also voted a constitutional amendment reinstating the office of president. See also ***Batllismo*; Colorado Party** (Uruguay); ***coparticipación***.

COLOMBIA, Republic of

Capital: Bogotá
Independence: (from Spain) 1819; break-up of Gran Colombia, 1830; became United States of Colombia, 1863, and Republic of Colombia, 1886; province of Panama seceded in 1903.
Area: 1,138,338 sq km
Population (1987): 29,942,000
Pop. growth rate (1980–5): 2.2%
Pop. density: 26.3/sq km
Infant mortality (1980–5): 53.3 per thousand
Life expectancy at birth (1980–5): 63.6
Literacy (1981): 82.1%
GDP per capita (1986e): US$1,330
Foreign debt per capita (1987e): US$518
Main exports (1985): coffee (50%); oil products (11.5%); gold (7%)

C

Political system

Constitution: first promulgated in 1886; amended several times. *Head of state/government*: Virgilio Barco Vargas (PL) (1986–); elected to succeed Belisario Betancur Cuartas (PC) (1982–6). General elections are held every four years (but on different dates) for president and a bicameral Congress, consisting of a 114-member senate and a 199-member house of representatives. The most recent elections were: (congressional) March 1986; (presidential) May 1986. Universal adult (18+) suffrage applies, with proportional representation employed for legislative elections. Party factions may present competing lists of candidates for the 23 multi-member constituencies: the votes of those failing to obtain an electoral quota are transferred to the party's most successful list. Re-election of the president is permitted, but not for consecutive terms. A 'first designate' (*primer designado*) to the presidency is elected by Congress and reconfirmed every two years, to occupy the presidency in cases of emergency. Since 1948 the country has often been governed under state of siege provisions, whereby many civil and political rights are suspended.

Political organisations

Political parties (seats in senate/house): Liberal Party/PL (58/98); New Liberal Movement (6/7); Social Conservative Party/PSC (43/80); Patriotic Union (7/14); Popular National Alliance/ANAPO; Christian Democrat Party/DC; Democratic Unity of the Left/UDI, coalition comprising Firmes, Communist Party of Colombia/PCC and Socialist Workers' Party/PST; Front for Popular Unity/FUP; Independent Revolutionary Workers' Movement/MOIR; Communist Party of Colombia–Marxist Leninist/PCC-ML.

Left-wing guerrilla groups: Revolutionary Armed Forces of Colombia/FARC (linked to PCC and UP; signed ceasefire agreement in 1984); National Guerrilla Coordinating Group/CNG alliance (comprising: 19 April Movement/M–19 (signed ceasefire in 1984 but resumed hostilities in June 1985); Popular Liberation Army/EPL (signed ceasefire, 1984; resumed hostilities 1985); National Liberation Army/ELN; Quintín Lame Movement; Free Homeland Movement; Revolutionary Workers' Party/PRT; Ricardo Franco Command–Southern Front; Ricardo Franco Front; Workers' Self-Defence Movement/MAO; Disaffected Youth of Colombia/JIC; Pedro León Arboleda Brigade/PLA; New Revolutionary Front of the People; Oscar William Calvo Column.

Main labour organisations (affiliation): (1) Unitary Confederation of Workers/CUT, comprising: Trade Union Confederation of Workers of Colombia/CSTC (PCC) and independent unions; (2) Democratic Trade Union Front/FSD, comprising Union of Workers of Colombia/UTC (ORIT, close to PC), Confederation of Workers of Colombia/CTC (ICFTU, close to PL) and General Confederation of Workers/CGT (Christian Democrat). *Main employers' organisation*: Colombian Confederation of Chambers of Commerce/CONFECAMARAS.

Colorado Party (Paraguay) (*Asociación Nacional Republicana*/ANR)

The ruling party under the regime of Gen. Alfredo Stroessner in Paraguay, the Colorados were originally created in 1870 by Triple Alliance war veteran Gen. Bernardino Caballero. After Paraguay's defeat by Argentina, Brazil, and Uruguay in the 1865–70 war, the Colorados emerged as the party closest to Brazilian interests (while the Liberals reflected Anglo-Argentine interests in the country). The Colorados retained power until 1904, after which followed a long period of Liberal rule until 1940. The regime of Gen. Higinio Morínigo, which had been sympathetic to the Axis powers, came under US pressure to democratise in 1946, and allowed the Colorados and the *Febreristas* a share in government. After Morínigo expelled the *Febreristas*, the Colorados successfully confronted the combined forces of Liberals, *Febreristas*, and Communists in the brief 1947 civil war. But there followed a series of coups and counter-coups as in-fighting between the *democrático* (moderate) and *guionista* (extremist) factions of the party broke out.

On 4 May 1954 Gen. Alfredo Stroessner overthrew the *democrático* government of Federico Chávez. Stroessner had himself nominated as the Colorado presidential candidate and duly elected in July 1954 – the first of what were to be many consecutive nominations and elections. In 1956 the president forced his main Colorado rival, the reformist Epifanio Méndez Fleitas, into exile. The party was subsequently reorganised, with Stroessner and his allies exercising tight central control. Dissidents were expelled; some formed MOPOCO, a rival Colorado group, in exile after 1959. A hierarchical, authoritarian structure was created, with party members expected to display unqualified allegiance to Stroessner.

The party is run through a 35-member *Junta de Gobierno* which controls a network of branches (*seccionales*) extending down to village and neighbourhood level. Local party militants, known as *py nandí*, perform a para-security role, carrying out surveillance of opposition forces. Civil servants, teachers, army officers and other professionals on the state payroll must be members of the party. *Patria*, the Colorado party newspaper, is paid for by compulsory deductions from civil servants' pay cheques. While Stroessner's central control has remained unchallenged, factions have continued to exist within the party. They include the *tradicionalistas*, led by an older generation which rose to power with Stroessner in 1954, and the neo-Colorados or *militantes*, a younger grouping which joined the party after the Stroessner era had begun.

At the party convention on 1 August 1987 the *militantes* successfully unseated Juan Ramón Chaves of the rival traditionalists, from the party presidency, installing their own leader, Sabino Montanaro, the interior minister. In general terms, the defeated traditionalists were believed to be more inclined towards political liberalisation; the victorious militants were more identified with the one-party state. Although both factions professed loyalty to Stroessner, their struggle was seen as a battle to control the succession.

See also **Paraguayan Civil War** (1947); **Popular Colorado Movement; *py nandí*; Stroessner**.

Colorado Party (Uruguay)

One of the two main political parties in the country, the Colorados trace their origins back to the nineteenth-century civil wars, during which they emerged from urban trading and business interests around Montevideo, in almost continual conflict with the rural landowners. In part these conflicts were based on a clash of economic interests: Montevideo, as city-port, acted as intermediary between the beef exporters and their final markets in Europe, and was often accused of taking too large a percentage. The party name (*colorado* = 'red') derives from the red flags used by the liberal faction in the 1836–8 civil war. The party's historic leader was José Batlle y Ordóñez, whose two presidencies (1903–7 and 1911–15) were used to introduce wide-ranging reforms and to end the cycle of civil wars. *Batllismo* was associated with the building of a welfare state, industrialisation, redistribution of income, and toleration of political opposition.

For most of the twentieth century power has been held by Colorado political leaders, with exceptions in 1959–66 (when the Blancos were in office) and 1973–85 (military rule). The party has developed many different internal tendencies or *sub-lemas*, ranging from the reformist through to the right-wing. Under President Jorge Pacheco Areco in the late 1960s/early 1970s, for example, the government became increasingly authoritarian and the cycle of protest, repression, and violence which was to culminate in the 1973 coup got under way. In the late 1970s and early 1980s the party underwent an internal revival in opposition to the military. In the 1982 internal elections the tendency associated with former President Pacheco Areco was defeated by those associated with Julio Sanguinetti (*Unidad y Reforma*) and Enrique Tarigo (*Libertad y Cambio*). The party won the November 1984 elections with 39% of the vote. Sanguinetti and Tarigo took office as president and vice-president in March 1985. Throughout most of the century the Colorados' electoral strength has been concentrated in the urban middle and working class, particularly in Montevideo.

See also ***batllismo*****; Bordaberry; Pacheco Areco; Sanguinetti**.

Communism

The earliest working-class parties with a generally Marxist orientation in Latin America date from around the time of World War I. Notable among them was the Socialist Workers' Party (POS), set up in Chile in 1912 by a group led by Luis Emilio Recabarren. This later became the Communist Party of Chile (PCCh), currently the region's most important communist party outside Cuba. It was in the early 1920s that the Soviet Union first took an interest in the development of Latin American communism and that communist parties as such began to be formed. By 1928, six countries from the region were represented at the 6th World Congress of the Communist International (Argentina, Brazil, Chile, Guatemala, Mexico, and Uruguay).

The development of the movement can be divided into periods corresponding to the directives of the Comintern and to splits in the world communist community. From 1928 to 1935 the Soviets viewed 'anti-imperialist and anti-feudal revolution' as the appropriate strategy for the undeveloped world. The parliamentary road was ruled out and alliances even with parties of the left were condemned. At this time some parties attempted insurrections, notably in Mexico (1929), El Salvador (1932), and Brazil (1935). In Peru, the communist intellectual José Carlos Mariátegui – regarded as the founder of Peruvian socialism – was highly influential. By the time the Brazilian communists, led by Luis Carlos Prestes, attempted their uprising the policy had changed to 'Popular Frontism' (1935–8), under which member parties were encouraged to form alliances with other 'progressive forces' against fascism and to abstain from revolution. In Chile the communists joined the Radicals (PR) and parties of the left in a Popular Front against the conservative Alessandri Palma government. This took power in 1938 under PR President Aguirre Cerda. A Popular Front was also successful in Cuba in 1940, while the Colombian Communist Party (f. 1930) joined a left-wing alliance backing the López Pumarejo government.

In the early years of World War II, following the Hitler–Stalin pact, communists collaborated with the Axis powers, switching to the Allied side in 1941 when Germany invaded the Soviet Union. This brought legalisation almost everywhere and communists joined the cabinet in Chile, Cuba, and Ecuador. Collaboration with the US in particular persisted briefly after the war, but at the onset of the Cold War most parties were driven underground or prevented from participating in legal politics. In Brazil the PCdoB (now known as the PCB) was at its height between 1945 and 1947, becoming the largest communist party in the Americas, with 17 seats in parliament and 10% of the vote, but in the latter year it was banned and Brazil broke off relations with the USSR. In 1948 the PCdoB deputies were expelled from parliament, and it was not until June 1985 that the party emerged from clandestinity (it now condemns armed struggle).

The 20th Congress of the CPSU (1956), which led to the 'de-Stalinisation' of the Soviet Union also brought greater autonomy to national parties, but with some exceptions they failed to make a major impact on electoral politics (the strategy endorsed by the Congress). Illegality certainly played a part in this failure: in South America it particularly affected the parties in Argentina, Bolivia, Brazil, Ecuador, Peru and Venezuela. Even where the parties were not formally banned, repression helped keep them ineffectual.

The question of armed struggle arose again in the 1960s as a result of the Sino-Soviet split and the Cuban revolution. The Cuban communists had played no part in Castro's victory, and despite its influence, pro-Soviet parties (with the qualified exception of the Colombian PCC, linked to the FARC guerrillas, and the Venezuelan Communist Party) refused to abandon the 'peaceful road' to socialism, which both Castroites and Maoists believed to be largely illusory. The Bolivian party gave only grudging support to Che Guevara's guerrilla *foco* in that country, and all over the continent pro-Chinese and pro-Cuban guerrilla movements sprang up. Between 1962 and 1965 Maoist splinter groups broke away from the communist parties of Bolivia, Brazil, Chile, Colombia, Ecuador and Peru. Only in the latter country did the Maoists attain significant influence, but the hegemony of orthodox communism over the Latin American left was permanently broken. It was left to the PCCh to carry the banner of the 'peaceful road' as the largest party in Chile's Popular Unity coalition government (1970–3). Although the strategy received a severe blow when the armed forces overthrew Popular Unity in 1973, outlawing all parties including the communists, the PCCh remains the biggest force on the Chilean left. Its opposition to armed struggle, however, has been modified and it has strong links with the FPMR guerrillas.

In the 1970s the so-called 'Eurocommunist' movement gained little

ground in Latin America, though it did influence the Venezuelans and the Brazilians. The contradictions arising from adherence to the Soviet line were evident in the refusal of the Argentine party to condemn the post-1976 military junta, for reasons directly linked with Soviet trading interests. The Bolivian party joined the government in 1982 as part of the UDP coalition but withdrew in late 1984. Elsewhere, the Peruvian 'Unity' communists have perhaps the best chance of forming part of government, as the United Left (IU) coalition gains electoral strength.
See also **Trotskyism**.

Communist Left (IC): see **Communist Party of Chile; Socialist Party of Chile**.

Communist Party (Argentina): see **Argentine Communist Party**.

Communist Party (Bolivia): see **Bolivian Communist Party**.

Communist Party (Brazil): see **Brazilian Communist Party**.

Communist Party (Paraguay): see **Paraguayan Communist Party**.

Communist Party (Peru): see **Peruvian Communist Party**.

Communist Party (Venezuela): see **Venezuelan Communist Party**.

Communist Party of Brazil (*Partido Comunista do Brasil*/PC do B) Founded by Mauricio Grabois and João Amazonas in 1962 as a Maoist split from the pro-Moscow *Partido Comunista Brasileiro* (PCB). It was illegal from the moment of its creation through to 1985. After the death of Mao the party broke with China and became pro-Albanian. The PC do B believed in armed struggle, and in the late 1960s tried to develop a rural guerrilla movement in the Araguaia region of Pará state, which was broken up by the armed forces. In 1976 three members of the central committee were killed and others arrested when the security forces raided a secret meeting the PC do B was holding in São Paulo. Exiled members of the PC do B were allowed to return to the country after the 1979 amnesty. In 1984/85 the party supported the Democratic Alliance.
See also **Brazilian Communist Party**.

Communist Party of Chile (*Partido Comunista de Chile*/PCCh) Founded in 1912 by Luis Emilio Recabarren as the Socialist Workers' Party (*Partido Obrero Socialista*). Initially strongest among nitrate workers in the north and the urban proletariat and artisans of the Santiago area, in 1917 it won control of the Grand Workers' Federation of Chile and renamed it the Workers' Federation of Chile. The POS became the PCCh at its 5th National Congress in 1922 and immediately joined the Third (Communist) International. Recabarren and another PC leader were elected deputies in 1921, but Recabarren killed himself in 1924 and Elías Lafertte became party leader. Party influence over labour declined with a 1924 law permitting legal unions: the PCCh would not allow those it controlled to register, and the FOCh was thus reduced to a minority of the labour movement. The government of Carlos Ibáñez (1926–31) outlawed the PCCh and exiled its leaders to Easter Island. In 1931 a faction under Senator Manuel Hidalgo split off and later became the Communist Left (*Izquierda Comunista*), which in 1937 joined the Socialist Party. The PCCh fiercely opposed the Socialist Republic of Marmaduke Grove (1932), in accordance with the Comintern line, but accepted the Moscow-imposed Popular Front policy in 1934–5, forming a front with the Radical (PR), Democratic (PD), Socialist (PS) and Radical Socialist (PSR) parties in 1936.

In 1937 the PCCh was banned, but as the Democratic National Party (PND) it won six seats in the lower and one in the upper chamber that year. In the 1938 presidential election the Popular Front chose Pedro Aguirre Cerda of the PR after the PCCh had blocked the nomination of Marmaduke Grove of the PS. Aguirre won, but the communists declined cabinet posts. Support for the Axis powers after the Hitler–Stalin pact brought another ban, and another break with the PS, but by adopting the name of National Progressive Party the PCCh again continued to function until the Soviet break with Germany caused a reversal of policy. In 1946 (by which time it was a well-established party, with strength not only in the unions but among students and intellectuals) it accepted three ministerial posts in the González Videla government, but in 1948 it was outlawed under González' Law for the Defence of Democracy (or '*Ley Maldita*'). The law was only repealed in 1958. Meanwhile the PCCh went partially underground, but gained influence in the unions after the socialists agreed to reunify the labour movement as the *Central Unica de Trabajadores* (CUT), which the PCCh came to dominate.

In the elections of 1952, 1958, 1964, and 1970 the party was allied with the PS behind the candidacy of Dr Salvador Allende, despite earlier hostility between the parties. In 1958 and 1964 the alliance was the Popular Action Front (FRAP) which included other left and centre-left forces such as the National Democratic Party (PADENA) and the Popular National Vanguard (VNP). For 1970 it was widened to include the Radical Party (PR) and its name changed to Popular Unity (UP). After the UP victory, which confirmed its status as the most important communist party in the western hemisphere (outside Cuba), the PCCh took the labour, finance, and public works and transport portfolios. It argued consistently for a more 'moderate' line, opposing land and factory seizures and seeking agreement with the Christian Democrat opposition and with the armed forces, which it declared were 'constitutionalist' and would not mount a coup. After the September 1973 Pinochet coup many of its leaders, including general secretary Luis Corvalán, were jailed, and many militants imprisoned or exiled, but the party was the only force on the left with a large underground organisation relatively intact.

Despite its previous reservations over armed struggle, since 1980 the party has adopted a policy of mass civil disobedience in which the use of armed actions plays an essential part, and it is unofficially linked to the Manuel Rodríguez Patriotic Front (FPMR) guerrillas. It became the leading force in the Popular Democratic Movement (MDP) opposition alliance, which opposed the National Agreement, though in July 1986

the PCCh stated that it would be willing to negotiate with a military regime which abandoned Gen. Pinochet. In mid-1987 it joined the United Left (IU) coalition which superseded the MDP, but initially opposed the IU position of registering voters according to government rules, while other members had reservations over the tactics of the FPMR. Only in June 1988 did the PCCh join the rest of the opposition in calling for a 'no' vote in the October plebiscite.
See also **Corvalán Lepe; Manuel Rodríguez Patriotic Front; National Agreement; Popular Democratic Movement; Popular Unity; Socialist Republic; United Left** (Chile).

Communist Party of Colombia (*Partido Comunista de Colombia*/PCC)
Founded as the Communist Group (*Grupo Comunista*) by a Russian emigré, Silvestre Savisky, in the mid-1920s, later becoming the Revolutionary Socialist Party (*Partido Socialista Revolucionario*/PSR). The PSR was dissolved in 1930, with the remnants of the membership founding the Communist Party of Colombia (*Partido Comunista de Colombia*/PCC) in the same year. PCC candidates were elected to parliament under Liberal (PL) governments, especially during the two terms of President Alfonso López Pumarejo (1934–8 and 1942–5), when the party attempted to form a Popular Front. In the pre-World War II era it enjoyed considerable support in the growing trade union movement, especially among dockers, seamen, and oil workers, as well as on the coffee and banana plantations, but developed its main strength in rural areas, organising land invasions and assisting peasants in armed defence. The party was also influential among students. It was severely repressed in the 1930s for its opposition to a war with Peru in the Amazon.

In the 1940s it chose to support the traditional wing of the PL against the populist leader Gaitán: this cost it support and helped bring about a 1947 split into several factions (under, respectively, Gilberto Vieira, Augusto Durán and Diego Montana Cuéllar). This was also due to followers of the Browderist tendency, who sought union with other progressive political forces. Communists were persecuted along with PL members in the late 1940s/early 1950s and their influence with organised labour declined. The party was outlawed under the Rojas Pinilla dictatorship, but restored to semi-legality after his departure. It backed the first National Front president, Lleras Camargo, but opposed the exclusion of third parties. Some candidates were elected on PL tickets and gained influence in the Liberal Revolutionary Movement (MRL) as well as regaining ground in the labour movement. A pro-Chinese faction expelled in 1965 formed the PCC–Marxist–Leninist (PCC-ML).

At its 10th party congress in 1966 the PCC adopted the Revolutionary Armed Forces of Colombia (FARC) as its armed wing. Manuel Marulanda ('Tirofijo'), who had led the FARC for many years, was already a member of the PCC central committee. PCC strategy has been flexible and pragmatic, and it did not adopt the openly hostile attitude to armed struggle which until recently typified most pro-Moscow parties in Latin

America, even though it never abandoned electoral politics. During the National Front period (when Liberals and Conservatives alternated in power) it formed electoral pacts with the Revolutionary Liberal Movement (MRL), and thereby obtained some representation at local level. Also in the mid-1960s, it formed its own trade union affiliate, the CSTC, based primarily in the sugar, oil, and construction industries, which was officially recognised in 1970.

By the end of the 1970s the PCC controlled unions representing about one-fifth of organised labour (especially in the cement, textiles, transport, brewing, and metallurgical industries), though the leadership of the party has always been middle class. In 1974 it joined the much smaller Independent and Revolutionary Workers' Movement (MOIR) and the Broad Colombian Movement (*Movimiento Amplio Colombiano*) in the National Opposition Union (UNO), winning only about 3% of the presidential vote. This was reduced to about 2% in 1978. In late 1979 it formed the Democratic Front (*Frente Democrático*) with the Firmes movement, and in 1982 this was expanded to include the Socialist Workers' Party (PST) and renamed the Democratic Unity of the Left (UDI), which gained a seat in each chamber of Congress. In 1985 the PCC and the FARC formed the Patriotic Union (UP) political party in response to peace proposals by the government of Belisario Betancur.
See also **Communist Party of Colombia–Marxist–Leninist; Patriotic Union; Revolutionary Armed Forces of Colombia**.

Communist Party of Colombia–Marxist–Leninist (*Partido Comunista de Colombia-Marxista Leninista*/PCC–ML)
A Maoist party founded in July 1965 by former members of the Moscow-line Communist Party (PCC) who had been expelled in 1964. Other groups, including the Liberal Revolutionary Movement (MRL) Youth and the Movement of Workers, Students, and Peasants (MOEC) were also involved. The leadership comprised students, intellectuals and lawyers. The PCC–ML launched the Patriotic Liberation Front (FPL) guerrilla group, which was later succeeded by the People's Liberation Army (EPL), in line with its policy of 'prolonged popular war', believing that the country was in a phase of 'incipient insurrection'. The PCC–ML operated largely clandestinely, although it was not formally banned. Its secretary general, Pedro León Arboleda, died in a shoot-out with police in Cali in July 1975 (his name was subsequently taken by another guerrilla group). Party militants were estimated at less than 1,000 in the early 1980s, by which time the Independent and Revolutionary Workers' Movement (MOIR) had taken over as the country's principal Maoist group.
See also **Communist Party of Colombia; People's Liberation Army**.

Communist Party of Ecuador (*Partido Comunista del Ecuador*/PCE)
A Moscow-line party, founded in 1926 as the Socialist Party of Ecuador (PSE), under the leadership of Ricardo Paredes and a group of young intellectuals. The issue of loyalty to the USSR caused a division in the ranks, with the pro-Moscow faction under Paredes (who had spent a year

in Russia) splitting off in 1927 and forming the PCE (which became a member of the Communist International) in 1931. The remainder of the membership retained the original name. It has been strong in the urban labour movement since its formation, and was responsible for the creation in 1944 of the Confederation of Ecuadorean Workers (CTE), to which most industrial unions belonged and which became the most powerful union body. In 1947 the CTE was taken over by the PSE, though it retained its affiliation to the communist CTAL/CPUSTAL international body. Communist control was restored briefly in the 1960s. During the 1970–2 Velasco Ibarra regime the CTE joined the Christian Democrat CEDOC in forming the United Workers Front (FUT). In 1963 a pro-Chinese faction of the PCE formed the PCE–Marxist–Leninist (PCE–ML).

The PCE was outlawed under the 1963–6 military junta and again from 1970 to 1973, but has often stood in elections, winning its first seat in 1928. It believes in an electoral strategy, leading to an eventual transition to socialism and has stressed nationalist issues (such as the recuperation of the Ecuadorean Amazon) as well as social concerns such as land reform and indigenous rights. Paredes stood for president in 1933 and Elías Gallegos in 1968, when the party formed the left-wing Democratic Popular Union (UDP) coalition to avoid challenges to its status. Since 1977–8 it has belonged to the Broad Left Front (FADI) with the Revolutionary Socialist Party (PSR), the Revolutionary Movement of the Christian Left (MRIC) and others. FADI came last in the 1978 election with only 5%. In the 1979 congressional election the PCE again stood under the UDP banner. It remains a member of FADI, of which its secretary general, René Mauge, is the leader. Mauge won a congressional seat in the 1986 elections. However, FADI's decision to back Gen. Vargas Pazzos for the presidency caused a dispute within the PCE, one faction of which supported the Democratic Left (ID) candidate, Rodrigo Borja. See also **Ecuadorean Socialist Party**.

Communist Party of Uruguay (*Partido Comunista del Uruguay*/PCU)

The PCU came into existence when a majority of the Socialist Party voted to join the Communist International in 1920. The party name was not formally changed until the following year, when PCU was adopted. Throughout its history the party has been closely identified with the Moscow line on international affairs and at home has been characterised by its dominant influence within the trade union movement and its commitment to electoral politics. In 1962 the PCU took part in the Left Liberation Front (*Frente Izquierda de Liberación*/FIDEL) the first attempt at a left-wing electoral coalition. Although FIDEL did not include all of the left and yielded only mixed results in terms of total votes, it was the precursor of the wider Broad Front (*Frente Amplio*) coalition, formed by the PCU and 16 other groups in 1971. The *Frente Amplio* obtained 18% of the votes in that year's presidential elections, a quantitative leap for the Uruguayan left. The party rejected armed struggle as inappropriate for the political conditions in Uruguay, and for that reason was highly critical of the Tupamaros guerrillas. Nevertheless, the party was a victim of the growing military repression in the late 1960s and early 1970s; in one incident alone nine militants were shot dead outside party headquarters by an army patrol.

After the 1973 military coup the PCU was declared illegal, and its members were imprisoned and tortured. PCU leader Rodney Arismendi was released from prison into exile in the Soviet Union in 1975, but other senior party figures remained in jail. When the military regime decided to call elections in 1984, it refused to lift the ban on the Communist Party. The PCU was nevertheless able to campaign within the *Frente Amplio*, which had been legalised, under the name of Advanced Democracy (*Democracia Avanzada*) – and obtained about 6% of the total vote in this manner. Arismendi returned to the country at the end of 1984 and in early 1985, after the return of civilian rule, the PCU recovered full legal status.

See also **Broad Front**.

Communist Proletarian Revolutionary Vanguard (VRPC): see **Shining Path**.

Compactación Obrera Nacional (*National Workers' Compact*): see ***velasquismo*** (Ecuador).

***comunidad/e de base*:** see **Medellín**.

Concentration of Popular Forces (*Concentración de Fuerzas Populares*/CFP)

An Ecuadorean political party, founded in 1946 (as the Popular Republican Union/UPR), which adopted its present name in 1948. From 1949 to 1960 it was led by the charismatic 'personalist' leader Carlos Guevara Moreno, a former Communist Party (PCE) member and briefly interior minister in the post-1944 government of José María Velasco Ibarra. A classic 'populist' party, the CFP defined itself from the beginning as 'not founded on a collection of abstract philosophical principles'. Its ideology is anti-imperialist and anti-oligarchic but tends towards authoritarianism (in the early 1950s it supported Argentina's Perón) and anti-communism. It has generally opposed foreign (especially US) investment, while stressing cooperative forms of organisation, progressive taxation, and the expropriation of idle lands (though not agrarian reform). Guevara was elected mayor of Guayaquil in 1951, and the party's main strength has always been in the coastal region centred on that city. Its main support is among workers, attracted by its emphasis on the need for social welfare and reform, but it also has some wealthy backers. It supported Velasco in his victorious presidential candidacy in 1952, despite the occasionally turbulent relations between Velasco and Guevara.

In 1956 the party stood alone and won 24% of the vote, compared with 29% for the victorious Conservative coalition. Guevara was subsequently involved in a scandal and went into exile. In 1960 the CFP fared badly when it stood with the PCE and the Revolutionary Socialist Party (PSR) behind the candidacy of Antonio Parra, who lost to Velasco. A second phase (1961–81) began under Assad Bucaram (mayor of Guayaquil from 1962) who turned the party into his own personal vehicle. In 1968 the CFP supported Liberal (PL) candidate Andrés Fernández Córdova, but from 1972 it put forward Bucaram himself. Under the military dictatorship of Gen. Rodríguez Lara, Bucaram called for free elections, but when they were finally held in 1978 his candidacy was vetoed on the pretext that his parents were foreign-born. Jaime Roldós Aguilera, related by marriage to Bucaram, was substituted and won convincingly in both rounds. The CFP (which was allied with the Christian Democrats/DP-UDC) also gained a majority of congressional seats. But a split developed between Bucaram and Roldós, who refused to be a mere front man and sought to redefine the party's ideology along social democratic lines. This weakened the CFP, especially after half its deputies joined a new party (People, Change and Democracy) set up in 1980 to back Roldós.

C

In 1982 – after the death of Roldós – the CFP joined the Christian Democrat government of Osvaldo Hurtado, but in 1984, when it obtained eight seats, it opted to back the ruling coalition of conservative President León Febres. In advance of the 1986 mid-term elections it withdrew from the coalition, but the tactic failed and its congressional seats were halved. The CFP's Angel Duarte was tipped as the right's presidential hope for 1988, but in the event he only managed fifth place.

See also **Bucaram; Communist Party of Ecuador; Roldós Aguilera; Velasco Ibarra**.

Cóndor Plan: see **Patriotic Union**.

Confederation of Peruvian Workers (CTP): see **APRA; Democratic Convergence.**

Confederation of Venezuelan Workers (*Confederación de Trabajadores de Venezuela*/CTV)

Founded in 1947, the CTV emerged as the country's main labour confederation, closely linked to Democratic Action (AD). During the 1945–8 *trienio* it enjoyed considerable influence, but was outlawed during the dictatorship of Gen. Marcos Pérez Jiménez, and suffered intense repression. It was nevertheless one of the prime moving forces in the general strike and popular uprising of January 1958 which led to the dictator's overthrow. The different trade union leaders came together to form the *Comité Sindical Unificado Nacional* (CSUN), but by 1959 the CTV had been re-established. Most major parties are represented on the CTV's executive council, although AD traditionally has a majority and controls the presidency. In 1984, for example, there were 10 members of AD, four of COPEI, two of MEP, and two of MAS on the CTV's executive council. PCV-affiliated unions split away from the CTV in 1963. Claimed membership is 2.5 million workers, although independent estimates suggest only 1 million. The CTV is affiliated to ORIT (the Interamerican Regional Organization of Workers) and CIOSL (the Inter-

american Confederation of Free Trade Unions); CTV leaders maintain links with their US counterparts in the AFL-CIO.
See also **COPEI; Democratic Action; ORIT; Movement of the Revolutionary Left** (Venezuela)**; People's Electoral Movement**.

Confederation of Workers of Latin America (CTAL): see **CPUSTAL**.

***conscientización/conscientização*:** see **Medellín**.

Conservative Party (Colombia): see **Social Conservative Party (PSC).**

Conservative Party (Ecuador) (*Partido Conservador*/PC)
Founded in 1855 by Gabriel García Moreno, the PC took shape during his dictatorship (1860–75), but acquired party status only in 1833, partly in response to the founding of the Liberal Party (PL). Closely associated in the past with both the Church and the army, its ideology has remained essentially unchanged. Led by landowners and merchants, with traditionally powerful support in the highlands (*sierra*) and among artisans, the PC promoted close Church–state cooperation, including state aid for religious and educational orders. It also traditionally favoured a unitary state. It was almost continuously in power from 1860 until the 1895–6 civil war, with occasional PL interludes after 1871–95. The PL then dominated the country until the 1931 Conservative presidency of Neptali Bonifaz, who was supported by PL dissidents. In 1933 he won the presidency again, this time in alliance with José María Velasco Ibarra.

In the constitutional debates of 1938 and 1947 legal parties were reduced to just three: the PC, the PL, and the Socialists (PSE). In 1944 the PC participated – with the PL, the PSE, the Velasquistas and, the Communists (PCE) – in the Democratic Alliance, which overthrew the Arroyo del Río presidency after the war with Peru. By 1952, when the party lost to Velasco but gained a majority in Senate, the progressive wing of the party had formed the Social Christian Movement (MSC). Rightist members of the 'Christian' tendency within the party had previously formed the Anti-communist Front for National Defence (FADN), which organised Christian militias to fight 'communists'. The 'fascist' tendency was represented by the Ecuadorean Nationalist Revolutionary Alliance (ARNE), founded in 1948 under the influence of Mexico's Sinarquista party and the Falange of Spain, whose supporters were mostly upper-middle-class youths. ARNE was militant and confrontational, though small in number.

In 1956 the PC joined the Popular Alliance backing Camilo Ponce of the ideologically similar Social Christian Movement (MSC), who became the main spokesman of the right. The PC won 28% of the vote, but the result was denounced as fraudulent and Ponce was compelled to have a PL majority in his cabinet. In the June 1962 congressional elections the party won 22 seats. In 1964 it joined the opposition Constitutionalist Front with the PSC against the military junta. In 1968 it stressed planned change as part of a pragmatic platform, backing Camilo Ponce for presi-

dent on the AP ticket, supported by other centre-right organisations. In 1978 and 1979 it supported the unsuccessful candidacy of Sixto Durán Ballén, winning nine seats (and becoming the third largest group) in the 1979 Congress. A severe internal crisis then deprived it of its small popular base, and it won only two seats in 1984, when it joined the winning National Reconstruction Front (FRN). These were reduced to one in 1986.
See also **National Reconstruction Front**.

Conservatives (Argentina)

C

The dominant political force in the late nineteenth century, the Conservative Party entered a long period of decline in the twentieth. Traditionally, it represented the interests of the landowning upper classes, identified with an economy geared to primary agricultural exports; through a restricted franchise and the use where necessary of electoral fraud, it sought to perpetuate its power. From the turn of the century, however, Conservative domination came under increasing threat from the emerging middle classes; after the advent of the Sáenz Peña law introducing universal male suffrage, the Radical Party (UCR) won the 1916 elections. Unable to recover power electorally, the Conservatives supported the 1930 coup against Hipólito Yrigoyen, the Radical Party president, ushering in the 'infamous decade' in which they ruled through electoral fraud and the support of the army. Out of power again after the 1943 coup, the party began to fragment. Many provincial Conservative groups ended up supporting or being absorbed by Peronism, the new alternative to the Radical Party.

By the 1960s and 1970s the Conservatives were no longer a major political force, despite numerous efforts by provincial and some national parties to re-create the party. It has often been argued that the emergence of an ideologically right-wing and interventionist army effectively took over the role of a Conservative party. In the September 1987 congressional elections, however, there were signs of a revival in civilian conservatism in the good performance by the Union of the Democratic Centre (UCD) party.
See also **Infamous Decade; Peronism; Radical Party; Union of the Democratic Centre; Yrigoyen**.

Constitutionalist Front: see **Conservative Party** (Ecuador).

Contadora process: see **Betancur Cuartas**.

continuismo

A practice whereby the incumbent president remains in office despite legal or constitutional provisions to the contrary. Notable exponents of *continuismo* in South America include Getúlio Vargas (Brazil, 1930–45), Gen. Juan Perón (Argentina, 1946–55), Gen. Augusto Pinochet (Chile, 1973–) and Gen. Alfredo Stroessner (Paraguay, 1954–). Most constitutions in the region forbid consecutive terms of presidential office: techniques for overcoming this problem include: the amendment of the constitution; plebiscites (usually fraudulent); the use of puppet presidents or juntas to provide a buffer period; and the replacement of the entire constitution by means of a constituent assembly or referendum. An alternative is the suspension of the constitution and rule by decree.

Contreras, Gen. Manuel: see **Letelier case**.

Contreras, Marcelo: see **MAPU**.

coparticipación

The name given in Uruguay to the share-out of government, state company, and other posts between the Blanco and Colorado parties. In one sense the system developed as a prolongation of the geographic division of the country during the nineteenth-century civil wars. Then, rival Blanco and Colorado leaders distributed the spoils of office by seizing control of different parts of the country by military means. But as more peaceful institutionally stable politics held sway in the twentieth century, the distribution of government posts became a matter for negotiation. It also served the important function of giving electoral losers a stake in the system, thus ensuring their respect for the rules of the game. If one party won elections, the *coparticipación* system ensured for its members a majority on a vast number of committees, boards of state companies, and so on; but the losing party was also ensured a minority voice and thus both an opportunity to influence policy and to distribute patronage. The system spread to almost all areas of government and reached its logical extreme when the unipersonal presidency was replaced by a nine-member collegiate executive, on which the ruling party had six seats and the opposition three. Although the unipersonal presidency was reintroduced in 1967, *coparticipación* at other levels of government remained widespread.
See also **Blanco Party; Colorado Party** (Uruguay)**; *Ley de Lemas***.

COPEI

One of Venezuela's two main parties, of essentially Christian Democratic inspiration, COPEI, sometimes also referred to as the Social Christian Party, is an acronym for Organising Committee for Independent Electoral Policy (*Comité de Organización Política Electoral Independiente*), the original title chosen at its founding on 13 January 1946 by Rafael Caldera and others. Caldera had long been active on the political scene, and had been seeking to create a movement opposed to the left-of-centre and Marxist currents in the Democratic Action (*Acción Democrática*) party and the Communist Party (PCV). Less than a year after its creation COPEI took second place in the constituent assembly elections of 27 October 1946, with 13% of the vote; and in the presidential elections of 14 December 1947 Rafael Caldera again came second, this time with 22%. At the end of the *trienio* of military/AD rule, COPEI was favourably disposed to the coup which removed the AD president, Rómulo Gallegos. But as Col. Marcos Pérez Jiménez consolidated his dictatorial control, the party moved into opposition.

After the popular uprising which ousted Pérez Jiménez in early 1958, COPEI joined the *Punto Fijo* accord with AD and the Democratic

Republican Union (URD) to protect the emerging new democracy. In 1958 and 1963 COPEI was again defeated by AD at the polls but in 1968, when AD was divided, Rafael Caldera narrowly won the presidency with 29% of the total vote. After a new AD victory in 1973, Luis Herrera Campins won the 1978 elections for COPEI with 47% of the total votes cast. The party is a member of the World Christian Democratic Organisation.
See also **Caldera; Christian Democracy; Herrera Campins; Pérez Jiménez; *Punto Fijo*.**

C

Cordobazo

An uprising in the Argentine province of Córdoba against the military regime and the local governor on 29–30 May 1969, during which violent clashes spread throughout the city and 14 people died. Prior to the uprising, trade union discontent with the regime of Gen. Juan Carlos Onganía and its economic policies had been growing. Students were also mobilising because of government repression on a national scale (including deaths of students in demonstrations in Corrientes and Rosario). There were also local grievances, such as the provincial government's attempts to introduce a corporative council and lengthen the working week. On 29 May workers and students took to the streets; when troops were sent in there was an uprising throughout the city, including widespread street fighting against the army's units. The *Cordobazo* led to the resignation of economy minister Adalberto Krieger Vassena, and was later seen to have marked the beginning of the end for the Onganía presidency.
See also **Argentine Revolution; Onganía.**

Cornejo Chávez, Héctor: see **Christian Democrat Party** (Peru).

coronelismo

A Brazilian clientilist system of political control and distribution of influence, originating during the Empire, and particularly marked in the Old Republic period (1889–1930), but still effective up to modern times. The name ('rule of the colonels') derives from the fact that in many rural municipalities the local political boss/landowner also had the title of colonel in the National Guard. These *coroneis* sought to deliver the vote in their area for state and federal leaders in return for patronage and favours. They were also seen by the local community as the channel for seeking improvements in facilities, mediating in family conflicts, and resolving other problems. Though *coronel* – client relationships were transferred from the rural areas in which they had first emerged to the urban shanty towns, they began to break down during the political liberalisation.

Corvalán Lepe, Luis

b. 1916. Secretary general of the Communist Party of Chile (PCCh) since 1958. Teacher, labour leader, and journalist. Editor of *El Siglo* (PCCh daily paper) 1961–9. Senator during the same period. A proponent of a non-violent, constitutional road to socialism, Corvalán backed the presi-

dential candidacy of socialist Salvador Allende in every election from 1952 to 1970. He was prominent during the Popular Unity (UP) government (1970–3), of which the PCCh was a major component. He strongly opposed the direct action over land and labour issues taken by some left-wing members of the UP and by the Revolutionary Left Movement (MIR), saying it was designed to divide the nation. After the 1973 coup he was captured as plans were being laid to smuggle him out of the country, and he spent the next few years in jail until in 1976 he was exchanged for the Soviet dissident Vladimir Bukovsky, whereupon he went to live in Moscow. Banned from returning to Chile until 1988, he nonetheless retained the post of secretary general.
See also **Allende Gossens; Communist Party of Chile; Popular Unity**.

COSENA: see **Alvarez, Gen. Gregorio; Bordaberry; *Proceso*.**

Costa, Miguel: see **Long March; *tenentes*.**

Costa, Sarney Araujo: see **Sarney.**

Costa e Silva, Gen. Arthur da

1902–69. Brazilian military leader and president 1967–9. Born in Taquari, Rio Grande do Sul. Studied at Porto Alegre Military College, Realengo Military School, and Fort Knox, US. During João Goulart's administration, Costa e Silva was dismissed from the command of the 4th Army for having cracked down on student protests. Considered a hard-liner, he was a prominent participant in the coup against Goulart in March–April 1964, with responsibility for the uprising in Rio de Janeiro. A signatory of Institutional Act 1, he became minister of war during the Castello Branco presidency.

Chosen to succeed Castello Branco, he took office on 15 March 1967 as the new constitution drawn up on the orders of the military came into force. Despite this, Costa e Silva was to sign a further eight Institutional Acts and 24 complementary decrees designed to further increase the powers of the presidency. His government was shaken by student protests and the emergence of left-wing guerrilla groups in 1968, and responded with the draconian Institutional Act 5. During this period serious human rights violations were committed by the political police and the security forces. Costa e Silva entrusted his vice president with the task of writing a new constitution to replace the 1967 text he had inherited; but by the time the new document was ready the president had suffered a thrombosis and was forced to hand power to a three-man military junta because of his rapidly deteriorating health. In early October 1969 the junta concluded that Costa e Silva's chances of a recovery were small and appointed a successor. Costa e Silva died two months later, on 17 December 1969.
See also **Institutional Acts.**

Coup of 1964 (Brazil)

A military uprising in Brazil against the elected government of President João Goulart in March–April 1964 which heralded a 21-year period of authoritarian military rule. Concern with Goulart's policies had been growing in the officer corps from 1963 – they saw his reform programme as dangerously radical, and were alarmed by the growth of trade union strength. The brief September 1963 revolt by army sergeants in Brasilia had fuelled fears in the high command that military discipline might be under threat. But even before this date many groups were seeking Goulart's removal. They included the Democratic Nationalist Union (UDN), business and financial interests (particularly groups in São Paulo, where *O Estado de S. Paulo*, owned by the Mesquita family, campaigned against the government) and the United States embassy. Middle-class opposition was also mobilised. Following Goulart's defiant speech and rally of 19 March 1964, conservative Catholic groups helped organise a rival 'March of the Family with God for Liberty'.

A key catalyst for the coup was the 25–27 March meeting of sailors and marines at the Guanabara Metalworkers' Federation. Senior officers considered it a manifestation of subversive indiscipline, and were furious when their attempts to crack down were frustrated by a more conciliatory line from the president. The coup was actually set in motion by Gen. Olimpio Mourão Filho, commander of the Fourth Military Region based in Juiz de Fora, Minas Gerais, who began to advance on Rio de Janeiro on 31 March. It was then that other military units controlled by Gen. Humberto Castello Branco (Chief of General Staff) and other officers joined the rebellion and that Gen. Amaury Kruel, head of the crucially important Second Army in São Paulo, who had earlier been undecided, finally declared himself against the government. Goulart left the country into exile on 4 April – even before his departure the United States had recognised the new government. Gen. Humberto Castello Branco was declared president on 11 April.
See also **Castello Branco; Democratic Nationalist Union; Goulart**.

COVEMA (Avengers of the Martyrs Commando) (Chile): see **death squad**.

CPUSTAL/*Congreso Permanente de Unidad Sindical de los Trabajadores de America Latina* (Permanent Congress for Trade Union Unity of the Workers of Latin America)
Founded in 1964 in Brasilia, as the Trade Union Coordination Committee of Latin American Workers, CPUSTAL replaced the Confederation of Workers of Latin America (*Confederación de Trabajadores de America Latina*/CTAL). The original move for its creation came from a conference in Santiago de Chile in 1962, called by the Chilean CUT (*Central Unica de Trabajadores*) and the Cuban CTC (*Central de Trabajadores de Cuba*). Its first secretariat was based in Santiago, but after the Chilean military coup of September 1973 it moved to Lima, Peru, and thence to Panama City. It is now based in Mexico City. In the late 1960s, CPUSTAL signed an accord with the communist World Federation of Trade Unions (WFTU), based in Prague, to work for the unity of the Latin American trade union movement. Headed by a general council and

a secretariat, it describes its aims as 'unitarian and anti-imperialist'. It does not publish membership/affiliates figures.

Crottogini, Juan José: see **Broad Front; Seregni.**

Cruzado

The name given in Brazil to both a new currency unit and an anti-inflationary programme launched by President José Sarney in February 1986. The new currency replaced the Cruzeiro; conversion was carried out at a rate of 1 Cruzado = 1,000 Cruzeiros. The package of economic policy measures announced at the same time included a wage and price freeze. Similar in inspiration to the Argentine Austral programme announced the previous year, it was initially more successful, leading to a consumption-led economic boom and significant redistribution of income. Inflation was initially halted, falling to a zero monthly rate from up to 15–16% a month (inflation in the 12 months before the plan was launched totalled 255%). The public responded enthusiastically, with neighbourhood groups forming to monitor compliance with officially sanctioned maximum prices (the so-called *fiscais do Sarney* – 'Sarney's inspectors'). The consumer boom was nevertheless allowed to continue for too long. It helped boost Sarney's popularity and win a landslide victory for the Brazilian Democratic Movement Party (PMDB) in the November 1986 state and congressional elections, but soon provoked a foreign payments crisis. Immediately after the elections the government was forced to authorise big price increases and in February 1987 it declared a moratorium on foreign debt payments. Economic growth slowed down and inflation rose again. By late 1987 inflation was again close to a 20% monthly rate and President Sarney's popularity ratings had collapsed.
See also **Austral; Sarney**.

cuartelazo

A military uprising; literally, 'a blow from the barracks (*cuartel*)'. The word *cuartelada* is also found.

Cubillos, Hernán: see **Party of National Renovation**.

Cue de Vargas, Ivete: see ***Trabalhismo***.

C

death squad (*esquadrão de morte/escuadrón de la muerte*)
A phrase coined in the 1960s in Brazil by unofficial units within the police which specialised in the torture and murder of beggars and alleged criminals and later (1969), with the aid of the army, added 'subversives' to their list of targets. The technique was adopted elsewhere in Latin America throughout the 1970s and 1980s by armies and security forces to eliminate their opponents while concealing their own identity. While governments have often sought to blame extreme right-wing groups for such activities, human rights groups suggest that most death squads are linked to armies or law enforcement agencies. 'Counter-terror' has been an integral part of the counter-insurgency doctrine taught by the US military to Latin Americans. More direct financial and organisational involvement in death squads on the part of the Pentagon and the Central Intelligence Agency (CIA) has often been alleged.

South American examples include:

American Anti-communist Alliance/Triple A (*Alianza Anticomunista Americana*/AAA)(Colombia) Founded in 1978 by military intelligence; tortured and killed guerrilla leader José Martínez Quiroz and other prisoners;

Argentine Anti-communist Alliance/Triple A (*Alianza Argentina Anticomunista*/AAA) Set up under the government of María Estela de Perón (1975–6) by José López Rega, her social security minister;

Avengers of the Martyrs Commando (*Comando Vengadores de Mártires*/COVEMA) (Chile) Founded in 1980 by detectives of the Investigations Service because of 'the inability of the security services and the police' to respond to violent opposition; known to have tortured to death a journalism student in 1980. Other names used by Chilean death squads include the Anti-Marxist Group (GRAPA), the Chilean Anti-communist Alliance (ACAA), the Movement Against the Marxist Cancer (MCCM), G–51, *Los Barbudos* (the Bearded Ones) and the 11 September Command. In 1986 Amnesty International accused the Chilean government of employing death squads.

Death to Kidnappers (*Muerte a Secuestradores*/MAS) (Colombia) Carried out several hundred killings of left-wing guerrillas (including some who were in jail), lawyers, trade union leaders, peasants, and human rights activists from 1981 onwards. MAS was a response by drugs bosses to attacks on them, but in 1983 59 army officers were indicted for involvement with MAS (none was convicted). After two years of sporadic activity the group re-emerged in 1985 and is now the largest of as many as 300 Colombian death squads, many allegedly linked to the armed forces.

Esquadrão de Morte (Brazil) By 1969 the death squads were publicly claiming responsibility for their actions, marking the bodies of their victims with a skull and crossbones. Total victims by 1970 were estimated at over 1,000. In 1972–6 a number of former policemen were convicted for their part in these murders, but initial attempts to bring charges against the reputed head of the organisation, police commissioner Sergio Fleury, failed. Fleury was a member of the São Paulo state political police (DEOPS) and was thought to be under the protection of his superiors partly because of his counter-insurgency work. In 1979 formal charges were laid, but Fleury died in a car accident before the trial. The death squads continued to operate, and killings rose sharply in Rio de Janeiro in September 1987 after the appointment of a new police chief to clean up corruption. In the four days after the appointment was announced, 60 bodies appeared in the streets.

See also ***desaparecidos***.

d

Death to Kidnappers (MAS) (**Colombia**): see **death squad**.

Debray, Régis: see ***foquismo***; **National Liberation Army** (Bolivia).

de la Puente Uceda, Luis: see **Movement of the Revolutionary Left** (Peru).

Delfim Netto, Antônio: see **Brazilian Economic Miracle**.

Delgado Chalbaud, Col. Carlos

1909–50. A Venezuelan army officer who took part in the 1945–8 revolutionary government as well as in the military regime which followed it. He supported the conspiracy against the government of Gen. Isaias Medina Angarita in 1945. At the age of 37 he became a member of the new Revolutionary Junta and minister of war and the navy. But the alliance between the military and Democratic Action (AD) in the 1945–8 period gradually broke down and Delgado Chalbaud, by then defence minister, was again a leading member of the conspiracy of 24 November 1948 which deposed the elected AD president, Rómulo Gallegos. He became president of the ruling three-man military junta, along with Lt-Col. Luis Felipe Llovera Páez and Lt-Col. Marcos Pérez Jiménez. The new government banned AD and closed the CTV union confederation, among other repressive measures. Delgado Chalbaud faced resistance in certain sectors of the army. But his qualities as an astute politician helped win over some opponents and create a group of supporters.

By mid-1950 there was speculation that the junta might call elections in which Delgado Chalbaud would be a candidate; some officers were being described as *delgadistas*. But on 13 November 1950 Delgado Chalbaud was assassinated on his way to the presidential palace at Miraflores by a group of nine men. Their leader was himself killed after his arrest

that same day, allegedly while trying to escape. Although there was never any conclusive proof, it was at the time suspected that Col. Marcos Pérez Jiménez was involved in the murder; certainly after Chalbaud's death Pérez Jiménez established dictatorial control of the country.
See also **Pérez Jiménez**; ***trienio***.

Demanda de Chile, la: see **National Civic Assembly**.

Demicheli, Alberto: see ***Proceso***.

Democracia Avanzada: see **Communist Party of Uruguay (CPU)**.

Democratic Action (*Acción Democrática*/AD)
Venezuela's main social-democratic grouping, *Acción Democrática*'s roots go back to the agitation against the dictatorship of Juan Vicente Gómez in the 1920s. Members of the 'Generation of 1928' such as Rómulo Betancourt were involved in its precursors, set up in the 1930s: ARDI (*Alianza Revolucionaria de Izquierda* – Revolutionary Alliance of the Left), ORVE (*Organización Revolucionaria Venezolana* – Venezuelan Revolutionary Organisation), and PDN (*Partido Democrático Nacional* – National Democratic Party), the latter set up in 1936. By 1941 the party was reorganised along the lines of a social democratic and national revolutionary movement, taking the AD name. Under the leadership of Rómulo Betancourt, AD led the successful revolution of 18 October 1945, in alliance with military officers. The party remained in control during the subsequent three-year period known as the *trienio*, winning overwhelming majorities in constituent assembly and presidential elections in 1946 and 1948. But President Rómulo Gallegos was deposed in a new military coup on 24 November 1948 which ushered in a 10-year period of repression directed against the party.

During the dictatorship of Gen. Marcos Pérez Jiménez many AD militants were imprisoned, tortured, and killed; the party was banned and its assets seized. It nevertheless played a key role in the popular uprising which toppled the Pérez Jiménez regime in January 1958. AD leaders signed the *Punto Fijo* accord with the other main parties in the same year; and Rómulo Betancourt was elected president for the 1959–64 period with 49.9% of the vote. Raúl Leoni again won the presidency for AD in the 1964–9 period with 32.8% of the vote. The party was defeated in the December 1968 elections by COPEI's Rafael Caldera, but returned victoriously with Carlos Andrés Pérez in December 1973 with 44.8%. After a further COPEI victory in December 1978, this time under Luis Herrera Campins, the party once more won the presidency in December 1983 under Jaime Lusinchi, with 56.8%.

AD's popularity has been based on its identification with land reform, oil nationalisation, industrial development, and income redistribution. The party has a claimed membership of about 1.5m, and the CTV, the country's largest trade union confederation, is affiliated. Traditionally various different political currents vie for position within the party – at various points in its history groups have broken away, generally on the left. They include the Movement of the Revolutionary Left (MIR) in the

early 1960s (which for a time took up guerrilla warfare) and the People's Electoral Movement (MEP) in 1967. *Acción Democrática* is affiliated to the Socialist International.
See also **Betancourt; Confederation of Venezuelan Workers; Generation of 1928; Gallegos; Leoni; Lusinchi; Oil nationalisation; Pérez, Carlos Andrés; Revolution of 1958** (Venezuela); ***trienio***.

Democratic Alliance (Brazil): see **Brazilian Democratic Movement Party (PMDB)**.

Democratic Alliance (*Alianza Democrática*/AD)
A Chilean opposition coalition, founded in August 1983, of which the most important member is the Christian Democrat Party (PDC). Its tactics have included support for street protest and mass mobilisation as a means of forcing the military government to the negotiating table, rather than overthrowing it by force. Its initial proposal was the resignation of Gen. Pinochet and elections to a constituent assembly. Talks between the AD and the government, with Church backing, held in August–September 1983, broke down and subsequent attempts were unsuccessful, leading to closer, though still informal, relations with the Communist (PCCh) led Popular Democratic Movement (MDP). However, despite its eventual support for the July 1986 general strike (in which it took part with the MDP), the AD had come under increasing pressure from the right (and from the US government, which gives it tacit support) to sever these links and abandon support for civil disobedience; especially after the signing of the National Agreement in 1985, which involved concessions to the right. No formal agreement between the two fronts had been reached, though both supported the idea of a transitional government to implement the short-term proposals of the National Agreement and the most urgent elements of the '*Demanda de Chile*'.

The September 1986 attempt on Gen. Pinochet's life by communist-linked guerrillas led to a further estrangement. By mid-1987 AD was proposing reform of the 1980 constitution, leading to 'free and open elections' for Congress and the presidency, and had condemned an MDP call for mass mobilisation. Member parties of AD are currently (1987): the PDC, the right wing of the Radical Party (PR), the Social Democrats (PDS), the Republican Right, the Popular Socialist Union (UPS), and the Liberal Movement. (The Socialist Party-Núñez was a member, but had left by January 1987.) All signed the National Agreement for Transition to a Full Democracy in August 1985.
See also **member parties; National Agreement; National Civic Assembly; Popular Democratic Movement; United Left** (Chile).

Democratic Alliance (Ecuador): see **Conservative Party** (Ecuador); **Ecuadorean Socialist Party**.

Democratic Convergence (*Convergencia Democrática*/CODE)
An alliance, founded in 1984, between two right-wing Peruvian parties, the Popular Christian Party (*Partido Popular Cristiano*/PPC) and the Hayista Base Movement (*Movimiento de Bases Hayistas*/MBH).

The PPC – which dominates the alliance – originated in 1966 as a right-wing breakaway faction of the Christian Democrat Party (PDC), led by the mayor of Lima, Dr Luis Bedoya Reyes (an ex-minister of justice). Its principal support is in the capital, among industrialists and the Lima upper-middle class, and its real power lies in the close relationship it enjoys with the industrialists' association, the *Sociedad Nacional de Industrias*. It also has strong links with the West German Christian Democrats. In 1978 (assisted by a decision to abstain on the part of its main rival, the Popular Action/AP party) the PPC won 25 out of 100 seats in the constituent assembly, becoming the second largest party. In 1980 it won only 5% of seats in the lower house. It was allocated two cabinet seats by the AP government from 1980 to 1984, in exchange for parliamentary backing, but this led to dissent within the party and the formation of the tiny National Integration Party (PADIN). Bedoya forced the ministers to resign in April 1984, aware of the government's plummeting popularity, but continued to back AP in parliament and even sought a joint slate of candidates for the 1985 elections. When this failed, the PPC joined the MBH in forming CODE.

The MBH (now of little importance) was founded in 1980 by a handful of right-wing dissidents from the APRA party, led by Andrés Tównsend who had been expelled after his failure to win control of APRA in a battle with Armando Villanueva. It was named after the founder and historical leader of APRA, Víctor Raúl Haya de la Torre, whose true political heir it claims to be.

Bedoya Reyes became the leader of CODE and was its presidential candidate in 1985, coming third with 10% of the vote. CODE's electoral platform stressed orthodox monetarism and denationalisation, but Bedoya also blamed 'American imperialism' for the debt problem. In December 1986 the PPC's national leaders all resigned, to facilitate a major internal reorganisation in the light of its poor electoral showing.
See also **APRA; Christian Democrat Party (Peru); Democratic Front; Haya de la Torre**.

Democratic Front (Colombia): see **Colombian Communist Party**.

Democratic Front (Peru) (Frente Democrático/Fredemo).
An alliance of three right-wing political groups, founded in Peru in February 1988 with the aim of presenting candidates for the 1989 municipal and 1990 presidential elections. The three members are the Popular Action (AP) and Popular Christian (PPC) parties and the Freedom Movement (*Libertad*), led by novelist Mario Vargas Llosa. The latter's apparent self-proclamation as presidential candidate of the alliance later caused friction with AP and the PPC.
See also **Popular Action; Popular Christian Party**.

Democratic Front of National Unity (FDUN): see **Morales Bermúdez Cerruti**.

Democratic Labour Party (*Partido Democrático Trabalhista*/PDT)
A Brazilian party created in 1980 by Leonel Brizola, who had shortly

before returned to the country under the terms of the 1979 political amnesty, the PDT considers itself to be a continuation of the *trabalhista* movement started by President Getulio Vargas in the 1940s. In the 1982 elections the PDT gained 24 seats in the Chamber of Deputies, thus becoming the largest labour-based party in congress. At the same time Brizola won the direct elections for governor of Rio de Janeiro, an office he held in 1983–7. The PDT campaigns for full employment, redistribution of income, and land reform. In Rio, Brizola channelled funds into education and other social programmes, but was widely criticised by conservative groups, who accused his administration of making populist gestures and of being corrupt.

In the 1986 state election campaign the PDT intensified its criticism of President José Sarney's Cruzado economic programme at a time when it was highly popular. This is believed to have been one of the major causes of the defeat of Darcy Ribeiro, the PDT candidate to succeed Brizola, who was beaten into second place by the PMDB. Brizola had hoped to use a renewed victory in Rio to turn the PDT into more of a national party, capable of helping him win the presidency.
See also **Brizola; *Trabalhismo***.

Democratic Left: see **Frei Montalva**.

Democratic Left (*Izquierda Democrática*/ID)
An Ecuadorean political party, founded in 1970 under the leadership of Rodrigo Borja Cevallos, a former member of the Radical Liberal Party (PLR). Much of its membership came from the Socialist Party (PSE), and its international links were with democratic socialists close to the Socialist International (to which it is affiliated). It won more votes than the PLR in the 1970 municipal elections. The leadership was primarily middle class and urban but it was backed by the Ecuadorean Labour Conferation of Free Trade Unions (CEOSL). Borja came fourth in the first round presidential elections in 1978, winning around 10%. The ID then backed the winner of the 1979 elections, Jaime Roldós of the Concentration of Popular Forces (CFP), and became the second largest party in Congress, with 15 (later reduced to 12) seats. It became more and more closely aligned with Roldós as splits emerged between the president and the CFP, and it joined the congressional majority backing him in 1980.

From 1982 to 1984 the ID supported Roldós' successor, the Christian Democrat Osvaldo Hurtado. In the 1984 presidential elections Borja came close to defeating the eventual winner, León Febres Cordero, and the party increased its seats to 24 (later reduced to 17 by defections and mid-term losses), making it the largest single party and the leading force in the Progressive Front (FP) opposition alliance. In the 1988 elections it presented Borja as its candidate and won both the presidency and 30 seats in Congress.
See also **Borja Cevallos; Progressive Front**.

Democratic Left Front (FID): see **Bucaram**.

Democratic Left Unity (*Unidad Democrática de Izquierda*/UDI)
A Colombian political alliance, formed to fight the 1982 elections. Members were the Communist Party (PCC), the Firmes movement and the Socialist Workers' Party (PST). Firmes had been founded in 1976 out of a pre-election campaign by a goup associated with the magazine *Alternativa*. It consisted largely of left-wing intellectuals, including novelist Gabriel García Márquez, whose aim was to channel popular discontent and rejection of the country's economic and political system into a unified left-wing party under working-class leadership, with a broadly socialist programme. The UDI presidential candidate in 1982, Gerardo Molina, polled only 1.2% of the vote.
See also **Communist Party of Colombia**.

d

Democratic National Party (PND): see **Communist Party of Chile**.

Democratic Nationalist Union (UDN): see **Coup of 1964** (Brazil).

Democratic and Popular Union (*Unión Democrática y Popular*/UDP)
A coalition of Bolivian parties, founded in April 1978. Led by Hernán Siles Zuazo's Nationalist Revolutionary Movement of the Left (MNRI), it also included the Communist Party of Bolivia (PCB); the Movement of the Revolutionary Left (MIR) and the Túpaj Katari Revolutionary Movement (MRTK). These were joined for the (ultimately aborted) 1978 elections by the Aponte wing of the Socialist Party (PS–Aponte) and the Movement of the National Left (MIN). When fresh elections were held in July 1979 the UDP was further expanded, gaining the support of the Popular Movement for National Liberation (MPLN), the Revolutionary Party of the Nationalist Left (PRIN), the PS–Atahuichi, the Alliance of the National Left (ALIN) and the Revolutionary Party of Bolivian Workers (PRTB). The MRTK, however, split over the issue of participation.

In the 1979 elections the UDP won 46 seats with 36% of the vote, but its lack of an overall majority led to a period of acute instability, including further military interventions, before a third poll in June 1980. This time the line-up consisted of: MNRI, MIR, PCB, MPLN, PS–Atahuichi, and the Workers' Vanguard (VO). During the campaign, the UDP's vice presidential candidate, Jaime Paz Zamora (MIR), was seriously injured, when a light plane the UDP had hired from a company controlled by the military crashed on take-off. The Front won 57 seats with 38% of the vote, but a further military intervention prevented the inauguration of Siles and Paz until October 1982. An attempt to set up a clandestine 'National Unity Government' (GUN) failed, and in the intervening years UDP leaders spent most of their time seeking foreign diplomatic support.

When the UDP was allowed to take office, the MIR took six cabinet seats, including finance, and the PCB the key positions of labour and mining, but tensions both within and among the member parties surfaced immediately. The MIR left the cabinet from January 1983 to April 1984, partly over economic issues, but also because of allegedly excessive MNRI

influence over Siles and insuffıcent efforts to abolish paramilitary groups. The PCB suffered serious internal divisions, as well as conflict with its partners, over the FSTMB union's decision to take over the mines. The shaky coalition eventually survived until the end of 1984, when both the MIR and the PCB, its only significant members apart from the MNRI, left the cabinet. With the MNRI itself split in three, Siles cut short by a year his term of office and called fresh elections for July 1985.
See also **Bolivian Communist Party; Movement of the Revolutionary Left (Bolivia); Siles Zuazo**.

Democratic Republican Union (*Unión Republicana Democrática*/URD)
A Venezuelan centre-left party founded in December 1945, and led from early 1946 by Jóvito Villalba. During the *trienio* the URD was critical of what it described as one-party rule by Democratic Action (AD); it was initially supportive of the 1948 coup, but later moved into opposition to the Gen. Marcos Pérez Jiménez dictatorship. In the 30 November 1952 constituent assembly elections, with AD banned, first results showed the URD leading; but the government intervened to alter the figures and put the pro-Pérez Jiménez party, the FEI, in the lead. In the end, the URD was granted 29 out of 104 seats; it was later persecuted by the regime, and took part in the struggle to oust Pérez Jiménez which culminated in 1958. In that same year the URD was one of the three signatories of the *Punto Fijo* accord, which gave it a share in the first elected government after the dictatorship, that of President Rómulo Betancourt. The party was nevertheless critical of Betancourt's growing anti-communism, withdrawing its ministers in October 1960.

In the 1 December 1963 elections Villalba stood as the party's presidential candidate, taking third place with 17.5%; the URD obtained seven senators and 29 deputies. Thereafter the party's electoral fortunes waned: its share of the Chamber of Deputies fell from 29 out of 179 seats in the 1963 elections, to 14 out of 188 in 1968, and five out of 203 in 1973. In 1978 the URD obtained only three deputies. In 1973 the party supported the Nueva Alternativa coalition presidential candidate, and increased its congressional representation to eight deputies and two senators.
See also ***Nueva Alternativa*; Pérez Jiménez; *Punto Fijo***.

Democratic Revolutionary Front–New Alternative (FDRNA): see **Christian Democrat Party** (Bolivia).

Democratic Social Party (*Partido Democrático Social*/PDS)
This Brazilian grouping was created as a right-wing organisation to succeed the pro-military government party, the National Renovating Alliance (ARENA). The PDS came into being after the 1979 political reforms introduced by President João Figueiredo; it took over ARENA's existing organisation and membership and inherited the built-in electoral advantages of the ruling party. By the end of 1980 the PDS had over 3,000 branches and held 213 out of 420 seats in the lower house and 37 out of 60 in the senate. After the 1982 elections it remained the largest

party, with 235 of the 479 deputies and 46 of the 69 senators; it also obtained 12 out of the 23 state governorships.

In 1984, however, many party members began leaving to form the dissident Liberal Front (PLF). The process accelerated after the PDS convention nominated the controversial Paulo Salim Maluf as its presidential candidate for 1985. Maluf lost the indirect elections in January 1985 to Tancredo Neves, the candidate of the opposition Democratic Alliance, who had obtained the support of the PLF breakaway. The PDS suffered badly in the November 1986 state and congressional elections, in which it was crushed by a Brazilian Democratic Movement Party (PMDB) landslide. Identified with the disgraced military regime, it was unable to win a single state governorship.
See also **National Renovating Alliance**.

***democráticos*:** see **Colorado Party** (Paraguay).

Democratic Union: see **Argentine Communist Party**.

desaparecidos

The 'disappeared ones' – the name given to victims of political persecution who, after being kidnapped, are never traced. The kidnapping of political opponents has a long history in Latin America's conflicts; but it was only after the 1950s that the practice of 'disappearances' was refined and used systematically for purposes of repression by the state.

The massive use of secret police and military units to kidnap and execute political dissidents, while the central government denied all involvement, made its appearance in Guatemala after the 1954 coup d'etat, although examples of this form of repression can be found under earlier Central American military regimes. Estimates of the total number of 'disappeared' in Guatemala in the three decades after 1954 range as high as 30,000. Disappearances were widespread under the Somoza dynasty in Nicaragua. The technique later moved to the Southern Cone of Latin America, appearing in Brazil (after the 1964 coup), Chile (after 1973), Uruguay (after 1973) and Argentina (from the early 1970s, but particularly after the 1976 coup). In Argentina's 'dirty war' a minimum of 9,000 people 'disappeared' although the actual figure is believed to be higher. In virtually all of these cases they were kidnapped by police and army personnel, wearing civilian clothes and driving unmarked cars. Military units maintained secret lists of names detailing those targeted for abduction, torture, and murder; the 'disappeared' were held in clandestine places of detention, known as *pozos* ('holes').

In the late 1970s large-scale disappearances began to take place in El Salvador, in a process linked to extreme state repression and the emergence of guerrilla insurgencies. They were also used in the 'dirty war' between the Peruvian military and the *Sendero Luminoso* (Shining Path) guerrillas in the 1980s, in which over a thousand people disappeared after being arrested by the military in areas of conflict. Even in more stable societies such as in Mexico politically motivated 'disappearances' have played a role in attempts to quell protest movements.

A separate phenomenon in both Peru and Colombia in the 1980s (though going back many years in the Colombian case) is the spread of 'commercial' kidnapping rings. Most countries in which the technique of 'disappearance' has been applied have also developed human rights organisations struggling either to trace the *desaparecidos* or at least to determine the circumstances of their deaths and the identity of those responsible. Among the better-known groups of relatives of the disappeared are the Mothers of the Plaza de Mayo in Argentina and the Mutual Support Group (GAM) in Guatemala.
See also **death squads; dirty war; due obedience; Mothers of the Plaza de Mayo**.

descamisados

Argentine name for the poor (literally: 'the shirtless ones') who supported Gen. Juan Domingo Perón and his policies of social justice and redistribution of income. They were often prominent in mass Peronist demonstrations, particularly during the first Peronist government (1946–55) when the state provided free transport to those wishing to attend. To Conservative opponents of Peronism the *descamisados* were an unorganised and violent rabble whipped up by populist leaders. There was also an element of racism in the upper classes' description of the *descamisados* as *cabecitas negras* (literally, 'black heads') because many were darker-skinned *mestizos*.
See also **Peronism**.

DIGEPOL: see **Betancourt**.

DINA: see **Letelier case**.

diretas já

The name of the massive opposition campaign in Brazil in the first half of 1984 in favour of direct presidential elections. The PMDB and other parties, backed by the Church, trade unions, and other organisations, sought to force the outgoing government of Gen. João Figueiredo to allow direct elections for his successor in January 1985, instead of an indirect choice through the electoral college, heavily weighted in the government's favour.

Demonstrations were held all round the country in support of the right to elect the next president. In Congress Dante de Oliveira put forward a constitutional amendment re-establishing direct presidential elections. Just before Easter, Figueiredo placed Brasilia and 10 surrounding satellite towns under a modified state of emergency, arguing that the move was necessary to prevent legislators coming under pressure from the demonstrators. The move was denounced by the opposition as a means of intimidating deputies. The government imposed strict censorship and surrounded Congress with army units; the vote on the de Oliveira amendment narrowly fell short of the two-thirds majority required to secure passage to the Senate. The *diretas já* campaign of mobilisations continued, however, with a turnout of 1 million people on 10 April 1984 in Rio de Janeiro and an estimated 1.5 million six days later in São Paulo, the largest political demonstration seen up to that time in Brazil. The campaign won the support of popular film stars and samba dancers.

While it was ultimately unsuccessful, the campaign succeeded in splitting the pro-government Democratic Social Party (PDS). One of the defectors was José Sarney Jr, who voted for the de Oliveira amendment despite the protests of his father, José Sarney Sr, who was himself later to become president and join the PMDB. Another was vice-president Aureliano Chaves. By July 1984 the breakaway faction of the PDS had re-named itself the Liberal Front (PLF) and moved into an alliance with the PMDB. This, and further divisions within the PDS over the choice of Paulo Salim Maluf as its presidential candidate, helped swing the vote in the electoral college on 15 January 1985 in favour of the opposition candidate, Tancredo Neves. While recognising the failure to achieve direct elections, Neves campaigned on the promise that his government would carry out a constitutional reform ensuring direct elections to the presidency for his successor.

d

See also **Brazilian Democratic Movement Party; Democratic Social Party; Figueiredo; Neves; Sarney**.

dirty war (*guerra sucia*)

The term used to describe a counter-insurgency campaign in which the state uses terror and violates human rights. The phrase was perhaps most closely identified with the conflict between the armed forces and the guerrilla movements in Argentina in the 1970s. Both sides operated outside the constitution and ignored restraints such as the Geneva Convention. The extensive use by the military of extra-judicial killings, abductions, and torture has also been referred to as state terrorism. It is estimated that more than 30,000 people were killed during this period, including at least 9,000 cases of 'disappearances'. Repression was most intense after the military coup of 24 March 1976. The army was influenced by the counterinsurgency campaigns of the French in Algeria, and the US in Viet Nam. Military commanders were given a free hand to operate in areas they controlled. 'Task forces' were deployed to kidnap, torture, and kill political opponents. The definition of the 'subversive enemy' was widened from the guerrillas to include almost all opponents of the government. Army and police units frequently operated in civilian clothes, using cars with no licence plates. Military-controlled judges failed to answer habeas corpus requests. The victims included trade unionists, artists, members of the liberal professions, teachers, human rights activists, and politicians. The National Commission on the Disappearance of Persons (Conadep), appointed by President Raúl Alfonsín after military rule ended in 1983, amassed evidence to indicate that at least 9,000 disappearances were the work of the security forces.
See also ***desaparecidos*; National Security doctrine**.

'disappeared': see ***desaparecidos***.

distensão

A Portuguese word meaning 'relaxation', which was used to refer to the

policy of gradual political liberalisation of the Brazilian military regime, initiated by President Ernesto Geisel in 1974. Its features included a reduction in censorship and police repression and moves to allow more genuine competition between the ruling National Renovating Alliance (ARENA) and the opposition Brazilian Democratic Movement (MDB) parties. Fears within the government that the MDB would make too much headway and might even be within reach of winning the indirect presidential elections of 1978, led Geisel to reverse the *distensão* process in 1977, tightening up again on censorship and political controls. It was only when the choice of another military man, Gen. João Figueiredo, as Geisel's successor was assured that he relaxed controls again, repealing the notorious Institutional Act 5.
See also ***abertura*****; Brazilian Democratic Movement; Figueiredo; Geisel; National Renovating Alliance**.

d

Doldán, Dr Enzo: see **Radical Liberal Party**.

dollar diplomacy

A phrase coined during the presidency of William Howard Taft (1909–13) to describe a financial technique whereby the US would grant loans to Central American and Caribbean nations with which they might repay onerous European debts, in exchange for US customs receivership. This method, which brought several nations (including Honduras, Nicaragua, Haiti, and the Dominican Republic at different dates) under US control, was excused by Taft as a means of avoiding the recovery of the debts by military force. It was eventually repudiated by President Franklin D Roosevelt in the 1930s. The phrase itself came to have a wider connotation, namely the use of US foreign policy to protect the interests of US transnational corporations in Latin America.
See also **good neighbour policy; Monroe doctrine**.

Dominican Republic Embassy siege: see **M–19**.

Duarte, Angel: see **Concentration of Popular Forces**.

Duarte de Perón, María Eva: see **Perón, Evita**.

due obedience

A legal concept applied in Argentina, under which military officers who carried out human rights violations on the orders of their superiors were exempt from prosecution, except in those cases where they had committed 'abhorrent acts'. The concept was first expressed by Dr Raúl Alfonsín in general terms during the 1983 presidential campaign, when he argued that a future Radical Party government would concentrate its efforts on the punishment of those military officers who had given the orders in the 'dirty war' of the 1970s, rather than on those who had carried them out. During the first years of the Alfonsín presidency, due obedience remained a general concept untested in the courts, as attention centred on the trials of the top military commanders. But as complaints against middle-ranking and junior officers worked their way through the legal system, the government came under increasing military pressure.

In December 1986 Alfonsín obtained congressional approval for the so-called 'full stop' (*punto final*) law, which gave the courts a 60-day deadline either to indict officers or to drop the cases against them. Conceived of as a way of putting a definite limit on both the number and the duration of the trials, the legislation nevertheless precipitated a crisis over the following months. Reacting to what many considered undue pressure from the executive, many judges actually stepped up the number of indictments prior to the February 1987 deadline. Consequently military resentment over the trials, rather than cooling, intensified. On 15 April 1987 a series of rebellions by middle-ranking officers broke out, in defence of colleagues who had refused to answer summons relating to human rights trials and who had been declared in contempt of court. Loyal troops sent to quell the risings by the government refused to move against the rebels. Alfonsín, backed by massive civilian demonstrations in support of democracy and against the uprising, eventually secured the surrender of the rebels on 19 April 1987 after flying to their headquarters by helicopter for direct negotiations. But the president had to make major concessions. One such was the immediate suspension of the trials, followed in mid-May 1987 by a government-submitted bill on 'due obedience'.

The proposed legislation exempted officers below the rank of colonel from prosecution on human rights charges, providing they had committed the violations in pursuit of orders received from higher up the chain of command. The Senate amended the text to extend the exemption to colonels and generals, provided they did not hold command posts at the time of the abuses. Once approved, the courts began applying the 'due obedience' argument, leading to the dismissal of many cases against named officers.

See also ***desaparecidos*****; dirty war; Mothers of the Plaza de Mayo**.

Durán, Augusto: see **Communist Party of Colombia**.

Durán Ballén, Sixto: see **Conservative Party** (Ecuador)**; Social Christian Party** (Ecuador).

Dutra, Gen. Eurico Gaspar

1889–1974. President of Brazil, 1946–51. One of the key army officers who engineered a process of political liberalisation after the end of the Second World War. Born in Mato Grosso state, Dutra entered the Porto Alegre military academy where in 1907 he joined the Castilhista Student Bloc, many of whose members, such as Gen. Pedro Goes Monteiro, went on to become influential officers in President Vargas' regime. In 1935, with the rank of general, Dutra played a prominent role in the suppression of a Communist Party revolt. He was appointed minister of war in 1936 and supported the creation of the authoritarian *Estado Nôvo* in 1937. Despite this he was later, with Goes, to become convinced of the need for democratisation. Dutra was one of the army leaders who forced Vargas to resign on 31 October 1945. He stood in elections held immediately afterwards as a candidate for the PSD (Social Democratic Party –

one of the two created by the Vargas regime). He won with 55% of the vote, after being endorsed by Vargas only four days before polling.

As president, Dutra took a strongly anti-communist line, declaring the Communist Party illegal in May 1947 and intervening in 143 trade unions to remove officials considered to be extremists. Economic growth in the first years led to a surge in imports and eventually to a balance of payments crisis; the later imposition of exchange controls, and an import licensing system helped promote a process of import-substituting industrialisation. During his presidency the constituent assembly sat to draw up the 1946 constitution, which granted the vote to women but maintained the exclusion of illiterates.
See also **Nationalist Democratic Union; Social Democratic Party; Vargas**.

'Dynamo, The' (el dínamo)

A collective term for the economic team appointed by Peruvian Prime Minister Manuel Ulloa in 1980. Comprising mainly young technocrats and bankers (including Pedro Pablo Kuczynski, Richard Webb, and Brian Jensen). The Dynamo group was largely US-trained and committed to neo-liberal, free market economics. Its strategy was to reduce state intervention and open up the Peruvian economy to international capital. Combined with President Belaúnde Terry's penchant for large, state-funded projects, their policies led to what Ulloa described as 'the worst economic crisis of the century' when world commodities prices collapsed, and Peru was forced to turn to the IMF in 1982. Ulloa resigned at the end of that year, but hard-line monetarism continued to prevail, despite the eventual appointment by Belaúnde of a group (dubbed 'the *Violeteros*' for their links with his wife) theoretically committed to the reactivation of the economy.
See also **Belaúnde Terry**.

ecclesial base communities (CEBS): see **liberation theology**.

Echeverría, Enrique: see **Free Nation Montoneras**.

Economic Commission for Latin America and the Caribbean (ECLAC) (*Comisión Económica para America Latina y el Caribe*/CEPAL)

A United Nations organisation set up in 1948 to coordinate policies for the promotion of regional economic development. The commission meets every two years. Its main work involves collaboration between governments to analyse economic development issues and formulate development plans. ECLAC headquarters are based in Santiago de Chile; the Executive Secretary is Norberto González of Argentina (who took over from Enrique Iglesias of Uruguay). The executive secretariat comprises divisions on development, statistics, documentation, and other specialist tasks.

The commission's member countries are: Antigua and Barbuda, Argentina, Bahamas, Barbados, Belize, Bolivia, Brazil, Canada, Chile, Colombia, Costa Rica, Cuba, Dominica, Dominican Republic, Ecuador, El Salvador, France, Grenada, Guatemala, Guyana, Haiti, Honduras, Jamaica, Mexico, Netherlands, Nicaragua, Panama, Paraguay, Peru, Portugal, St Christopher and Nevis, St Lucia, St Vincent and the Grenadines, Spain, Suriname, Trinidad and Tobago, United Kingdom, USA, Uruguay, and Venezuela. ECLAC economists have established a reputation for a structuralist analysis of local economies (as distinct from a monetarist analysis), stressing the need for the removal of production bottlenecks in resolving problems such as inflation and balance of payments disequilibria.
See also **Latin American Economic System**.

ECUADOR, Republic of

Capital: Quito (Largest city: Guayaquil)
Independence: (from Spain) 1822; (fom Gran Colombia) 1830
Area: 270,670 sq km
Population (1987): 9.92m (53.2% urban)
Pop. growth rate (1980–5): 2.9%
Pop. density: 36.66/sq km
Infant mortality (1980–5): 69.6 per thousand

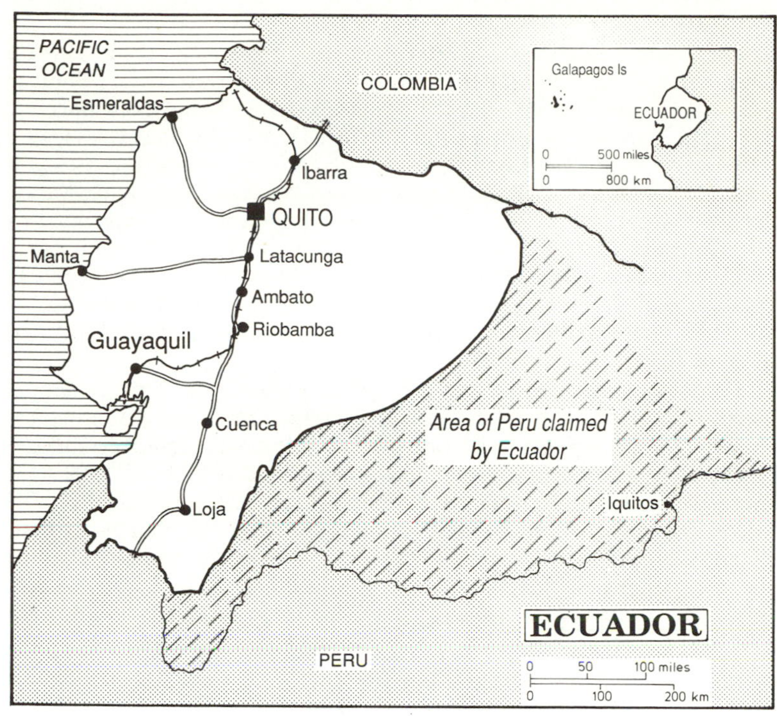

Life expectancy at birth (1980–5): 64.3
Literacy (1981): 85.2%
GDP per capita (1986e): US$1,326
Foreign debt per capita (1987e): US$1,000
Main export (1985): crude oil (68%); fish products (11%); bananas (7%); coffee (7%)

Political system

Constitution: 1979. *Head of state/government*: Rodrigo Borja Cevallos (ID) (1988–), elected to succeed León Febres Cordero Rivadeneiro (PSC) (1984–8). Elections are held every four years for president and a 71-seat, single-chamber legislature (National Congress). Twelve 'national deputies' are elected for four-year terms (two from each province with over 100,000 inhabitants, one from every other province); and 59 deputies for two years. The last full legislative and presidential elections were in 1988. There is universal compulsory adult (18+) suffrage and illiterates have had an optional vote since 1977. Candidates must belong to a legal political party. Re-election is permitted for deputies but not for the presidency.

Political organisations

Legal political parties (seats after January 1988): Democratic Left/ID (30); Social Christian Party/PSC (8); Concentration of Popular Forces/CFP (6); Radical Alfarist Front/FRA (2); Popular Democracy/DP (7); Ecuadorean Roldosista Party/PRE (8); Popular Democratic Movement/MPD (2); Broad Left Front/FADI (2), comprising Ecuadorean Communist Party/PCE, Revolutionary Socialist Party/PSR, Movement for the Unity of the Left/MUI, and Revolutionary Movement of the Christian Left/MRIC; Conservative Party/PCE (1); Liberal Party/PLE (1); Socialist Party/PSE (4); People, Change and Democracy/PCD (0); National Republican Coalition/CNR (0); Ecuadorean Popular Revolutionary Action/APRE (0); Democratic Institutionalist Front/CID (0); Revolutionary Nationalist Party/PNR (0).

There are two active armed opposition groups: the Popular Armed Forces–Eloy Alfaro (aka Alfaro Lives!) and the Free Nation Montoneras.

Main labour organisations (affiliation): Workers United Front/FUT (comprising Confederation of Ecuadorean Workers/CTE (CPUSTAL), Ecuadorean Confederation of Working Class Organisations/CEDOC (CLAT), and Ecuadorean Confederation of Free Trade Unions/CEOSL (ORIT)); Workers' Catholic Central; Public Servants' National Confederation/CONASEP; National Educators' Union/UNE. *Main employers' organisations*: National Businessmen's Association/ANDE; National Federation of Chambers of Commerce of Ecuador.

Ecuadorean Democratic Alliance (ADE): see **Velasco Ibarra**.

Ecuadorean Labour Federation of Free Trade Unions (CEOSL): see **Democratic Left**.

Ecuadorean Nationalist Revolutionary Alliance (ARNE): see **Conservative Party** (Ecuador).

Ecuadorean Popular Revolutionary Alliance (APRE): see **National Reconstruction Front**.

Ecuadorean Popular Revolutionary Union (URPE): see **Broad Left Front**.

Ecuadorean Revolutionary Socialist Party (PSRE): see **Ecuadorean Socialist Party**.

Ecuadorean Socialist Party (*Partido Socialista Ecuatoriano*/PSE) Founded in 1926 by a group of dissident Liberal intellectuals and professionals inspired by the Russian revolution, the PSE was the first party to provide an alternative to the Conservatives (PC) and Liberals (PL). In 1927 it split in two: the minority, pro-Moscow faction went on in 1931 to found the Ecuadorean Communist Party (PCE), and the majority eventually (1933) formed a new PSE. In the late 1930s the latter joined the de facto regime of Gen. Henríquez, under which reformist laws, including the Ecuadorean labour code, were introduced. A law giving equal parliamentary representation of Left, Right, and Centre meant the PSE held a third of the seats in Congress. It strongly supported trade unions and rights for indigenous Ecuadoreans, but failed to achieve consistent mass support in the labour movement. However, its supporters played a role in the 1944 establishment of the Ecuadorean Workers' Confederation (CTE), and in 1947 briefly took control of the organisation from the PCE. In 1944 the PSE took part in the overthrow of President Carlos Arroyo, and subsequently held cabinet posts under President José María Velasco Ibarra, withdrawing when he began to rule as a dictator. When he too was overthrown the party supported Galo Plaza, and later held posts in his government.

In 1952 the PSE joined the PCE and others in the Democratic Alliance, which fared poorly. It then took part in the centre-left National Democratic Front alliance with the PL and independents in 1956 and 1960. Internal strains again emerged in the 1950s; and in 1960, when the majority backed the candidacy of PL candidate Galo Plaza, a pro-Cuban wing broke away and (in 1961) formed the Revolutionary Socialist Party (PSRE), which eventually declared itself Marxist-Leninist. In 1968 the party joined the FID coalition with the PL and others. In this period it seemed threatened with extinction, having lost many members to other groups. It supported the PL candidate in 1978 and won no seats in the 1979 congressional elections, but in 1984 it elected one deputy and joined the Progressive Front (FP) bloc in parliament. In 1988 it won four seats. See also **Communist Party of Ecuador; Revolutionary Socialist Party**.

e

Eisenhower, Gen. Dwight D.: see **Monroe doctrine**.

Elbrick, Burke: see **Action for National Liberation**.

11 September Command: see **death squad**.

Eloy Alfaro Popular Armed Forces: see **Alfaro Lives!**

Emanuels, S. D.: see **National Party of Suriname**.

Emperor Pedro II: see **Old Republic**.

Enríquez, Miguel: see **Movement of the Revolutionary Left (Chile)**.

Erro, Enrique: see **Broad Front**.

***escuadrón de la muerte*:** see **death squad**.

Esguerra Barcenas Treaty: see **San Andrés dispute**.

ESMACO: see **Alvarez, Gen. Gregorio**.

Espinosa, Col. Pedro: see **Letelier case**.

***esquadrão de morte*:** see **death squad**.

Essequibo dispute

A long-standing territorial dispute in which Venezuela claims ownership of the Essequibo, a 159,000 square kilometre area of Guyana. The disputed territory represents two-thirds of Guyana's total area. Guyana originally consisted of three separate Dutch colonies – Essequibo, Demerara, and Berbice – which were ceded to Britain in 1814. The three areas were integrated into a single colony, British Guiana. Venezuelan claims to the Essequibo were advanced in the late nineteenth century; Britain, in turn, made competing claims to what are now the eastern and northeastern regions of Venezuela. With strong US support, Venezuela succeeded in obtaining British agreement to international arbitration; the decision of a specially appointed court (consisting of two Americans, two Britons, and a Russian president) was to be respected by all parties. The court gave its ruling in October 1899, conceding Venezuelan claims at the mouth of the Orinoco river, but confirming British rights in the Essequibo. Venezuela accepted the ruling and took part in a mixed border commission which demarcated the new boundary in 1905.

However, in 1949 Sevro Mallet-Prevost, one of the US lawyers who had acted for Venezuela in the court proceedings, died; in his will he had left instruction for the posthumous publication of a memorandum alleging that the 1899 ruling had been illegal, the product of a behind-the-scenes political deal. In 1951 Venezuela questioned the validity of the arbitration decision on the basis of the Mallet-Prevost memorandum; and at the United Nations General Assembly in 1962 it announced it could no longer accept the decision and wished to register that it still had an outstanding dispute with the neighbouring British colony, which was soon to be granted independence. Britain agreed to a re-examination of documentary evidence on the dispute. The talks led to the Geneva agreement of February 1966 in which the need for new substantive negotiations was accepted. The British colony became independent on 26 May 1966, taking the name of Guyana. Border incidents with Venezuela took place at various times, particularly in October 1966 and February 1970. Failure to break the deadlock led both governments to sign the Protocol of Port of Spain of 18 June 1970, which placed a 12-year moratorium on the dispute.

In October 1978 Carlos Andrés Pérez became the first Venezuelan head of state to visit Guyana, where he was welcomed by Prime Minister (later President) Forbes Burnham. But despite some signs of progress, relations worsened abruptly after Burnham paid a return visit to Pérez's successor, Luis Herrera Campins, in April 1981. Immediately after the visit the Guyanese president said his government would not 'cede an inch' of the Essequibo; Herrera Campins announced that Venezuela's claim would be kept alive, and his government would not, as had been expected, extend the moratorium on its expiry. Venezuela's more aggressive stance on the dispute and the 1982 Argentine occupation of the Falklands/Malvinas led to Guyanese fears of an invasion, and the government obtained the backing of Cuba and Brazil. Subsequently both Venezuela and Guyana agreed to mediation by UN Secretary-general Javier Pérez del Cuellar. In March 1987 President Desmond Hoyte of Guyana visited Caracas and signed economic cooperation agreements with President Jaime Lusinchi which were described as creating a positive

climate for progress on the dispute. Both leaders promised to develop bilateral contacts 'to assist the work of the secretary-general'.
See also **Gulf of Venezuela dispute; South Atlantic War**.

Estado Nôvo (New State)
A period of dictatorship in Brazil which began with the 10 November 1937 declaration by President Getulio Vargas of a new constitution, under which he assumed decree powers for six years. Modelled on Italian and Portuguese fascism, the *Estado Nôvo* did not survive the removal of Vargas in a military coup in 1945.
See also **Integralism; Vargas**.

Eurocommunism: see **Brazilian Communist Party (PCB); Communism**.

Falklands/Malvinas

A South Atlantic island archipelago, the subject of a long-running sovereignty dispute between Argentina and Britain. The English name was first used by Captain John Strong, who landed on the islands in 1690 and named the Falkland Sound after the then Admiralty Commissioner, the 3rd Viscount Falkland. The name Malvinas is derived from the French *Les Malouines*, after Breton sailors from St Malo who were involved in fishing and sealing on the islands in the early eighteenth century. Claims of initial discovery are disputed, being variously attributed to Amerigo Vespucci in 1504, John Davis, and Richard Hawkins. The first settlement was established by France, but it ceded the islands to Spain in 1767. A rival British settlement was maintained until 1774, when it was withdrawn because of its high cost. The British left behind a plaque asserting their claim to ownership. After Argentine independence from Spain, the newly independent government in Buenos Aires extended its claim to the islands. In 1824 the new republic granted a concession to develop Isla Soledad (East Falkland) to Louis Vernet, who was appointed governor in 1829. But the USS Lexington attacked and sacked the island settlement after a dispute with Vernet over whaling rights. The British warships Clio and Tyne then seized the islands on 3 January 1833, beginning an almost uninterrupted period of British control.

The Argentine claim to sovereignty, asserted since the loss of the islands by force in 1833, rests on an inheritance of Spanish rights, geographical proximity, and the location of the islands on the Argentine continental shelf. The Argentine claim received backing in Resolution 2065 of the UN General Assembly in December 1965, which described the islands' status as colonial and called for peaceful negotiations to resolve the conflict with reference to the interests of the islanders. The British claim is based on continuous occupation since 1833. Sheep farming was traditionally the main economic activity, accounting for 99% of exports, and controlled mainly by the Falkland Islands Company (FIC), the main employer and an important land owner. The population is almost entirely of British descent, about three-fifths born on the islands. After reaching a peak in the 1930s, the population declined steadily thereafter in step with the general neglect of the islands by Britain. It had dwindled to 1,813 by the time of the 1980 census.

After the Argentine military occupation of the islands in April–June

1982 and the subsequent recapture by British forces, a UK military garrison approximately 3,000-strong was established, together with additional civilian support and administrative staff. Efforts were also made to attract new settlers from Britain and to diversify the economy. After the establishment of a fishing conservation zone in February 1987 and a licensing system for visiting trawlers, income from this source increased sharply. New investments included the building of the Mount Pleasant airport, capable of taking wide-bodied jets. Following the 1982 South Atlantic War, successive UN General Assembly resolutions called on the UK and Argentina to negotiate a solution to the sovereignty question, but the British government refused to commence talks on the subject.
See also **South Atlantic War**.

fascism: see **Integralism**.

Fatherland and Freedom: (*Patria y Libertad*/P & L)
An extreme right-wing, neo-fascist organisation, founded in Chile in 1970 in response to the electoral victory of the left-wing Popular Unity (UP) coalition and the rise of the Movement of the Revolutionary Left (MIR). Its leaders were Dr Pablo Rodríguez Grez and Walter Roberto Thieme. It was small in size, but disproportionately influential inside the armed forces. It organised middle-class districts of Santiago into self-defence ('PROTECO') committees against the alleged threat from the left. Its paramilitary forces fought the left in the streets and engaged in sabotage and terrorism, coming to prominence during the December 1971 demonstrations against Fidel Castro's visit to Chile, after which they organised street violence. The group was involved in gun-running from Argentina and military training in Bolivia and southern Chile. Rodríguez fled to Ecuador and Thieme to Argentina in mid-1973 after a P & L attempt to kill the loyalist Gen. Carlos Prats. It was also deeply involved in the military uprising ('*tancazo*') of 29 June 1973, following the failure of which its leaders sought refuge in the Ecuadorean embassy; and it subsequently participated in the 11 September 1973 coup d'etat led by Gen. Augusto Pinochet.

Pablo Rodríguez became one of Pinochet's closest advisers. In the 1980s he joined the National Action Movement (MAN), a pro-government party, but resigned when MAN opted to back Gen. Pinochet's candidacy in the 1988/89 elections. MAN has since been dissolved and many of its leaders have joined the National Advance (*Avanzada Nacional*) party, created by the security and intelligence services, which is noted for its close links with Gen. Pinochet. P & L itself was revived in the late 1980s under Javier Andrade.
See also **Popular Unity; *tancazo***.

Fayad, Alvaro: see **M–19**.

Febreristas **(Febrerista Revolutionary Party)** (*Partido Revolucionario Febrerista*/PRF)
The PRF takes its name from the coup of 17 February 1936 which

installed a radical nationalist government under Colonel Rafael Franco. Franco's government had the support of veterans of the Chaco War as well as members of the Communist Party, and introduced a programme of land reform. Franco was deposed in a counter-coup on 13 August 1937, and the PRF remained banned until 1946, when the liberalisation process under the Morínigo regime led to the formation of a Colorado–Febrerista government. After a period of political freedom, the *guionista* faction of the Colorados, in alliance with Morínigo, expelled the Febreristas and began a reign of terror against them and the opposition in general. The Febreristas led a counter-rebellion in early 1947 with the backing of some army units. The rebels, who by then included Communists and Liberals, seized the northern city of Concepción on 8 March 1947. But in the ensuing civil war the insurgents under Col. Franco were defeated by central government forces and most of the leadership was either killed or exiled. The survivors in exile purged the party of left-wingers and adopted a more moderate political stance.

Although banned inside Paraguay, the PRF, together with the Liberals, tried to organise a boycott of the 1960 elections. In 1959 a small group within the party organised the *Vanguardia Febrerista* guerrilla column, which was rapidly defeated by the army. The PRF regained its legal status in the mid-1960s, participating in elections in 1967–8 and gaining one seat in the Chamber of Deputies. But it reverted to boycotting elections after that, a policy confirmed when it joined the National Accord (*Acuerdo Nacional*) opposition coalition in 1979. The PRF became the only legally recognised party not to be represented in Congress. The PRF is affiliated to the Socialist International.

See also **Chaco War; Franco; National Accord; Paraguayan Civil War**.

Febres Cordero Rivadeneiro, León

b. 1931. President of Ecuador 1984–8. Member of a powerful Guayaquil clan; descendant of an independence hero of the same name and of the tenth US president, John Tyler. Trained as mechanical engineer. Millionaire industrialist and cattle rancher; owner of a salt factory and a cardboard box company. Former manager of the US-owned electricity utility EMELEC. Won many trophies as a pistol shot, a skill perfected at a US military academy. Past president of the Chamber of Guayaquil Industrialists, the National Federation of Chambers of Industry, and of the Association of Latin American Industrialists. Served three terms as a congressman between 1966 and 1984.

A representative of the financial and agro-industrial oligarchy of Guayaquil, allied to US interests, Febres Cordero was the victorious presidential candidate of the Social Christian Party (PSC) in the 1984 elections. He was backed by the National Reconstruction Front (FRN) coalition, an alliance of the parties of the traditional right which he played a major part in bringing together. His victory was based on support in the coastal provinces, while the remainder of the country helped ensure an opposition majority in Congress for most of his term. He imposed strict monetarist, pro-business economic policies, challenged many aspects of the Andean Pact (from which he threatened at one point to withdraw), and fought OPEC production quotas. In the first two years of his presidency, 26 'emergency' economic decrees transformed the economy, opening it up to foreign and domestic private capital. Closely aligned with the United States in foreign policy, he broke relations with Nicaragua in October 1985 after a verbal clash with President Daniel Ortega, while cultivating friendly relations with South Africa. He aroused many constitutional controversies by his attempts to concentrate more power in the hands of the executive and blur the separation between the branches of government, for example by vetoing all congressional resolutions of which he disapproved.

In June 1986, after failing in attempts to alter the electoral system in order to ensure control of the legislature, he sought to amend the constitution in order to allow the election of independents to Congress, but was heavily defeated. The most severe challenges to his rule came from air force chief Gen. Frank Vargas Pazzos, who in March 1986 seized the Manta air base in protest at alleged corruption within the high command. He was jailed after his protest turned into an attempt to overthrow the government; but in January 1987 air force commandos loyal to Vargas kidnapped Febres and held him, his defence minister, and others hostage for 11 hours until they secured the general's release. Opposition parties subsequently called unsuccessfully for Febres' resignation. A severe earthquake, also in early 1987, caused an estimated US$1bn in losses and destroyed large parts of the country's oil pipeline, halting exports and causing the government (hitherto considered a model debtor) to suspend all private foreign debt repayments. A sharp drop in the price of crude oil (the country's main export) had already brought a 44% decline in oil earnings.

Febres was accused by human rights organisations of presiding over a marked increase in torture and extra-judicial killings. His administration was also marred by accusations of corruption, and there were moves to bring criminal charges against him after he stepped down.
See also **National Reconstruction Front; Social Christian Party; Vargas Pazzos rebellion**.

Fernández, Edmundo: see ***trienio***.

Fernández, Lorenzo: see **Pérez, Carlos Andrés**.

Fernández, Sergio: see ***Gremialismo***; **Party of National Renovation**.

Fernández Córdova, Andrés: see **Concentration of Popular Forces**.

Fernández Gasco, Gonzalo: see **Movement of the Revolutionary Left** (Peru).

Fernández Larios, Maj. Armando: see **Letelier case**.

Ferreira, Joaquim Cámara: see ***abertura***.

Ferreira Aldunate, Wilson

1919–88. A leading Uruguayan politician, from the Blanco Party. From a traditional landowning family, he became known as a good orator while serving as deputy and later senator (1967–72) for the Blancos. He was minister for agriculture and livestock in 1963 under the Blanco administration. He set up his own tendency or *lema* within the party, *Por la Patria*, which, in alliance with the *Movimiento de Rocha* presented him as its presidential candidate for the November 1971 elections. Ferreira Aldunate's political platform was considerably removed from traditional Blanco conservatism, including proposals for land reform, the nationalisation of the banking system, and social reforms designed to alleviate conditions which, it was felt, had helped engender the MLN-Tupamaros guerrilla movement. His opposition to the increasing militarisation of the country under the presidency of Jorge Pacheco Areco made for a harshly fought election campaign. Ferreira Aldunate emerged as the single most popular candidate – but under the workings of the *Ley de Lemas* he was defeated because the aggregate of votes for the Colorados was greater than that for the Blancos (41% against 40%). The Blancos claimed that there had been electoral fraud, an allegation supported by independent observers.

After the new president, Juan María Bordaberry, was sworn in, Ferreira Aldunate became an outspoken parliamentary critic of human rights violations in the counter-insurgency campaign, and was forced to flee the country after the 27 June 1973 coup d'etat. He later testified on human rights violations in Uruguay before a committee of the US Congress, a testimony which helped persuade congressmen to cut off military aid to the country and earned Ferreira Aldunate the hatred of the regime. He remained in exile in Argentina until 1976 when he narrowly escaped abduction. He then moved to Britain, returning to Argentina in 1984. By that time *Por la Patria* and *Movimiento de Rocha* had established virtual control of the Blanco Party, but the regime refused to allow Ferreira to stand as a candidate in the planned elections. On 16 June 1984 he returned to Uruguay on board a specially chartered ship, accompanied by journalists; Blanco supporters organised demonstrations. He was arrested on arrival and imprisoned on a string of charges, including aiding subversion and undermining the morale of the armed forces. Despite the efforts of his supporters, Ferreira Aldunate was kept in prison until just after the November 1984 elections. The elections were won by the Colorados; after the return to constitutional rule in March 1985, Ferreira Aldunate remained active as leader of the Blancos.

See also **Blanco Party; *Proceso***.

Figueiredo, Gen. João Baptista de Oliveira

b. 1918. Brazilian military leader and president 1979–85, the last in the cycle of military rulers in the 1964–85 period. Born in Rio de Janeiro, he had a military education and was posted to Army General Staff in 1958. During the presidency of Janio Quadros, Figueiredo was head of the Federal Information and Counter-Information Service and general-secretary of the National Security Council. In 1964 he was appointed head of the SNI intelligence agency in Rio, and was promoted to the rank of brigadier-general. In 1969 he was appointed commander of Third Army General Staff, and became head of President Garrastazu Medici's Military Household. In 1974 Figueiredo took overall control of the SNI.

In October 1978, shortly after rising to the rank of four-star general, he was ratified by the Electoral College as the next president. He took office in March 1979, inheriting the gradual political liberalisation process initiated by his predecessor, Gen. Ernesto Geisel. The Figueiredo administration also inherited a rapidly worsening economic crisis; it proved increasingly difficult to service the country's foreign debt, inflation rose to an annual rate of over 200%, and there was a severe economic recession in 1983/84. A series of corruption scandals also troubled the administration which was facing growing popular dissatisfaction with military rule and demands for full democracy. Figueiredo introduced the 1979 political amnesty which led to the return of many exiles, and reformed the political party system in the same year. His government also allowed direct elections of governors in 1982, the first time since 1965. In the last years of his term in office, Figueiredo prepared the way for the election of a civilian successor; with both the ruling PDS and the opposition Democratic Alliance nominating non-military candidates. But Figueiredo refused to budge on opposition demands for direct presidential elections, despite the mass *diretas já* (direct elections now) campaign of 1984. Figueiredo stepped down in March 1985, handing power to José Sarney. See also ***abertura***; **amnesty (Brazil, 1979)**; ***diretas já***; **Neves**; **Sarney**.

f

Figueroa, Emiliano: see **Ibáñez del Campo**.

Filho, Alexandre Marcondes: see ***Trabalhismo***.

Firmenich, Mario: see **Montoneros**.

Firmes: see **Colombian Communist Party**; **Democratic Left Unity**.

First of March Organisation: see **Politico-Military Organisation**.

***fiscais do Sarney*:** see **Cruzado**.

Fleury, Sergio: see **death squad**.

FLN/FALN (National Liberation Front/Armed Forces of National Liberation)

The political and military wings of a Venezuelan guerrilla movement active in the 1960s. The FALN were created on 20 February 1963, grouping together the various guerrilla organisations which had sprung up around the country in the previous year and were fighting a common enemy, the Democratic Action (AD) government of President Rómulo Betancourt. The signatories of the declaration announcing the creation of the FALN justified their action by citing the constitutional duty to 'rise up against arbitrary abuses of power . . . especially when as in our case they have led to the setting up of a despotic, sectarian, and anti-national government.' The FALN's first commander was a rebel from the regular army, Captain Manuel Ponte Rodríguez. At the insistence of the Communist Party (PCV) a National Liberation Front (FLN), which was to have responsibility for political decisions affecting the guerrilla struggle, was also created. The FLN was initially dominated by the PCV and to a lesser extent by the Movement of the Revolutionary Left (MIR), the two left-wing parties most committed to the insurgency. The FALN was involved in both rural and urban guerrilla actions.

In November 1963, as part of its campaign for a boycott of the elections due later that year, the FALN called a two-day general strike and protests – in the ensuing street fighting 20 people died. But the failure of the campaign against the elections was a setback for the organisation. By 1965, with the PCV moving away from armed struggle, the FLN/FALN was reorganised by the guerrilla commanders who wanted to continue the war. Douglas Bravo of the José Leonardo Chirinos Front in Falcón state became the FALN's main *comandante*, with Fabricio Ojeda (later to be killed by the security forces) and Américo Martín as president and secretary-general of the FLN. As the split between the PCV and the FLN/FALN worsened, Fidel Castro expressed support for the guerrilla commanders. But the insurgency did not prosper and by the late 1960s the FLN/FALN was isolated and reduced in size. After President Rafael Caldera took office in 1969, the MIR too renounced armed struggle and the FALN was narrowed down to Bravo's group, which held out in the hills until the late 1970s, for most of which time it was militarily ineffective.

See also **Betancourt; Bravo; Movement of the Revolutionary Left** (Venezuela); **Venezuelan Communist Party**.

Fly, Claude: see **National Liberation Movement-Tupamaros**.

Fonseca, Marshal Deodoro da: see **Old Republic**.

foquismo

A theory of guerrilla war which emerged from the Cuban revolution, was refined by Ernesto 'Che' Guevara and popularised by the French Marxist philosopher Régis Debray (though Debray later acknowledged its limitations). Its essence, as expressed by Guevara, was that 'it is not necessary to wait until all conditions for making a revolution exist; the insurrection can create them'. In practice, this meant starting a guerrilla '*foco*' (centre, or nucleus) in a remote, preferably mountainous, region, which could provide the model for the rural population and eventually a catalyst for mass revolt. Both Guevara and Debray stressed that this should not be considered in isolation from work amongst the urban proletariat, though they tended to minimise this requirement, and this was a prime factor in the downfall of most *foquista* experiments. The theory began to lose credibility after the failure of Guevara's 1967 Bolivian *foco*, which led to his death.

In South America, the theory was put into practice by (among others) the People's Revolutionary Army (ERP) in Argentina (1974–7), the National Liberation Army (ELN) and Armed Forces of National Liberation (FALN) in Venezuela (1962–70), the National Liberation Army

(ELN) in Colombia (from 1965), and the Movement of the Revolutionary Left (MIR) in Peru (1965). The failure of all these experiments led to a profound reassessment, with different results in different countries. In some (e.g. Argentina) the guerrillas were effectively wiped out as a political force. In others (Peru, Venezuela) they were generally reincorporated into civilian politics; while in Colombia, for example, they adapted their strategies and continued the struggle.
See also **Guevara; National Liberation Army** (Bolivia).

14 May Movement: see **guerrilla invasions** (Paraguay).

Franco, Col. Rafael

1897–1973. Charismatic Paraguayan army officer who as president in 1936–7 after the Chaco War implemented important socio-economic reforms. As commander of the 2nd Army Corps during the war he was considered an excellent officer and his humane treatment of the troops inspired their loyalty. The army came out of the war feeling it had defended the country successfully in spite of the Liberal government's indecision – and its resentment was sharpened by the authorities' refusal to grant pensions to disabled war veterans. Franco was involved in conspiracies against the government from his new position as head of the Military College. But when, in February 1936, he was arrested and deported to Argentina, an army uprising overthrew the government and Franco became the new president.

In office he initiated a land reform programme and introduced a progressive labour code which for the first time guaranteed the right to strike and provided important social welfare benefits for workers. But his government suffered from internal factional fighting. In August 1937 a new army rebellion led to Franco's downfall and exile in Argentina.

He was not able to return to the country until 1945, after the dictatorship of Gen. Higinio Morínigo promised elections and invited the Colorados and Franco's followers – by now known as *Febreristas* after the February 1936 revolution – into a coalition government. Once again this coalition fell victim to infighting, with Morinígo and the *Guión Rojo* faction of the Colorados plotting to delay the elections. The coalition collapsed in January 1947, when Morínigo declared a state of siege and began rounding up opposition leaders. Franco and other leading *Febreristas* were arrested and deported. But on 7 March 1947 a *Febrerista* revolt broke out, sparking off an army revolt in support of Franco, centred on the Concepción garrison. Franco flew to that city from Argentina to take command of the rebel forces. In the ensuing civil war, the rebel alliance of *Febreristas*, Communists, and Liberals, despite laying siege to Asunción, was eventually defeated with great loss of life. Franco once again left for exile, although the *Febreristas* continued to work underground within Paraguay.

In 1956 Franco made an unsuccessful attempt to fly back to the country for talks with the regime of Gen. Alfredo Stroessner. In exile his movement, known by its initials PRF, began to lose its dynamism. Franco opposed the more radical members of the movement who took up guer-

rilla struggle inside Paraguay. At the party's national convention in 1962 Franco's group expelled the radicals; as a result Stroessner decided to legalise the party in August 1964. Franco returned to Paraguay under the terms of an amnesty but after a few years decided to retire from active politics. He died in October 1973.
See also **Chaco War; *Febreristas*; Morínigo**.

Free Nation Montoneras (*Montoneras Patria Libre*/MPL)
An Ecuadorean guerrilla group which emerged in January 1986 with the theft from a Quito museum of weapons used by independence fighters. In May 1986 ten members held hostage Enrique Echeverría, President Febres' representative on the Constitutional Guarantees Tribunal (TGC), for six days before surrendering. Their demands included a political trial for President Febres, whom the MPL accused of failing to fulfil promises of 'bread, housing, and jobs'. The group has been disowned as 'adventurist' by the country's senior guerrilla organisation, Alfaro Lives, of which it is said to be a splinter group. (*Montonera* is a Latin American word for a band of mounted rebels.)
See also **Alfaro Lives!**.

f

Frei Montalva, Eduardo
1911–82. President of Chile 1964–70. Born in Santiago, the son of a Swiss immigrant book-keeper on a farm. Educated at the Institute of Humanities and the Catholic University Law School (graduated 1933). Elected president of the National Association of Catholic Students, 1933, and of the Chilean Catholic Action Youth in the same year. Represented Chile at a congress of Catholic youth in Rome in 1934. Manager of *El Tarapacá* daily newspaper in Iquique after graduation. A founder member of the Falange Party, based on the Conservative Youth section, Frei ran twice for deputy in Iquique, receiving the highest vote in Tarapacá province in 1937, but was not elected due to the national proportional representation system. He returned to Santiago in 1937 to develop his law practice and work for the newspaper *El Diario Ilustrado*. Frei argued for cooperation between the Falange and the Communists (PCCh). He was professor of labour law at the Catholic University from 1940–5 and minister of roads and public works for nine months in 1945–6 under President Juan Antonio Ríos, resigning after a crowd of demonstrators was fired on. He was elected senator for Atacama and Coquimbo in 1949 and was a Chilean delegate to the UN in 1950. Elected senator for Santiago in 1957, the year in which the Falange merged with the Social Conservative Party to become the Christian Democrat Party (PDC), Frei was PDC presidential candidate in 1958, when he came third.

In 1964 he was elected president on the 'Democratic Left' ticket (comprising the PDC backed by the New Democratic Left and part of the Agrarian Labour Party), with the slogan 'revolution in liberty'. In office he proceeded with the partial nationalisation (*chilenización*) of the copper industry (which was agreed by its foreign owners in exchange for tax concessions) and small-scale agrarian reform. His reputation as a reformer was tarnished, however, when a 24-hour strike in November

1968 was met with force and five people were shot, a pattern repeated during the 1966 copper strike. In line with its 'communitarian' philosophy, the government promoted neighbourhood committees (*juntas de vecinos*) under a programme called '*promoción popular*'. Since Frei was constitutionally prevented from standing again in 1970, his place was taken by left-winger Radomiro Tómic, who lost to Salvador Allende of the Popular Unity (UP) coalition. Elected senator again in 1973, the former president was a supporter of the September 1973 coup which overthrew Allende, though he subsequently became estranged from the military regime. On his death in 1982, the Pinochet regime declared three days of mourning, but the Frei family boycotted the memorial ceremony and held their own, attended by thousands of supporters and addressed by the archbishop of Santiago.
See also **Christian Democrat Party** (Chile).

FREJULI: see **Justicialist Liberation Front**.

French Guiana/Guyane

French overseas departement (province)
Capital: Cayenne
First French settlement 1604; departement from 1946
Area: 90,910 sq km
Population (1988e): 90,240 (75% urban)
Pop. growth rate: 3.6%
Pop. density: 1/sq km
Infant mortality (1984): 22.6 per thousand
Life expectancy at birth (1979): 66.6.
Literacy (1982): 82%
GDP per capita (1981): US$3,086
Main export (% of 1987 merchandise exports): shrimps (57%), timber, rice

f

Political system

A prefect/commissioner appointed by and sent from Paris for (generally) a two-year term governs in consultation with a 19-member General Council and (since 1981) a 31-member Regional Council (with fewer powers), both elected for six years. Guiana is represented in the French parliament by two National Assembly deputies and one senator. *Prefect/commissioner*: Jean-Pierre Lacroix (1988–). *President of General Council*: Elie Castor (PSG) (1985–). *President of Regional Council*: Georges Othily (PSG) (1983–). *Deputies*: Elie Castor (PSG) (1981–); Léon Bertrand (1988–). *Senator*: Raymond Tarcy (PSG) (1980–). *Last elections*: June 1988 (National Assembly), October 1988 (General Council), March 1986 (Regional Council).

Political organisations

Parties (leader) (seats in General/Regional Councils): Guianese Socialist Party/PSG (Gérard Holder) (9/15), f. 1956; Rally for the Republic/RPR (Léon Bertrand) (2/9), f. 1946; Union for French Democracy/UDF

(Serge Patient) (2/3), f. 1979; Guianese Democratic Action/ADG (André Lecante) (1/4). Left-wing independents hold two seats on the General Council. *Parties with no elected representatives*: Party for Guianese Progress/PPG (Claude Ho A Chuck) f. 1974; Guianese Popular National Party/PNPG (Alain Michel), f. 1985; Front de la Lutte Anti-Colonialiste/ FULAC (Michel Kapel); Panga (Michel Kapel). *Trade unions*: Guianese Workers' Union/UTG (sec. gen., Paul Cécilien); local branches of the three main French union federations.

Fresno, Cardinal Juan Francisco: see **National Agreement for a Transition to Full Democracy**.

Friedman, Milton: see **Chicago Boys**.

Frigerio, Rogelio: see **Frondizi; Movement for Integration and Development**.

Frondizi, Dr Arturo

b. 1908. Argentine lawyer and politician, identified with *desarrollista* (developmentalist) policies, whose 1958–62 presidency was characterised by almost uninterrupted crises in relations with the armed forces, leading in the end to his removal by a military coup. Active in student politics, he was imprisoned in 1930 for his opposition to the military coup against the Radical Party (UCR). Frondizi was appointed professor of law at the University of Buenos Aires in 1932. He was elected on the Radical ticket to the Chamber of Deputies, in 1946, and was a vice-presidential candidate in the 1952 elections.

Although he initially supported the anti-Peronist Liberating Revolution, he later began to take a more critical line. Frondizi was strongly influenced by the thinking of Rogelio Frigerio, who believed that the Peronist constituency could be integrated into a wider alliance based on a programme of industrialisation and development. This position led to growing tensions within the UCR, as the other groupings in the party were more favourably disposed to the military government. After the UCR congress nominated Frondizi as the party's presidential candidate in 1956, rival factions led by Dr Ricardo Balbín broke away, forming the People's Radical Party (UCRP). Frondizi's wing took the name of Intransigent Radical Party (UCRI). In the July 1957 constituent assembly elections the UCRI took second place behind the UCRP. In the February 1958 general elections the UCRI emerged victorious, after reaching a secret understanding with Gen. Juan Perón.

Frondizi's presidency was marked by a new surge in industrialisation and the development of the oil industry. But the military saw the president as dangerously pro-Peronist and left-wing. During his administration there were over 30 *planteos* or military ultimatums. The army was particularly incensed when Argentina abstained in an OAS vote to expel Cuba, while Frondizi's later decision to break diplomatic relations with Havana alienated the left. These tensions came to the fore when Peronist candidates won elections in five provinces (including Buenos Aires) in March 1962. Faced with a military backlash, Frondizi ordered federal intervention in the five, but his cabinet resigned in protest. On 29 March 1962 the armed forces deposed the president.

Frondizi remained politically active, supporting the National and Popular Front coalition in 1966. But disagreements over the party's role in the coalition led to a split in the UCRI. As a result Frondizi created the Movement of Integration and Development (MID). Frondizi's opposition to the UCRP administration installed in 1963 led him to support Gen. Onganía's coup in 1966. In the 1973 elections the MID joined the Peronist-dominated Justicialist Liberation Front (FREJULI) alliance. In 1983 Frigerio stood as the MID's presidential candidate, with Frondizi acting as its elder statesman.

See also **Frigerio; Liberating Revolution; Radical Party** (Argentina).

Gaitán, Gloria: see **Gaitán, Jorge Eliécer.**

Gaitán, Jorge Eliécer

1898–1948. Reformist/populist leader of the Colombian Liberal Party (PL). Barrister; author of *Socialist Ideas in Colombia* (1924). Gaitán came to prominence through his defence of workers involved in the 1929 banana strike against the United Fruit Co. He founded the National Union of the Revolutionary Left (UNIR) in 1934 in an attempt to create an independent socialist party, but was forced to rejoin the PL in order to regain lost support. He was presidential candidate for the left of the PL in 1946, when the split in the party led to the election of the Conservative president Ospina Pérez. After his electoral defeat Gaitán won over large numbers of Liberals, and even the Communist Party (PCC), which had previously labelled him a 'fascist'. He had a majority in parliament, but did not assume sole leadership of the PL until shortly before his death in 1948.

He was a renowned orator, with a gift for communicating in the language of ordinary people, and his political thinking was Marxist-influenced. It has been argued that, had his movement developed, he could have been 'the Fidel Castro of Colombia'. Under Ospina the period known as 'the violence' began, much of it directed at Gaitán supporters: in April 1947 Gaitán presented a protest memorandum detailing acts of violence in 56 towns, and in February 1948 he made an 'Oration for Peace' at a large rally in the capital, Bogotá, calling for the restoration of public order. He was assassinated in Bogotá on 9 April 1948 by a gunman whose motives remain unknown (he was immediately lynched by the crowd). Gaitán's death sparked the days of rioting known as the *Bogotazo*. His daughter, Gloria Gaitán, and her husband, Luís Emiro Valencia, later headed a short-lived left-wing movement favouring armed struggle, called the United Revolutionary Action Front (FUAR).
See also ***Bogotazo***; **Liberal Party** (Colombia); ***violencia, la***.

Gaitania: see **Marquetalia** (Colombia).

Galán Sarmiento, Luis Carlos: see **New Liberalism**.

Galindo, Eudoro: see **Nationalist Democratic Alliance**.

Galindo, Dr Francisco Baptista: see **Gómez, Gen. Juan Vicente**.

Gallegos, Elías: see **Communist Party of Ecuador**.

Gallegos, Rómulo

1884–1969. Prominent novelist and teacher who became Venezuela's first elected president in 1948, only to be ousted in a coup that same year. Born in Caracas, in 1909 he founded a weekly magazine, *La Alborada*, which carried essays on literature, art, and politics – it lasted for three months before being closed down by the dictatorship of Gen. Juan Vicente Gómez. He was also involved with other artists in the *Círculo de Bellas Artes* which grouped together those seeking cultural and political enlightenment. His novels included *Reinaldo Solar* (1920) and *Doña Barbara* (1929). The latter was so appreciated by Gen. Gómez that Gallegos was appointed Senator for Arágua. Faced with rumours that the dictator was about to make him minister of education or president of Congress, Gallegos left Venezuela in 1931 to avoid the choice of having to collaborate with or oppose Gómez. He returned in 1936 and became minister of education under the administration of Gen. López Contreras; he was a member of the Chamber of Deputies (1937–40), and president of the Caracas municipal council. In 1941 Gallegos, along with Rómulo Betancourt, was a founding member of *Acción Democrática* (AD). He stood as a 'symbolic' presidential candidate for AD in the indirect elections that same year.

After the 1945 revolution, which brought power to a combination of AD members and military officers, Gallegos stood as the party's candidate in the December 1947 elections, winning with a landslide 74%. He thus became the first popularly and freely elected president in Venezuelan history. Taking office in February 1948, he continued the reformist policies implemented by AD in the preceding years, but inherited a troubled relationship with the army. The conflict came to a head on 24 November 1948, when the military conspirators arrested Gallegos and took power. Forced into exile for the duration of the military regime, Gallegos returned to Venezuela on the fall of Gen. Marcos Pérez Jiménez in 1958. See also **Democratic Action; *trienio***.

Galtieri, Gen. Leopoldo Fortunato

b. 1926. Argentine army leader and president, 1981–2, who ordered the ill-fated military occupation of the Falklands/Malvinas islands. Of Italian descent, Galtieri entered the Military College in 1943, achieving the rank of colonel in 1967, and general in 1972. He was commander of the 9th and 7th Infantry Brigades, Commander 2 (Operations) at Army General Staff and head of the 2nd Army Corps (in 1976 – the year of the coup which brought the Process of National Reorganisation military regime to power). During his time at the 2nd Army Corps in Rosario there were severe violations of human rights in the counter-insurgency campaign. By this time he had established a reputation for a brash style and driving ambition.

In December 1979 he became Commander-in-Chief of the Army and a member of the ruling junta. From this position he destabilised the government of Gen. Roberto Viola, who had headed the army before him. Galtieri was reported to have sent Argentine military advisers to Central America in cooperation with the CIA, but without Viola's knowledge or approval. In mid-1981 he ordered the closure of all land borders with Chile, provoking a new crisis in relations over the Beagle Channel dispute, again acting unilaterally without the president's knowledge. Galtieri helped engineer Gen. Viola's removal in December 1981 – initially described as being due to ill-health but in reality a palace coup.

As president from 22 December 1981 Galtieri retained the two key positions of army commander and junta member. Faced by growing demands for information on the fate of the 'disappeared' and an intensifying economic crisis, he began to look for some kind of foreign military intervention capable of distracting attention from these domestic problems. The military occupation of the Falklands/Malvinas on 2 April 1982 was initially successful in mobilising nationalist sentiment behind the government; but Britain's counter-attack and eventual recapture of the islands on 14 June was fatal for Galtieri's administration. He was deposed on 16 June, only 48 hours after Argentine forces had surrendered in the South Atlantic. In 1983 he was frequently placed under disciplinary arrest by the army high command. Under the administration of President Raúl Alfonsín, Galtieri was placed on trial on charges of crimes against humanity along with eight other former commanders and junta members. Although he was acquitted in December 1985 he was sentenced to 12 years' imprisonment in May 1986 in a separate trial of top military officers for their role in the conduct of the South Atlantic War.
See also **Beagle Channel dispute; dirty war; South Atlantic War**.

g

gamonal

A Latin American term for a political boss, or *cacique*, usually in a small town or rural area. In the northern Andean countries, more particularly a large landowner. *Gamonalismo* in Bolivia, Ecuador, and Peru refers to the exploitative use by such landowners of rural labourers, usually indians.
See also ***cacique***; ***latifundio***.

García Márquez, Gabriel: see **Democratic Left Unity (UDI)** (Colombia).

García Meza Tejada, Gen. Luis: see **Bolivian governments post-Bánzer**.

García Moreno, Gabriel: see **Conservative Party** (Ecuador).

García Pérez, Alan

b. 1949. President of Peru 1985 – . Son of an accountant and a primary-school teacher, both of whom were APRA activists. His father was several times a political prisoner in El Frontón jail. Obtained a law degree from the University of San Marcos, Lima. García had joined the APRA youth section (JAP) at the age of 12 and become a disciple of the APRA founder, Haya de la Torre, the following year. From 1972–7 he was in Europe, where he studied in Geneva, Madrid, and Paris, obtaining a doctorate in law and befriending European socialist democrats such as the future head of the Spanish government Felipe González. On his return he took a university teaching post and became organisation secretary of APRA. As Haya de la Torre's political heir, García was elected to the constituent assembly in 1978 and to parliament in 1980. In the internal party feuds of subsequent years, he opted for the reformist wing, but enjoyed the backing of prominent conservatives, notably Luis Alberto Sánchez. Elected secretary general of APRA in October 1982, leapfrogging a whole generation of APRA leaders, he succeeded in uniting the party. In parliament, to which he was elected in 1980, he won a reputation as the champion of the opposition and a powerful orator.

In 1985 he made history by becoming the first *aprista* president as well as the youngest in Peruvian history, having won 46% of the vote in the April first round elections. García was appointed to the newly-created post of president of APRA in the same year and strengthened his grip on the party. At his inauguration he promised: to limit repayments on Peru's US$14bn foreign debt to 10% of export earnings for the first year; to cut arms purchases; to reduce tax exemptions for multinational companies; to reorganise the corrupt police forces; to establish a peace committee to resolve the guerrilla war and reassert the country's non-aligned role in foreign policy. Relations with the US became strained over a number of issues. Disbursements of official aid were suspended for a time for non-payment of debt arrears, and the expropriation in December 1985 of the country's second largest oil producer, Belco Corp of New York, also created tension. Belco had refused to come to an agreement over outstanding tax liabilities. García was instrumental in creating the 'Lima Group' of four nations which backed the Contadora peace process for Central America. At home, he confronted the military establishment with his plan to create a unified defence ministry, and proposed replacing Peru's 25 local government departments with 12 regions. But the rebellion led by the *Sendero Luminoso* ('Shining Path') guerrillas worsened. The peace commission resigned after a few months, claiming García had not given them enough authority. A new one was set up in February 1986, but the Catholic church and the left refused to participate. In June 1986 some 300 *Sendero* prisoners, held in two Lima jails, were killed in cold blood by security forces after they had rioted, in an incident which severely damaged García's domestic and international standing, especially since the Socialist International was meeting in Lima at the time. The new peace commission resigned.

In August 1986 the IMF declared Peru ineligible for further lending, but GDP growth reached an historic 8.5% that year. By mid–1987 the government admitted that debt servicing had risen to 17–18% of export earnings and inflation was taking off. In June the economic team known as '*los audaces*' ('the bold ones') took up the reins, relaunching heterodox policies. They re-established the 10% debt repayment ceiling except for short-term and private debt, but their ascendancy was short-lived. On the political front García sought to improve relations with the right- and left-wing opposition, and 28 United Left militants accused of subversion

were released from jail. In August 1987, in a surprise move, he introduced legislation to nationalise banks and financial services. This backfired badly, however as the plan became bogged down in the courts and the right-wing opposition successfully capitalised on its unpopularity. As inflation headed for 500% a year, 1988 saw a return to economic orthodoxy, with massive devaluations and price rises. A tougher counter-insurgency policy was also introduced. Under new Prime Minister Armando Villanueva the influence of the APRA hierarchy over the government was strengthened.
See also **APRA; Lima Group: Lurigancho massacre**.

Garrastazú Medici, Gen. Emílio

1905–85. A right-wing Brazilian army officer and military president, 1969–74. Born in Rio Grande do Sûl, he was head of General Staff, head of the Second Army and commander of the Agulhas Negras military academy. Garrastazú Medici played an important part in the 1964 coup against President João Goulart. He was appointed chief of the National Intelligence Service (SNI) in 1967; then, in 1969, he became commander of the Third Army. Chosen to succeed Gen. Arthur da Costa e Silva as president by the military leadership, his term coincided with the so-called 'Brazilian Economic Miracle', a period of annual GDP growth in the region of 10%, and of high confidence inside the military regime, which sought to capitalise on events such as the Brazilian soccer team's victory in the 1970 World Cup. The government carried out a series of prestige capital projects, such as the building of the Transamazonic highway and the Rio-Niteroi bridge, which were later criticised for being excessively ambitious and ill thought-through. It was also in this period that press censorship was tightened and government repression increased sharply as the regime sought to crush small armed guerrilla groups. Torture and other human rights violations by the security forces became widespread.

g

Garretón, Oscar: see **MAPU**.

Geisel, Gen. Ernesto

b. 1908. Brazilian army officer and military president, 1974–9. Born in Rio Grande do Sûl, he followed an army career and was appointed military attache at the Brazilian mission to Uruguay in 1948. After the 1964 military coup, he was made head of President Humberto Castello Branco's Military Household. Promoted to general in 1966, Geisel sat on the Supreme Military Tribunal in 1967–9 and was later appointed director of Petrobras, the state oil company. Chosen to succeed President Garrastazú Medici by the military leadership, he was ratified by Congress and took office on 15 January 1974.

During his administration human rights violations continued, although at a lesser rate than under his predecessor. But as a result of the new emphasis on human rights observance by the Carter administration in Washington, Brazil–US relations entered a particularly tense period. Another factor cooling relations with Washington was the nuclear cooperation agreement with West Germany, involving what the Carter adminis-

tration considered to be sensitive technology transfer. Gen. Geisel was responsible for beginning a slow and cautious process of political relaxation, known as *distensão*. During his term the much-hated Institutional Act 5 was repealed and replaced by less draconian regulations. While politicans still suffered the loss of their rights under Geisel, he did undertake reforms of the judiciary and the electoral system, consistent with the policy of gradual relaxation. Also during his presidency, Brazil suffered the economic impact of the 1973–4 oil price shock and the subsequent international recession.
See also ***distensão*; Institutional Acts**.

Gelli, Licio: see ***Propaganda Due***.

General Confederation of Bolivian Workers (CGTB): see **COB**.

General Confederation of Labour *(Confederación General del Trabajo*/CGT)
The main Argentine labour confederation, founded in 1930, initially under communist, socialist, and to some extent anarchist influence. It was involved in labour struggles during the authoritarian regimes of the 1930s; after 1943 it began moving closer to the emerging Peronist movement. During the 1946–55 presidency of Gen. Juan Domingo Perón, the Peronist party's control of the CGT was consolidated through labour and social reforms, the distribution of government posts to union officials, but also the persecution of non-Peronist union members. The 1955 military coup inaugurated a long period of repression of the CGT. At the first post-coup CGT Congress in 1957, allowed despite the military *intervención* of the confederation, a split emerged between 62 unions expressing continuing loyalty to Gen. Perón and 32 led by socialists, radicals, and independents. Henceforth the Peronist union block with the CGT was known as the '62 organisations', although the actual number varied.

In 1964 the CGT supported a 'struggle plan' (*plan de lucha*) of strikes and factory occupations during the People's Radical Party (UCRP) administration of President Arturo Illia. The growing power of Augusto Vandor, leader of the engineering workers, led the CGT into negotiations with military officers; the confederation supported the 1966 coup d'etat led by Gen. Juan Carlos Onganía. Opposition to Vandor led to a split in 1968 with the formation of a 'CGT of the Argentines' (CGT-A), a more radical grouping, under the leadership of Raimundo Ongaro.

Following the May 1969 *Cordobazo* and the assassination of Vandor in June of the same year, the CGT-A was banned by the military government and its top leaders were imprisoned. The CGT was finally re-unified at a 1970 Congress. The return of a Peronist administration in 1973–6 restored CGT influence and power, but the top leadership was increasingly involved in the violent Peronist factional struggles. After Gen. Perón's death and replacement by his widow Isabel, the CGT under the influence of the new engineering workers' leader, Lorenzo Miguel, began opposing the government's economic policies.

During the 1976–83 military regime the CGT was again placed under military *intervención* and its top leaders were jailed. The confederation split into numerous factions, but the essential division was that between supporters of 'hard' and 'soft' lines on relations with the armed forces. Following the return of civilian rule in 1983, a process of re-unification and union elections commenced. Saúl Ubaldini, who had been a leader of the more hard-line sectors of the labour movement under the military, was appointed general secretary. The CGT had called numerous strikes at the tail-end of military rule in 1982–3, and continued to mount protests and industrial action over President Alfonsín's economic austerity programmes in the following years. The CGT claims a membership of 5 million, grouped in approximately 800 unions although independent observers believe the real numbers are smaller.
See also **Ubaldini**.

Generation of 1928 (Venezuela)

From the 1930s to the 1980s Venezuelan politics have been profoundly influenced by a group of public figures known collectively as the 'Generation of 1928'. The group takes its name from the February 1928 student protests against the dictatorship of Gen. Juan Vicente Gómez. The student activists of that year included future presidents such as Rómulo Betancourt and Raúl Leoni; Jóvito Villalba, later to lead the Democratic Republican Union (*Unión Republicana Democrática*/URD); and the nuclei of the future Democratic Action (AD) and COPEI parties. The students of 1928 have also been described as the first generation to discard the old nineteenth-century political dichotomy between liberals and nationalists, and in that sense to usher Venezuela into the twentieth century. Gen. Gómez responded both to the student protests and to a related attempt at a military rebellion on 7 April 1928 by imprisoning all those involved and later sending many of them into exile. The Generation of 1928 thus began its political apprenticeship with what was to be the first of many periods of enforced exile – a feature which helped make it more international in outlook.
See also **Betancourt; COPEI; Democratic Action; Generation of 1958** (Venezuela)**; Gómez, Gen. Juan Vicente; Leoni**.

Generation of 1958 (Venezuela)

The group of Venezuelan political leaders who grew up during the dictatorship of Gen. Marcos Pérez Jiménez and whose initiation came in the January 1958 revolution against him. Often contrasted with the 'Generation of 1928' – those who created the country's main contemporary political parties – the Generation of 1958 took more radical and nationalist positions. Indeed, it is possible, if simplistic, to describe much of Venezuelan politics as a struggle between those two generations.

Prominent members of the younger generation included José Vicente Rangel, a Democratic Republican Union (URD) member who was active in the *Junta Patriótica*, leaving the party in 1964 and eventually standing as a presidential candidate for the Movement Towards Socialism (MAS). Teodoro Pétkoff became an important PCV leader involved in the guer-

rilla insurgency in the 1960s (as was his brother Lubén), during which time he was twice captured by government forces and twice led daring escapes from prison. In 1971 he led a split from the Communist Party (PCV) to set up MAS. Douglas Bravo, who came from the PCV to lead the FALN guerrillas and emerge as one of the principal guerrilla commanders, was another member of the same generation. He persisted with his rebellion long after the PCV and other groups had decided on pursuing the peaceful road to socialism. Américo Martín, another contemporary, led the split from Democratic Action (AD) to form the Movement of the Revolutionary Left (MIR). Argelia Laya moved from AD to the PCV, became a guerrilla commander in Lara state in the mid-1960s (under the *nom de guerre* of *Comandante Jacinta*) and later became one of the founder-members of MAS.
See also **Bravo; FLN/FALN; Generation of 1928** (Venezuela)**; Movement of the Revolutionary Left** (Venezuela)**; Movement towards Socialism; Pérez Jiménez; Venezuelan Communist Party**.

Geneva Convention: see **dirty war**.

Gomes, Eduardo: see **Nationalist Democratic Union**.

Gómez, Gen. José Vicente: see **Gómez, Gen. Juan Vicente**.

Gómez, Gen. Juan C.: see **Gómez, Gen. Juan Vicente**.

Gómez, Gen. Juan Vicente

g

1857(?)–1935. Venezuelan dictator who ruled the country for 27 years between 1908 and 1935. He came to power from the vice-presidency, carrying out a coup to depose the president, Gen. Cipriano Castro. In this he had the support of both the Liberal and Nationalist parties, who believed they could use him for their own ends. But Gómez began systematically to eliminate all challenges to his authority, forcing his defeated rivals into exile. By 1913 he had begun building a new army whose key officers, like others in the central administration, came from his home state of Táchira. In the 1914–22 period Gómez left the presidency in the hands of a provisional occupant, Dr Victorino Márquez Bustillos, while he remained 'president-elect' and commander-in-chief of the army. He left Caracas to live in Maracay; after 1922 he again formally occupied the presidency, but this time appointed Dr Francisco Baptista Galindo as interior minister to look after the day-to-day matters of government in Caracas. The dictator cracked down on student protests in 1918, which were followed in 1919 by an unsuccessful uprising led by young military officers. This and other movements – such as attempted invasions by exiles – were all crushed and their leaders imprisoned and tortured.

In 1922, worried by the succession, Gómez had Congress create the first and second vice-presidencies. Gen. Juan C. Gómez, the president's brother, was appointed first vice-president; Gen. José Vicente Gómez, his son, was made second vice-president. Within government circles different factions had been forming around the two candidates for the succession (supporters of the dictator's brother were known as *juanchistas* while those who backed his son were the *vicentistas*). In June 1923 Juan Gómez was stabbed to death in his bed in the presidential palace. Although the government later said that those guilty of the murder had been arrested, it was believed to have been the result of an internal family quarrel; many speculated on the involvement of the dictator's estranged wife, mother of the second vice-president. In 1928 a new wave of student protests was followed by another military uprising, also unsuccessful. This time the dictator suspected that his son was involved; shortly afterwards José Vicente Gómez left for Europe and the post of vice-president was abolished completely. In 1929 Gómez again stepped down from the presidency while retaining power, installing Dr Juan Bautista Pérez in office, while he remained commander-in-chief of the army. But the arrangement only lasted to 1931 when, in response to a conspiracy by the Táchira group of officials (who resented their loss of influence), Gómez again took over the presidency. He remained in office until his death in December 1935 after a long illness.

Gómez, Laureano

1889–1965; President of Colombia 1950–3. Co-founder of *El Siglo* newspaper; leader of the Conservative Party (PC) and Falangist. He was elected unopposed in 1949 after the Liberal Party (PL) had declined to present a candidate amid the turmoil following the *Bogotazo*. During his term of office the bloodshed known as *la violencia* reached its peak. He was overthrown in a military coup in June 1953 by Gen. Gustavo Rojas Pinilla. In exile in Spain, he signed the Pact of Benidorm and the subsequent Sitges Declaration which led to the National Front agreement between the PC and the Liberal Party.
See also **National Front; Social Conservative Party**.

Gómez Hurtado, Alvaro: see **Barco Vargas; López Michelsen; M–19; Social Conservative Party** (Colombia).

González, Juan Bautista: see **Workers' Self-Defence Movement**.

González Juan Natalicio: see **Morínigo; Paraguayan Civil War**.

González, Norberto: see **Economic Commission for Latin America and the Caribbean**.

González Videla, Gabriel: see **Communist Party of Chile (PCCh); Socialist Party of Chile; Socialist Republic**.

Gonzalo, Comrade/President: see **Shining Path**.

good neighbour policy

A 'non-interventionist' stance adopted by US presidents Herbert Hoover and Franklin D. Roosevelt towards Latin America in particular (though as originally formulated it referred to international relations in general). Espoused by Hoover with his acceptance of the 1928 Clark Memorandum on the Monroe doctrine. Mentioned by FDR in his inaugural address in

1933, and formally stated to be official policy by Secretary of State Cordel Hull at the 7th Pan American Congress in Montevideo that same year. Hull declared that 'no government need fear any intervention on the part of the United States'. In Montevideo he signed the Convention on the Rights and Duties of States, Article 8 of which affirmed that 'No state has the right to intervene in the internal affairs of another'. The policy led to the abrogation of the Platt Amendment relating to Cuba, the withdrawal of US troops from Haiti, and the 1936 signing of a non-intervention pact by the US and Panama.
See also **Monroe doctrine**.

gorilas

The name used in a number of countries to denote extremely right-wing, pro-US factions of the military. More precisely, the usage can be traced to Argentina, where it was applied to an extreme anti-Peronist army faction active after the 1955 Liberating Revolution. The name was taken from the lyrics of a song popular at the time of the coup. The faction's immediate aims were the removal of officers considered to have cooperated with the ousted Peronist administration and the reinstatement of those purged during the same period. The *gorilas* were also associated with ultra-liberal economic policies and a Cold War ideology in which Peronism and Communism were considered virtually identical. The *gorilas'* demands effectively led to the increased politicisation of the armed forces, with promotions more a function of political stance than professional ability. Many of the young *gorila* officers of the second half of the 1950s later, as generals, joined the *Colorado* faction in the conflicts of the early 1960s.
See also ***Azules* and *Colorados*; National Security doctrine**.

g

Goulart, João Belchior Marques

1918–76. President of Brazil 1961–4. Born in Rio Grande do Sûl, into a wealthy landowning family. He joined the Trabalhista Party (PTB) in 1945, and was elected a federal deputy in 1947. Goulart was appointed labour minister under President Vargas in 1953. His announcement of a 100% increase in the minimum wage helped establish his credentials both as a popular leader among the poor and as a dangerous radical among the rich; following the outcry over the announcement he resigned from the ministry. He served as vice-president twice; first under Kubitschek in 1955, then under Quadros in 1960.

On an official visit to China when Quadros presented his surprise resignation in August 1961, Goulart returned to find conservative and military factions trying to block his constitutional succession to the presidency. In the end these groups permitted him to take office only on condition that a parliamentary system of government be introduced, which, it was believed, would act as a necessary check on his power. The crisis in August–September 1961 ended when Congress approved by the necessary two-thirds majority an amendment to the Constitution creating the role of prime minister, a post which was entrusted to Tancredo Neves. In his initial period in the presidency, much of Goulart's effort was aimed at recovering the powers he felt had been unjustly removed from his office at the outset. At first his policies were decidedly conciliatory; they included a continuation of the orthodox financial measures begun under Quadros. But as the president mapped out his plans for growth, redistribution of income, and a nationalist foreign policy, a process of polarisation set in.

In a referendum in January 1963 an overwhelming majority voted in favour of a full return to the presidential system. But later that year tension rose over the president's attempts to push through a moderate land reform programme. Goulart's generally populist style was unpredictable, with many of his allies on the left often distrustful of his intentions. The economic situation worsened rapidly, with higher inflation, zero growth, and growing foreign payments difficulties. In September 1963 there was an unsuccessful rebellion by air force and navy officers; the following month Goulart tried but failed to impose a state of siege which would have given him emergency powers. In early 1964 clashes between landowners and peasants increased. Under pressure, the president swung to the left, defiantly announcing wage increases and an intensification of land reform. There was a new rebellion by navy officers which merged with a wider coup plan led by the heads of the three services, who deposed Goulart on 31 March 1966. Forced into exile in Uruguay, Goulart returned to farming and ranching. He died of a heart attack in 1976.

See also **Coup of 1964** (Brazil); ***Trabalhismo*****;** **Vargas**.

g

Grabois, Mauricio: see **Communist Party of Brazil (PCdoB)**.

Gran Acuerdo Nacional **(GAN):** see **Argentine Revolution; Lanusse**.

GRAPA (Anti-Marxist Group) (Chile): see **death squad**.

Great National Accord (GAN): see **Argentine Revolution; Lanusse**.

Green, Hamilton

b. 1934. Prime minister and first vice president of Guyana since August 1985. Born in Georgetown, Green is a former civil servant and trade union official who became minister of works and hydraulics (1969–72). From 1972 to 1974 he held the public affairs portfolio, and from 1975 to 1981 that of cooperatives and national mobilisation. In 1981 he was appointed one of five vice-presidents, with responsibility for public welfare and labour, switching to agriculture the following year. In August 1984 he was named first deputy prime minister, and on the death a year later of President Forbes Burnham he replaced Prime Minister Desmond Hoyte, who became president.

Gremialismo

Derived from *gremio*, a term similar to the English 'guild', often used as a synonym for trade unions (*sindicatos*), but also to refer to professional and business associations, including lawyers', doctors', and small traders' organisations and those of landowners and industrialists. In Chile, the *Gremialista* Movement was founded in 1967 by conservative Catholic academics and students at the Catholic University to counter the influence of the left. *Gremialistas* favoured a corporatist society in which political parties would be replaced by *gremios*; their theories bore a strong resemblance to the Integralism of the 1930s and 1940s, and many were closely linked with the right-wing Society for the Defence of Tradition, Family and Property (TFP).

'*Gremialismo*' (along with nationalism and the armed forces) was a rallying cry for the right during its fight to destabilise the Popular Unity (UP) government (1970–3). The *gremio* system helped maintain a sense of common class identity and purpose between middle and upper classes, and increased the impact of the bosses' strikes aimed at destabilising the government (including the lorry owners' strike of 1973). After the 1973 military coup some on the right wished to see the *gremios* take on a governing role in a corporativist state, but the junta rejected this and most *gremios* in any case gradually distanced themselves from the military regime. Those *gremialistas* who have played an important role in the regime (e.g. interior minister Sergio Fernández) espouse not a corporatist social theory but one which stresses the primary role of the market as in orthodox monetarism. The political party which most strongly reflects their views is the Independent Democratic Union (UDI), now part of PARENA.
See also **Integralism; Party of National Renovation; Popular Unity**.

gremio: see ***Gremialismo***.

Grove, Marmaduke: see **Allende Gossens**.

Gueiler Tejada, Lidia: see **Bolivian governments post-Bánzer**.

g

guerrilla insurgency (Venezuela)

A guerrilla war against central authority was waged in 1962–9; the campaign is estimated to have cost up to 6,000 lives. Fighting petered out in the early 1970s as a result of the guerrillas' failure to build mass support and the decision by left-wing parties to revert to non-violent campaigning. The first guerrilla groups were formed by participants in the 1958 revolution against Gen. Marcos Pérez Jiménez who felt frustrated by the rightwards drift of President Rómulo Betancourt's AD administration and who were inspired by the example of Cuba's 1959 revolution. In April–May 1960 Américo Martín and Domingo Alberto Rangel had led a leftist split from AD to form the Movement of the Revolutionary Left (MIR). The government responded by arresting some of the leaders of the new party on charges of subversion, which in turn led to student protests and repression (*el popularazo* of October–November 1960). President Betancourt suspended constitutional guarantees and initiated proceedings against MIR and Communist (PCV) leaders.

By early 1962 the first clashes between the security forces and the incipient guerrilla organisations began to take place. At first the guerrillas spread out, opening almost 20 different fronts; but by the end of 1962 most of these had been destroyed, leaving only two or three which were consolidated. The guerrilla *focos* were formed by members of the PCV and MIR, parties which actively promoted armed rebellion; individual members of the Democratic Republican Union (URD); and leftist deserters from the armed forces, many of whom joined the rebels after taking part in some of the failed army rebellions against the Betancourt administration (such as those at the Carupana and Puerto Cabezas navy bases in May and June 1962). In 1963 the Armed Forces of National Liberation (FALN) and the National Liberation Front (FLN) were created, initially under the dominant influence of the PCV. The emphasis in that year shifted from the rural fronts to urban guerrilla actions in Caracas. The FLN/FALN called for a boycott of the December 1963 elections, organising a two-day general strike and violent street fighting. The government intercepted a shipment of arms from Cuba, which it said was part of a FALN plan to seize Caracas. But despite the boycott there was a 90% turnout in the 1 December 1963 elections and Raúl Leoni led AD to a second victory. The failure of the boycott campaign led some of the PCV and MIR's political leaders to question the strategy of armed struggle. Others, such as Douglas Bravo in Falcón state, established control of the FALN and pressed ahead with the guerrilla war.

The rebels suffered losses as a result of a government counter-offensive in 1966. In April 1967 the 8th plenum of the PCV central committee decided to drop armed struggle and expelled Bravo from the party. Fidel Castro, the Cuban leader, condemned the decision and supported Bravo. But the Falcón *foco* was unable to expand and began to experience its own internal disagreements. The Leoni administration, meanwhile, was offering amnesties to guerrillas who laid down their arms. After President Rafael Caldera took office in March 1969, amnesty offers were extended to guerrillas in the hills. The MIR eventually accepted the peace proposals, although Douglas Bravo's FALN held out. In January 1970 Bravo accused Castro of deserting Latin American guerrillas to concentrate on building up the Cuban economy. It was not until the election of Luis Herrera Campins in 1978 that Bravo finally agreed to lay down arms, although his group had been inactive for some time.

See also **Betancourt; FLN/FALN;** ***foquismo; popularazo, el.***

guerrilla invasions (Paraguay)

In 1958–60 Paraguayan exiles made various unsuccessful attempts to enter the country secretly and initiate a guerrilla war against the regime of Gen. Alfredo Stroessner. They were inspired by the successes of Fidel Castro's guerrilla movement in Cuba, and hoped in this way to overcome the failures of other forms of opposition to the regime. One of the first attempts was made by the 14th May Movement, a group of dissident Liberals led by Benjamín Vargas Peña. It attacked the Coronel Bogado police garrison on 1 April 1958, making off with a number of arms. The movement briefly joined up with a splinter from the *Febrerista* tradition, the Febrerista Vanguard (*Vanguardia Febrerista*) led by Arnaldo Valdovinos. But both movements went their separate ways after the two leaders had quarrelled. A group which split away from the 14th May Movement under the leadership of José Rotela then organised a two-pronged guer-

rilla invasion of the country on 12 December 1959, aimed at taking over the city of Encarnación. But both contingents – over a thousand men – were intercepted and heavily defeated by government troops; there were few survivors. Rotela was among those killed. After another disastrous invasion in April 1960 the 14 May Movement was a spent force. The *Febrerista* guerrillas also lost effectiveness after they were expelled from the mainstream of the party. The initiative then passed to the communist-dominated United National Liberation Front (FULNA), whose forces crossed the frontier three times in May–December 1960. On each occasion, however, they were detected and destroyed by government troops. Among the reasons given for the failure of the guerrilla invasions were the hostility of the peasantry (many of whom were members of the ruling Colorado Party's *py nandí* militias), the ruthless efficiency of the government troops, and the fact that the exile community was thoroughly infiltrated by government spies.
See also ***py nandí; Stroessner***.

guerrilla movements (Brazil)

A number of guerrilla movements emerged in opposition to the Brazilian military regime in the late 1960s. One of the first to take up armed action was the Maoist PC do B, but its efforts were on a relatively small scale in Pará state. Former soldiers and nationalists who had been linked to Leonel Brizola formed the MNR (Nationalist Revolutionary Movement), which also tried to set up a guerrilla campaign in the Serra do Caparão in early 1967. Many of the groups involved emerged from student politics and were very small and prone to a process of fragmentation and re-formation. They included the MAR (Armed Revolutionary Movement), MR–26 (26 July Revolutionary Movement, named after the date of Fidel Castro's attack on the Moncada barracks in Cuba) and POLOP (Workers' Politics). POLOP split in 1967, with most of its São Paulo members going on to form the VPR (Popular Revolutionary Vanguard – led by Carlos Lamarca). Members from Minas Gerais together with some from Rio formed COLINA (Commando of National Liberation) which later fused with another splinter group from VPR to form VAR-Palmares (Armed Revolutionary Vanguard; 'Palmares' referred to the seventeenth-century slave republic in northern Brazil). Other groups to emerge in this period included the ANL (Action for National Liberation, led by Carlos Marighela and other dissidents from the Communist Party), MR–8 (8 October Revolutionary Movement) and MRT, the Tiradentes Revolutionary Movement, led by Dimas Antônio Cassemiro. After the rise and later repression of student protest in 1968 these and other groups turned to armed struggle.

VAR-Palmares was one of the more effective forces in early 1969, taking part in a series of bank raids and armed actions. In September 1969 MR–8 kidnapped C. Burke Elbrick, the US ambassador to Brazil, exchanging him for the release of 15 political prisoners. The effect of these and other actions were largely counter-productive, however, as they served to unify the military leadership, at the time involved in a

series of bitter internal quarrels. Already in 1969 the security forces had scored an important victory by killing Carlos Marighela of the ANL. In October 1970 his successor, Joaquim Câmara Ferreira, died in prison shortly after being arrested. In the same month most of the São Paulo branch of VAR-Palmares was arrested. In November the government launched Operation Birdcage, in which 5–10,000 suspects were arrested. Counter-insurgency operations were marked by the widespread use of torture and beatings; many detainees died in prison as a result of this brutal treatment. The December 1970 kidnapping of the Swiss ambassador Giovanni Bucher by the ANL led to the release of 70 political prisoners in an exchange, but the security forces intensified their pursuit of the guerrilla organisations. In early 1971 the regime inflicted further heavy blows on the armed opposition by killing the leaders of the VPR and the MRT. In August 1971 Carlos Lamarca of VPR was tracked down to Bahia and killed. By late 1971 the guerrilla groups had been effectively defeated by the regime, although despite this the security forces continued to use torture and violent repression.
See also **Communist Party of Brazil (PC do B); Marighela; MR–8**.

Guevara Arze, Walter

b. 1912. Interim president of Bolivia 1979–80. Born in Cochabamba. Educated at the University of San Andrés (law degree, 1932). Congressional deputy in the late 1930s. President of the Banco Minero, 1939. Professor of sociology, University of San Andrés (1940). Founder member of the Revolutionary Nationalist Movement (MNR), 1941. Secretary general of government, 1944. Foreign minister, 1952–6, 1960, and 1967–8. Ambassador to France, 1956–8. Minister of the interior 1958–9. Ambassador to the UN, May 1969. Guevara, a leader of the right within the MNR, split with the party leadership in 1960 after being denied the presidential candidacy. He founded the Authentic MNR (MNR-A – renamed the Authentic Revolutionary Party/PRA in 1961) as a vehicle for his political ambitions and challenged Víctor Paz Estenssoro for the presidency in 1960, winning 14% of the vote. The PRA was critical of trade union influence over the MNR. In March 1961 Guevara was exiled to Chile. In 1964 the PRA abstained in the presidential elections and backed the subsequent Barrientos/Ovando military coup which overthrew Paz Estenssoro. It supported Gen. Barrientos' candidacy in the 1966 elections and took part in the ruling coalition under him (1966–9). Guevara served as ambassador to the UN under the military government of Gen. Hugo Bánzer, but the PRA opposed Bánzer after 1974 and Guevara was exiled to Paraguay. He was vice-presidential running mate to Víctor Paz in 1978.

In 1979 he became president of the new senate, and was appointed interim president for one year, after elections brought no clear victor. He named a cabinet of conservative technocrats and his attempts to govern independently and to introduce controversial, deflationary economic policies lost him support both in Congress and among the powerful trade unions. He was overthrown in November by Col. Alberto Natusch

Busch and prevented from resuming the presidency even after Natusch in turn was removed. Encouraged by the increased popularity stemming from his resistance to the Natusch regime, he stood for the presidency on an independent PRA ticket in 1980, but won less than 3% of the vote. A faction of the PRA under Jorge Ríos Gamarra split away in the early 1980s.

See also **Revolutionary Nationalist Movement**.

Guevara de la Serna, Dr Ernesto Che

1928–67. Argentine-born revolutionary and guerrilla leader. Born in Rosario into a well-to-do family, Guevara's early schooling was sporadic, due to the asthma which persisted throughout his life, but he graduated from the Buenos Aires School of Medicine in 1953. His parents were both involved in left-wing politics. As a student he travelled through several Latin American countries and spent a month in Miami. On his return he took part in a failed anti-Peronist plot. He had intended to go after graduation to Caracas, Venezuela, to work in a leper colony, but instead found himself eventually in Guatemala during the period of the US-backed overthrow of the Arbenz government. After taking a small part in the resistance, but failing in his attempt to be sent to the front, he was forced to flee via the Argentine embassy to Mexico, where he met Fidel Castro in 1955.

He agreed to join Castro in an attempt to overthrow the Batista government in Cuba, and set out on the *Granma* expedition in November 1956. Nicknamed 'Che' after the familiar Argentine form of address, he initially acted as a doctor but soon took up arms, gaining the highest rank (*comandante*, or major) and command of the 2nd (later renamed the 4th) Column in the Sierra Maestra campaign. Two books based on these experiences (*Guerrilla Warfare* and *Reminiscences of the Cuban Revolutionary War*) became classics in their field. After the victory of the guerrilla forces in 1958 he toured widely (especially in the communist nations) explaining the nature of the revolution.

Naturalised as a Cuban (under the name Ernesto Che Guevara) in January 1959, he held the following posts: industrial director of the agrarian reform agency INRA; president of the National Bank; head of the Department of Instruction in the armed forces ministry (responsible for the development of the militias); director of the National Planning Board; and Minister of Industries. He may also have helped set up the G2 secret police unit. In 1961 he headed the Cuban delegation to the Punta del Este conference at which the Alliance for Progress was enacted. From April–December 1965, under the code-name 'Tatu' he fought with 200 Cuban troops in the Congolese civil war, in which the US Central Intelligence Agency and Cuban exile mercenaries were involved on the other side. There followed two years of planning for guerrilla campaigns on the mainland of South America, the aim being (as he put it) to create 'two, three, many Vietnams'. Having decided on Argentina as the ideal location for a guerrilla *foco* he later changed his mind and opted for Bolivia, setting up the National Liberation Army (ELN) training base at

Ñancahuazú. The campaign, however, was a failure. Neither the local population nor the Bolivian Communist Party provided the necessary support, and with CIA help, Bolivian army rangers tracked down and annihilated the guerrillas. Guevara was captured on 8 October 1967 and after being identified by CIA Cuban agents was executed the next day by Sgt Mario Terán. His body was buried secretly, but his severed hands and his campaign diary were later sent clandestinely to Cuba.
See also ***foquismo***; **National Liberation Army** (Bolivia).

Guevara Moreno, Carlos: see **Concentration of Popular Forces**.

Guiana, British: see **GUYANA, Republic of**.

Guianese Socialist Party (PSG): see **Castor**.

Guido, José María: see ***Azules* and *Colorados***.

Guimarães, Ulysses

b. 1916. As a Brazilian federal deputy and later senator, Guimarães played an often central role in national politics from the 1960s into the 1980s. A member of the Social Democratic Party (PSD) at the time of the 1964 coup d'etat, he emerged as one of the leading forces in the Brazilian Democratic Movement (MDB, later renamed PMDB) and established his credentials as an outspoken opponent of military rule. Guimarães played a key role in the *diretas já* campaign and the transition to civilian rule in 1984/85. He was president of the constituent assembly in 1987/8 and in 1988 was considered a possible contender in the presidential elections planned for 1989.
See also **Brazilian Democratic Movement; *diretas já*; Social Democratic Party**.

g

***Guión Rojo*:** see **Franco; Paraguayan Civil War**.

***guionistas*:** see **Colorado Party** (Paraguay).

Gulf of Venezuela dispute (Colombia, Venezuela)

A territorial conflict in the Gulf of Venezuela. The land border between the two countries, based on the old division between the Spanish captaincies-general of Venezuela and Granada, was not fixed until 1932, as a result of arbitration by the Swiss Federal Council. But the frontier in the Gulf remained the subject of competing claims, particularly in the area around the Los Monjes islands, near the Guajira peninsula. The conflict had been fuelled by the discovery of oil in Lake Maracaibo to the south, in the 1920s. The islands were occupied by Venezuela during the Pérez Jiménez dictatorship in the 1950s. In 1965 both governments agreed to talks on the definition of offshore limits. By 1968 Venezuela had established its position that a large sector of the Gulf ('the submarine areas . . . south of the parallel through Castilletes and Punta Salinas in their entirety . . .') was non-negotiable.

In April 1973 Colombia broke off the talks, claiming that the Los Monjes islands did not have their own continental shelf. As expressed by President López Michelsen in July 1975, Colombia's claim to part of the continental shelf was based on the fact that the Gulf 'is not exclusively surrounded by Venezuelan territory'. In November 1968 the Colombian government revealed that bilateral talks on limits in the 'Gulf of Maracaibo' (of Venezuela) were underway in a 'spirit of cordiality and understanding'; both sides rejected the appointment of a tribunal to arbitrate in the conflict. In early 1979 Colombia recognised Venezuelan sovereignty over Los Monjes. Venezuela responded that this was a 'positive factor' in the talks but nevertheless insisted on pointing out that the status of the islands had never been part of the agenda for negotiations. On 21 October 1980 the terms of a draft treaty were revealed by the Colombian authorities. Colombia was to be granted limited rights in the Gulf. There were provisions for a 50/50 split of the output of oil fields which could be shown to straddle the boundary, with a similar sharing of production costs, and there were also clauses guaranteeing the 'innocent passage' of either country's shipping through the area. However, the draft was opposed by nationalists in both countries – in Venezuela in particular there was a backlash against what was seen as a treaty which would give away parts of the national territory. President Luis Herrera Campins had said he would only approve the draft if a national consensus formed in favour of it. This failed to emerge and in November 1980 further talks were suspended. Despite periodic mentions of the desirability of a solution by both countries, the issue remained essentially deadlocked in the following years.

In May 1987, however, President Virgilio Barco of Colombia proposed invoking the 1939 Treaty of Non-Aggression, Conciliation, Arbitration, and Judicial Negotiation signed by both countries. The terms of the treaty provide for judicial adjudication by the International Court of Justice if arbitration has failed; arbitration in turn is invoked only when it can be shown that conciliation has failed. In August 1987 tension between the two countries rose sharply after a Colombian Navy corvette, *ARA Caldas* took up position in the disputed area, in what Venezuela described as a 'provocation'. The ship was eventually withdrawn after both governments agreed in principle to further talks aimed at resolving the dispute.

Gutiérrez, Gustavo: see **liberation theology**.

Gutiérrez, Dr Mario: see **Bolivian Socialist Falange**.

Gutiérrez, Nelson: see **Movement of the Revolutionary Left** (Chile).

Gutiérrez Ruiz, Héctor: see **Blanco Party**.

GUYANA, Republic of

Capital: Georgetown
Independence (from Britain): 1966
Area: 214,970 sq km
Population (1988): 756,000 (27% urban)
Pop growth rate (1980–5): 2%.
Pop density: 3.5/sq km

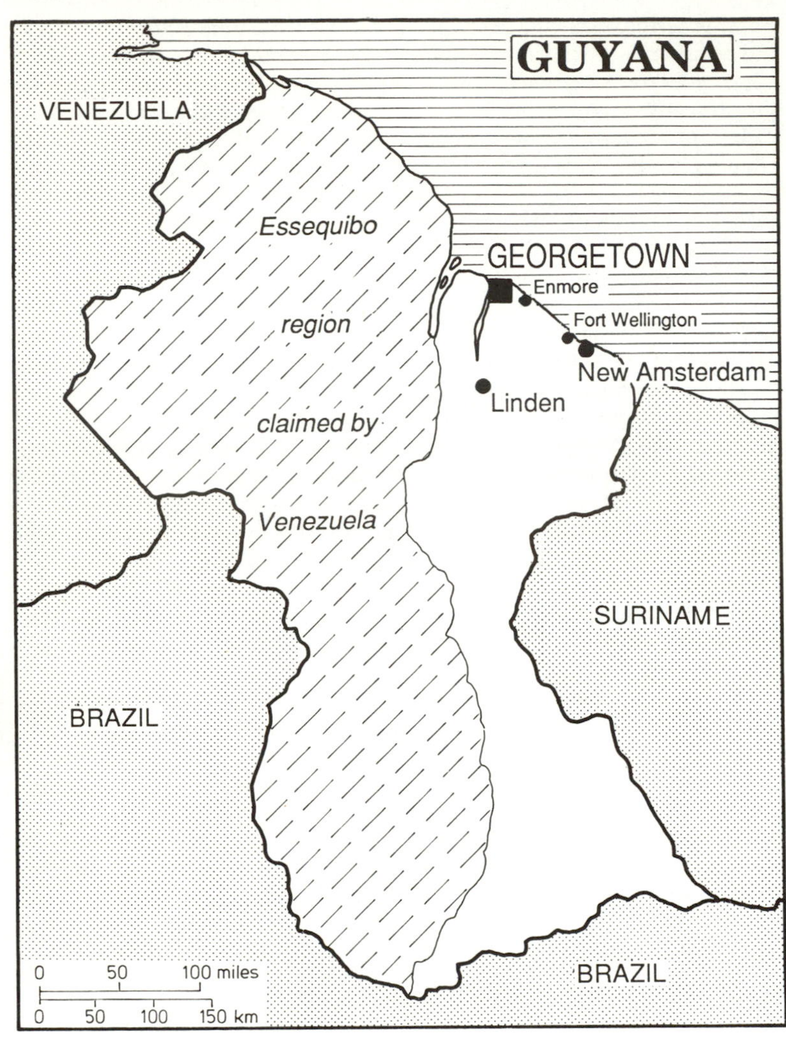

g

Infant mortality (1986): 65 per thousand
Life expectancy at birth (1986): 60
Literacy (1980): 91.3%
GDP per capita (1987e): US$874
Foreign debt per capita (1988e): US$2,250
Main exports: bauxite, alumina, sugar, rice

Political system

Constitution: 1980 creating an executive presidency (became republic 1970). *Head of state*: President Desmond Hoyte (1985–), constitutionally succeeded Forbes Burnham on the death of the latter in August 1985;

elected November 1985 for a five-year term. Prime minister: Hamilton Green (August 1985–). The 53-member National Assembly is elected every five years by proportional representation. *Last elections* (parliamentary): December 1985.

Political organisations

Parties (seats in parliament) (leaders): People's National Congress/PNC (42) (Desmond Hoyte), f. 1957; People's Progressive Party/PPP (8) (Cheddi Jagan), f. 1950; United Force/UF (2) (Fielden Singh), f. 1957; Working People's Alliance/WPA (1) (Rupert Roopnaraine, Eusi Kwayana), f. 1974. *Parties not represented in parliament*: Democratic Labour Movement/DLM (Paul Tennassee), f. 1983; People's Democratic Movement/PDM; National Democratic Front/NDF. The Patriotic Coalition for Democracy /PCD, f. 1986, comprises the PPP, WPA, DLM, PDM, and NDF.

Trade Unions: Trades Union Congress/TUC (Joseph Pollydore); Guyana Agricultural and General Workers' Union/GAWU (Komal Chand); Guyana Mineworkers' Union/GMU; National Association of Agricultural, Commercial and Industrial Employees/NAACIE (N.K. Gopaul); Clerical and Commercial Workers' Union (B. Philadelphia), National Workers' Union, Public Service Union. *Employers' organisations*: Guyana Manufacturers' Association; Consultative Association of Guyanese Industry; Guyana Rice Producers' Association.

Guzmán, Abimael: see **Shining Path**.

Haig, Gen. Alexander: see **South Atlantic War**.

Haya de la Torre, Víctor Raúl

1895–1979. Founder-leader of the American Popular Revolutionary Alliance (APRA) and the Peruvian Aprista Party (APRA, aka PAP). Born in Trujillo, of middle-class origins. Studied at Trujillo National University (1915) and San Marcos University (1917), but did not graduate. President of the student federation at San Marcos and a leader of the 1919 student – worker strike. During a period of exile from 1923 to 1930, Haya visited the Soviet Union and decided that the Soviet system was inappropriate for Latin America (or 'Indo-America' as he chose to call it). He then founded (in Mexico in 1924) what was intended to be a continent-wide anti-imperialist movement, APRA. His sources of inspiration included the Mexican revolution and the Chinese Kuomintang. The key problem for Indo-America, as Haya saw it, was the alliance between feudalism and international capitalism. He focused on the growing middle classes, in whom he saw the possibility of creating an authentic native capitalism.

Only in his native Peru did the movement take off, becoming the country's first large disciplined political party after its foundation in 1930. A populist, nationalist party in its early days, it found itself in constant conflict with the military and was frequently banned. Whenever it was permitted to stand in elections, Haya was its presidential candidate (1931, 1962, and 1963). In 1931 he was officially awarded 35% of the vote, but the party regarded this as fraud and staged an unsuccessful uprising. Haya was then imprisoned from 1932 to 1933. Gradually he moved to the right, abandoning his opposition to 'yankee imperialism' during the US administration of F. D. Roosevelt. During the dictatorship of Odría (1948–56) he was forced to spend five years in the Colombian embassy and a further three in exile.

In 1962 he polled the highest number of votes but failed to reach the percentage required for automatic election. The military stepped in to abort the process and in fresh elections the following year Haya lost to AP's Fernando Belaúnde Terry. He chose to join forces with ex-president Gen. Manuel Odría's supporters in Congress in blocking Belaunde's legislative programme, thus helping bring about the 1968 coup. During the military government Haya, who remained the titular and inspirational

leader of APRA, spent much of his time in Paris. In 1979, despite being close to death, he was elected president of the constituent assembly of 1979. Alan García, currently APRA leader and president of Peru, is regarded as his political heir.
See also **APRA; García Pérez**.

Hayista Base Movement (MBH): see **Democratic Convergence.**

Heder, Leopold: see **Holder.**

Henríquez, Gen.: see **Ecuadorean Socialist Party.**

Herrera Campins, Luis

b. 1925. A founding member of Venezuela's Social Christian party, COPEI, and president of Venezuela 1979–84. Born in Acarigua, Portuguesa state, of middle-class parents, Herrera Campins attended university in Caracas and went on to study at the University of Santiago de Compostela in Spain, graduating in both political science and law. While at university in Caracas in 1946 he was among the founders of COPEI. In 1948 he was elected a deputy in the Portuguesa state assembly. But by 1952, as Col. Marcos Pérez Jiménez established dictatorial control and cracked down on the political parties, he was arrested and imprisoned for seeking to organise a student strike. After four months in the Carcel Modelo in Caracas, Herrera Campins was sent into exile in Europe, where he developed links with Christian Democratic parties; in 1956 he acted as COPEI representative at the first world conference of Christian Democratic parties.

After the end of the Pérez Jiménez regime in 1958, he was elected federal deputy and became chairman of the COPEI bloc in the Chamber of Deputies, a position which he held until 1973 when he was elected to the Senate. Herrera Campins had generally difficult relations with Rafael Caldera; Caldera saw him as a potentially dangerous rival for control of the party and therefore intervened to stop him getting the presidential nomination in 1973.

He was successful, however, in getting his party's backing for the 1978 election, defeating the AD candidate Luis Piñerúa by 47% to 43% of the vote. During the electoral campaign Herrera Campins had accused the incumbent AD president, Carlos Andrés Pérez, of squandering the country's oil riches on prestige projects and corruption, while failing to invest in housing and other socially necessary areas. Nevertheless, once president, his popularity wore off quite rapidly as the economy remained stagnant and inflation failed to come down. By the end of his term in 1984 COPEI's standing in the opinion polls had slumped and the party proved unable to stave off a new AD victory.
See also **Caldera; COPEI**.

Hidalgo, Manuel: see **Communist Party of Chile**.

Hindustani-Javanese Political Party (H-JPP): see **Lachmon.**

Holder, Gérard
b. 1929. Mayor of Cayenne, French Guiana; secretary general of the Guianese Socialist Party (PSG). A school headmaster in Cayenne, Holder joined the city council in 1965 and became mayor in 1978 on the death of PSG leader Léopold Héder. He was elected to Guiana's General Council in 1979 and in 1983 to the Regional Council, from which he resigned soon afterwards. He became PSG secretary general in 1985.

Hoover, Herbert: see **good neighbour policy**.

***Hora del Pueblo, La*:** see **Hour of the People, The**

Hour of the People, The (*La Hora del Pueblo*)
A political coalition formed in Argentina on 11 November 1970 to press the Argentine Revolution military regime to step down and call elections. The group was formed by the Peronist, Radical, Progressive Democratic, Bloquista, Popular Conservative, and Socialist parties. It emerged in response to President Roberto Levingston's plans to 'deepen' the Argentine Revolution and appeal over the heads of the party leaders to an 'intermediate generation' supposedly ready to collaborate with the regime. The formation of *La Hora del Pueblo* effectively cut short the Levingston presidency; and thereafter the military regime did begin to pave the way for free elections, which were eventually held in 1973.
See also **Argentine Revolution; FREJULI; Onganía.**

Hoyte, Desmond
b. 1929. President of Guyana 1985 – . A Georgetown-born teacher and lawyer, Desmond Hoyte was elected to parliament in 1968. He served as minister of home affairs (1969–70), finance (1970–2), works and communications (1972–4), and economic development (1974–81). In 1981 he was named as one of five vice-presidents, with responsibility for economic planning, finance, and regional development. He succeeded Ptolemy Reid as prime minister in August 1984 and was also named as first vice-president. He became president on the death of Forbes Burnham in August 1985 and was elected to the presidency in November of the same year.

h

Hull, Cordell: see **good neighbour policy**.

Hurtado Larrea, Dr Osvaldo
b. 1939. President of Ecuador 1981–4. A lawyer and a prolific writer on Ecuadorean politics, Hurtado founded the Christian Democrat Party in 1964 out of sympathetic groups which had emerged in Guayaquil, Quito, Cuenca, and Loja, together with dissidents from the youth wing of the Social Christian Party (PSC), dissatisfied with the latter's conservatism. His politics are on the social democratic side of the movement, and the party he founded had no direct links with the Catholic church. After participating in the Velasco Ibarra government in 1968, the PDC lost some of its left wing, which went on to form the Christian Left (IC). In 1972, however, it formed an electoral front with Marxist parties. Hurtado led the party into an alliance in 1977 with the progressive wing of the

Conservative Party and two other groups which was known as the Popular Democratic Coalition (CPD). However, the electoral authorities refused recognition to the CPD, and (under the name of Popular Democracy-Christian Democrat Union) it eventually participated in the 1978–9 elections in alliance with the victorious Concentration of Popular Forces (CFP). Hurtado became vice president to Jaime Roldós, playing a relatively low-key role but providing vital international contacts via the Christian Democrat movement.

In May 1981 Roldós was killed in an air crash and Hurtado served out the remainder of his term to 1984. The government moved to the right and the new president sought to consolidate his hold on Congress with support from the CFP (which had previously moved into opposition) and the Democrat Party (PD), though he never won a clear majority. The CFP's *roldosista* wing, which had become the People, Change and Democracy (PCD) party, withdrew its support from him in January 1982. Hurtado was plagued with economic difficulties arising from falling oil revenues, a large fiscal deficit and a US$5bn foreign debt, and was forced into a substantial devaluation of the currency. Social unrest and frequent protest strikes led to the declaration of a state of emergency on a number of occasions. Later Hurtado played a leading role in the opposition to the Febres Cordero government, and has been tipped as a possible secretary general of the Organisation of American States (OAS) or the UN's Economic Commission for Latin America (ECLAC/CEPALC)

See also **Popular Democracy**.

I

Ibáñez del Campo, Col. Carlos

1877–1960. President of Chile 1927–31 and 1952–8. Born in Chillán. Graduated from the military academy (*Escuela Militar*) in 1896 and became a career officer. Took part in 1924 and 1925 uprisings aimed at securing constitutional change and the return of President Arturo Alessandri. Appointed minister of war by Alessandri in 1925. Minister of the interior under President Emiliano Figueroa, whom he succeeded constitutionally on the latter's resignation. Called fresh elections, which he won with army backing; when in power he rewarded his supporters with higher pay and new equipment for the armed forces.

Ruling as a dictator, he banned the Communist Party (PCCh), controlled the press, launched a huge public works programme and established a new Chilean nitrate company. He sought to improve the labour laws, increased wages and attempted a small-scale agrarian reform. During his first presidency a settlement was achieved of the dispute with Peru over the Tacna and Arica region, whereby Peru obtained Tacna and Chile kept Arica. Ibáñez was forced to resign in 1931 after popular demonstrations sparked by a dramatic collapse of export earnings due to the world depression were violently put down. From 1931–8 he was in exile. He stood again for the presidency in 1938 but was forced to withdraw after the Nazi Party (MNSC – one of his backers) was involved in violent incidents.

He was again unsuccessful in 1942, but was returned to power in 1952 with broader support, even from among the left. The Popular Socialists (PSP) briefly joined his cabinet. He promised to legalise the PCCh (though this did not happen until 1958) and institute a minimum wage law. The Chilean national bank was founded during his second term. His populist stance was replaced by repression when fresh economic problems, stemming largely from the decline in copper prices, appeared after the end of the Korean War. A state of emergency was declared on the pretext of 'communist subversion' in 1955. The left united in the Popular Action Front (FRAP) to oppose Ibáñez in 1956, but it was a right-wing president, Jorge Alessandri, who succeeded him in 1958.
See also **Popular Front**.

Iglesias, Enrique: see **Economic Commission for Latin America and the Caribbean (ECLAC)**.

Illia, Dr Arturo Umberto

1900–83. Leading member of Argentina's Radical Party (UCR) and president from 1963 to 1966. He trained as a medical doctor, and went into private practice in the small rural town of Cruz del Eje, Córdoba. Illia was elected to the senate of Córdoba province for the UCR in 1936; later he became vice-governor of Córdoba. Elected governor of the province in March 1962, he was unable to take up the post because the elections were annulled due to military pressure. The People's Radical Party (UCRP) selected him as its presidential candidate for the July 1963 elections. Top party leaders had chosen him when it appeared that the UCRP had little chance of winning. But in the event, Dr Illia topped the poll with 25% of the vote; the Peronists were not allowed to take part.

As president, he went a considerable way to restoring civil liberties, by declaring an amnesty for political prisoners and lifting the state of siege. Illia's government cancelled oil exploration and exploitation contracts signed during the 1958–62 Frondizi administration, arguing that they infringed on Argentine sovereignty. In 1965 he secured United Nations General Assembly resolution 2065, calling for negotiations between Britain and Argentina over sovereignty in the Falklands/Malvinas islands. Domestically he was criticised for having a slow-moving, provincial-style administration; opponents caricatured Illia as a tortoise. The General Confederation of Labour (CGT), led a wave of strikes and sit-ins known as the *plan de lucha*. In December 1964 Gen. Juan Domingo Perón attempted to return to the country, but was turned back in Brazil at the request of the Illia government. In the March – April 1965 congressional elections the Peronists received 36% of the vote against 29% for Illia's UCRP. A sector of the trade union leadership under Augusto Vandor began expressing support for a military coup against Dr Illia by army commander Gen. Juan Carlos Onganía.

On 26 June 1966 Dr Illia was deposed by the new Argentine Revolution regime led by Gen. Onganía. After his overthrow, Dr Illia remained in Argentina, although he was not very active politically. By the early 1980s his period in office was looked back upon as one of the best in terms of civil liberties. On his death in January 1983 he received widespread tributes as a symbol of morality in politics and respect for the constitution. See also **Argentine Revolution; *Azules* and *Colorados*; Onganía; Radical Party (Argentina)**.

Independent Liberal Movement (MLI): see **ANAPO.**

Independent and Revolutionary Workers' Movement (*Movimiento Obrero Independiente y Revolucionario*/MOIR)

Founded in September 1969 in Colombia by former members of the Movement of Workers, Students and Peasants (MOEC). The split had its origins in dissent expressed at the 2nd Congress of MOEC (1965) over the movement's rigid Marxist – Leninist stance. MOIR's initial policy was to foment a 'national democratic' rather than an overtly socialist revolution. It was later infiltrated by Maoists, who succeeded in diverting it in the direction of a mass-based Maoist party. It took part in the 1974 and 1978 general elections as a member of the National Opposition Union (UNO) front, led by the Communists (PCC). In 1982 it stood alone in the congressional elections, but its candidate for the presidency, Consuela de Montejo, withdrew on account of its poor showing. Its leader in 1985 was Diego Betancur Alvarez (son of Belisario Betancur, president of Colombia, 1982–6).

indigenismo

A twentieth-century intellectual and political movement concerned with the revival of indigenous culture in the Americas. Its greatest contribution to politics was in post-revolutionary Mexico, especially under President Lázaro Cárdenas (1934–40) and in the APRA movement created by the Peruvian Víctor Raúl Haya de la Torre, who proposed that Latin America should be renamed 'Indo-America'. Although the *indigenistas* challenged the theory of white racial supremacy, hardly any of them were indians themselves, and the movement was in many respects paternalistic. One of its tenets was that the mixing of the races in the Americas would result in a superior '*raza cósmica*' (cosmic race).
See also **APRA**.

Infamous Decade (*Década Infame*)

A period of conservative rule in Argentina in the 1930s, marked by economic recession, anti-labour policies, and the exclusion of the Radical Party (UCR) from elections. It began with the 6 September 1930 military coup which deposed the elected UCR President Hipólito Yrigoyen, and installed Gen. José Félix Uriburu in his place. This coup has been considered the originator of the twentieth-century cycle of military interventions in politics. Uriburu's corporativist leanings and sympathies for fascist ideals led him to try and prolong his rule, but an opposing military faction forced elections in November 1931, which were won by Gen. Augustín P. Justo. British companies were given preferential access to the local market under the Roca – Runciman pact of 27 April 1933, in return for guaranteed minimum levels of purchases of Argentine beef and grain exports.

Roberto Ortiz, a pro-British civilian and anti-Yrigoyen Radical, succeeded to the presidency in 1938 in fraudulent elections. But his own attempts to crack down on corrupt electoral practices alienated the conservatives, and he was replaced due to illness by Vice-President Ramón Castillo in July 1940. Castillo, a conservative, adopted a neutralist stance in World War II, but faced continual and conflicting pressures from pro-Allied and pro-Axis military factions. Castillo selected a controversial pro-British sugar mill owner, Robustiano Patrón Costas, for the presidential succession in 1944, but this generated widespread military and civilian opposition. The internal political struggle over the succession and the war led to the 4 June 1943 coup, out of which Peronism was eventually to emerge.
See also **Peronism; Radical Party** (Argentina); **Yrigoyen**.

Institutional Acts

Government decrees introduced by the 1964–85 Brazilian military regime which, while in theory continuing to uphold the 1946 constitution, in reality suspended its workings and allowed a concentration of powers in the executive. Institutional Act 1 proclaimed the legitimacy of the coup and served notice that 'the revolution is not seeking to legitimise itself through congress. Rather, it is the latter which receives its legitimacy from this Institutional Act, by means of the exercise of that constituent power inherent in all revolutions.' The Act enabled the government to cancel the mandate of congressmen and elected members of state assemblies and municipal councils, stripping them of political rights for up to 10 years. Although it provided for congressional election of the president, by the time the legislature ratified Gen. Humberto Castello Branco, 39 deputies and one senator had already been removed from its midst.

In October 1965 Institutional Act 2 dissolved all existing political parties and put an end to direct presidential elections. This led to the creation of a restricted two-party system, with the government represented through ARENA and the opposition through the MDB. Institutional Act 3 in early 1966 banned the direct election of governors, who were henceforth to be chosen by the state legislatures. But the most notorious was Institutional Act 5 of December 1968, which gave the executive sweeping powers to intervene in state and municipal government, suspend the political rights of citizens, and terminate the mandates of elected officials (through the *cassações*). Other military regimes, such as the 1973–85 *Proceso* in Uruguay, also used Institutional Acts.

See also ***cassações***; ***Proceso***.

Integralism

An authoritarian political doctrine developed in Brazil in the 1930s by Plínio Salgado, who founded Brazilian Integralist Action (AIB) in 1932. Although described as an original Brazilian philosophy, it was modelled on European fascism. Integralists used the sigma as an emblem, wore green shirts, and were organised in cells controlled by the 400-member Integralist Chamber personally chosen by Salgado. AIB claimed a membership of 400,000 in 1935 but independent estimates suggest there were approximately 250,000 members in 1937. One leading AIB theorist, Gustavo Barroso, published anti-semitic tracts, but anti-semitism was not otherwise prominent in the movement's propaganda. The top leadership was made up of middle-class professionals, intellectuals, and army officers. The AIB demanded radical reforms of the economic system, integration of all aspects of national life, discipline, authority, and hierarchy.

Integralism attracted some Catholics opposed to the corruption of the Old Republic but unable to accept the atheism of Marxism. One such early supporter was Helder Cámara, later Archbishop of Recife and Olinda, associated with leftist criticism of the post-1964 military regime and known as an exponent of liberation theology. Although the AIB supported the declaration of the *Estado Nôvo* by President Vargas in

1937, it was dissolved with all the other parties in 1938, and its influence on the regime waned. Following an AIB-inspired coup attempt on 10 April 1938, including an unsuccessful attack on Guanabara Palace, the movement was repressed. Salgado left for exile in Portugal. The influence of Integralism survived the demise of the AIB however, and can be traced to the ideology of the post–1964 military regime.

Inter-American Defense Board

An advisory committee of the Organisation of American States (OAS) dealing with military cooperation issues. Originally created after the Rio de Janeiro foreign ministers' meeting of January 1942 to coordinate the Allied war effort in the Americas during World War II. Headquartered in Washington, it liaises with member governments to plan the joint defence of the western hemisphere. It also runs the Inter-American Defense College.

See also **Organisation of American States; Rio Treaty**.

Inter American Development Bank (IDB)

Created in 1959 within the framework of the Inter American system, the IDB provides project finance to public and private sectors in the region. Its aims are defined as the promotion of development in the region by the funding of economic and social enterprises, and the provision of technical assistance. The membership includes 44 countries: Argentina, Austria, Bahamas, Barbados, Belgium, Bolivia, Brazil, Canada, Chile, Colombia, Costa Rica, Denmark, Dominican Republic, Ecuador, El Salvador, Finland, France, Guatemala, Guyana, Haiti, Honduras, Israel, Italy, Jamaica, Japan, Mexico, Netherlands, Nicaragua, Panama, Paraguay, Peru, Portugal, Spain, Suriname, Sweden, Switzerland, Trinidad and Tobago, United Kingdom, USA, Uruguay, Venezuela, West Germany, and Yugoslavia. The Board of Governors is the main decision-making body; it meets annually and is composed of one governor and one alternate for each member country. The US holds 35% of the votes on the IDB board. In 1988 Enrique Iglesias (Uruguay) was elected president to replace the long-serving Antonio Ortiz Mena (Mexico). The cumulative total of IDB lending to end-1985 was US$31.5bn, of which most was destined for projects in the energy sector (27%), followed by agriculture and fisheries (21.2%), industry and mining (17.6%), transport and communications (12.6%), and others. IDB capital is replenished every four years – the sixth replenishment in 1983 raised authorised capital to $35bn.

See also **Economic Commission for Latin America; Latin American Economic System**.

International Federation of Christian Trade Unions (IFCTU):

see **CLAT**.

Intransigent Party (*Partido Intransigente*/PI)

An Argentine left-of-centre grouping, the PI emerged in the early 1960s under the leadership of Oscar Alende as a result of factional fighting within the Radical Party (UCR). Alende had joined the Intransigent

Radical Party (UCRI) after the Radical Party split of the late 1950s. After the Frondizi administration was toppled by a military coup in 1962, the UCRI joined the National and Popular Front alliance with the Peronists and others for the 1963 elections. But after disagreements over the choice of candidate, Alende announced he would stand for the presidency alone under the UCRI label. In the July 1963 elections Alende obtained 16.5% of the vote, taking second place. By later that year differences between the *frentistas* and the *alendistas* within the UCRI had increased. Frondizi and his supporters broke away to form a new party, eventually to be known as the Movement of Integration and Development (MID). The group faithful to Alende took the name of Intransigent Party; it developed into a left-wing and anti-imperialist grouping, popular among students and the young in urban centres, but without much influence in the organised trade union movement. In the March 1973 elections Alende stood for the presidency at the head of a new left-wing alliance including the Communist Party and the Popular Revolutionary Alliance (APR), receiving 7.4% of the vote. After the 1976 military coup the PI, like the other parties, suffered from the ban on political activity and its militants were persecuted. In the October 1983 elections Alende stood for the presidency and received 2.3% of the total vote.
See also **Alende**.

Intransigent Radical Party (UCRI): see **Frondizi; Movement for Integration and Development.**

Isunza, Jaime: see **Popular Democratic Movement.**

J

Jacinta, Comandante: see **Generation of 1958** (Venezuela).

Jackson, Sir Geoffrey: see **National Liberation Movement-Tupamaros**.

Jagan, Cheddi

b. 1918. Premier of British Guiana 1961–4; leader of the opposition, Guyana. Born in Port Mourant, Jagan is a dentist by profession. He founded a Marxist group, the Political Affairs Committee, in 1946 which evolved in 1950 into the People's Progressive Party (PPP). Jagan was elected to the legislative council in 1947 as its first anti-establishment member. After the PPP won the 1953 elections he led a government (as leader of the House of Assembly and agriculture minister) for four and a half months before being removed by British colonial authorities alarmed at his radicalism. He was jailed for sedition for six months in 1954, but the PPP again won parliamentary elections in 1957 and he was named to lead a new government as minister of trade and industry.

He became premier when the post was created in 1961 and minister of development and planning at the same time. Strikes and unrest later documented as having been organised by the CIA and British intelligence, as well as changes in the electoral system, led to his defeat in the 1964 elections and replacement by his one-time ally, Forbes Burnham. He has been official leader of the opposition since 1964, except for the period 1973–6, when the PPP boycotted parliament, accusing the government of having rigged the 1973 elections with the help of the army. One of the world's first freely-elected Marxist government leaders, Jagan maintains close ties with Moscow.

See also **People's Progressive Party**.

Jarpa, Sergio Onofre: see **Party of National Renovation.**

Jarrín, Arturo: see **Alfaro Lives!**

Jarrín, Capt. Gustavo: see **military governments (Ecuador/1961–79).**

Jordán Pando, Roberto: see **Revolutionary Nationalist Movement.**

juanchistas: see **Gómez, Gen. Juan Vicente**.

Juárez Celman, Miguel: see **Radical Party (Argentina).**

Julião, Francisco: see **Peasant Leagues**.

Jungle Commando/Suriname National Liberation Army (SNLA)
A group of several hundred rebels, led by a young former army private, Ronnie Brunswijk, based among the Bush Negro/Bosneger ethnic group of eastern Suriname and backed by anti-government exiles in the Netherlands and (tacitly) by the authorities in neighbouring French Guiana. Brunswijk, a former bodyguard to Surinamese ruler Desi Bouterse, has vague political ideals but speaks of racial discrimination and ending military involvement in politics. The rebels first appeared in May 1986. Though poorly armed, they fought government troops, destroyed bridges, vehicles and factories, and hijacked a plane.

In January 1987 they blew up power lines supplying the bauxite smelter at Paranam and closed down the country's main industry. The rebels, who include a handful of white mercenaries, had earlier seized the bauxite mining town of Moengo for several weeks. Brunswijk declared a unilateral ceasefire after the November 1987 elections which were to return the country to civilian rule. But the army dismissed his demands for the military's total withdrawal from power and for soldiers who had killed civilians in the fighting to be tried. The government, helped by the churches, negotiated a formal ceasefire with the rebels in June 1988 despite army objections. But fighting broke out again and Paramaribo accused France of allowing rebel leaders to pass freely through neighbouring French Guiana and of giving them other help. In August, France and Suriname agreed on a UN-unsponsored repatriation of the more than 10,000 refugees who have fled from the fighting to French Guiana. Since the revolt began, at least 500 people have died in government–rebel clashes and in a number of massacres of civilians by the army.

junta
Literally 'board, council, or executive committee'; the word has characteristically been used to denote the body exercising de facto control of state power, often in military regimes. Historically some of the first ruling juntas came into being in the nineteenth-century independence struggle against Spain. In the twentieth century there were also civilian – military juntas, such as the seven-man junta (five civilians, two military officers) set up after the 18 October 1945 coup in Venezuela, which inaugurated the period known as the *trienio*. But from the 1950s onwards, juntas were most frequently entirely military affairs, associated with the spread of militarism around the continent. In Argentina the coups of 1955, 1966, and 1976 all involved the seizure of power by three-man military juntas, made up of the army, navy, and air force commanders. Despite the pre-eminence of Gen. Augusto Pinochet in the post-September 1973 military regime in Chile, he operated from the outset with a four-man military junta (composed of the commanders of the army, navy, air force, and carabineros) which approved all legislative initiatives. Under the 1976–83 military regime in Argentina, the three-man junta of service chiefs was the highest executive authority, to whom the president was subordinate.

For part of the period, the army commander was both president and simultaneously a member of the junta. But as a result of the ebb and flow of inter-service rivalries these two roles were separated, with the presidency going to a retired army officer not on the junta (the so-called 'fourth man' arrangement) and then re-united again. There were numerous military juntas in the 1960s and 1970s in Bolivia, Peru, Ecuador, El Salvador, and Guatemala.

Junta Patriótica

A Venezuelan anti-government alliance formed during the dictatorship of Gen. Marcos Pérez Jiménez. The *Junta Patriótica* was set up by members of the Democratic Republican Union (URD), the Social Christians (COPEI) and Democratic Action (AD) in June 1957, defining its objectives as 'fighting for observance of the national constitution, against the re-election of Marcos Pérez Jiménez, for free elections and for the establishment of a democratic government which will respect citizens' rights'. The grouping played a prominent part in the clandestine campaign against the 15 December 1957 plebiscite for the re-election of the president and in the popular uprisings in January 1958 which led to the collapse of the dictatorship. The *Junta Patriótica* was represented at the signing of the *Punto Fijo* accord in October 1958.
See also **Pérez Jiménez; *Punto Fijo***.

Justicialist Liberation Front (FREJULI)

The *Frente Justicialista de Liberación* was formed in Argentina on 14 December 1972, less than a month after Gen. Juan Perón's return to the country, as a Peronist-dominated electoral front. Its members included the Movement for Integration and Development (MID), Popular Conservatives, Popular Christians, and other smaller parties. In the 11 March 1973 elections Gen. Perón was barred from standing, so FREJULI nominated Héctor Cámpora as its candidate. On the slogan of '*Cámpora al gobierno – Perón al poder*' ('Cámpora in the government – Perón in power') FREJULI won the presidential elections with 49.6% of the vote (against 21.3% for the Radical Party candidate). In the Senate FREJULI took 43 out of 69 seats and in the Chamber of Deputies it had 145 out of 234. Cámpora took office on 25 May 1973, but resigned on 13 July to allow new elections in which Perón could stand. These were held on 23 September, with FREJULI backing what was known as the Perón – Perón formula: Gen. Perón for the presidency, his wife Isabel Perón for the vice-presidency. This time FREJULI won the presidential race with 61.9% of the vote. Gen. Perón took office on 12 October 1973, governing the country until his death on 1 July 1974, when he was succeeded by his wife. By December 1975 FREJULI had split, as the Isabel Perón administration faced growing internal quarrels.
See also **Cámpora; Perón, Gen. Juan Domingo; Peronism**.

Justicialist Party: see **Peronism.**

Justo, Gen. Augustín P.: see **Infamous Decade.**

K

Kennedy, John Fitzgerald: see **Alliance for Progress; Monroe doctrine**.

Klinger, Gen. Bertoldo: see **São Paulo revolt**.

Kolle Cueto, Jorge: see **Bolivian Communist Party (PCB)**.

Konrad Adenauer Foundation: see **Christian Democracy**.

Krieger Vassena, Adalberto: see ***Cordobazo***.

Kruel, Gen. Amaury: see **Coup of 1964** (Brazil).

Kubitschek de Oliveira, Juscelino

1902–76. President of Brazil in 1956–61 and the driving force behind the building of Brasília, the new federal capital. Born in Minas Gerais, he studied medicine and was elected as a deputy in 1934. Appointed the mayor (*prefeito*) of Belo Horizonte in 1940, Kubitschek was elected governor of Minas Gerais in 1950. Following the death of President Vargas in 1954, he stood as the presidential candidate for the *trabalhista*–Social Democratic Party (PTB–PSD) alliance, made up of the two groupings set up with official backing towards the end of the Vargas period. He won the elections against strong opposition from the right, in the shape of the Nationalist Democratic Union (UDN). Yet Kubitschek fell short of an outright majority, gaining only 36% of the vote. Because of this, strenuous efforts were made by his defeated opponents and certain sectors of the military to stop him taking power. Finally a military movement led by Gen. Henrique Teixera Lott ensured that he would after all take office as laid down in the constitution.

As president from January 1956 Kubitschek emphasised the development of the steel, motor vehicle, and shipbuilding industries, and made an attempt to develop the impoverished north-eastern region. But his best known achievement was the creation of a new federal capital, Brasília, designed by the architect Oscar Niemeyer. Construction work began in 1957 and the city was officially opened in 1960. Politically, Kubitschek's presidency was characterised by considerable congressional opposition and a number of military revolts, the most important of which occurred in Jacareacanga (1956) and Aragarcas (1959). After stepping down from the presidency, he was elected as a senator for Goias state. Following the 1964 military coup, Kubitschek moved into opposition to the regime.

As a result his political rights were suspended and he lost his position in the Senate. He died in a car crash in 1976.

L

Lacerda, Carlos

1914–77. Despite an association with Brazil's communists in the 1930s, Lacerda is remembered as a maverick of the political right. As an anti-government newspaper owner he was directly involved in the August 1954 crisis which led to the suicide of President Getúlio Vargas. A group of the president's supporters, angered by Lacerda's bitter attacks, tried to assassinate him. The attempt failed – he was only wounded while an air force officer who had been with him was killed. In the uproar which followed Lacerda redoubled his attacks on Vargas. Although the president denied any involvement in the assassination attempt, the armed forces demanded his resignation; Vargas then shot himself. Later that year Lacerda was elected federal deputy for the conservative Nationalist Democratic Union (UDN). In the 1955 elections he emerged as an outspoken supporter of a military coup to prevent Juscelino Kubitschek from taking office. The anti-Kubitschek conspiracy was frustrated by the 'constitutionalist coup' led by Gen. Henrique Lott. Faced with this blow Lacerda and some military allies sailed out of Rio de Janeiro on board the cruiser *Tamandare* in the hope of heading for Santos and gathering support for a counter-coup. This too failed.

In the 1960 elections Lacerda persuaded the UDN to back Jânio Quadros for the presidency. After Quadros took office Lacerda, who had been elected governor of Guanabara, was involved in the political crisis which led to the president's unexpected resignation in August 1961, having quarrelled with him because among other things Quadros had bestowed a decoration on Che Guevara. Lacerda played a key part in rallying opposition to Quadros' successor João Goulart. He was involved from an early stage in the consultations which led to the 1964 coup against Goulart. After the coup Lacerda became associated with the hard-line tendency within the officer corps and supported the removal of the political rights of many politicians particularly those who, like Kubitschek, might emerge as rivals for the presidency. But by late 1966, when it was clear that a succession of military men would block his hopes of reaching the presidency, Lacerda began to seek an alliance with old enemies such as Kubitschek and Goulart in a broad front (*Frente Ampla*) against the regime. The plan received less than enthusiastic support. In December 1968 the military regime stripped Lacerda of all political rights.

Lachmon, Jaggernath

b. 1916, Nickerie. Surinamese politician. After becoming the country's first Hindustani barrister in 1946, Lachmon founded the Hindustani-Javanese Political Party (H-JPP) in 1947 and joined the call for universal suffrage. In 1949 he formed the United Hindustani Party, later known as the Vatan Hitkarie Party (VHP) and then the Progressive Reform Party, and became a member of parliament. He formed an alliance with Johan Pengel, leader of the country's other main party, the National Party of Suriname (NPS) in 1953, and the two men ruled the country in coalition from 1958 to 1967, although Lachmon himself never held ministerial office. He was speaker of parliament from 1964 to 1973. In 1974–5 he opposed plans for independence from the Netherlands, accepting them only at the last minute. Forced out of politics by the 1980 coup, Lachmon resumed his activities when the ban on political parties was lifted in 1985. After the November 1987 parliamentary elections, when the VHP won the largest number of seats, he again became speaker of the national assembly. He wields considerable power as political patriarch of Suriname's largest ethnic group.

ladino

Originally a pejorative term for a 'latinised' (i.e. hispanicised) indian in Spanish America. Later, the term came to refer to any individual not identifiably indian in dress or behaviour, including those of Spanish descent. It is also used to mean a sly or cunning person in some countries. The opposite is '*indio*' (a usually pejorative term) or '*indígena*'. Nowadays the term is most widely used in Guatemala, where pure-blooded indians are a larger proportion of the population than elsewhere in the region. '*Ladinización*' means the adoption of 'western', or hispanic, dress and customs.

Lafertte, Elías: see **Communist Party of Chile**.

Laíno, Domingo

b. 1935. Paraguayan opposition politician and leader of the Authentic Radical Liberal Party (PLRA). Laíno first rose to prominence within the Radical Liberal Party (PLR), where in the controversial 1971 convention he represented the reformist wing, arguing for both democracy and socio-economic change. A popular figure with the party youth, he used his position as a member of the Chamber of Deputies to denounce the corruption and contraband activities of members of the regime of Gen. Alfredo Stroessner. He was denounced by the right, however, as being a communist in the pay of Moscow (an allegation which was never substantiated).

In 1975 he was sacked from his job as a university lecturer. Laíno was president of the PLR in 1975–7, but he lost control of the party in 1977 after a court case brought by conservative Liberals with tacit government support. In response he set up the PLRA in 1978, which, although growing to become the largest Liberal group, was nevertheless denied legal recognition. After criticising the government's human rights record

during a trip to Washington, Laíno was briefly arrested; he was imprisoned again in 1979 and 1980. In 1982 he was charged with insulting the memory of the former Nicaraguan dictator Anastasio Somoza (who had been killed in Asunción in 1980) and deported. He made five attempts to return to the country, but was forcibly turned back on each occasion. On one of these attempts, in June 1986, despite being accompanied by former US ambassador Robert White and Argentine and Uruguayan politicians, he was physically attacked by members of the police. Laíno was finally allowed back into the country in April 1987, but was still the subject of police harassment.
See also **Authentic Radical Liberal Party; Liberals** (Paraguay).

Lamarca, Carlos: see **guerrilla movements** (Brazil).

Lami Dozo, Brig. Basilio: see **South Atlantic War**.

Lanusse, Gen. Alejandro Augustín

b. 1918. Argentine army officer and military president in 1971–3 who called the first free elections in the country in two decades. Born in Buenos Aires, as a young officer he supported the failed anti-Peronist uprising in September 1951, and was imprisoned. But after the 1955 coup he resumed his military career, with postings as Chief of Staff, 3rd cavalry Division (1960) and Deputy Director, Superior War School (1960–2). In the internal struggle which broke out within the army, Lanusse supported the *Azules* faction (legalists) led by Gen. Onganía. He was posted to the Army command and supported Gen. Onganía's 1966 coup. He became head of the 3rd army (Córdoba) in 1967, and overall army commander in 1968. But Lanusse became critical of the Onganía administration, particularly after the 1969 protests known as the *Cordobazo*. As head of the army, he pressed for a military return to barracks and new elections. Given Gen. Onganía's refusal to accept this, Lanusse led the June 1970 palace coup, representing the army on a new three-man junta which installed Gen. Roberto Levingston in the presidency.

Dissatisfaction with Levingston's performance led to his removal and replacement by Lanusse on 26 March 1971. From his new position, Lanusse set about organising a political agreement to make the elections possible – known as the Great National Agreement (*Gran Acuerdo Nacional*/GAN). For the first time since the 1955 coup the Peronists were to participate. Gen. Lanusse also allowed Gen. Perón to return to Argentina in November 1972, although outstanding court cases were invoked to exclude him from standing. The victory of the alternative Peronist candidate, Dr Héctor Cámpora, in March 1973, and the re-election of Gen. Perón himself in September were seen by many army officers as a defeat. The younger generation of officers also accused Gen. Lanusse of permitting conditions in which the guerrilla groups grew.

Members of the Process of National Reorganisation military regime which took power in 1976 were ill-disposed towards Gen. Lanusse. In 1977 he was briefly arrested on corruption charges, later dropped by the courts. In the last years of the military regime and after the return to

democracy in 1983, Gen. Lanusse criticised its members for human rights violations, particularly the kidnapping and disappearance of his former press secretary, Edgardo Sajón. He was a witness for the prosecution in the 1985 trial of military commanders on human rights charges.
See also **Great National Agreement; Liberating Revolution; Onganía**.

Lara Bonilla, Rodrigo: see **Betancur Cuartas**.

Lara Parada, Ricardo: see **National Liberation Army** (Colombia).

Larrazábal, Adm. Wolfgang: see **Venezuelan Communist Party**.

Larrota, Antonio: see **Movement of Workers, Students and Peasants**.

latifundio

A large, private agricultural estate, sometimes only partially worked, which may take the form of a plantation, ranch or hacienda, and which typically depends for seasonal labour on landless, or semi-landless peasants. Hence, '*latifundismo*' which is a land tenure system based on large estates. The *latifundio* is usually associated with the '*minifundio*', which is defined as a plot too small to support a family and whose owner or tenant must therefore seek employment from the large landowner. This is sometimes known as the '*latifundio–minifundio* complex'. In many countries and regions of Latin America the bulk of land is taken up by *latifundia*, while the vast majority of farms are *minifundia*, the latter often forming part of the large estate. Forms of labour are frequently (but not always) semi-feudal, in that a cash wage may not be paid, or may be only part of the remuneration. The *latifundio* has been the target of many land reform programmes, but even when broken up it sometimes reappears when rich landowners find ways of circumventing the law; a process defined as '*neo-latifundismo*'. The large landowner, known as a '*latifundista*', naturally has better access to credit, irrigation, and modern technology than the smallholder, as well as to centres of political power.
See also ***gamonal***.

Latin American Bishops' Council (*Consejo Episcopal Latinoamericano*/CELAM)

Founded in 1955 with four stated objectives: to study matters of interest to the Catholic Church in Latin America; to coordinate activities; to promote and assist Catholic initiatives; and to prepare conferences of Latin American bishops, to be convened by the Holy See. Its members are the bishops' conferences of South and Central America and of the Caribbean. In addition to the general secretariat (based in Bogotá, Colombia) there are five under-secretariats, dealing with (i) the preservation and propagation of the faith; (ii) the supervision of diocesan clergy and religious institutions; (iii) the dissemination of religious education for youth; (iv) the apostolate of the laity and (v) social action/social assistance.

In 1968 Pope Paul VI became the first pontiff to visit Latin America when he attended the second conference of Latin American bishops in Medellín, Colombia. Pope John Paul II followed him when he addressed

the third, in Puebla, Mexico, in 1979. In recent years, CELAM has suffered from deep divisions between left and right. The most prominent conservative is Cardinal Alfonso López Trujillo of Colombia, while Cardinal Aloisio Lorscheider, Archbishop of Fortaleza, Brazil, is usually considered the leading progressive.
See also **liberation theology; Medellín; Puebla**.

Latin American Economic System (*Sistema Económico Latino Americano*/SELA)
Set up in 1975 largely on the initiative of presidents Luis Echeverría of Mexico and Carlos Andrés Pérez of Venezuela. The group includes all Latin American countries, and is conceived as a coordination and consultation body. SELA places great emphasis on the need for joint Latin American action on a number of issues, independently of the different forms of economic or political organisation of member states. Unlike other regional organisations, SELA excludes the United States but includes Cuba in its membership. It sees itself very much as representing the South in terms of the North–South dialogue. SELA has sought to promote joint marketing of Latin American commodities, so as to defend international price levels; it has also campaigned against protectionism in the industrialised countries and has tried to promote the formation of bi- or multinational companies through which local producers might compete more effectively on world markets. In the early 1980s SELA also took an active interest in the foreign debt problem. The top decision-making body within SELA is the Latin American Council, which meets annually and is composed of ministers from each member state. The permanent secretariat is based in Caracas.
See also **Andean Pact; Latin American Integration Association; Organisation of American States**.

Latin American Energy Organisation (*Organización Latinoamericana de Energía*/OLADE)
Founded in November 1973 at the Third Latin American Consultative Meeting of Ministers of Energy and Petroleum, held in Lima, Peru. The Lima Convention, setting up the organisation, came into effect on 18 December 1974 and was signed by the following countries: Argentina, Brazil, Colombia, Cuba, Costa Rica, Chile, Dominican Republic, Ecuador, El Salvador, Guatemala, Guyana, Honduras, Jamaica, Mexico, Nicaragua, Panama, Paraguay, Peru, Trinidad and Tobago, Uruguay, and Venezuela. Since then, Barbados, Bolivia, Dominica, Grenada, Haiti, and Suriname have joined, while Argentina now has only observer status.

OLADE's objectives are: to promote joint action in the utilisation and defence of the natural resources of each country and the region as a whole, including the identification and resolution of specific energy problems which constitute a barrier to development; to promote the rational exploitation and conservation of energy resources; to develop a Latin American energy market and a common regional approach to energy issues; and to develop a financial arm to channel funds into energy projects. It collaborates with the UN Development Programme on the Latin American Energy Cooperation Programme. OLADE's executive secretariat has its headquarters in Quito, Ecuador. The annual meeting of ministers is the body's highest authority. It elects a committee of six ministers on a geographical basis.

Latin American Federation of Christian Trade Unionists (CLASC): see **CLAT**.

Latin American Integration Association (LAIA) (*Asociación Latinoamericana de Integración*/ALADI)
Created in August 1980 to replace the Latin American Free Trade Association (LAFTA), which had been in existence since February 1960. The objectives of LAFTA had been: to increase trade between members; to promote regional integration and development; and to lay the basis for what would eventually become a Latin American Common Market. But progress towards these aims was slow – the tariff reduction programme in particular proved problematic, with LAFTA agreements accounting for only 14% of trade among members by 1980. The change to LAIA on expiry of the original LAFTA protocols was designed to create a less ambitious, more flexible association. The LAIA framework stresses a regional tariff preference for goods coming from other member countries, economic preference areas, and partial scope agreements (involving specific goods and groups of member countries).

LAIA comprises the 11 original LAFTA members, now grouped into three categories: most developed – Argentina, Brazil, Colombia, and Mexico; intermediate – Chile, Peru, Uruguay, and Venezuela; and least developed – Bolivia, Ecuador, and Paraguay. Tariff treatment varies by category, with the least developed countries getting the best terms. The main decision-making body is the Council of Ministers – made up of foreign ministers of member countries. The Secretariat, LAIA's technical body, is based in Montevideo, Uruguay.
See also **Andean Pact**.

Latin American Peasant Federation (FCL): see **CLAT**.

Law for the Defence of Democracy: see **Communist Party of Chile**.

Laya, Argelia: see **Generation of 1958** (Venezuela).

Lechín Oquendo, Juan
b. 1914. Bolivian labour leader and politician. Born in Corocoro, La Paz department; his parents were middle-class and of Lebanese origin; his half-brother, Juan Lechín Suárez, is a leading right-wing general. Lechín fought as a sergeant in the 1930s Chaco War and was subsequently employed as a clerk in the mining town of Catavi (he never worked as a miner). Executive secretary of the Mineworkers' Federation (FSTMB) (1944–86) and of the trade union confederation COB (1952–86), he became minister of mines and petroleum, 1952–6; senator, 1956–60; and vice president of Bolivia, 1960–2. He was 'exiled' as ambassador to Italy (December 1962–November 1963) after being falsely implicated in a drugs

scandal. Lechín had joined the Nationalist Revolutionary Movement (MNR) in the late 1940s, becoming the leader of its left wing (eventually known as the 'Leftist Sector') after a period of involvement with the Trotskyist Revolutionary Workers' Party (POR). When the left was denied a voice in the selection of MNR candidates for the 1964 election, he withdrew his delegates from the party convention, announced the formation of the Revolutionary Party of the National Left (PRIN) and stood for the presidency as its candidate.

Most of the period from 1965 to 1978 was spent in exile, including periods in Paraguay, Chile, Argentina, and Venezuela (where the Lechín family has appreciable commercial interests). In 1970, during the brief presidency of left-wing general Juan José Torres, Lechín was elected president of the Popular Assembly, an attempt at a 'people's parliament'. During the 1980 García Meza coup, he was arrested with other left-wing leaders, later appearing on television to call for an end to civil resistance, before once more being sent into exile. Under the Paz Estenssoro government (1985–) Lechín several times declared that the time was ripe for popular insurrection. During a period of state of siege (September 1985) he was banished to a remote Amazonian town, where he staged a hunger strike. Lechín resigned as leader of the FSTMB 'to dedicate himself to politics' in 1986, apparently because the organisation had lost much of its political muscle with the decline of the tin industry. He was succeeded by independent Victor López Arias. In 1987 he did not stand for re-election to the leadership of the COB, and the post went to Simón Reyes, head of the Communist Party (PCB). Lechín remains a highly popular figure and may stand for president in 1989. He has taken on the role of spokesman for the militant coca growers.
See also **COB; Revolutionary Nationalist Movement; Revolutionary Party of the Nationalist Left**.

Lechín Suárez, Juan: see **Lechín Oquendo**.

Left Liberation Front (FIDEL): see **Communist Party of Uruguay**.

Left Revolutionary Front (FRI): see **Revolutionary Party of the Nationalist Left**.

Léhder Rivas, Carlos: see **Barco Vargas; National Latin Movement**.

Leigh, Gen. Gustavo: see **Pinochet**.

Leniz, Fernando: see **Chicago Boys**.

Leoni, Raúl

1905–72. Founding member of Venezuela's Democratic Action (AD) party and president in 1964–9. Born in Upata, Bolívar state, Leoni was a member of the 'Generation of 1928'. For taking part in the anti-government protests of that year he was exiled to Colombia where he enrolled in university in Bogotá to study law. On the death of the dictator Gen. Juan Vicente Gómez in 1936, he returned to set up the *Organización Revolucionaria Venezolana* (ORVE) together with Rómulo Betancourt.

Leoni's election as a deputy for the state of Bolívar was annulled by the government of Gen. Eleázar López Contreras, together with that of 46 other opposition figures. Exiled for a second time to Colombia, he completed his law studies in 1938 and returned to set up the National Democratic Party (PDN), the forerunner of AD, in 1941. He participated in the 18 October 1945 coup against Gen. Isaías Medina Angarita which installed Betancourt as provisional president. Under the new AD government Leoni became a member of the ruling revolutionary junta and minister of labour. Following the 24 November 1948 coup by Col. Marcos Pérez Jiménez, Leoni was imprisoned and again forced into exile, this time for 10 years during which he lived in the United States, Costa Rica, Peru, and Bolivia.

On the overthrow of the Pérez Jiménez regime he returned to Venezuela and organised Betancourt's successful 1958 presidential campaign. Leoni himself was elected senator for Bolívar, president of the Senate (1959–62) and president of AD (1959–63). Nominated by AD as its candidate to succeed Betancourt, Leoni won the 1 December 1963 elections with 33% of the votes. He took office on 11 March 1964, promising to maintain friendly relations with the US and support the Alliance for Progress, while continuing to fight the guerrilla groups. The Leoni presidency was politically more stable than the previous Betancourt administration; although the guerrilla insurgences continued in the first years of his rule, they did so with lessening intensity. After ending his presidential term in 1969, Leoni died on 5 July 1972.
See also **Betancourt; Democratic Action; guerrilla insurgency** (Venezuela).

Letelier case

On 26 September 1976 Orlando Letelier, a former cabinet minister in the 1970–3 Popular Unity government of Chile, was killed by a car bomb in Washington DC, along with an assistant, US citizen Ronni Moffit. The case was to have a long-term negative effect on US–Chilean relations, and effectively prevented Washington from lifting the arms embargo on Chile. Letelier, who had served as ambassador in Washington and as foreign minister and defence minister, had been organising international opposition to the military regime of Gen. Pinochet in Chile. His murder was carried out by agents of the Chilean secret police (DINA), including US citizen Michael Townley, who subsequently confessed and was extradited from Chile, tried and sentenced to 10 years in jail. Townley named three Chileans, including the head of DINA, Gen. Manuel Contreras, a close associate of Pinochet, as having been involved in the plot. He also implicated five US-based anti-Castro Cubans.

Despite US pressure, the Chilean supreme court in 1979 turned down an extradition request for the Chileans, citing the political nature of the crime. The DINA was dissolved by Pinochet in 1977 and replaced by a similar organisation, the CNI. Gen. Contreras retired. In 1987 one of the accused, Maj. Armando Fernández Larios, gave himself up to the US authorities and confessed his involvement in preparations for the

murder. His testimony implied that it had been ordered by Pinochet himself. Fernández Larios was given a light sentence, and the US government asked the Chilean authorities to expel Contreras and the other prime suspect, Col. Pedro Espinoza, but the response was negative.
See also **Pinochet Ugarte**.

Levi Ruffinelli, Carlos and Fernando: see **Liberals** (Paraguay).

Levingston, Gen. Roberto Marcelo: see **Argentine Revolution; The Hour of the People; Lanusse**.

Ley de Lemas

The name given to Uruguay's unusual electoral system, which permits established parties to field more than one presidential candidate each. The *Ley de Lemas* can be translated as 'law of the parties' although the mechanism has also been described as the 'double simultaneous vote'. Traditionally, the system has operated to allow each sub-group within the Blanco and Colorado parties (known as *sub-lemas*) to present its own presidential candidate. The most-voted candidate within a party then receives the votes of his unsuccessful rivals as second preferences. The presidency is therefore won by the most-voted candidate within the most-voted party. The system has been used in other Latin American countries, most notably in Honduras for the 1985 elections. The *Ley de Lemas* has been widely criticised, not least because of the frequently large political differences within each party. A vote cast for a conservative Blanco candidate can end up helping a reformist Blanco to win. In some cases candidates from different parties have had more in common with each other than candidates within the same party.

In 1971 the *Ley de Lemas* produced a controversial result when Wilson Ferreira Aldunate of the Blancos was the single most-voted candidate in the country, but failed to win the presidency because the aggregate vote for his party was just below that of the rival Colorados. Juan María Bordaberry, the most voted candidate within the Colorados, was declared the winner. During the 1973–85 military regime, the armed forces frequently described the *Ley de Lemas* as one of the features of the corruption of the political system which they said had prompted the coup. But despite this, when a decision was taken to allow new elections in 1985, the *Ley de Lemas* was reintroduced with only marginal modifications. A move to single candidates per party at that moment would have been beneficial to the more radical opponents of military rule.
See also ***autogolpe***; ***coparticipación***.

Ley Maldita: see **Communist Party of Chile**.

Liberal Front Party (*Partido da Frente Liberal*/PFL)

A Brazilian centre-right party founded in July 1984 as a split from the ruling Democratic Social Party (PDS). The dissidents were opposed to the PDS choice of Paulo Salim Maluf as a presidential candidate. They decided to throw their weight behind the opposition candidate, Tancredo Neves. The PFL and Neves' Brazilian Democratic Movement Party

(PMDB) between them created the Democratic Alliance. As part of the accord the PLF secured the vice-presidential nomination for José Sarney. The Neves–Sarney formula was chosen on 15 January 1985 by the electoral college. Neves, however, died in April 1985 and Sarney became President. The PMDB–PFL coalition lasted until September 1987, when the PFL formally withdrew from the coalition. Some PFL members nevertheless continued to serve as ministers on an individual basis.

Liberal Movement: see **Democratic Alliance**.

Liberal Party (Colombia) (*Partido Liberal*/PL)
More informally known as the 'Red' or 'Colorado' party. Founded in the 1840s by members of the Democratic Societies formed by farmers and artisans as political discussion clubs and pressure groups, and young aristocrats grouped around the Republican School. Influenced by European liberal and utopian socialist ideas, opposed to monopoly capitalists and the traditional landowning class, Liberals favoured free trade, federalism, curbs on Church power, and the abolition of slavery. The party effected a liberal reform in the mid-nineteenth century which ended state monopolies and slavery (provoking a Conservative uprising in 1851), reduced the power of the Church, decentralised government, and modernised the treatment of indians. In the late nineteenth and the first three decades of the twentieth century the party played a minor opposition role to the powerful Conservative Party (PC), but in 1930 (with the PC split under the impact of the worldwide economic crisis) it came to power under moderate president Enrique Olaya Herrera, who had been ambassador to Washington and who first formed a bipartite administration. Thereafter, new-style leaders temporarily took the initiative, moving the party in the direction of a mass movement.

The 'Liberal Republic' lasted from 1934 to 1946, and under President Alfonso López Pumarejo many reforms were enacted, affecting land tenure, labour law, education, fiscal policy, and social welfare. Restrictions on suffrage were lifted and trade unions were allowed to operate more freely. A breach opened up between the old-guard Liberals and the reformers, whose most powerful and radical representative was Jorge Eliécer Gaitán. The right, led by Gabriel Turbay, sought to block Gaitán's campaign for the masses to seize control of the party under his leadership, but by 1947 his promises of profound agrarian reform, democratisation, and radical social measures brought him the party leadership. In 1948 Gaitán was assassinated. The era of 'the violence' ('*la violencia*') had already begun, and Liberal oligarchs joined the PC (now in power) in putting down the uprising which followed his death. The PL finally withdrew its support from the extreme right-wing PC administration and backed Gen. Rojas Pinilla's 1953 army coup against it, but the general's plans did not match the interests of the traditional parties and the PC and the PL came together to devise the National Front plan under which they alternated in power from 1958 to 1974. (Conservatives were also included in PL administrations from 1974 to 1982, even though the National Front was formally at an end.) The PL has its greatest mass support in urban areas and a strong voice in the trade unions – it effectively controls the third largest confederation, the CTC. Ties to industrial and financial capital have traditionally predominated, however, despite the populist elements in the party, such as the 1960–8 Liberal Revolutionary Movement (MRL), led by Alfonso López Michelsen, which was communist-(PCC-)influenced.

In the 1970s the party was divided into three tendencies: the right-wing party 'machine' controlled by Julio César Turbay (president 1978–82) and his allies; the moderate Carlos Lleras Restrepo wing, which had ties to more progressive elements in the PC; and the López Michelsen wing. Divisions, however, were less ideological than cliquish: only in the 1982 elections was the party sufficiently divided (between the traditional wing and the 'New Liberalism' of Dr Luís Carlos Galán) to let the PC win the presidency. The PL has also maintained a consistent congressional majority in recent times (the National Front provisions relating to Congress were suspended in 1960). When in power, its policies are largely dictated by pressure groups (including the armed forces). Its traditional strongholds have been the departments of Cauca, Cundinamarca, and those on the Caribbean coast, and the towns of Bogotá, Barranquilla, Cartagena, and Pereira. Splits in the PL led to a poor performance in the 1988 mayoral elections, blamed by many on lack of leadership by President Barco.
See also **Barco Vargas; Gaitán; Liberal Revolutionary Movement; López Michelsen; National Front; Turbay Ayala**.

Liberal Party (Ecuador): see **Conservative Party** (Ecuador).

Liberal Party (Paraguay) (*Partido Liberal*/PL)
A legally recognised parliamentary party, the PL has played the role of 'loyal opposition' to Gen. Stroessner's Colorado Party. It is one of various competing Liberal parties. It stood in elections in 1963, 1968, 1973, 1978, 1983 and 1988. Official election results gave it 3.1% of the total vote in 1988. The party describes itself as favouring democratisation and free enterprise. Critics accuse it of giving credibility to Gen. Stroessner's claims that Paraguay is a democracy by taking part in fraudulent elections.
See also **Liberals** (Paraguay).

Liberal Revolutionary Movement (Colombia) (*Movimiento Revolucionario Liberal*/MRL)
A progressive, quasi-socialist tendency within the Liberal Party (PL) from 1960 to 1967, led by future president (1974–8) Alfonso López Michelsen. Opposed to the National Front arrangement under which the PL and the Conservatives (PC) alternated in power and excluded third parties, the MRL was close to the Communist Party (PCC), which helped establish it and with which it acted jointly on some issues. It favoured agrarian and urban reform and greater political and economic independence and was strongest among rural voters. The MRL was committed to an electoral strategy and operated for tactical purposes under the terms of the

National Front, though in 1963 a more radical sector under Alvaro Uribe broke away over the issue of separation from the PL.

In 1962, at the height of its influence, it received 36% of the PL vote in the congressional elections. Most of the membership (led by López, who accepted the foreign ministry under the Lleras Restrepo government in 1968) rejoined the main PL for the 1968 elections. A small, left-wing group stood as the People's MRL in alliance with the PCC, winning two seats in Bogotá and Cali.

See also **Liberal Party** (Colombia)**; López Michelsen; New Liberalism**.

Liberals (Argentina)

Political groups identified with free market policies and the opening up of the economy to foreign capital. Traditionally drawn from the landowning establishment, sectors of banking and commerce, and some tendencies within the armed forces. In contrast to international usage, in Argentina the term is used in its economic, rather than political, sense. In fact, free market economic policies have more often than not been identified with repressive military rule. The political opposite of 'liberal' is 'nationalist'.

Liberals (Paraguay)

The Liberals came into being in 1887 after the War of the Triple Alliance, as a largely pro-Argentine grouping, and held power almost without interruption between 1904 and 1940. On the death of Marshal Estigarribia, the Liberal leader, Gen. Higinio Morínigo came to power, eventually aligning himself with the rival Colorados and outlawing the Liberal Party in 1942. Dissident Liberals took part in the unsuccessful 1947 rising against Morínigo, along with *Febreristas* and communists. The party then had to come to terms with the establishment of a dictatorship under Gen. Alfredo Stroessner and the Colorado Party from 1954 onwards. Young members of the party in exile formed a guerrilla column which entered the country in 1959, but after a series of defeats the policy of armed struggle against the Stroessner regime was dropped in 1961. In that year the party regrouped, although by 1963 new divisions began to make themselves felt.

The Renovationist wing broke away, and was granted official recognition by the authorities under the name of Liberal Party (*Partido Liberal*/PL). Under the leadership of Carlos and Fernando Levi Ruffinelli until 1977, and others after that date, the PL was widely seen as collaborationist with the regime. The party mainstream, on the other hand, achieved legal recognition in 1967 under the name of Radical Liberal Party (*Partido Liberal Radical*/PLR). The PLR suffered growing internal tensions between rival factions in 1971. The conservative tendency, which favoured taking part in elections, won control of the party amid accusations of vote-rigging. Accordingly, the PLR took part in the 1973 elections, winning 12% of the vote. In 1975 the left, led by Domingo Laíno, took control of the party.

In 1977 the PLR and the main faction in the PL (led by the Levi Ruffinellis) were able to re-unite on a platform of opposition to the regime, forming the United Liberal Party (*Partido Liberal Unido*/PLU).

But the conservative PLR faction which had been displaced by the left in 1975, with government backing, challenged the legal status of the new party in the courts. These ruled that the PLU had no legal status and that the conservatives should regain control of the PLR. Laíno consequently lost his parliamentary immunity and was briefly arrested after criticising the government's human rights record. In 1978 he set up the Authentic Radical Liberal Party (*Partido Liberal Radical Auténtico*/PLRA) which has boycotted elections and been refused legal recognition. For their part the Levi Ruffinelli brothers regrouped by forming the Teeté Liberal Party (*Partido Liberal Teeté*/PLT) which did obtain legal recognition and participated in the 1978 elections. In 1979 the PLRA became a founding member of the National Accord opposition coalition. Laíno was arrested on various occasions, and was deported in 1982. In the 1983 and 1988 elections only the PLR and the PL presented candidates to Congress. The PLT and the PLRA did not take part. In 1988 the PLR obtained 7.2% and the PL 3.1% of the total vote, according to official results.
See also **Authentic Radical Liberal Party; Laíno**.

Liberating Revolution (*Revolución Libertadora*)

The name taken by the Argentine military regime which took power in the 16 September 1955 coup against the administration of Gen. Juan Domingo Perón. The main conspirators were Gens Pedro Aramburu and Eduardo Lonardi. Gen. Lonardi began the uprising in Córdoba; after 11 days of negotiations and military manoeuvres, including a threat by the radically anti-Peronist Navy to bombard Buenos Aires, Gen. Perón left the country. Gen. Lonardi was sworn in as the new president. In office, he sought to adopt a conciliatory line towards supporters of the previous government, proclaiming that there would neither be victors nor vanquished (*no habrá vencedores ni vencidos*). But this was opposed by Gen. Aramburu, and the sharply anti-Peronist *gorila* faction of the military. These groups were dissatisfied with Lonardi's failure to ban the Peronist-dominated General Confederation of Labour (CGT), and with what they saw as his excessive reliance on ultra-Catholic and nationalist advisers and ministers.

On 13 November 1955 Gen. Lonardi was deposed and replaced by Gen. Aramburu. The new government immediately intensified measures against the Peronists. 27 military and civilian conspirators in a failed pro-Peronist uprising of 8–9 June 1956 were shot by firing squad, the first government-ordered political execution in almost a century. The leaders of the regime insisted that their intention was to restore liberal democracy, but that there could be no place for the Peronists. Elections to a constituent assembly were held in July 1957, to modify the 1853 constitution (the government having already annulled the 1949 constitution by decree). Blank ballots – cast by the Peronists – took the largest share of the poll, with the People's Radical Party (UCRP) in second place and the Intransigent Radical Party (UCRI) in third. UCRI constituents walked out of the assembly's first session, in protest at the exclusion of

the Peronists. The remaining delegates ratified the annulment of the 1949 constitution and added a new clause on social rights before the departure of additional small parties led to a loss of quorum, forcing the dissolution of the assembly. The government pressed on with its promise to hold elections in February 1958. These were won by Dr Arturo Frondizi of the UCRI, who in a secret pact had obtained the support of Gen. Perón. The Liberating Revolution regime came to an end when Dr Frondizi took office on 1 May 1958.
See also **Aramburu; Peronism**.

liberation theology

The popular name for an approach to the expression of Catholic beliefs developed by Latin American theologians, both priests and laypeople. Their inspiration came from the teachings of Pope John XXIII, the documents of the Second Vatican Council (1962–5) and the Second General Conference of Latin American Bishops at Medellín (Colombia) in 1968. (The term was popularised by Peru's best-known theologian, Gustavo Gutiérrez, in the title of a book published in 1971.) Among its key concepts are the 'preferential option for the poor', and their liberation from all forms of oppression, including 'institutionalised violence', to which the violence of the poor is a sometimes justifiable response.

Liberation theologians adopted as an analytical tool some of the methodology of Marxism. Their ideas were derived in large measure from the everyday experience of the 'ecclesial base communities' (*communidades eclesiales/eclesiais de base*, or CEBs) in which ordinary people came together to reflect on their lives in the light of the teachings of the Bible. The Vatican has looked askance at certain aspects of liberation theology as practised in Latin America, in particular its links with Marxism. Cardinal Joseph Ratzinger, head of the Vatican's Congregation for the Doctrine of the Faith, has been pursuing its exponents with particular hostility since the 1970s. In 1985, in a lengthy criticism deplored by Brazilian bishops, the Congregation described a book by Brazilian theologian Leonardo Boff as 'unsustainable' and as 'placing at risk the sound doctrine of the faith'. Boff had in September 1984 become the first theologian ever to be summoned to Rome to be personally confronted. A year's silence was imposed on him (1985–6), during which he was not to give lectures to those outside his religious community; however, this was cut short after 11 months.
See also ***comunidad de base*; Latin American Bishops' Conference; Medellín**.

L

Libertad y Cambio: see **Colorado Party** (Uruguay).

Lima Group (*aka* Contadora Support Group)
Four South American nations came together on 29 July 1985 to form this group, which backs the four-nation Contadora Group in its search for peace in Central America. The initiative came from President Alan García of Peru, at whose inauguration the agreement was sealed. The other three nations are Argentina, Brazil, and Uruguay, all of them

recently restored to civilian rule. On 24–25 August 1985 the Lima Group met the Contadora foreign ministers in Cartagena, Colombia, to discuss implementation of the Contadora Act. On 11–12 January 1986 foreign ministers of the eight issued the Caraballeda Message, defining the conditions for lasting peace in Central America and calling for a fresh impetus to the peace talks. This message was subsequently supported by the Central American nations and welcomed by the European Community. The Lima Group has taken part in many subsequent meetings of the Contadora Group.

Lim A Po, F. H. R.: see **National Party of Suriname**.

Lins de Barros, João Alberto: see **São Paulo Revolt; Long March**.

***Lista 99*:** see **Broad Front**.

Lleras Restrepo, Carlos: see **Liberal Party** (Colombia).

Llovera Páez, Col. Luis Felipe: see **Delgado Chalbaud**.

Lodge Corollary: see **Monroe doctrine**.

Lonardi, Gen. Eduardo: see **Aramburu; Liberating Revolution.**

Long March

A two-year, 14,000 mile march through the Brazilian wilderness by a rebel column in 1925–7. Its origins lay in the failed *tenente* uprising in São Paulo and Rio Grande do Sûl in July and October 1924. 3,000 rebels from São Paulo under the command of Juárez Távora withdrew to near the Iguaçu falls in Paraná state, where they were joined by the remnants of the Rio Grande do Sûl group under Luis Carlos Prestes (later to become the country's main communist leader) and João Alberto Lins de Barros. Another prominent leader was the São Paulo *tenente* Miguel Costa. Casualties and desertions reduced the rebel forces to about 1,600 men, facing persecution by a 15,000 strong federal army. But the rebel leaders nevertheless decided to march through Paraguay before re-entering Brazil in an attempt to spark off new uprisings.

In the following two years, the column moved through Paraguay, the Brazilian states of Paraíba, Ceará, Alagoas, Bahia, Goiás, and Matto Grosso, and then into Bolivia. It clashed not only with the army but also with bandits (*cangaçeiros*) in the north-east and gunmen in the pay of the landowners. The rebels printed a broadsheet titled *O Libertador*, advocating land reform and calling for a peasant uprising. The Long March failed to spark off the type of rural revolution its leaders sought, but the rebel column managed to survive until the end of the Artur da Silva Bernardes presidency. Prestes, disillusioned with the potential for a rural revolution, sought to concentrate on the urban working class after 1930, through the Communist party.

See also **Brazilian Communist Party; *tenentes***.

López Arias, Víctor: see **Lechín Oquendo**.

López Contreras, Gen. Eleázar

1883–1972. The minister of war during the final yars of the Venezuelan dictatorship of Juan Vicente Gómez, López Contreras took over as president on Gómez's death in December 1935, a position he held until 1941. His government was marked by relative liberalisation, although the essential authoritarian structure of the regime remained intact. Opposition groups were allowed more open activity, but many left-wingers were sent into enforced exile in 1937. During his presidency López Contreras initiated a series of reforms to the labour code; the central bank was also created. He chose Gen. Isaias Medina Angarita (who had been his secretary during the Gómez years) to succeed him, but the two men fell out. It was a conflict between ex-President López Contreras and President Medina Angarita over the choice of a candidate for the succession which created conditions favourable to the coup of 18 October 1945, led by members of Democratic Action (AD) and young army officers.

See also **Democratic Action; Gómez, Gen. Juan Vicente; Medina Angarita;** ***trienio*****.**

López Michelsen, Alfonso

b. 1913. President of Colombia 1974–8. Son of former President (1934–8 and 1942–5) Alfonso López Pumarejo. Lawyer, teacher, and Liberal Party (PL) politician. Educated at Nuestra Señora del Rosario University, where he took a law degree. Congressional deputy 1960–2. Unsuccessful PL candidate for the presidency in 1962. Senator 1962–6. Governor of César department 1967. Editor of the newspaper *El Liberal*, organ of the PL. López was the leader of the left-wing Revolutionary Liberal Movement (MLR) from 1958 to 1967, opposing the National Front arrangement under which the PL and the Conservatives (PC) alternated in power. He became foreign minister (1968–71) under Presidents Carlos Lleras Restrepo and Misael Pastrana. López Michelsen scored a massive victory over Alvaro Gómez Hurtado of the PC in 1974, after overcoming intense opposition to his candidacy from the traditional wing of the PL; but by this stage he was no more than a moderate reformer. He agreed to govern with the PC, abandoning his former opposition to power-sharing.

Early in his presidency he sought to reach a ceasefire agreement with the communist guerrillas of the FARC, but was frustrated by the military hierarchy. Like most Colombian presidents since the '*violencia*' period, he eventually resorted to the imposition of a state of siege, as guerrilla activity increased. His presidency acquired a reputation for chaos, and much of his popularity evaporated in the course of it. At one point, after the collapse of his cabinet over his alleged mishandling of a general strike, he was reported to be considering resigning. At least 13 people died in the strike, which López described as 'an uprising'. In 1977 he again threatened to resign, raising fears of a military takeover, when his two sons were charged with improper receipt of government funds. In 1982 he once more stood for the presidency, but was defeated by the Conserva-

tive (PC) Party's Belisario Betancur due to the split in the Liberal vote. He remains a powerful voice in the PL and could make a comeback. Under Betancur he accepted the job of attempting to revive the truce with the guerrillas which had effectively collapsed.
See also **Liberal Party** (Colombia); **Liberal Revolutionary Movement; National Front;** ***violencia, la***.

López Pumarejo, Alfonso: see **Communist Party of Colombia; Liberal Party** (Colombia); **López Michelsen**.

López Rega, José: see **death squad**; **Perón, Isabel**.

López Suárez, Armando: see **Workers' Self-Defence Movement**.

López Trujillo, Cardinal Alfonso: see **Latin American Bishops' Council**.

Lorscheider, Cardinal Aloisio: see **Latin American Bishops' Council**.

Lott, Gen. Enrique Teixera: see **Kubitschek de Oliveira**.

Lúder, Dr Italo: see **Alfonsín**.

Luis, Washington: see **Old Republic**.

Lula (Luis Inâcio da Silva)

b. 1945. A charismatic Brazilian trade union and political leader who first rose to prominence in the metalworkers' strikes in São Paulo in 1978. The son of poor parents from the north-east Luis Inâcio da Silva, known by his nickname 'Lula', had become a toolmaker at Villares. One of his brothers was a trade unionist sympathetic to the PCB. Lula became a substitute member on the executive of the São Bernardo metalworkers' federation, then under the leadership of Paulo Vidal, an official deeply influenced by AFL-CIO-style economicist trade unionism. In 1975 Vidal nominated Lula as his successor in the presidency; but after being elected, Lula broke with his old mentor, negotiating a separate deal with the employers.

In 1977 he launched a novel campaign, demanding compensation for the government's 'falsification' of the inflation index used to adjust wages in previous years. The union estimated that since 1974 its members had been cheated out of pay roughly equivalent to 34% of June 1977 wage levels. The campaign captured the rank-and-file's imagination and attendance at union meetings grew dramatically. In May 1978 a strike broke out at the Saab-Scania plant and rapidly spread throughout the motor vehicle industry in the industrial outskirts of São Paulo known as the ABC area. It was the first strike of significance in 10 years, and under Lula's leadership favourable settlements were obtained in many plants.

A new strike in 1979 led to government intervention of the São Bernardo metalworkers' union, and the suspension of Lula; but the move was only temporary and his leadership of the movement was unaffected. A further strike in 1980 was met by military repression – Lula and 14 other union leaders were arrested. Faced with massive counter-demonstrations the army withdrew from the ABC area. In the wake of the strike Lula and other leaders of the movement founded the Workers' Party (PT) – this had been a long planned objective which provoked the hostility of both the *pelego* union leaders and left-wing parties such as the PCB (which considered itself the natural workers' party).

In 1981 ten PT leaders including Lula were sentenced to 2–3½ years in prison on charges of incitement to murder. The charges arose from speeches they had made at the funeral of a peasant leader shot by opponents of land reform. Lula and four other co-defendants were acquitted in 1984. In the November 1986 state and congressional elections, after the return of civilian rule, Lula was elected a federal deputy for the PT in São Paulo with one of the highest vote totals in the country. See also ***pelegos;*** **Workers' Party**.

Lurigancho massacre

In June 1986 prisoners belonging to the Shining Path (*Sendero Luminoso*) guerrilla movement staged a coordinated revolt in three Peruvian prisons – Lurigancho, El Frontón prison island, and the Santa Bárbara women's prison in Callao – claiming there was a 'genocide' plot against them by the military. The government put the army, the navy, and the paramilitary police in charge, and they responded with artillery, mortars, bazookas, and rockets. All 124 mutineers in Lurigancho died, and despite military denials it emerged that over 100 had been executed after surrendering. Of at least 154 prisoners at El Frontón, only 35 were said to have survived. According to Amnesty International, a further 35–60 were taken away to be tortured and murdered.

It emerged that the military had been planning for some time to move against the *Sendero* organisation within the prisons, which they believed was coordinating urban guerrilla operations. Many bodies were secretly buried. The Peruvian government of President Alan García denied that it had sought to cover up the killings, as Amnesty claimed. 95 Republican Guard (GR) personnel were arrested for executing prisoners, but jurisdiction over the case was granted to military courts and no military or police personnel were eventually convicted. No criticism was levelled at the responsible army and navy officers. However, the justice minister, the head of the prison service, and the head of the GR resigned from their posts.

Domestically the incident damaged relations with the parliamentary left, while internationally it dented García's progressive image. He had been hosting a meeting of the Socialist International in Lima at the time. The government-appointed peace commission, which had sought to mediate, resigned en bloc. A parliamentary commission under left-wing Senator Rolando Ames, could not agree on the issue of presidential responsibility. A minority, opposition report found García directly responsible for the killings, however.
See also **García Pérez; Shining Path**.

Lusinchi, Dr Jaime

b. 1924. Venezuelan politician, paediatrician, and president 1984– . Born in Anzoátegui, he went to university in Barcelona in eastern Venezuela. Lusinchi was politically active from an early age, joining the Democratic Action (AD) party in the year it was founded, 1941. In 1948 he was elected president of the legislative assembly for Anzoátegui state; but after the coup that year which brought the AD *trienio* to an abrupt end he joined the underground opposition. In April 1952 he was arrested and deported, beginning a six-year exile in Chile, Argentina, and the United States. He returned to Caracas in 1958 after the overthrow of the Marcos Pérez Jiménez regime. Lusinchi rose steadily through the party, becoming at one stage a protege of Carlos Andrés Pérez.

In 1977 he tried unsuccessfully to win the AD presidential nomination. On his second attempt, in January 1982, he succeeded in winning 75% of the party's internal primary votes and securing the nomination for the December 1983 elections. In those elections he won comfortably with 57%, against COPEI's Rafael Caldera with 34.5%. Once in office Lusinchi's administration was mainly preoccupied with a lengthy rescheduling of the foreign debt and the need to impose domestic economic austerity. Falling international oil prices placed severe strains on the economy, and with unemployment on the increase, the AD-dominated union confederation, the CTV, became increasingly critical of the government. Within the party Lusinchi also faced a strong challenge from Carlos Andrés Pérez, who beat the president's favoured candidate to secure the party's presidential nomination in 1987 (to run for president a second time, in 1988).

See also **Democratic Action; Pérez, Carlos Andrés**.

M–19 (19 April Movement/*Movimiento 19 de Abril*)
A Colombian guerrilla movement, founded in 1973 and named after the elections of 19 April 1970 which were claimed by the loser, Gen. Gustavo Rojas Pinilla, to have been rigged against his ANAPO party. Its original leaders were left-wing ANAPO dissidents, of whom the most prominent was former congressional deputy Dr Carlos Toledo Plata (assassinated in 1984). Its principal military commander (until his death in a plane crash in 1983) was Jaime Báteman Cayón, a widely-travelled Marxist–Leninist with little formal education, who had previously (1966–70) spent time with Revolutionary Armed Forces of Colombia (FARC).

The movement's first public act (repudiated by ANAPO) was the seizure of Simón Bolívar's sword and spurs on 17 January 1974. Its ideology is a rather incoherent mixture of radical liberalism (it claims to represent the tradition of Jorge Eliécer Gaitán, assassinated in 1948), Marxism, and social democracy. Its structure is similar to that of the Uruguayan Tupamaros (who are said to have assisted in its formation), with separate 'columns' in different cities, each divided into cells.

In February 1976, M–19 kidnapped and later assassinated the trade union leader José Raquel Mercado, whom it accused of links with US Central Intelligence Agency. This was followed in succeeding years by further kidnappings and sabotage, aimed particularly at foreign multinational companies. In January 1979 it captured 5,000 weapons (all subsequently recovered) from a Bogotá arsenal by tunnelling into the building. In 1980 it held 15 ambassadors and 42 others hostage for 61 days at the Dominican Republic embassy in Bogotá, obtaining a large ransom and safe passage to Cuba, but not the release of imprisoned comrades. Colombia has accused Cuba and Nicaragua of giving arms and training to M–19, and in 1981 broke diplomatic relations with the former over the issue.

M–19's openness to peace talks with the government led in 1981 to the formation of the breakaway National Base Coordinating Group (CNB), committed to continuing the armed struggle. The government held direct talks with M–19 leaders in November 1982 and October 1983, and despite sabotage attempts by the armed forces and dissident guerrillas a one-year ceasefire was signed in August 1984, allowing open political activity by M–19. The agreement finally broke down in June 1985, following which the M–19 and the armed forces resumed all-out war. In November 1985

35 M–19 members seized the Supreme Court building in Bogotá, taking several hundred hostages. The army attacked with helicopters and tanks, and over 100 people – including 12 members of the Supreme Court – died in a 28-hour battle. In 1985 M–19 formed the guerrilla front known as the CNG, which grew to include all significant armed groups by late 1987. Also in 1985, with the Túpac Amaru guerrillas of Peru and 'Alfaro Lives!' of Ecuador, the group formed the America Batallion, comprising recruits from several Latin American countries.

In early 1987 M–19 proposed peace talks with the Barco government, on condition that indigenous communities in its stronghold of Cauca were given the leading role in framing 'rehabilitation' programmes. There was speculation that the organisation might be split between those for and those against a truce. M–19 has lost three top commanders since 1983: Báteman (d. 1983), Iván Marino Ospina (d. 1985) and Alvaro Fayad (d. 1986). Twelve of its leaders were killed during the Betancur presidency (1982–6). Carlos Pizarro Leongómez took over from Fayad. In May 1988 M–19 kidnapped leading Conservative politician Alvaro Gómez Hurtado. Held for 53 days, he was eventually released in return for national peace talks, in which the government declined to take part.
See also **America Batallion; ANAPO; National Guerrilla Coordinating Group**.

Machado, Gustavo: see **Venezuelan Communist Party**.

***Madres de la Plaza de Mayo*:** see **Mothers of the Plaza de Mayo**.

Maira, Luis: see **Christian Left**.

Mallet-Prévost, Sevro: see **Essequibo dispute**.

Mallet-Prévost memorandum: see **Essequibo dispute**.

Maluf, Paulo Salim: see **Democratic Social Party; Sarney**.

Mandujano, Manuel: see **Socialist Party of Chile**.

Manuel Rodríguez Patriotic Front (*Frente Patriótico Manuel Rodríguez*/FPMR)
Usually regarded as the armed wing of the Chilean Communist Party (PCCh), though it claims to be autonomous and does have links with other groups. PCCh members are formally required to leave the party before joining the guerrillas. Founded in 1983 with the aim of creating a nationwide military organisation to both lead and complement popular resistance and, by making the country ungovernable, cause the collapse of the Pinochet dictatorship, the FPMR is expected to disband once this is achieved, although its statements on this have been inconsistent. In mid-1987, disagreement over this issue contributed to a split in the organisation.

The FPMR is named after a hero of the resistance to Spanish colonial rule. Its activities range from armed propaganda to sabotage and assassination. In September 1986 25 members staged a machine-gun and rocket

attack on President Augusto Pinochet in which five of his bodyguards were killed. Shortly before this, the government had announced the discovery of over US$10m worth of arms and explosives hidden in underground caches, and the associated arrest of 21 alleged FPMR and communist militants.
See also **Communist Party of Chile**.

MAPU/*Movimiento de Acción Popular e Unificada* (Popular Action Movement)
A Chilean party, founded in 1969 by left-wing dissidents from the Christian Democrat Party (PDC), led by Jacques Chonchol, who were particularly unhappy with the party line on agrarian reform. It participated in the left-wing Popular Unity (UP) coalition from its formation in 1969 to the coup d'état of 1973, though Chonchol joined the Christian Left (IC) party (also part of UP) after its formation in 1971. MAPU had split into two factions before the coup: MAPU-Garretón (after its secretary general, Oscar Garretón) and Worker/Peasant MAPU (MAPU *Obrero-Campesino*/MAPU-OC), led by Marcelo Contreras as secretary general inside Chile. The former has been a mainstay of the Socialist Bloc since its formation as an opposition coalition in September 1983; while the latter split again, with one faction also joining the Socialist Bloc and the other joining the more radical, Communist-led Popular Democratic Movement (MDP). In 1985 the Socialist Bloc MAPU-OC merged with the Núñez faction of the Socialist Party (PS). Both remaining factions now belong to the United Left alliance.
See also **Christian Democrat Party** (Chile); **Popular Democratic Movement; Popular Unity; Socialist Bloc; United Left** (Chile).

Mariátegui, José Carlos: see **Communism**.

Marighela, Carlos
1911–69. A Brazilian left-wing activist and intellectual who broke with the Communist Party in the 1960s and set about developing armed opposition to the military regime. Born in Bahía, he joined the PCB in the late 1920s, and remained inside the party until 1967. In 1945 he was elected federal deputy for Bahía, and represented the PCB in Congress until the party was banned in 1947. Based mainly in São Paulo, he became editor of the party journal *Problemas*. In 1953–4 he spent a year in the People's Republic of China. Marighela was initially associated with the 'Arruda' group inside the party (named after Diogenes Arruda Camara) which supported the election of Luis Carlos Prestes as secretary-general. But after the 1964 coup he and some others went on to form an internal tendency calling for a more aggressive political strategy known as the 'Bahía group'. In May 1964 Marighela was shot and seriously wounded by the security forces. The party's official line of stressing the 'bourgeois revolution' and thus seeking to associate itself in a subordinate role with business and middle-class opposition to the regime provoked growing internal dissatisfaction.

Marighela was expelled from the party in December 1967. He described the party's belief that the Brazilian bourgeoisie was the moving force of the revolution as 'the sheerest historical fatalism . . . denying the people all initiative and making them the plaything of events'. Outside the party Marighela became leader of the ALN (Action for National Liberation) guerrilla group. His *Handbook of Urban Guerrilla Warfare* described the theory and practice of armed revolutionary action. He died in a police ambush in São Paulo on 4 November 1969.

Marino Ospina, Iván: see **M–19**.

Marquetalia

An 'autonomous guerrilla republic' in southern Tolima department, Colombia, 1949–64. Originally set up as 'Gaitania' at the beginning of the period known as '*la violencia*' by Fermin Charry Rincón (aka '*Charro Negro*', d. 1960) and later led by Manuel Marulanda (aka '*Tiro Fijo*'). It was the largest of several such peasant 'republics' set up during this period, most of which were brought back under government control by military action in 1964–5.

See also **Revolutionary Armed Forces of Colombia; *violencia, la***.

Márquez, Pompeyo: see **Movement towards Socialism**.

Márquez Bustillos, Dr Victorino: see **Gómez, Gen. Juan Vicente**.

Martín, Américo: see **FLN/FALN; Generation of 1958** (Venezuela); **guerrilla insurgency** (Venezuela); **Movement of the Revolutionary Left (MIR)** (Venezuela).

Martínez, Pablo: see **Authentic Radical Liberal Party**.

Martínez de Hoz, José

b. 1926. A businessman from a wealthy Argentine family, Martínez de Hoz served as economy minister under the Argentine Revolution and Process of National Reorganisation (PRN) military regimes. Educated at Eton and at university in the United States, he was economy minister briefly during the military regime in the late 1960s, and again during the presidency of Gen. Jorge Rafael Videla from 1976 to early 1981. His efforts to reduce inflation and open up Argentina to the international economy were initially praised by foreign bankers and orthodox economists. But he was bitterly criticised for his policy of overvaluing the peso and allowing high domestic interest rates, which led to widespread bankruptcies in industry while encouraging financial speculation. Martínez de Hoz's opponents accused him of deliberately setting out to 'de-industrialise' the country, forcing a return to its role as a primary commodity exporter.

His period in office was also one of a massive inflow of foreign loans, which increased the country's indebtedness. In 1980, the year before he stepped down, there was a spate of domestic bank failures; this was followed in 1981 by a new inflationary surge and in 1982 by a foreign debt crisis. Nevertheless Martínez de Hoz continued to justify his policies thereafter. His opponents variously described him as a 'Chicago boy'

(after the Chicago school of monetarist economics) or a representative of the 'financial motherland' (*patria financiera*), the name used for finance capital. See also **Liberals** (Argentina); **Process of National Reorganisation**.

Martínez de Perón, María Estela: see **Perón, Isabel**.

Marulanda Vélez, Manuel: see **Communist Party of Colombia; Marquetalia; Revolutionary Armed Forces of Colombia**.

Marxist-Leninist Nuclei: see **Shining Path**.

Marxist-Leninist Revolutionary Vanguard (VRPM): see **Shining Path**.

massacre of the valley: see **Bánzer Suárez**.

Massera, Adm. Emilio

b. 1926. Argentine navy commander and member of the ruling junta (1976–9) during the Process of National Reorganisation government; he was involved in 'dirty war' human rights violations and in a number of political scandals. Under his orders, the Navy Mechanical School was used as a torture centre. Massera retired from active service in 1979, but retained political ambitions, founding the *Partido Democracia Social* which sought a neo-Peronist political line; its leader was intensely critical of the economic policies that had been pursued by José Martínez de Hoz (economy minister during the period of Massera's membership of the junta). But in this period a series of revelations damaged the admiral's political image beyond repair. It was revealed that he had been a member of the *Propaganda Due* Italian secret masonic lodge. Put on trial by the civilian government of Dr Raúl Alfonsín, Massera was found guilty on charges of homicide, illegal detention, and other human rights violations in December 1985. He was stripped of military rank and sentenced to life imprisonment.

See also **dirty war; Process of National Reorganisation; *Propaganda Due***.

Mateus Puerto, Oscar: see **Workers' Self-Defence Movement**.

Mauge, René: see **Broad Left Front**.

Meany, George: see **American Institute for Free Labor Development**.

Medellín (Second General Conference of Latin American Bishops)

This conference, held in Medellín, Colombia, in 1968 (and usually referred to as 'Medellín' or 'CELAM II'), has been described as the single most important milestone in the recent development of Latin American Catholicism. The deliberations of the Second Vatican Council (Vatican II, 1962–5) had led to the incorporation into the Church's social doctrine of analyses drawn from contemporary social science. This led to an emphasis on 'development' issues and the promotion of social justice, closely associated with the growth of the Christian Democrat movement in Latin America in the 1960s. Moreover, Vatican II's acceptance of the notion of historical change, summed up in the description of the Church

as a 'Pilgrim People of God', freed it from automatic association with conservative forces and allowed traditional concepts of hierarchy and authority to be challenged. The emphasis was shifted away from rank towards 'testimony' and 'witness' as sources of authority, and thus towards action and shared experience.

By the time of the Medellín conference, which was to apply Vatican II to Latin America, Catholics in the region had expanded significantly on these ideas, often adopting Marxist categories of analysis and even acting in concert with Marxists. A certain disillusionment with Christian Democracy had also become evident. Medellín itself came to controversial conclusions, especially on questions of violence and poverty. Pope Paul VI, addressing the conference, rejected violence as un-Christian, but the bishops introduced the concept of 'institutionalised violence' and the sin inherent in unjust structures. This opened the way to an acceptance by some of revolutionary violence as a legitimate response in certain circumstances. Notions of endurance and resignation were swept away, to be replaced by an active 'option for the poor', identified by some radicals with the Marxian proletariat. The promotion of awareness ('*conscientización*'), 'participation', and 'liberation' were also stressed.

Medellín gave impetus to the creation – throughout the continent, but particularly in Brazil, Chile, Paraguay, and Central America – of Christian 'base communities' (*comunidad/comunidade de base*). These lay groups, whose spread was partly due to the crisis in priestly vocations, encouraged self-help and were often seen as subversive by the authoritarian regimes which dominated Latin America in the 1970s. They also came to be seen as representing the 'popular Church', as distinct from the hierarchy. Divisions within the Church were sharpened by Medellín, and the Third General Conference, at Puebla, Mexico, in 1979, saw a sharp clash between left and right, with the latter seeking to reverse the trend. The final documents of Puebla reflect this conflict without resolving it.

See also **Christian Democracy; Latin American Bishops' Council; liberation theology**.

Medellín cartel: see **National Latin Movement**.

Medina, Fernando Abal: see **Montoneros**.

Medina Angarita, Gen. Isaías

1897–1953. President of Venezuela 1941–5. As a colonel, Medina Angarita had been secretary to Gen. Eleázar López Contreras, the minister for war who took over the presidency on the death of the dictator Gen. Juan Vicente Gómez in December 1935. While in reality a prolongation of the authoritarian regime that had preceded it, the Medina Angarita government sought cautious reforms. Opposition parties were allowed greater freedom and a pro-government party, the *Partido Democrático Venezolano* (PDV), was created. Among the reforms introduced by the government were a new Petroleum Code (1943) and income tax. As a result of the Soviet Union's alignment with the Allies in the Second

World War, Medina Angarita's PDV cooperated with the *Unión Popular* (the legal expression of the Venezuelan Communist Party, PCV) in the September 1944 municipal elections, a development sharply criticised by former President Gen. López Contreras. López Contreras and Medina Angarita became increasingly involved in a power struggle focused on the choice of the next president, due to take over in 1946. In the midst of this conflict, Medina Angarita was taken by surprise by the military revolt of 18 October 1945, backed by Democratic Action (AD), which toppled his government.
See also **Gómez, Gen. Juan Vicente; López Contreras**.

Méndez, Aparicio: see ***Proceso***.

Méndez Fleitas, Epifanio: see **Colorado Party** (Paraguay). **Popular Colorado Movement**.

Menem, Carlos Saúl
b. 1935. Chosen in Argentina as the Peronist party's presidential candidate for the 1989 elections. A provincial lawyer of Syrian descent, he joined the Peronist Youth in the 1950s. Under the 1973–6 Peronist administration he was elected governor of his home province of La Rioja, but was arrested during the 24 March 1976 military coup and held in jail until 1978, under house arrest until 1982. Re-elected governor of La Rioja in 1983, he was associated with the *renovadores* (reformists) within the party, although his own ambitions clashed with those of Antonio Cafiero, the leader of this sector. In September 1987 he was re-elected La Rioja governor for the third time with over 60% of the vote. In contrast to Cafiero's more modern, technocratic image, Menem adopted a flamboyant populist style reminiscent of Peronism's earlier era. Menem was backed by a heterogeneous alliance of interest groups including orthodox trade union leaders, the far right, and former Montonero guerrillas. In July 1987 he won the party's first direct primary elections with 53% of the vote. His campaign promises included wage increases, a foreign debt moratorium, and the introduction of the death penalty for drug traffickers.
See also **Montoneros; Peronism**.

Menéndez, Gen. Luciano Benjamín: see **Viola**.

Mercado, José Raquel: see **M–19**.

Michelini, Zélmar: see **Broad Front**.

Miguel, Benjamín: see **Christian Democrat Party**.

Miguel, Lorenzo: see **Army-Union Pact; General Confederation of Labour; Ubaldini, Saúl**.

***militantes*:** see **Colorado Party** (Paraguay).

military governments (Ecuador/1961–79)
The 1960s and 1970s in Ecuador were dominated by military regimes.

Between 1960 and 1984 no elected president succeeded in handing power to an elected successor. The process began with the 1961 overthrow of President Velasco Ibarra, who was replaced by his vice president, Carlos Julio Arosemena, with the assistance of the progressively-inclined officers of the air force. In 1963, Arosemena himself was replaced by a four-man military junta on the grounds that he was pro-communist and a drunkard. The junta modified the tax system and brought in a mild agrarian reform law. However, it was forced to resign after 33 months and party leaders were asked by the High Command to choose an interim president. They opted for Clemente Yeroví, a plantation owner and businessman who had been economy minister under President Galo Plaza. Elections were scheduled for July 1966, but they were cancelled and a constituent assembly was voted in later that year. Otto Arosemena Gómez, whose centrist supporters held the balance of power in the assembly, was able to secure election as provisional president with the backing of the right.

With the return to free elections in 1968 Velasco was once more voted in (though narrowly on this occasion), only to be ousted again in 1972. Facing a hostile Congress, he had ruled as a dictator since 1970 and, more importantly, was intending to hold free elections in 1972 which would almost certainly have brought victory to populist Assad Bucaram of the Concentration of Popular Forces (CFP), a figure unacceptable to the military. This time Velasco was replaced by a junta under Gen. Guillermo Rodríguez Lara, which proclaimed itself 'revolutionary and nationalist' though it was largely conservative in outlook. The Communist Party (PCE) was among the first groups to express support for the junta. However, this period did see the development of the Ecuadorean state oil company, Cepe, and the country's admission to the oil exporters' cartel, OPEC. The radical minister of natural resources, Capt. (later Adm.) Gustavo Jarrín, who was responsible for oil policy, was even considered by the PCE as a possible 'broad front' presidential candidate.

In 1976 a more right-wing junta under Adm. Alfredo Poveda Burbano took over, but public pressure eventually forced a return to civilian rule. From 1977 to 1979 there was intense and sometimes violent political activity, in the course of which one presidential candidate (Abdón Calderón Muñoz) was shot dead in November 1978 in mysterious circumstances. A referendum approved the drafting of a new constitution, which for the first time gave the vote to illiterates (over a quarter of the population) and provided for a run-off election if no presidential candidate obtained an overall majority. The military regime blocked the candidacies of a number of politicians of whom it disapproved, including former president Velasco and Assad Bucaram. Civilian rule was finally restored in August 1979 with the inauguration of President Jaime Roldós. See also **Bucaram; Velasco Ibarra**.

minifundio: see *latifundio*.

Miranda, Julio César de: see **National Party of Suriname**.

Miranda, Gen. Rogelio: see **Torres González**.

Miranda Pacheco, Mario: see **Socialist Party** (Bolivia).

Mitrione, Daniel: see **National Liberation Movement-Tupamaros**.

Moffitt, Ronni: see **Letelier case**.

MOIR: see **Independent and Revolutionary Workers' Movement**.

Molina, Gerardo: see **Democratic Left Unity**.

Molina, Sergio: see **National Agreement for a Transition to Full Democracy**.

momio

A pejorative term used in Chile for reactionary members of the bourgeoisie and upper middle class. Its literal translation is 'mummy'.

Monroe doctrine

A unilateral foreign policy statement by US President James Monroe in his 2 December 1823 State of the Union address (drafted by Secretary of State John Quincy Adams), whereby the US rejected the colonisation of the Americas by European powers, in exchange for non-interference by the US in the colonial affairs of the latter. Monroe stated that any attempt 'to extend their system to any portion of this hemisphere' would be considered 'dangerous to our peace and safety'.

The enunciation of the doctrine was prompted by European threats to intervene in order to suppress independence movements in the Spanish colonies. It has remained a major (though largely tacit) element in US foreign policy, despite modifications (such as Roosevelt's 'good neighbour' policy of the 1930s) to its interventionist overtones and the support ultimately given to the UK against Argentina in the 1982 Falklands/Malvinas war. It was restated and strengthened by President James K. Polk in 1845 over the attempt by Yucatán to secede from Mexico to Britain and Spain. The curb on British plans in Central America imposed by the Clayton-Bulwer Treaty of 1850 was one of the doctrine's most important practical applications. In 1895 Secretary of State Richard Olney coined the Olney Corollary to the doctrine, over a border dispute between Venezuela and British Guiana. He described the US as 'practically sovereign on this continent'.

The Roosevelt Corollary, set out by President Theodore Roosevelt in 1904, extended the doctrine to cover US intervention in Latin America in response to 'chronic wrongdoing, or an impotence which results in a general loosening of the ties of civilised society'. This justification ostensibly lay behind subsequent US 'police actions' in Haiti, the Dominican Republic, and Nicaragua. On 12 August 1912, Congress approved the Lodge Corollary, drafted by Sen. Henry Cabot Lodge, which further extended the doctrine to cover an Asian country (Japan) and a private company in that country (which had sought to acquire Magdalena Bay in Baja California, Mexico). The Roosevelt Corollary was repudiated in the 1928 Clark Memorandum. President Eisenhower affirmed the relevance of the doctrine over Soviet involvement with the Castro regime

in Cuba, but his successor John F. Kennedy never invoked it. However, Secretary of State George Schultz confirmed as recently as 1987 (apropos of Soviet support for Nicaragua) that the doctrine was still considered valid.
See also **dollar diplomacy; good neighbour policy**.

Montana Cuéllar, Diego: see **Communist Party of Colombia**.

Montanaro, Sabino: see **Colorado Party** (Paraguay).

Monteiro, Gen. Pedro Góes: see **Dutra**.

Montejo, Consuela de: see **Independent and Revolutionary Workers' Movement**.

Montenegro, Carlos: see **Revolutionary Nationalist Movement**.

***Montoneras Patria Libre*:** see **Free Nation Montoneras**.

Montoneros

An Argentine guerrilla group which emerged from within Peronism in the late 1960s, reaching its high point in political and military terms in 1970–6, before being crushed in the dirty war of 1976–9. The *montoneras* were groups of irregular peasant horsemen active in the war of independence and the regional conflicts in the first half of the nineteenth century. The name was then adopted by the essentially middle-class urban guerrillas of the 1970s. The leadership was drawn from student activists, Catholic intellectuals, and former right-wing extremists. Mario Firmenich and Fernando Abal Medina, the two main leaders, had been members of the Catholic Youth. Montonero ideology was a loose mixture of nationalism, Peronism, and socialism.

The movement's first armed action on 29 May 1970 was the kidnapping and (later) killing of Gen. Pedro Eugenio Aramburu. But the Montoneros also targeted what they considered to be reactionary elements within Peronism, especially the conservative trade union bureacracy. In August 1972 top Montonero leaders were among those who managed to escape Trelew prison, in an incident in which 16 prisoners were killed (allegedly after they had surrendered).

The Montoneros took part in the electoral campaign in 1973, and welcomed the inauguration of Dr Héctor Cámpora as president in May 1973. Their leaders held positions of influence in his administration. They also benefited from the Cámpora administration's amnesty for political offenders. But Cámpora's resignation to allow Gen. Perón himself to stand for the presidency coincided with an increasingly violent factional war. On 20 June 1973 right-wing Peronists opened fire on leftists during a mass rally at Ezeiza airport intended to welcome Gen. Perón on his return to the country. Although the death toll was never established, it is widely believed to have been over 100. The Montoneros hit back by assassinating the Peronist general-secretary of the General Confederation of Workers (CGT), José Rucci. Relations between Gen. Perón and the Montoneros steadily worsened. After Gen. Perón's death and replacement by his widow Isabel, Montonero attacks on police and army targets increased, as did abductions of businessmen to raise funds (a record US$60 million was received in ransom for the brothers Juan and Jorge Born in June 1975). In 1975 the Authentic Peronist Party (*Partido Peronista Auténtico*/PPA) was created under Montonero influence in an attempt to regroup the Peronist left, but was banned after nine months. In warfare with the security forces and the right-wing death squads/Peronist right, the Montoneros became increasingly isolated from the mass political movement.

After the 1976 military coup the organisation suffered heavy losses during the counter-insurgency onslaught. Top leaders were either killed or went into exile. The last major Montonero attacks took place in 1979. By 1980 splits had emerged among exiled Montonero leaders. After the return to civilian rule Mario Firmenich was extradited in 1985 from Brazil to stand trial in Argentina, and was sentenced to life imprisonment in 1987.

See also **dirty war; People's Revolutionary Army; Peronism**.

MOPOCO: see **Popular Colorado Movement**.

Morales Bermúdez Cerruti, Gen. Francisco

b. 1921. President of Peru 1975–80. Born in Lima. Graduated from the Chorrillos military academy as a sub-lieutenant (engineering) 1943. Graduated from the Escuela Superior de Guerra and CAEM, 1967. A member of the so-called 'earthquake generation' of officers. Brigadier-general, 1968. Division general, 1972. A trained economist, Morales served as minister of finance and economy under President Fernando Belaúnde from March to May 1968, before returning to military duties as logistics director on the general staff. After the 1968 coup of Gen. Velasco Alvarado he was appointed army commander in 1969, and is said to have been the architect of the agrarian reform programme under Velasco's presidency, for part of which he served as economy minister.

Morales assumed the presidency in 1975, when Velasco became terminally ill and was removed in a 'palace coup'. He steered the country away from the radicalism of the Velasco era, while continuing to pay lip-service to some of its main themes. He cut public spending, downplayed the importance of the 'social property' sector of the economy, put a brake on the agrarian reform and eased restrictions on profit remittances by foreign companies. Progressives among the officer corps were removed from key positions. With the encouragement of the International Monetary Fund, Morales set about implementing an economic stabilisation policy which was highly deflationary, with drastic effects on wages, prices, and unemployment levels. A balance of payments crisis led him to seek IMF assistance in 1976. Mass protests were met with repression, and in 1976 a state of emergency was declared which was to last a year. Popular pressure eventually compelled him to offer a return to civilian rule, via the election of a constituent assembly in 1978 and parliamentary elections in 1980. He formally handed back power in July 1980 to the president whom Velasco had overthrown in 1968, Fernando Belaúnde of

Popular Action (AP). In 1985 Morales was the presidential candidate of the newly-founded Democratic Front of National Unity, but failed to make any impact, and retired from politics in 1986.
See also **Velasco Alvarado**.

Moreira Ostría, Gastón: see **Bolivian Socialist Falange**.

Morínigo, Gen. Higinio

b. 1897. Paraguayan military ruler who held power in the 1940s and led the government side in the 1947 civil war. In 1940, Morínigo, who had been serving as defence minister, was made president by a faction of the army and the Liberals, who thought he would be easily controlled. But the new president quickly established his own power base in the army and turned against his original Liberal backers. In this first stage of his rule he relied on pro-fascist military officers, and initiated a ruthless persecution of opponents. Morínigo nevertheless generated some real popular support, portraying himself as a down-to-earth man from the countryside and speaking Guaraní to the indian peasants. Following the Allied victory in World War II, he bowed to international pressure for liberalisation, inviting *Colorados* and *Febreristas* into a coalition government which was to call elections. Yet he was soon backing one faction of the *Colorados*, the *guionistas*, in a campaign of violent intimidation of the other parties.

In January 1947 the coalition collapsed; Morínigo declared a state of siege and police began arresting *Febreristas*, Communists, and Liberals. In March 1947 the *Febreristas* led a rebellion which received the backing of many army units in the Chaco. In the ensuing civil war Morínigo was eventually able to prevail, with the help of the Colorado militias. At the end of the civil war the government prepared elections, with Morínigo favouring the *guionista* leader, Natalicio González. Given the extent of the repression, González was elected unopposed in February 1948. It was rumoured, however, that Morínigo would retain considerable power, perhaps even becoming the new army commander under González. Unhappy with such a prospect, a coalition of army officers and ambitious *guionistas* deposed him in a bloodless coup on 3 June 1948.
See also **Colorado Party** (Paraguay); ***Febreristas***; **Paraguayan Civil War**.

Mothers of the Plaza de Mayo (*Madres de la Plaza de Mayo*)

Human rights group formed in Argentina by mothers of those 'disappeared' persons in the state's 'dirty war' against opponents of the Process of National Reorganisation military government. The group carried out its first public demonstration against repression in April 1977 when a small number of mothers marched around Plaza de Mayo (facing Casa Rosada, government house, in central Buenos Aires) wearing white headscarfs and demanding information on the fate of their relatives. Thereafter the white scarfs and the vigil in Plaza de Mayo every Thursday became trade-marks of the movement. The *Madres* were also known as *locas de la Plaza de Mayo* ('madwomen' in literal translation, but the term can also mean 'prostitutes' in Argentine slang); the term was used by officials in the regime in an attempt to ridicule and discredit the movement.

Members of the group suffered arrest and imprisonment, and in some cases were abducted and killed. In 1979 the related Grandmothers of the Plaza de Mayo was formed, playing a prominent role in trying to trace children of victims of the 'dirty war', some of whom had been secretly given away for adoption. After the advent of civilian rule, the *Madres* continued their Thursday demonstrations, and kept up the demand for investigations. They criticised the government of Raúl Alfonsín for not pursuing the investigations and the trials of military officers to the fullest possible extent. The *Madres* were particularly opposed to the 'due obedience' legislation of 1987 which had the effect of stopping many of the trials.

See also ***desparecidos*****; dirty war; Process of National Reorganisation**.

Mourão Filho, Gen. Olimpio: see **Coup of 1964** (Brazil).

Movement Against the Marxist Cancer (MCCM): see **death squad**.

Movement of Integration and Development (*Movimiento de Integración y Desarrollo*/MID)

An Argentine 'developmentalist' party which came into being in 1963 as a split from the Intransigent Radical Party (UCRI). The MID was identified with the policies of Arturo Frondizi, who had been president from 1958 until he was deposed by a coup in 1962. The party's name reflected the main plank in Frondizi's platform: integration (in other words the incorporation of the Peronists, disenfranchised after 1955) and development (taken to mean the rapid expansion of industry and particular sectors of the economy, such as oil).

Frondizi had long resented the support the People's Radical Party (UCRP) gave to the coup against him in 1962, and the MID had its revenge when it supported the 1966 coup against the UCRP. One of the peculiarities of MID has been its use of leftist, even Marxist, jargon and concepts, to pursue policies aimed at generating capitalist growth. The MID has also been seen by its critics as a party of the elite, more interested in exerting influence than in mass appeal. Despite this criticism, the MID has participated in most elections. In the two elections in 1973 the party joined the victorious FREJULI alliance, dominated by the Peronists. In October 1983 the MID stood alone, but obtained only 1.6% of the vote. Its presidential candidate, Rogelio Frigerio, had campaigned on a platform of increased industrialisation, lower interest rates, higher wages, and the encouragement of both domestic savings and foreign investment.

See also **Frondizi; Justicialist Liberation Front; Radical Party** (Argentina).

Movement of the National Left (MIN): see **Democratic and Popular Union**.

Movement of the Revolutionary Left (Bolivia) (*Movimiento de la Izquierda Revolucionaria*/MIR)
Emerged in the late 1960s out of the Christian Democrat (PDC) youth wing, as the Revolutionary Christian Democrat Party (PDCR). It took its present name in September 1971 when the PDCR merged with the Spartacus Revolutionary Movement (MRE) and individuals from the left of the Revolutionary Nationalist Movement (MNR). The MIR, which was formed in opposition to the right-wing coup of 1971, was initially radical Marxist in stance. Its goal was the creation of a politico-military organisation, but it never developed a military wing and was somewhat confused as to which sector was to play the vanguard role: this led by 1972 to the formation of two wings of the party. It had strong links with the Catholic Church (many members regarded themselves as Christian democrats) and was also closely linked in its early days with the National Liberation Army (ELN) and strongly supported by many students. It took control of the national student body (CUB). Later, it abandoned much of its Marxist platform, losing many left-wing members in the process.

The MIR was persecuted (and remained clandestine) during the Bánzer regime (1971–8). It joined the short-lived Anti-imperialist Revolutionary Front (FRA) in 1973–4 and the 1978 centre-left Democratic and Popular Union (UDP) electoral alliance (with the MNRI, the PCB, and the MRTK). In the 1979 and 1980 elections, Jaime Paz Zamora, leader of the MIR, was vice-presidential running mate of the UDP's Hernán Siles Zuazo, but the armed forces intervened on both occasions. In January 1981 a meeting of MIR leaders was raided by the Special Security Service (SES) under interior minister Arce Gómez and eight leading party members were tortured and then shot dead. Later that year, in contrast to its previous stance on alliances with 'progressive military sectors', the party called for a 'national convergence' movement, including officers opposed to the García Meza dictatorship, which would overthrow the government. In 1982 the UDP, which had won the 1980 elections, was allowed to take office, with Paz Zamora as vice-president. Six '*miristas*' were appointed to the cabinet.

From January 1983 the party effectively withdrew all support from the Siles government, though Paz remained as vice-president until December 1984, when he resigned to campaign for the presidency. Paz won 8.8% of the vote in the 1985 elections, and the party gained 16 congressional seats. Its support for Víctor Paz Estenssoro helped ensure his victory over Hugo Bánzer in the presidential confirmation vote in Congress. Two dissident MIR groups stood against the main party: the MIR-Bolivia Libre (f. January 1985, formerly the centrist faction) and the MIR-Masas (f. 1984, the left wing), both of them as part of the United People's Front (FPU). Nowadays the supporters of the MIR itself (which is a consultative member of the Socialist International) belong primarily to the disaffected middle class of the cities, though the party is seeking to build its strength among the working class and peasantry as well as in the business

community. Its ranks were swelled in 1986–7 by disaffected members of Bánzer's ADN party, further alienating it from the left.
See also **Democratic and Popular Union**.

Movement of the Revolutionary Left (Chile) (*Movimiento de la Izquierda Revolucionaria*/MIR)
Founded in 1965 by a group led by Miguel Enríquez, most of whom were students at the University of Concepción who in 1963 had split from the Socialist Party (PSCh). In 1967 the MIR staged bank raids to accumulate funds and began political work in shanty towns outside Santiago. Some militants went to Cuba for training. It remained an urban guerrilla group during the Frei presidency (1964–70), refusing to participate in electoral campaigns, and remained outside the left-wing Popular Unity (UP) coalition which took office in 1970. The MIR then adopted a stance of 'critical support' towards the UP, while pursuing a popular mobilisation policy which included seizures of land and factories, often in alliance with the left of President Salvador Allende's own PS. Allende (who legalised the MIR and pardoned jailed members) held both private and public talks with the movement. His nephew, Andrés Pascal Allende (now secretary general of the MIR), was among its leaders.

In the March 1973 elections the MIR offered public support to the PSCh, whose majority had moved closer to its position. After the attempted coup ('*tancazo*') of 29 June 1973 the movement went underground to prepare for confrontation with the armed forces. It has participated in armed resistance during and since the overthrow of Allende. In December 1973 it signed a declaration in Rome with all UP parties, establishing a broad Anti-fascist Front. In February 1974 it published a statement that only armed struggle would end the Pinochet regime, and announced an alliance with the ERP guerrillas of Argentina. It lost most of its central committee, including Miguel Enríquez, in military actions, and in November 1975 Andrés Pascal Allende sought asylum in the Costa Rica embassy, later spending several years in Cuba before returning clandestinely to Chile.

In recent years the MIR has placed more emphasis on mass political work, while continuing sporadic military actions. It joined the Popular Democratic Movement (MDP) opposition coalition and later the broader United Left (IU) alliance. It announced the formation of the Armed Forces of Popular Resistance (FARP) in November 1984. The MIR favours the establishment of a single revolutionary party by all left-wing forces. In 1987 it held a party congress inside Chile, at which it split in two, with the bulk of the membership following a minority leadership faction under Nelson Gutiérrez.
See also **United Left** (Chile).

Movement of the Revolutionary Left (Peru) (*Movimiento de la Izquierda Revolucionaria*/MIR)

Founded in 1959 as Rebel APRA (*APRA Rebelde*), a breakaway from the APRA party led by Luis de la Puente Uceda (d. 1965), who had been expelled from APRA for questioning coexistence ('*convivencia*')

with right-wing forces. The new party took the MIR name in conscious imitation of Democratic Action (AD) dissidents in Venezuela. It called for a general amnesty and thorough agrarian reform, but convinced of impotence of electoral politics, sought to give armed support to the radical peasant movement. It joined the Trotskyist-controlled Revolutionary Left Front (FIR) in 1962, but left almost immediately for fear of jeopardising its relations with the Communist Party (PCP). In 1965 de la Puente embarked on a clandestine struggle, and with other rural leaders established three guerrilla *focos*, beginning in the mountains near Río Andamarca. By early 1966 all had been crushed by the army.

The MIR survived as a political movement, but split into factions - at one time as many as eight. In 1978, MIR–5 (consisting of five of these which had merged again) joined the Revolutionary Vanguard in the Popular Democratic Unity (UDP) alliance. MIR-Peru, led by a survivor of the 1960s guerrilla, Dr Gonzalo Fernández Gasco, belongs to the Union of the Revolutionary Left (UNIR). Another group, MIR-Militant (*MIR-El Militante* – also in the UDP), was formed by dissident members of the Revolutionary Socialist Party (PSR) who favoured armed struggle, and subsequently joined up with another PSR splinter, the PSR–Marxist Leninist, both of which in the early 1980s backed Maoist guerrillas known as the Unified Marxist–Leninist Communist Committee (CCUML). A faction known as MIR-FUI joined the United Left Front (FUI).
See also **APRA**.

Movement of the Revolutionary Left (Venezuela) (*Movimiento de la Izquierda Revolucionaria*/MIR)

A leftist political movement set up in May 1960 as a breakaway from the Democratic Action (AD) party, then in government. The new party was led by Domingo Alberto Rangel and Américo Martín. Both men had been critical of President Rómulo Betancourt's centre-right policies in general, and of the terms sought by AD in a new wages contract for workers employed by foreign oil companies in particular. The MIR was inspired by the Cuban revolution and defined itself as a revolutionary party. But despite its allegiance to Marxism–Leninism, it remained ideologically flexible. By October 1960 some of its members were being arrested on charges of subversion. In 1962–4 it took up armed struggle in rural areas, participating in the formation of the FALN. But after the failure of the guerrilla experiment, top MIR leaders opted for a return to legal politics. Banned in 1962, the party was allowed to take up legal activities again in 1969, as part of President Rafael Caldera's pacification programme.

In the 1973 presidential elections the MIR supported the Movement towards Socialism (MAS) and obtained one seat in the Chamber of Deputies. In 1978 the MIR presented its own candidate, Américo Martín, who obtained under 1% of the total vote; but it increased its representation in the Chamber of Deputies to four seats. Américo Martín subsequently led a breakaway group from the party into the *Vanguardia*

Unitaria coalition. In the 1983 elections the MIR again supported the MAS candidate, gaining two seats in the Chamber of Deputies.
See also **Democratic Action; FLN/FALN; Movement towards Socialism**.

Movement towards Socialism (*Movimiento al Socialismo*/MAS)
A Venezuelan leftist party which came into being in January 1971 as a result of a major split in the Communist Party (PCV). Teodoro Pétkoff and other PCV members had become increasingly critical of the party line. Pétkoff's books, criticising the Soviet invasion of Czechoslovakia in 1968 and proposing a peculiarly Venezuelan form of socialism, were condemned by the PCV Central Committee; he was described as an 'adventurer' who 'denies the role of the party, using subjective and mistaken analyses'. The issue came to a head when 21 of the 68 members of the Central Committee, including Pétkoff and Pompeyo Márquez, broke ranks to convene a separate 4th party congress; on 23 January 1971 they founded a new party, the MAS. The party has been called 'Eurocommunist'; in reality it is committed to 'elaborating a Venezuelan theory for a Venezuelan revolution'. In the December 1973 elections the MAS candidate, José Vicente Rangel, came fourth with 4.2% of the vote.

In December 1978 Rangel again stood as the MAS candidate, coming third with 5.1% of the vote; the party improved its congressional vote and made further gains in municipal elections. But the MAS suffered a serious split in the run up to the December 1983 elections. While Pétkoff argued that the party should again fight the elections alone, Rangel sought a common front on the left, taking his faction first into the *Coordinadora Nacional de Izquierda* coalition and then into the *Vanguardia Unitaria*; it was this group which finally took part in the *Nueva Alternativa* front, which presented Rangel as its presidential candidate. Pétkoff, standing as the MAS candidate, obtained 4.2% of the vote (more than Rangel's 3.3%); in the congressional elections his party secured 5.8%, giving it 10 seats in the Chamber and two in the Senate.
See also **Venezuelan Communist Party**.

Movement of Workers, Students and Peasants (*Movimiento de Obreros, Estudiantes y Campesinos*/MOEC)
A student-based, far-left organisation founded in Bogotá, Colombia, in January 1960, originally to protest an increase in urban transport fares. MOEC, which favoured armed insurrection and urban terrorism, was led by student leader Antonio Larrota until his murder in May 1961 brought to an end a brief guerrilla campaign (one of several attempted by the movement) in Valle del Cauca. His successor, Federico Arango, was later also killed. In 1965 MOEC initially supported, but later distanced itself from, Camilo Torres' United Front, which it considered insufficiently committed to a Leninist strategy. It subsequently merged with the pro-Chinese Colombian Communist Party (Marxist–Leninist) (PCC–ML) and gave birth to the People's Liberation Army (EPL). Fabio Vásquez Castaño, who founded the National Liberation Army (ELN), also emerged from MOEC.

See also **Communist Party of Colombia Marxist–Leninist; Independent and Revolutionary Workers' Movement; National Liberation Army** (Colombia); **People's Liberation Army; Torres Restrepo**.

Movimiento de Rocha: see **Blanco Party; Ferreira Aldunate**.

movimiento generacional**:** see **Bolivian governments post-Bánzer**.

MR–8 (8 October Revolutionary Movement)
One of the Brazilian guerrilla groups active in the late 1960s/early 1970s. It took its name from the date of the death of Ernesto 'Che' Guevara in Bolivia in 1967. Its members were responsible for the kidnapping of the US ambassador to Brazil, C. Burke Elbrick, for three days in September 1969. He was released after the government conceded MR–8's demand that 15 political prisoners be freed into exile. Imprisoned members of MR–8 were among 70 released into exile in January 1971 in exchange for the Swiss ambassador, who had been kidnapped by another guerrilla group, Action for National Liberation (ALN). One former MR–8 member, Fernando Gabeira, was among those who returned after the 1979 amnesty; he became a member of the Green Party (*Partido Verde* – PV) and stood as a candidate for governor of Rio de Janeiro in November 1986, taking third place.
See also **guerrilla movements** (Brazil).

MR–26 (26 July Revolutionary Movement): see **guerrilla movements** (Brazil).

Multipartidaria**:** see **Christian Democrat Party** (Chile).

Natale, Remo di: see **Christian Democrat Party** (Bolivia).

National Accord (*Acuerdo Nacional*)
A coalition, formed in 1979, of four Paraguayan parties opposed to Gen. Stroessner's regime. The members are the Popular Colorado Movement (MOPOCO), the Christian Democrats (PDC), the Authentic Radical Liberals (PLRA), and the *Febreristas* (PRF). Of the four, only the PRF is legally recognised by the Paraguayan authorities. The *Acuerdo* has generally called for a boycott of elections held under the Stroessner regime. In its programme launched in August 1984 it called for the lifting of the state of siege, the release of all political prisoners, measures to defend human rights, the abolition of repressive laws, freedom of expression, an independent judiciary, and new legislation covering the conduct of elections and the role of political parties. The *Acuerdo* has a collective leadership, composed of the leaders of its four constituent parties.
See also **Authentic Radical Liberal; Christian Democratic Party** (Paraguay); **Febreristas; Popular Colorado Movement; Stroessner**.

National Action (AN): see **National Party** (Chile).

National Action Movement (MAN): see **Fatherland and Freedom**.

National Advance (*Avanzada Nacional*): see **Fatherland and Freedom**.

National Agreement for a Transition to Full Democracy
A document signed by a large number of Chilean opposition leaders in August 1983 and sponsored by the Archbishop of Santiago, Cardinal Juan Francisco Fresno; Fernando Leniz, former economy minister under Gen. Pinochet; and Juan Zavala, president of the Christian Businessmen's Association. The Agreement called for the restoration of full constitutional rights, the creation of an electoral register, an end to the ban on political activity, free elections for public office and a referendum to legitimise its proposals. The 21 signatories were from the following groups: National Party (PN); National Union (UN) party; Democratic Alliance (AD, comprising Christian Democrat Party/PDC, Radical Party/PR, Social Democrat Party/PSD, Republican Right/DR, Popular Socialist Union/USOPO, Socialist Party/PS-Briones, and Liberal

Movement/ML); and Socialist Party/PS-Mandujano. The proposals were also supported by the Socialist Bloc coalition (comprising the United Popular Action Movement/MAPU and the Christian Left/IC as well as the PS-Briones) and by the Social Democrat Movement/MSD, the Radical Union, and the National Action Movement/MAN.

Parties of the left grouped in the Communist-led Popular Democratic Movement (MDP) eventually decided not to sign the Agreement, while those loyal to the government rejected it out of hand. The left objected to its failure to condemn the 1980 constitution, to call for the resignation of Gen. Pinochet, and to set time limits for its demands. (Some also opposed the terms on which human rights cases would be dealt with and the constitutional proposals for the economy.) Pinochet himself refused to consider the document, although some members of the ruling junta appeared less anxious to reject it, and Air Force representative Gen. Matthei openly welcomed it, fuelling speculation over possible splits in the government. The United States and other Western nations, along with sectors of the European social democrat movement, welcomed it as a basis for a peaceful transition to democracy. In September 1986, in an attempt to attract the left to the Agreement, it was modified in a document entitled 'Bases of Support for the Democratic Regime: an Extension of the National Agreement'. This was a reflection of the popular pressure generated by the National Civic Assembly. In the following month the coordinator of the Agreement, Sergio Molina, proposed the nomination of an opposition candidate for the 1988 elections. This was rejected as 'premature' by the PDC.
See also **National Civic Assembly**.

National and Popular Front: see ***Azules* and *Colorados;* Intransigent Party.**

National Base Coordinating Group (CNB): see **M–19**.

National Civic Assembly (*Asamblea Nacional de la Civilidad*)
An opposition body in Chile, launched in April 1986, comprising 22 of the country's main labour, professional, and community organisations, including doctors, lawyers, and teachers, student and shanty-town groups, and owners of lorries and small businesses. The Assembly's underlying political aim was to provide a framework for a more stable relationship between the Christian Democrats (PDC) and the Communists (PCCh). It presented the Pinochet government with a series of demands, summarised in a 50-point document entitled '*La Demanda de Chile*' which called for a democratically approved constitution and social and economic reforms. When the junta did not respond by the deadline of 31 May, the Assembly organised a two-day general strike in July 1986 as 'a warning', as well as calling for non-payment of bills and a boycott of companies sponsoring news programmes on state television. The stoppage, which was widely observed, met with severe repression. Among the eight dead was a student from Washington DC, Rodrigo Rojas, burned alive by troops in an incident which created an international scandal. 14 Assembly

leaders were jailed for a month on state security charges for having called the strike. The Assembly was subsequently eclipsed by disagreements between the Christian Democrats (PDC) and the Communists (PCCh), though there were attempts to revive it.
See also **'*quemados*' case**.

National Civic Democratic Movement (MCDN): see **Plaza Lasso**.

National Commission on the Disappearance of Persons (Conadep): see **dirty war**.

National Confederation of Workers (CNT) (Peru): see **Democratic Convergence**.

National Democratic Front (FDN): see **Ecuadorean Socialist Party; Plaza Lasso**.

National Democratic Party (PADENA) (Chile): see **Communist Party of Chile**.

National Democratic Party (Suriname): see **Bouterse**.

National Democratic Party (PDN) (Venezuela): see **Democratic Action; Leoni, Raúl**.

National Falange: see **Christian Democrat Party** (Chile).

National Front (*Frente Nacional*)
A pact between the Colombian Liberal (PL) and Conservative (PC) parties, forged in 1958, under which the two would alternate in the presidency and share public appointments equally between them. (Similar pacts had been a feature of Colombian history.) Conceived as a means of ending the dictatorship of Gen. Gustavo Rojas Pinilla, it was the outcome of a series of agreements, later formalised as statutes and approved by referendum on 1 December 1957. Originally intended to run for 16 years (four presidential terms), its influence was to last until 1982, when Belisario Betancur formed the first modern, single-party government. For most of this period, successive governments ruled under state of siege, with many constitutional guarantees suspended. The pact is generally felt to have benefited the PC more than the PL. It met widespread opposition from political groups excluded from the pact, as well as from the Liberal Revolutionary Movement (MLR) within the PL. One of its most noticeable effects was to reduce voter participation to between 30% and 40% in most elections.
See also **Liberal Party** (Colombia); **Rojas Pinilla; Social Conservative Party**.

National Front (Peru): see **APRA**.

National Front of the People: see **Allende Gossens**.

National Guerrilla Coordinating Group (*Coordinadora Nacional Guerrillera*/CNG)

Founded in Colombia in October 1985 by the 19 April Movement (M–19), the Ricardo Franco Front (made up of dissidents from the FARC), and the indian-based Quintín Lame Movement, by early 1986 the CNG had expanded to include the National Liberation Army (ELN), the People's Liberation Army (EPL), the Free Nation Movement (*Patria Libre*), and the Revolutionary Workers' Party (PRT). The Ricardo Franco Front was 'irrevocably' expelled, however, in January that year after its leaders admitted executing 164 alleged 'infiltrators'. The CNG called for electoral abstention in 1986 and carried out armed actions during the March and May elections. In August it rejected peace talks with the Barco government and stepped up its military campaign.

In July 1987 it held preliminary talks with the Revolutionary Armed Forces of Colombia (FARC) on a plan to unite all the country's guerrilla groups, and this appeared to have been achieved in October that year, when a communique signed by the FARC, M–19, the PRT, the EPL, Quintín Lame, and the Camilista Union (for the ELN) announced the formation of the Simón Bolívar Guerrilla Coordinating Group. It was estimated that if the plan to unite the guerrilla armies were successful it would involve 60 fronts and some 30,000 combatants, but many observers were doubtful that ideological differences could be overcome. In August 1988 the FARC and members of the Coordinating Group agreed to respond jointly to President Barco's amnesty offer.

See also **member organisations; Revolutionary Armed Forces of Colombia**.

National Integration Party (PADIN): see **Democratic Convergence; United Left (Peru)**.

Nationalist Democratic Action (*Acción Democrática Nacionalista*/ADN)

A Bolivian political party, founded in 1979 as a vehicle for ex-President Hugo Bánzer and the interests of the Santa Cruz region. The ADN rapidly became the main right-wing political force, taking over much of the constituency of the Bolivian Socialist Falange (FSB) among the urban middle classes. It polled between 15% and 17% in 1979 and 1980, expanding from Bánzer's Santa Cruz power-base to embrace some peasant and small business sectors. It initially backed the García Meza coup of 1980, but withdrew its support in 1981.

Its platform for the 1985 elections included: curbing union power; abolishing worker co-management of the mining corporation Comibol and dividing it into profitable units; reversing Andean Pact restrictions on foreign investment, and legalising cocaine exports. Bánzer won more than 28% of the vote in the 1985 elections, narrowly beating Víctor Paz Estenssoro, and the ADN took 51 congressional seats. However, Congress confirmed Paz as president under the terms of the constitution and he went on to outflank the ADN on the right. Bánzer was persuaded by the presidents of Argentina, Uruguay, and Colombia to accept his defeat, and a 'Pact for Democracy' was agreed between the ADN and Paz Estenssoro's MNR[H] on 16 October 1985. Despite subsequent rows

over such issues as armed forces promotions, the pact survived, and the ADN accepted cabinet posts in 1986. Its long-term plan was to reduce the country's legal political parties to the three biggest (MNR[H], ADN, and MIR). A split occurred in 1986 when Bánzer''s former right-hand man, Eudoro Galindo, who opposed the pact, was expelled and went on to form his own, extreme right party, the Nationalist Democratic Front (FDN), whose main power base is in Cochabamba. A number of ADN deputies left to join the new party, and Galindo spoke of reviving the congressional inquiry initiated by the Socialist Party (PS–1) in 1979 into Bánzer's activities in government.
See also **Bánzer Suárez; Bolivian Socialist Falange**.

Nationalist Democratic Front (FDN): see **Nationalist Democratic Action**.

Nationalist Democratic Union (*União Democrática Nacionalista*/UDN)
A conservative Brazilian political coalition, originally formed to oppose President Getúlio Vargas; it played a key role in the 1964 military coup against President João Goulart. The coalition first made its appearance in April 1945 as a heterogeneous grouping of political figures who had fought President Vargas in the previous 15 years and lost. Its members were nevertheless able to play an important role in convincing army officers to withdraw their support from Vargas in October 1945, forcing his resignation. The UDN developed into an essentially conservative, upper-class body, radically opposed to reformist or redistributionist movements such as *Trabalhismo*, which it tended to equate with Communism. Another constant feature was its involvement in conspiracies against elected governments, which it described as necessary to protect democracy. Eduardo Gomes stood as UDN presidential candidate in the 1945 elections, taking second place with 34.7% of the vote after the victorious Eurico Dutra. In sympathy with Dutra's anti-communist stance, the UDN gained ministerial representation as a result of an agreement with his PSD party. But in the 1950 elections both these groups split the anti-Vargas vote between them. Gomes again came second, this time with 29.6%, with Vargas at the head of the PTB recovering the presidency.

The party used its influence to the utmost against the government in the August 1954 political crisis which culminated in the military's demand for the resignation of the president and Vargas' suicide. Throughout the 1950s and 1960s the UDN welcomed and adapted to the Cold War ideology. One sector of the party, typified by Carlos Lacerda, used this to justify repeated attempts to organise coups. These included trying to stop President-elect Juscelino Kubitschek taking office in 1955, and to stop Vice-president João Goulart doing the same after Janio Quadros' resignation in 1961. Although both these attempts failed, the UDN again played a decisive role in the March–April 1964 coup against Goulart, which ushered in 21 years of authoritarian military rule.
See also **Goulart; Lacerda; Vargas**.

Nationalist Popular Front (FPN): see **Bánzer Suárez**.

Nationalist Revolutionary Movement (MNR) (Brazil): see **guerrilla movements** (Brazil).

National Labour Front (FNT): see **Party of National Renovation (PARENA)**.

National Latin Movement (*Movimiento Latino Nacional*/MLN) (aka *Movimiento Cívico Latino Nacional*) An ultra-nationalist Colombian political movement with neo-fascist overtones, founded in 1982 by former senator Carlos Léhder Rivas, one of the key figures in the Medellín drugs cartel. The Medellín cartel, a group of four major traffickers, is held responsible for most of the illegal cocaine entering the US. The MLN's principal campaign was for the repeal of the extradition treaty between Colombia and the United States. It was dissolved on 4 October 1983, and Lehder himself was extradited in February 1987 to face trial and imprisonment in Florida on drugs charges.

National Left Coordinating Group (CNI): see **Movement towards Socialism**.

National Left Front (FIN): see **Bolivian governments post-Bánzer**.

National Left Movement (MNI): see **Bolivian Socialist Falange**.

National Liberation Army (Bolivia) (*Ejército de Liberación Nacional*/ELN)
A guerrilla movement founded in Cuba in 1966 by Ernesto 'Che' Guevara with the original aim of fomenting revolution in his native Argentina. Bolivia was chosen as the route for infiltration, with assistance from the Bolivian Communist Party (PCB), but Guevara then decided (against PCB advice) that conditions were more favourable for a guerrilla *foco* there than in Argentina. With the help of PCB members Inti and Coco Peredo, some 40 combatants (including some Cubans) were trained at the Ñancahuazú farm in Santa Cruz province. The first phase of operations lasted from March to October 1967, when Guevara was captured and killed by Bolivian army Rangers (assisted by US Special Forces). Only five ELN members (including Inti Peredo) escaped alive. The local population had been found to be largely hostile and jungle conditions very harsh. French Marxist philosopher Régis Debray, who had travelled with the ELN for a time and was captured in April 1967, was put on trial in September and sentenced to 30 years imprisonment. He was released by the Torres government after serving three years. Peredo tried to resurrect the ELN in 1969, but was killed by the military.

In July 1970 – after gathering support particularly among students – the ELN made a fresh attempt at rural operations with the Teoponte campaign in northern La Paz department under the command of a third Peredo brother, Osvaldo ('Chato'). After eight weeks, all but eight of the original 75 combatants were dead. The leaders were exiled to Chile (whence Peredo returned in 1971), and later operations were exclusively

n

urban. Nuclei remained in La Paz and Cochabamba, but the network was uncovered in 1972. Peredo lived in Cuba until a 1978 amnesty. The ELN was largely inactive during the period of Gen. Bánzer's dictatorship (1971–8), despite the February 1974 formation of a revolutionary coordinating body (JCR) by the ELN, the MIR (Chile), the ERP (Argentina) and the MLN/Tupamaros (Uruguay). Peredo was again arrested in August 1978. The current political heir to the ELN (though no longer *foquista* in outlook) is the Bolivian Revolutionary Workers' Party (PRTB), founded in 1972 as the political wing of the movement.
See also **Guevara de la Serna**.

National Liberation Army (Colombia) (*Ejército de Liberación Nacional*/ELN)
A pro-Cuban guerrilla group, founded in 1964 by a group of students led by Fabio Vásquez Castaño, a former bank worker and member of the Movement of Workers, Students, and Peasants, MOEC. It set up its operations in Santander department (north-east Colombia). Overtures to the established guerrillas of the FARC initially met with a cool response, and an attempt at merger in 1967 did not succeed. The ELN attracted international attention when revolutionary priest Camilo Torres joined its ranks in 1965. The group had hoped that Torres' urban organisation, the People's United Front, would complement its rural guerrilla actions, but the Front collapsed. Torres was to die in his first battle and the ELN began to decline in importance shortly afterwards.

The ELN broke up into warring factions after a major army offensive in 1973. Vásquez left the country, while fellow leader Ricardo Lara Parada was captured. Its strength has waxed and waned, but its activities have included the occasional spectacular blow such as the assassination of army inspector general Gen. Rincón Quiñones in 1975. In November 1983 it held the brother of President Betancur hostage for two weeks. The ELN rejected the ceasefire offer by Betancur in 1984, maintaining its objective of seizing power militarily, but several fronts belonging to the organisation accepted the amnesty. On 26 November 1985 (following the return, after a 10-year absence, of Vásquez) the group executed Lara Parada, who had resigned and later taken up the offer. At around the same time it joined the rejectionist National Guerrilla Coordinating Group (CNG). Now commanded by the Spanish-born former priest Manuel Pérez, the ELN has undergone a resurgence in recent years, becoming Colombia's most active guerrilla group. Estimated to have obtained up to $18m in ransoms and protection money from foreign oil companies, it carried out over 100 attacks on the main oil pipeline between 1985 and 1988, in support of its campaign for oil nationalisation. Its combatants are put at 600–1,000.
See also **Movement of Workers, Students and Peasants; National Guerrilla Coordinating Group; Revolutionary Armed Forces of Colombia; Torres Restrepo**.

National Liberation Front (FLIN): see **Bolivian Communist Party; Socialist Party** (Bolivia).

National Liberation Movement – Tupamaros (*Movimiento de Liberación Nacional – Tupamaros*/MLN-T)
A Uruguayan guerrilla movement which challenged successive governments in the 1960s and early 1970s before suffering military defeat at the hands of the security forces. Broadly speaking, the Tupamaros came into being as a result of the frustration with electoral politics felt within many strands of the left, and the example of the guerrilla victory in Cuba. Its first members, who began organising in 1962, included people with roots in socialist, communist, and anarchist traditions. There were also people from Catholic groups. Although the movement began to take shape as a result of union struggles by impoverished cane cutters from the north of the country (known as *peludos*) it was later to turn into an essentially urban guerrilla movement with many middle-class members.

MLN leaders such as Raúl Sendic, who had begun working with the cane cutters as a labour lawyer, reacted against what they described as the excessive theorising of the Uruguayan left, which was believed to be little more than an excuse for inaction. One of the popular early theories of the Tupamaros was that in the process of taking up arms to destroy the existing order they would gradually, through the dialectic of revolutionary action, develop an idea of what to put in its place. The first guerrilla actions included robberies and 'Robin Hood' style operations in which, for example, food was distributed to the poor. But following the increased social and political tensions caused by the economic crisis, particularly after 1968, the movement stepped up its activities. Against a background of student and worker unrest, the MLN carried out a series of kidnappings which brought it international attention.They included: the abduction of a US agronomist, Claude Fly; the abduction and killing of a US CIA agent, Daniel Mitrione, in 1970; and the abduction and later release of the British ambassador, Geoffrey Jackson (January–September 1971). Other diplomats and right-wing Uruguayan politicians were also taken and held in 'people's prisons'. Top MLN leaders managed on various occasions to break out from prison. Yet despite the movement's initial humiliation of the police, the growing involvement of the army and the use of generalised repression and the torture of guerrilla prisoners began to change the military balance.

By early 1972 the defection of a top MLN leader, Héctor Amodio Pérez, gave the security forces key information which was used to break up the organisation. Sendic and other leaders were captured later that year. Following the 1973 military coup, nine MLN leaders were held by the army as hostages, and threatened with death if guerrilla activities resumed. When civilian rule was restored in 1985, all imprisoned Tupamaros were released under the terms of a political amnesty. The MLN then reorganised, announcing that it was taking up non-violent politics, and obtained political party status.
See also ***autogolpe***; **Pacheco Areco;** ***Proceso***; **Sendic**.

National Opposition Union (UNO): see **ANAPO; Colombian Communist Party**.

National Party (Chile) (*Partido Nacional*/PN)
The original PN (f. 1851) merged into the newly-united Liberal Party (PL) in 1933. A second version, with close links to the upper ranks of the government bureacracy, existed briefly from 1956–8. The modern PN (f. 1966) dates from the merger of the United Conservative Party (PCU) and the PL, which had operated a de facto alliance since the 1930s, with the small National Action (*Acción Nacional*) party. In the 1970 election PN presidential candidate Jorge Alessandri won 34.9% of the vote, only 1.4% behind the victorious Salvador Allende of the Popular Unity (UP) coalition, whose ratification as president the PN refused to endorse. At this period the party was among those receiving covert funding from the US Central Intelligence Agency. Its leaders were landowners and industrialists, with strong support among the middle classes worried about the radical trend of Chilean politics. It strongly supported the military coup which overthrew Allende in 1973, after which it dissolved itself on the grounds that the Pinochet government (which many members had joined) represented its interests.

It re-emerged in 1983–4, by which time former PN members had formed the National Union Movement (MUN, later UN), which was to become more important than the PN. Another PN splinter became the National Unity Movement (MUN). The new National Party has had close contacts with the Christian Democrat-led Democratic Alliance, as well as with other right-wing parties, in an attempt to forge an opposition consensus, although it declined to join three parties of the right in forming the Party of National Renovation in early 1987. It signed the National Agreement for Transition to a Full Democracy in 1985. The PN rules out a pact with the Communist Party (PCCh), but has wavered over support for its banning. The election in 1987 of Patricio Phillips as party leader was expected to lead to a cooling of relations with the Christian Democrats. In 1988 the PN called for a vote against Pinochet in the October plebiscite, after its call for a civilian 'consensus candidate' was rejected.
See also **Alessandri Rodríguez; National Agreement for a Transition to Full Democracy; PARENA**.

National Party (Uruguay): see **Blanco Party**.

National Party of Suriname (*Nationale Partij Suriname*/NPS)
A conservative Surinamese political party largely representing the Creole (Afro-Surinamese) community. Founded in 1946 by G. J. C. van der Schroeff, it won most seats in the 1949 general election and named Julius Cesar de Miranda as premier. In 1950, F. H. R. Lim A Po became party chairman. After winning the 1951 election the NPS named J. A. E. Buiskool as premier. Johan Pengel became party leader in 1953 and formed an alliance with the country's other main party, the United Hindustani Party (VHP) of Jaggernath Lachmon. The NPS was defeated in the 1955 election, but won most seats in 1958 and governed in coalition with the VHP under NPS premier S. D. Emanuels. It won again in 1963 and Pengel became premier. After winning in 1967, Pengel broke with the

VHP, but strikes forced him to resign in 1969 and the party lost the election in the same year.

Henck Arron became party leader on Pengel's death in 1970 and led it to victory in the 1973 elections at the head of a four-party coalition which became the country's first post-independence government in 1975. Arron and the NPS won re-election in 1977 leading a reshuffled coalition and retained power until an army coup in February 1980, after which, along with all other parties, the NPS was banned. Arron was jailed for several months. The ban was lifted in 1985 and the party resumed activities, joining with the VHP and the country's third main party, the KTPI, in a Front for Democracy and Development. The NPS won 14 seats at the November 1987 elections to the national assembly, which elected Arron vice-president of the republic in January 1988. Arron was also named prime minister in a coalition government formed by the Front at the same time.

See also **Arron**.

National Patriotic Front (FPN): see **Vargas Pazzos rebellion**.

National Popular Front: see **Peronism**.

National Progressive Party: see **Communist Party of Chile**.

National Reconstruction Front (*Frente de Reconstrucción Nacional*/FRN)

A coalition of Ecuadorean parties representing traditional conservative and liberal currents which came together to support the successful candidacy of León Febres Cordero in the 1984 presidential elections. Apart from Febres Cordero's own Social Christian Party (PSC), members were: the Conservative Party (PC), the Radical Liberals (PLR), the Revolutionary Nationalists (PNR), the Democratic Institutionalist Coalition (CID, now the National Republican Coalition, CNR), the National Velasquista Party (PNV), and the Ecuadorean Popular Revolutionary Alliance (APRE). Fusion into one party was at one point considered, but the idea did not prosper.The FRN initially held a minority of seats in Congress, but by June 1985 it had acquired a slim majority. This was achieved with the support of the Concentration of Popular Forces (CFP) and the Radical Alfarist Front (FRA), and through defections from the opposition Progressive Front (FP). It was lost in the mid-term elections of 1986, when the combined FRN parties won only 19 seats.

See also **Febres Cordero Rivadeneiro; member parties**.

National Renovating Alliance (*Aliança Renovadora Nacional*/ARENA)

A pro-government party created by the Brazilian military in 1965, ARENA held a majority in congress for its entire lifetime, up to its replacement by the PDS in 1979. ARENA came into being as a result of Institutional Act 2 of November 1965, which abolished all existing political parties. It quickly attracted almost all the former Nationalist Democratic Union (UDN) congressmen, most of the former Social

Democratic Party (PSD) members, and many from the smaller parties. The new party inherited and expanded an effective electoral machine, aided with government backing and a clientilist network in rural areas. The government also used other mechanisms to ensure that ARENA would have a built-in advantage over the opposition Brazilian Democratic Movement (MDB), such as banning certain MDB politicians or continually altering electoral regulations. ARENA proved to be a docile organisation, generally rubber-stamping military decisions. There were, however, some exceptions, such as when many ARENA congressmen protested at the introduction of Institutional Act 5 by the administration of Gen. Costa e Silva in 1968. ARENA ceased to exist as a result of the political reforms of 1979, which led to the creation of the Democratic Social Party (PDS) as the new ruling group.
See also **Democratic Social Party; Institutional Acts; Nationalist Democratic Union; Social Democratic Party** (Brazil).

National Republican Coalition (CNR): see **National Reconstruction Front**.

National Revolutionary Party: see ***tenentes***.

National Security doctrine

An authoritarian ideology much favoured by the military regimes of the 1960s and 1970s. Although subject to many variants, the main thrust of the doctrine was to cast the armed forces as the ultimate custodians of national objectives, empowered to use all the resources of the state against external threat and internal subversion. National objectives were themselves to be defined not by democratic debate but by the military 'science' of geopolitics. The doctrine assumed a world divided into two antagonistic power blocks. It was deeply influenced by US Cold War thinking, as taught in institutions such as the US-controlled School of the Americas in the Panama Canal Zone. National security doctrine assumed that international Communism was seeking to undermine Western societies from within, through subversive movements. It was therefore justified for the continent's armies to concentrate less on the defence of the frontiers and more on the 'enemy within'. The national security regimes repeatedly widened the definition of subversion until it became synonymous with almost all forms of opposition to military rule. The regimes were also characterised by systematic human rights violations, over-developed domestic intelligence services and the use of psychological warfare techniques. A high priority was placed on isolating 'subversive elements' from the mass of the population – by building strategic villages in the countryside or by using the techniques of extra-judicial killings and 'disappearances' in the cities. The doctrine also emphasised the need for economic growth to fend off subversion; it claimed that 'there can be no security without development and no development without security'.
See also ***desaparecidos*; dirty war**.

National Union of the Revolutionary Left (UNIR) (Bolivia): see **Socialist Party** (Bolivia).

National Union of the Revolutionary Left (UNIR) (Colombia): see **Gaitán**.

National Union of the Revolutionary Left (UNIR) (Peru): see **United Left** (Peru).

National Unity Government (GUN): see **Democratic and Popular Union.**

National Unity Movement (MUN): see **National Party** (Chile); **Party of National Renovation** (Chile).

National Velasquista Federation (FNV): see **Velasco Ibarra**.

National Velasquista Party (PNV): see **Velasco Ibarra**.

Natusch Busch, Col. Alberto: see **Bolivian governments post-Bánzer**.

Nazi Party (MNSC) (Chile): see **Ibáñez del Campo**.

Neves, Dr Tancredo de Almeida

1910–85. Brazilian politician and architect of the return to civilian rule in 1985. Although elected president, he fell ill only hours before he was due to take office on 15 March 1985, and was hospitalised until his death on 22 April 1985. Neves studied law and went into politics in 1934, when he was elected councillor in his home town. He was removed from office, and briefly imprisoned when President Getúlio Vargas imposed the authoritarian *Estado Nôvo* in 1937. When a democratic constitution was re-established in 1945, Neves became a leader of the conservative Social Democratic Party (PSD) in Minas Gerais. He was elected a PSD federal deputy in 1948. When Vargas returned to the presidency in 1950, Neves served as his justice minister, saying he was happy to work with his old opponent because this time he had been constitutionally elected.

Neves became Prime Minister in 1961–2 during the brief experiment with a parliamentary system under president João Goulart. After the 1964 military coup he refused to support the new regime, but remained in the moderate opposition sector within the newly formed Brazilian Democratic Movement (MDB). Following the liberalisation of the military-controlled two party system in 1979, Neves left the party (by now re-named PMDB) to create his own Popular Party (PP). He sought a PP–PMDB alliance in the November 1982 state elections but when the authorities banned alliances he dissolved the PP and re-joined the PMDB. He was elected governor of Minas Gerais for the PMDB, stepping down in August 1984 to campaign for the presidency.

Neves played a key role in mass mobilisations demanding direct presidential elections, but faced with government intransigence he finally decided to accept an indirect contest through the electoral college, promising if victorious to convene a constituent assembly and ensure constitutional reforms to guarantee direct elections for his successor. Neves was regarded as the founding father of the broad Democratic Alliance

coalition; he skilfully incorporated dissident factions from the government party and created a multi-class appeal. He was elected president on 15 January 1985 by 480 to 180 votes in the electoral college. He appointed a politically balanced ministerial team, and mapped out a policy of gradualist social, economic, and political reforms, together with a planned renegotiation of the foreign debt. His popularity was such that his untimely illness and death was perceived as a national tragedy–there were scenes of hysteria and mass mourning. His successor was Vice-president José Sarney, who re-affirmed Neves' commitment to constitutional rule and to the concept of an emerging 'New Republic'.
See also **Democratic Alliance; Sarney**.

New Democratic Left: see **Frei Montalva**.

New Liberalism (*Nuevo Liberalismo*)
A minority tendency within the Colombian Liberal Party (PL), led by Senator Luis Carlos Galán Sarmiento, with support from former President Dr Carlos Lleras Restrepo. Opposed to the two-party system and to the re-election of former presidents, but lacking a coherent programme and national organisation, the tendency emerged in the early 1980s and is strongest in urban areas. Galán was minister of education from 1970 to 1972 when in his late twenties. He split the PL in 1982, when he stood against its official candidate, Alfonso López Michelsen, and won nearly 11% of the vote, thus allowing the Conservative (PC) candidate, Belisario Betancur, to emerge victorious. Galán's followers were given several important posts in the Betancur administration, but after threatening to forge alliances with independents, dissident Liberals and Conservatives, the tendency was denied congressional posts by the PL leadership. Talks with the pro-communist Patriotic Union (UP) broke down in 1985. Galán's decision to stand again in 1986 caused a split in his own movement and after it polled poorly in the municipal and congressional elections of March that year he decided to pull out, despite his personal popularity. The tendency (which holds eight seats in the Senate and seven in the lower house) announced that it would continue to be active in local and congressional politics.
See also **Liberal Party** (Colombia).

Nixon's visit
The visit paid to Venezuela by the US Vice-president, Richard M. Nixon, in May 1958 led to widespread public disorders. He arrived in the country only four months after the fall of the dictatorship of Marcos Pérez Jiménez. On 10 May 1958 students at the Central University described Nixon as *persona non grata*, arguing that he represented 'a policy of supporting dictatorships which oppress the peoples of Latin America' and that his government had bestowed its highest decorations on Pérez Jiménez and granted the deposed dictator asylum. The motorcade bringing Nixon and other officials into Caracas on 13 May was surrounded by demonstrators, stoned, and spat upon. Unable to pay his respects at the tomb of Simón Bolívar because of the protesters, Nixon was forced

to suspend the official programme and take refuge in the US embassy. In Washington the Venezuelan ambassador was summoned and asked to guarantee the Vice-president's safety, while there were reports that US marines and paratroopers had been placed on alert. On 14 May, under heavy guard, Nixon was accompanied by the members of the governing junta to Maiquetia airport from where he left for Puerto Rico.

Non-Aligned Movement (NAM)

Founded in 1961 by emerging Third World nations with the aim of avoiding involvement in the east–west conflict, the movement comprises (1987) 100 sovereign states and two movements (the PLO and SWAPO), It has four basic principles: (1) peaceful coexistence; (2) non-participation in military pacts; (3) no bases for the superpowers; (4) support for national liberation struggles. Today it is most closely identified with the struggle for a New International Economic Order (NIEO), the principles of which were drawn up at the Algiers summit of 1973. They were based on the 'centre-periphery' analysis pioneered by leading Latin American economist Raul Prébisch. The NAM also maintains funds for agricultural development, the maintenance of buffer stocks of commodities, and the enhancement of food production. NAM is run by the 17-member Coordination (or 'Coordinating') Bureau of the Non-Aligned Countries (or 'Movement').

Cuba was a founding member, but remained alone among western hemisphere nations until 1970. In 1979, Havana hosted the 6th Non-Aligned Summit and took over the chairmanship of the organisation for the next three years. The Havana summit, which focused on the concept of non-alignment, was dominated by ideological disputes, notably over the desire of the Cubans to re-direct the movement towards the Soviet camp. The final declaration, however, stressed the 'authentic, independent, non-bloc' character of the NAM. Peru is due to host the 1989 summit.

Of the countries dealt with in this volume, the following are now members: Argentina; Bolivia; Colombia; Ecuador; Guyana; Peru; and Suriname. Venezuela has observer status. The Non-Aligned Movement opposes what it calls the 'colonial' status of the Falklands/Malvinas islands.

Nueva Alternativa

A Venezuelan left-wing electoral coalition formed in July 1982, *Nueva Alternativa* grouped 12 parties which, while retaining their separate identities, supported a single presidential candidate, Dr José Vicente Rangel. Rangel, who had earlier left the Movement Towards Socialism (MAS) in a dispute over electoral strategy, received 219,368 votes, or 3.3% of the total. One seat in the Chamber of Deputies, together with a number in the state legislatures and municipal councils, were won in the name of *Nueva Alternativa*. The main members of the coalition included: *Vanguardia Unitaria* (VU – Unity Vanguard) which had split from the Communist Party (PCV) in 1974; *Constancia Gremial* (Union Steadfastness), a leftist labour group; *Movimiento Patria Socialista* (MPS – Socialist Home-

land Movement), set up by dissident members of MAS; and *Movimiento Revolucionario Popular* (MRP – Popular Revolutionary Movement). Rangel's presidential campaign was also supported by the PCV, URD, MEP, and minor leftist groups such as *Causa R* and *Grupo de Acción Revolucionaria* (GAR – Revolutionary Action Group) although each of these was much more loosely associated with the coalition itself.
See also **Movement of the Revolutionary Left** (Venezuela)**; Movement towards Socialism; Venezuelan Communist Party**.

***Nueva Fuerza*:** see **People's Electoral Movement**.

Núñez, Ricardo: see **Socialist Party of Chile**.

Odría, Gen. Manuel: see **Haya de la Torre**.

Oil nationalisation (Venezuela)

The nationalisation of 16 foreign oil companies operating in Venezuela became law on 1 January 1976, under the administration of Carlos Andrés Pérez. After years of tough bargaining between successive governments and the foreign companies, the nationalisation had come to be regarded as largely inevitable by the private sector, and there was little concerted opposition to the measure. The 1973 OPEC oil price increase had strengthened the government's hand by generating windfall profits and affirming nationalist sentiment. Compensation of $1bn was paid to the head offices of the 16 companies involved. Fedecámaras, the Venezuelan private sector federation which in the past had acted as an ally of the foreign companies, raised no serious objections. From its inception the new state holding company *Petróleos de Venezuela* (Petroven, later also known as PDVSA) had to move to make up for the lack of investment by its predecessors, particularly in offshore drilling. Although the initial idea was to keep Petroven free from political intervention, in later years there was a series of tussles over its policies, often between a management seeking full decision-making autonomy and the ministry of energy and mines.
See also **Pérez, Carlos Andrés**.

Ojeda, Fabricio: see **FLN/FALN**.

Olaya Herrera, Enrique: see **Liberal Party** (Colombia).

Old Republic

The Brazilian political system dating from the fall of Emperor Pedro II in 1889 to 1930. The revolt against the Empire had been fuelled by the growth of São Paulo economic interests opposed to slavery and by the politicisation of the army following the 1865–70 war against Paraguay. The military were responsible for the 1889 coup, which declared a republic and installed Marshal Deodoro da Fonseca as president; but divisions between military factions placed the new system in civilian hands by 1893. The 1891 constitution vested considerable autonomy in the 20 states, allowing them wide taxation powers, and the right to keep their own military forces, distinct from the national army. The Chamber of deputies was chosen on the basis of a limited electorate: property-holding male citizens over 21.

The Old Republic was characterised by the elitist control exercised by landowning interests, wealthy economic groups linked to the coffee growers in São Paulo and cattle ranchers in Minas Gerais. The alternation of presidents from these two dominant states was known as a policy of 'coffee and milk' (*café com leite*). Politics were marked by electoral fraud and a clientilist system of control. There were frequent conflicts between states over the nomination of the president. The Old Republic was ended by a military coup in 1930 following the insistence of the outgoing President Washington Luis on appointing a successor who, like him, was from São Paulo. The coup was also in part a reaction to the local economic problems caused by the Great Depression.

Oliveira, Dante de: see ***diretas já***.

Olney Corollary: see **Monroe doctrine**.

Onganía, Gen. Juan Carlos

b. 1915. A key figure in the Argentine military during the political crises of the early 1960s who became leader of the Argentine Revolution military regime, and president during its first phase. Onganía was a prominent member of the legalist (*Azul*) military faction, which suffered an initial blow as a result of the August 1962 uprising by the rival (*Colorado*) group. But the situation was reversed when tanks under Onganía's command led a September 1962 uprising in the name of professionalism and the principle of the subordination of the military to the elected authorities. Onganía's forces crushed pockets of *Colorado* resistance. A new *Colorado* uprising led by navy units in April 1963 was also crushed when Onganía's tanks overran navy bases at Punta de Indio. The defeat of the *Colorados* removed obstacles to the July 1963 elections, although the newly-dominant military faction continued the electoral ban on the Peronists. Onganía was promoted to army commander, a post which he held for most of the 1963–6 Arturo Illia presidency.

Onganía was removed in November 1965 after disagreements with Illia, and despite his earlier commitment to constitutionalism he emerged as the leader of the 28 June 1966 *Revolución Argentina* coup. As president until June 1970 he led a repressive military regime, influenced by right-wing Catholics and corporatists in groups such as the Opus Dei. His opposition to political liberalisation and an apparent desire to perpetuate himself in power led to his removal by an army leadership committed to a new political opening (which eventually led to elections in 1973).
See also **Argentine Revolution; *Azules* and *Colorados*; *Cordobazo*; *gorilas*; Illia**.

Operation Birdcage: see **guerrilla movements** (Brazil).

Operation Pan America: see **Alliance for Progress**.

Organisation of American States (OAS)

The main inter-American regional organisation, designed to strengthen political, economic, and social ties and defend sovereignty, territorial integrity, and independence. Its origins lie in: (i) the First Congress of American States, convened by Simón Bolívar in Panama City in 1826, attended by Colombia, United Provinces of Central America, Peru, and Mexico; and (ii) the International Union of American Republics, set up in 1890, later re-named the Pan American Union (PAU). The 9th Inter-American Congress under the PAU framework in Bogotá set up the OAS in April 1948. The OAS charter was modified in 1970, establishing the General Assembly as the dominant body in the organisation, and replacing the Inter-American Conferences.

The main OAS bodies are the following: the General Assembly, which meets annually and operates on basis of one country – one vote; the consultative meeting of foreign ministers, which is convened to consider urgent problems; the Inter-American judicial committee; the Inter-American Commission on Human Rights; and the General Secretariat (based in Washington). In 1962 the OAS supported the USA in its demands for the removal of Soviet nuclear missiles sited in Cuba; and the organisation voted to suspend Cuban membership. In 1964 member states voted to impose sanctions against Cuba. Interventions in other regional political conflicts included: mediation in the US–Panama dispute of 1964; backing for an Inter-American Peace Force in the Dominican Republic in 1965; investigation of human rights violations and recommendation of a cease fire in the El Salvador–Honduras war of 1969; condemnation of the military coup in Bolivia in 1980; a call for a cease fire in the Peru–Ecuador border clashes of 1981; and a request to Britain and Argentina in 1982 to cease hostilities over the Falklands/Malvinas islands and negotiate a settlement, taking account of Argentina's 'rights of sovereignty' and the interests of the islanders. In November 1984 the General Assembly recognised the need to 'revitalise' the organisation.

General Secretary: João Clemente Baena Soares (Brazil – succeeded Alejandro Orfila of Argentina). Assistant general secretary: Val McComie (Barbados). Membership: Antigua and Barbuda, Argentina, Bahamas, Barbados, Bolivia, Brazil, Chile, Colombia, Costa Rica, Cuba (suspended), Dominica, Dominican Republic, Ecuador, El Salvador, Grenada, Guatemala, Haiti, Honduras, Jamaica, Mexico, Nicaragua, Panama, Paraguay, Peru, St Christopher and Nevis, St Lucia, St Vincent and the Grenadines, Suriname, Trinidad and Tobago, USA, Uruguay, Venezuela.

See also **South Atlantic War**.

Organising Committee for Independent Electoral Policy: see **COPEI**.

***Organización Revolucionaria Venezolana* (ORVE):** see **Betancourt**.

ORIT/Interamerican Regional Organization of Workers (*Organizacion Regional Interamericana de Trabajadores*)

A trade union international, founded in 1951 by the International Confederation of Free Trade Unions (ICFTU) as its western hemisphere branch, and with the specific aim of combating 'communist infiltration' in the labour movements of the region. It is headquartered in Mexico City, from where it coordinates anti-communist unions throughout the Americas (including the USA and Canada). Its sub-regional organisations include the Confederation of Central American Workers (CTCA) and the Caribbean Confederation of Labour (CCL).

Despite taking a stand in its early days against dictatorships of the right (e.g. that of Trujillo in the Dominican Republic), ORIT has been linked with US-backed coups against left-leaning governments, including those of Jacobo Arbenz (Guatemala, 1954), João Goulart (Brazil, 1964), and Cheddi Jagan (Guyana, 1964). There have been frequent accusations that it serves as a tool of US foreign policy and the CIA. The AFL-CIO of the US is by far the dominant organisation within ORIT (though it withdrew from the ICFTU in 1969), and other member organisations have expressed opposition to its close identification with US interests. Even the ICFTU had distanced itself in recent years from its affiliate. ORIT's Congress meets every four years (most recently in Mexico City in 1985). The organisation is run by a 22-member executive council and a 12-member executive committee. It has (1987) 33 full members and claims to represent around 32 million workers in 24 countries and territories.
See also **American Institute for Free Labor Development**.

Ortiz, Roberto: see **Infamous Decade**.

Ortiz Mena, Antonio: see **Inter-American Development Bank**.

Ospina Pérez, Mariano: see **Social Conservative Party**.

Ospina Rodríguez, Mariano: see **Social Conservative Party**.

Ossio, Luis: see **Christian Democrat Party** (Bolivia).

Ovando Candia, Gen. Alfredo: see **Torres González**.

P

Pacheco Areco, Jorge

b. 1920. President of Uruguay 1967–72. A right-wing Colorado Party politician who presided over a period of economic crisis and growing social tension. Elected vice-president in the 1966 elections, Pacheco became president on the death of Gen. Oscar Gestido in the following year. Faced with a deteriorating economic situation, in February 1968 he signed an agreement with the IMF and in June imposed a wage freeze. Pacheco declared a state of siege (*Medidas Prontas de Seguridad*) in response to the wave of protest strikes: workers were subject to military discipline. The state-of-siege measures were maintained as guerrilla actions by the MLN-Tupamaros grew – these included the kidnapping of the British ambassador, Geoffrey Jackson, and the kidnapping and killing of a CIA agent, Dan Mitrione. Civil liberties were restricted by the government. Pacheco survived attempts by the parliamentary opposition to impeach him on charges of violating the constitution. Shortly before his term in office ended he placed the military in direct command of the counter-insurgency campaign. In the November 1971 elections Pacheco's attempt to secure re-election – which required approval of a constitutional amendment – failed, but Juan María Bordaberry, from the same right-wing sector of the Colorados, was declared the winner.

After stepping down in March 1972, Pacheco became an ambassador, serving in Spain, the US, and Switzerland for most of the 1970s, after the establishment of a military regime. He returned to take part in the November 1982 internal party elections, when his tendency within the Colorados was pushed aside by groups which had refused to collaborate with the dictatorship. Nevertheless his group obtained a number of parliamentary seats in the November 1984 elections.

See also ***autogolpe***; ***Batllismo***; **Colorado Party** (Uruguay); **MLN–Tupamaros;** ***Proceso***.

Pact for Democracy: see **Bánzer Suárez; Paz Estenssoro**.

Padilla Arancibia, Gen. David: see **Bolivian governments post-Bánzer**.

Palace of Justice siege: see **Betancur Cuartas**.

Palma, Aníbal: see **Radical Party** (Chile).

PARAGUAY, Republic of

Capital: Asunción
Independence (from Spain): 1811
Area: 406,752 sq km
Population (1986): 3.8m (43.9% urban)
Pop. growth rate (1970–86): 3.2%
Pop. density: 8.6/sq km
Infant mortality (1985): 48.9 per thousand
Life expectancy at birth (1985): 68
Literacy (1984): 92%
GDP per capita (1986e) US$1,829
Foreign debt per capita (1986e): US$475
Principal export commodities (% of total 1985 exports): cotton (49%), soya (33%), timber (3%)

Political system

Constitution: 1967 (amended 1977). *Head of state/government*: President Alfredo Stroessner (Colorado Party/ANR) (1954–). General Stroessner was re-elected in 1958, 1963, 1968, 1973, 1978, 1983, and 1988. Under

the constitution, the president serves a five-year term in office; since 1977 there are no limits on the number of consecutive terms that can be served. The bicameral National Congress is composed of a Senate and a Chamber of Deputies, of at least 30 and at least 60 seats respectively. The party that wins the presidential election automatically obtains two-thirds of the seats in both houses of Congress.

Political organisations

Parties (seats in Senate/Chamber of Deputies): Colorado Party/ANR (20/40); Radical Liberal Party/PLR (6/13); Liberal Party/PL (4/7). *The following parties have no congressional representation*: Teeté Liberal Party/PLT, Communist Party/PCP, Colorado Popular Movement/MOPOCO, Christian Democrat Party/PDC, Authentic Radical Liberal Party/PLRA, Febrerista Revolutionary Party/PRF. The PDC, PLRA, PRF, and MOPOCO together make up the National Accord/AN opposition alliance. Of the four, only the PRF is legally recognised.

Main labour organisations: Paraguayan Confederation of Workers/CPT (government-controlled); Inter-union Workers' Movement/MIT (independent). *Main employers' organisation*: Federation of Production, Industry, and Commerce/FEPRINCO.

Paraguayan Civil War (1947)

An armed conflict following the break-down of a coalition government, involving rival parties and sections of the armed forces. In 1946 the military regime of Gen. Higinio Morínigo had announced plans to call elections, inviting the *Colorados* and *Febreristas* into a coalition government. But rivalries within the new coalition grew rapidly; Morínigo began to ally himself with a sector of the *Colorados* led by Juan Natalicio González, which built up a storm-trooper organisation, the *guión rojo* (Red Banner). The *guionistas* began a campaign of intimidation against other parties, seeking among other things to wrest control of the labour movement from *Febreristas* and Communists.

In January 1947 Morínigo dissolved the coalition, declared a state of siege and began arresting his opponents. In March the *Febreristas* responded with an attack on the Asunción police headquarters, which in turn sparked a rebellion by dissident army units in Concepción. Most of the officer corps, together with *Febrerista*, Liberal, and Communist irregulars, fortified themselves in Concepción. In Asunción Morínigo had the support of the *Colorados* and their peasant militias, the *py nandí*. In April 1947 the navy garrison in Asunción rebelled, but this rising was crushed with heavy artillery. In July government troops recaptured Concepción. Most of the rebels had nevertheless outflanked them and managed to lay siege to a now under-defended Asunción. The government was, however, able to hold out and the rebels were eventually caught by the rest of the loyal troops returning from Concepción. The siege collapsed in mid-August after great loss of life, with many of the rebels fleeing to exile in Argentina. Some estimates put total emigration

during and immediately after the civil war (when there was a *Colorado* terror campaign) as high as 300,000 people – about one-third of the population.
See also **Colorado Party** (Paraguay); ***Febreristas*; Franco; Morínigo**.

Paraguayan Communist Party (*Partido Comunista Paraguayo*/PCP)
Set up in 1929, the PCP was involved in establishing a short-lived 'revolutionary commune' in Encarnación in 1931, which was crushed by government forces. The PCP opposed the 1930–5 Chaco War and supported the *Febrerista* coup of early 1936. After a brief period of legality, the party returned to clandestinity, organising strikes against the Morínigo regime after 1940. In August 1947 the party joined forces with *Febreristas* and Liberals in the civil war against the government. After the rebels were defeated, many PCP members were arrested or exiled. Following the advent of the Stroessner regime in 1954, the PCP concentrated its clandestine activity in urban areas. It took part in the August 1958 general strike, but three of its top members, Antonio Maidana, Julio Rojas, and Alfredo Alcorta, were arrested and spent the following two decades in prison. In the wake of the failure of the general strike, the PCP switched briefly and unsuccessfully to a guerrilla strategy in 1959–61.

A group critical of general secretary Oscar Creydt broke away in 1963 to form the *Partido Comunista Leninista Paraguayo*, which in 1965 changed its name to the Committee for the Defence and Reorganisation of the PCP. The committee obtained the recognition of the Soviet Communist Party and in 1967 announced the re-formation of the PCP and the expulsion of Creydt. Creydt and 50 supporters formed a Maoist group. The Moscow-line PCP was the larger of the two, and continued to operate inside Paraguay against Stroessner. In 1975 about 70 party members were arrested in a new security crack-down. Miguel Angel Soler, the general secretary, and two central committee members, died under torture. Antonio Maidana became the new general secretary on his release from prison in February 1977. However, in August 1980 he was kidnapped in Buenos Aires by Argentine security forces and was thought to have been handed back to Paraguay; he was presumed dead.
See also **Stroessner**.

Pardo Buelvas, Rafael: see **Workers' Self-Defence Movement (MAO)** (Colombia).

Pardo Leal, Jaime: see **Patriotic Union**.

Paredes, Ricardo: see **Communist Party of Ecuador**.

PARENA: see **Party of National Renovation**.

Parra, Antonio: see **Concentration of Popular Forces**.

Parra Durán, Luis Guillermo: see **Barco Vargas**.

Party for Democracy (*Partido por la Democracia*)
A socialist-based 'umbrella' party, created in Chile in 1988 with the aim

of overcoming the obstacles to legal political activities presented by the Law of Political Parties and campaigning for a 'no' vote in the October 1988 plebiscite. Ricardo Lagos, of the Nuñez wing of the Socialist Party (PSCh), became the president of the new party, which was registered with 45,000 adherents. Other parties, most notably the Christian Democrats (PDC), opted to register in their own names.

Party for the Government of the People: see **Broad Front**.

Party of National Renovation (*Partido de Renovación Nacional*/PARENA)

In Chile, three small, pro-government parties, respresentative of major business interests, coalesced to form the PARENA alliance in March 1987 in order to register under the new Law of Political Parties, which requires a minimum of 35,000 members. They were: the National Union Movement (MUN, now known simply as National Union/UN), led by Andrés Allamand; the Independent Democratic Union (UDI), led by Sergio Fernández (later appointed interior minister for a second time); and the National Labour Front (FNT), led by another former Pinochet minister, Sergio Onofre Jarpa. Independent right-winger Ricardo Rivadeneira, a lawyer and government adviser, was appointed president, while the three parties shared the vice-presidencies.

The MUN, the strongest right-wing party in the universities and a signatory of the National Agreement, has sought to build a constituency among the business sectors which have emerged under the military regime; while the members of the UDI, which has strong backing in local government throughout the country, include the mayors of the three biggest cities. The National Party (PN) declined an invitation to join PARENA, preferring to seek closer relations with the Christian Democrats (PDC). Internal battles, especially over economic policy, began immediately, although the MUN and UDI agreed on the need for promulgation of the 1984 party law, an end to political exile, and the return of the universities to civilian control. Although the MUN was clearly opposed to the candidacy of Gen. Pinochet in the 1988 plebiscite, the other parties initially supported this. However, in April 1988 the FNT also came out against an endorsement of Pinochet, causing a serious split in PARENA. See also ***Gremialismo*****; National Agreement for a Transition to Full Democracy; National Party** (Chile).

Party of the Revolutionary Left (*Partido de la Izquierda Revolucionaria*/PIR)

A Stalinist party founded in 1940 in Bolivia, around a group of Cochabamba intellectuals. It became the focus of the major left-wing currents of the time, and its candidate, José Antonio Arze, polled well against the official candidate, Gen. Enrique Peñaranda, in the 1940 elections. The PIR was highly orthodox, though not formally linked with Moscow. Following Comintern strategy (and that of the Chilean CP, which its leaders admired), the PIR joined the 'anti-fascist coalition' against the Villarroel government (1943–6) but found itself allied with the tin barons in overthrowing him, thus losing most of its growing trade union influence and almost destroying itself. This process was completed by the bloody armed conflict of January 1947 between the PIR and the Potosí miners, formerly its strongest supporters.

In 1950 a breakaway faction founded the Bolivian Communist Party (PCB). The PIR dissolved itself after the 1952 revolution but was revived in 1956 as a 'radical socialist' alternative to the Revolutionary Nationalist Movement (MNR). It joined the military government of Gen. Barrientos (1966–9), holding cabinet posts, but never regained any popular credibility. Its leader, Ricardo Anaya, was foreign minister to Gen. Pereda in 1978, but the party is now moribund.

See also **Bolivian Communist Party**.

Party of the Venezuelan Revolution (PRV): see **Bravo**.

Pascal Allende, Andrés: see **Movement of the Revolutionary Left**(Chile).

Pastrana, Misael: see **ANAPO; Social Conservative Party**.

Patriotic Union (*Unión Patriótica*/UP)

The third biggest party in Colombia, founded in 1985 by the semi-legal Communist Party (PCC) and its armed wing, the Revolutionary Armed Forces of Colombia (FARC). The latter was among the guerrilla groups to sign peace accords with the Conservative government of President Belisario Betancur in 1984. In March 1986 the UP won 21 congressional seats and in May its presidential candidate, high court judge Jaime Pardo Leal, won 4.5% of the vote. Incoming President Virgilio Barco appointed 329 UP councillors in areas where the party was strongest.

At the end of 1986 the party withdrew from parliament on the grounds that its representatives' physical safety could not be guaranteed. It alleged a systematic attempt to wipe out its members (the 'Condor Plan'), and demanded the establishment of a 'court of guarantees' to investigate attacks on the opposition; the dismantling of up to 40 paramilitary groups; and 'effective guarantees' for its members' safety. Otherwise, it said, it would withdraw from local government as well and take steps to 'mobilise the people' in protest. Its congressional representatives soon returned to parliament, but the killing did not stop: by late 1987 over 450 UP members, including four congressmen and two senators, had been assassinated, and on 11 October 1987 Pardo Leal himself was gunned down, causing mass protests. Earlier that year it had asserted that it was 'not the spokesman for the FARC', and said its legal political activities would continue if the FARC–government truce were broken. The move was seen in the light of the party's desire to consolidate electoral alliances with groups to its right. Despite these, however, it fared badly in the mayoral elections of 1988, which were marred by extreme violence against UP candidates and others. The UP's support is strongest in the departments of Antióquia, Bolívar, and Santander.

See also **Communist Party of Colombia; Revolutionary Armed Forces of Colombia**.

Patrón Costas, Robustiano: see **Infamous Decade**.

Paz Estenssoro, Víctor

b. 1907. President of Bolivia 1952–6; 1960–4; 1985– . Born in Tarija into a landowning family. Studied economics and law at the Universidad Mayor de San Andrés (UMSA). Fought in the 1930s Chaco War as an NCO. Worked in the ministry of finance 1932–3 and 1936–7. Professor of economic history at UMSA, 1939–43. Minister of the economy for one week in 1941. Leader of the Revolutionary Nationalist Movement (MNR) from its official founding in June 1942. Nicknamed '*el mono*' (the monkey), Paz served as minister of finance during most of the Villarroel government (December 1943–July 1946). He went into exile in Argentina (1946–52) after its overthrow. From exile he won the 1951 election, backed by an alliance of the MNR and the Workers' Revolutionary Party (POR), but the military intervened and installed a junta in May of that year.

In 1952 his supporters overthrew the junta and Paz became president, embarking on a programme of fundamental economic and social reform, including the nationalisation of the major tin mines (October 1952) and agrarian redistribution. Despite his radicalism, he was supported by the US, which gave him substantial economic assistance. The following year saw several revolts against his rule, but he served out his term to 1956 (the first president to do so since 1930). From 1956–9 he was ambassador to the UK, before being elected to a second term as president. This was characterised by economic problems and labour disputes, and Paz lost much of his support on the left. Having announced a 10-year economic plan in 1962, he was elected to a third term in May 1964, but the armed forces overthrew him six months later.

He was exiled in Peru from 1964 to 1971. Paz returned to Bolivia in 1971 and backed the military government of Gen. Bánzer, but was later exiled again to Argentina. In 1985, as leader of the Historic MNR (MNR-H), which he had founded out of his faction of the party, he was again elected president and embarked on a drastic austerity programme aimed at curbing Bolivia's acute economic crisis, exacerbated by the collapse of the world tin price. Among other measures, the peso was devalued by 95%, fuel prices were raised tenfold, state sector workers laid off, wages frozen, and price subsidies on basic goods removed. Restrictions on foreign investment were lifted. Inflation was reduced to double figures from 24,000% in September 1985, but real wages were halved and unemployment passed the 30% mark. However, the New Economic Programme (NPE) won praise from the World Bank and donor nations.

In January 1987 six noughts were struck from the peso (which had reached 1.9 million to the dollar) and it was renamed the boliviano. The tin-mining industry was restructured and several mines closed; while the state mining company Comibol more than halved its workforce. Faced with widespread labour unrest, the Paz government twice suspended civil rights and used troops against the workers. In July 1986 it aroused controversy by allowing US troops to enter the country for an operation officially described as an assault on drugs trafficking (the country's main source of income). The opposition argued that the constitution had been violated and that the operation was ineffectual. Further controversy was aroused in 1988 by the introduction of a narcotics control law which proposed the eradication of most of the country's coca crop. Violent clashes between police and coca growers left several dead and led to widespread labour unrest.

Although he owed his confirmation by Congress in large measure to a desire to prevent that of Bánzer (who had won more votes), Paz did not hesitate to forge an alliance (the 'Pact for Democracy') with Bánzer's ADN in 1985. This was still in force by late 1987 and led the opposition to assert that the ADN was sharing in government.
See also **Bánzer Suárez; Revolutionary Nationalist Movement**.

Paz Zamora, Jaime: see **Democratic and Popular Union; Movement of the Revolutionary Left** (Bolivia).

Peasant Leagues

Associations of poor Brazilian peasants, mainly in the north-east of the country, in the late 1950s and early 1960s, often cited as an important sign of rural radicalisation prior to the 1964 military coup. The first Leagues sought to provide seeds, fertilisers, and other services to the peasants, but later took a more overt role in challenging the power of the large landowners and campaigning for land reform. Different leagues came under the influence of Francisco Julião (the man most associated with their growth), Catholic activists, and the Communist Party. Julião was himself a landowner and lawyer whose role as an adviser to the leagues laid the basis for a political career and his election to Congress as a federal deputy. In exile after the 1964 coup, Julião presented the Leagues as a kind of rural revolutionary vanguard, and while conservatives generally agreed on their radical nature, there is much evidence to suggest that the main aims of the movement were more reformist in nature. The Leagues supported the campaign by wage-earning rural workers in the sugar industry for an increased minimum wage, which succeeded in wresting concessions from the employers after a strike in November 1963. Before the 1964 coup they had begun to move with other rural unions towards the formation of a national confederation of rural workers, within the *Trabalhista* model.
See also **Coup of 1964** (Brazil); ***Trabalhismo***.

Pedro León Arboleda Brigade: see **People's Liberation Army**.

pelegos

The name used in Brazil for trade union officials who, while claiming to represent the workers' interests, were in fact more closely tied to those of the federal government and the corporatist trade union system created by President Getúlio Vargas in the 1940s. *Pelego* was originally the term used for a sheepskin placed between a saddle and the horse, to make the horseman's ride more comfortable. The analogy was therefore with union leaders placed between capital and labour to reduce friction between the

two. Although originating in the paternalist aspects of the Vargas/PTB tradition, the concept of the *pelego* and *peleguismo* was later used more loosely to describe pro-company or pro-government unionism.
See also ***Trabalhismo*; Vargas**.

peludos: see **National Liberation Movement-Tupamaros**.

Pengel, Johan: see **Arron; Lachmon; National Party of Suriname**.

Peñaranda, Gen. Enrique: see **Party of the Revolutionary Left** .

People, Change and Democracy (PCD): see **Hurtado Larrea; Progressive Front**.

People's Committee: see **Broad Left Front**.

People's Democratic Committee: see **Revolutionary Party of the Nationalist Left**.

People's Electoral Movement (*Movimiento Electoral del Pueblo*/MEP)
A Venezuelan left-wing party which emerged in December 1967 as a split from Democratic Action (AD). The split had developed as a result of a battle for the presidential nomination between Gonzalo Barrios and Luis Beltrán Prieto. Prieto was expelled from AD and his supporters followed him into the MEP. In the December 1968 elections Prieto took fourth place with 19% of the vote; in the Chamber of Deputies the MEP was the third largest group. Thereafter, however, its electoral fortunes declined, as the party proved unable to carry the traditional AD electorate with it. In December 1973 the MEP entered the New Force (*Nueva Fuerza*) coalition with the URD and the Communist Party (PCV). In the December 1982 elections, the MEP supported the *Nueva Alternativa* left-wing coalition presidential candidate.
See also **Democratic Action; *Nueva Alternativa***.

People's Front: see **Popular Front**.

People's Liberation Army (*Ejército Popular de Liberación*/EPL)
A Colombian guerrilla group launched in January 1968 by the pro-Chinese Communist Party (the PCC-ML) after two years of organising among peasants in southern Córdoba province. It survived heavy losses due to counter-insurgency operations and for a time in the mid-1980s was considered to be the third strongest of the armed groups on the left. With other groups, it signed a truce with the Conservative government of Belisario Betancur in August 1984, but this broke down in mid-1985. On 20 November of that year the group's leader, Oscar William Calvo was murdered by 'Death to Kidnappers' (MAS). In late 1985 the EPL joined other guerrilla groups in the National Guerrilla Coordinating Body (CNG). Strongholds include Sucre in the north-west. An associated urban guerrilla group, the Pedro León Arboleda Brigade (PLA), ended two years of inactivity in July 1987 with a bomb in central Bogotá which injured seven people. In 1988 the EPL joined the National Liberation

Army (ELN) in a series of coordinated kidnaps of jounalists and foreign representatives.
See also **Communist Party of Colombia–Marxist-Leninist; death squad; National Guerrilla Coordinating Body**.

People's National Congress (PNC)
Guyana's ruling party. Founded in 1957 by Forbes Burnham as successor to the People's Progressive Party faction he led after splitting with PPP founder Cheddi Jagan in 1955. The faction won three out of 14 parliamentary seats in the 1957 general election, after which it adopted its present name and based itself in the Afro-Guyanese community. It won 11 out of 35 seats in the 1961 election, and after winning 22 of 53 seats in 1964 took power in coalition with the small, right-wing United Force (UF) party. It won an absolute majority in elections in 1968, 1973, 1980, and 1985, which it is widely considered to have rigged with the help of the army.

Soon after he came to power, Burnham declared a vaguely socialist 'cooperativism' as the official doctrine. In 1974, though, he took a sharper turn left in the 'Sophia Declaration', in which he announced the PNC's paramountcy over the government. As his grip on the country tightened, top officials of the opposition PPP defected to the PNC, notably Ranji Chandisingh, who became PNC general secretary. The party is currently led by Desmond Hoyte.
See also **Burnham; Hoyte**.

People's Party: see **APRA**.

People's Progressive Party (PPP)
Guyana's main opposition party, based in the majority East Indian population. Founded in 1950 by Marxist Cheddi Jagan, the PPP won 18 out of 24 legislative council seats in the 1953 elections. Jagan led the government for nearly five months until it was forcibly removed by the British colonial authorities, fearful of Communism. The party split in 1955 when one of its co-founders, Forbes Burnham, encouraged by US and British officials, broke away and formed his own party. But the PPP won nine out of 14 elected seats in the 1957 parliamentary elections and Jagan governed until 1964, when the party lost its majority. The PPP charges that Burnham and his PNC party rigged the subsequent elections. The PPP boycotted parliament in protest between 1973 and 1976. Its calls for a PNC–PPP 'government of national unity' to tackle the country's severe economic problems have gone unheeded. Cheddi Jagan remains party leader.
See also **Burnham; Jagan; People's National Congress**.

People's Radical Party (UCRP): see **Frondizi**.

People's United Front (FUP): see **Torres Restrepo**.

Pereda Asbun, Gen. Juan: see **Bolivian governments post-Bánzer**.

Peredo, Coco: see **National Liberation Army** (Bolivia).

Peredo, Inti: see **National Liberation Army** (Bolivia).

Peredo, Osvaldo: see **National Liberation Army** (Bolivia).

Pereira, José: see **Bolivian Communist Party**.

Pérez, Carlos Andrés

b. 1922. Democratic Action (AD) politician and Venezuelan president 1974–9, who campaigned on North–South issues and nationalised the local petroleum industry. Born in Rubio, Tachira state; studied at Liceo Andrés Bello and Central University. A participant in the October 1945 revolution, he became private secretary to the AD leader and provisional president, Rómulo Betancourt. Elected a deputy in 1946, he also became secretary to the Council of Ministers. After the November 1948 coup Pérez was imprisoned for a year in Caracas and then deported to Colombia. He was again captured on trying to re-enter Venezuela, and after another period in prison, went back into exile, this time in Cuba and Costa Rica.

On the fall of the dictatorship of Gen. Marcos Pérez Jiménez in January 1958, Pérez returned to the country and was again elected a deputy. In 1960–1 he was director general at the ministry of the interior. He became minister in 1962, taking over responsibility for the bitterly fought counter-insurgency campaign against leftist guerrillas. The severe repression of that period earned him a reputation as a hard-liner. He resigned from the ministry in August 1963, joining AD's national executive committee. In the December 1963 polls he was re-elected as a deputy for Tachira, becoming president of AD's congressional bloc in 1964–7 and again (after another re-election as deputy) in 1969–73. Regarded as a Betancourt protégé, Pérez was nominated AD presidential candidate in August 1972, and went on to win the elections in December the following year with 49% of the vote, against 37% for his COPEI rival, Lorenzo Fernández.

Taking office in 1974 after the first big OPEC price rise, Pérez received both the benefits and the disadvantages of the 'petro-dollar' boom. The iron and steel industry was nationalised on 1 January 1975, followed by the oil industry on 1 January 1976. But the rise in oil revenues led to inflation and an overheating of the economy. The government was plagued by accusations of corruption (particularly over the May 1977 purchase of a refrigerated ship, the *Sierra Nevada*) and by signs of a guerrilla revival (such as the February 1976 kidnapping of US businessman William Niehous). In foreign policy, Pérez helped set up SELA, improved relations with Cuba, supported Panama's efforts to secure a new Canal treaty, and backed the Sandinista guerrillas in Nicaragua. He championed the interests of the South in the North–South debate and moved AD into closer contact with the Socialist International. After he had stepped down from the presidency in 1979 a congressional investigation into his role in the *Sierra Nevada* affair concluded that he was neither morally nor administratively guilty for the irregularities, but was responsible for fomenting a general climate of political corruption. Pérez remained politically active both as a senator and as a leading figure

within AD. In 1987 he won the AD presidential nomination for the elections due in December 1988.
See also **Democratic Action; Latin American Economic System. Oil nationalisation** (Venezuela).

Pérez Jiménez, Gen. Marcos

b. 1914, President of Venezuela 1952–8. Educated at the Colegio Gremios Unidos in Cúcuta, Colombia, the Escuela Militar in Caracas, and the Superior War School in Lima, Peru. Pérez Jiménez took part in the October 1945 coup which inaugurated the reformist *trienio* of rule by young army officers and the Democratic Action (AD) party. But he turned against AD and was involved in the November 1948 coup which ousted President Gallegos. As minister of defence and a member of the new three-man junta, he helped organise the wave of repression against members of AD, the CTV union confederation, and other parties. Following the assassination of junta leader and president Col. Carlos Delgado Chalbaud on 13 November 1950, Pérez Jiménez emerged as the driving force behind the regime and organised elections to a constituent assembly, from which AD and the Communist Party (PCV) were excluded. The pro-government electoral front was declared the winner by a large margin, after signs of fraud against the front runner, the Democratic Republican Union (URD). Pérez Jiménez was proclaimed the new president in December 1952. The assembly drafted a new constitution in 1953, and granted him extraordinary powers.

His rule was characterised by systematic and ruthless repression of AD, PCV, and other parties; thousands were imprisoned and many who became involved in attempted uprisings or attacks on barracks were killed. At the same time Pérez Jiménez used growing revenues from oil exports to expand public works and housing programmes, developing a populist political style. In 1957 he organised a plebiscite on his rule, declaring himself re-elected for a second term, which was to have covered the 1958–63 period. But the opposition had gathered strength in the plebiscite campaign. A military rebellion broke out in Caracas and Maracay on 1 January 1958. Although it was defeated, it sparked off a mass popular uprising. A general strike against the regime began on 21 January. Police machine-gunned a demonstration in Caracas, but by 23 January with army units in Caracas and the navy joining in the anti-government camp, Pérez Jiménez was forced to flee the country into exile.

In August 1963 he was extradited from the United States and imprisoned in Venezuela until 1968. On his release he went into voluntary exile in Madrid. In the December 1968 elections the Nationalist Civic Crusade, a party which described itself as '*perezjimenista*' nominated him as its candidate for the Senate. Although winning sufficient votes *in absentia*, his election was declared void by the Supreme Court, on the grounds that he had not registered to vote.
See also **Delgado Chalbaud; Revolution of 1958** (Venezuela)**;** ***trienio***.

Perón, Evita (María Eva Duarte de Perón)

1919–52. Co-founder of and charismatic figure in Argentina's Peronist movement. Evita was a powerful orator adored by her supporters, and reviled by her opponents. She developed a career in radio and film in the 1930s and 1940s. Evita met Perón when he was an aspiring young colonel. She influenced him to use his position as secretary of labour to develop a following among the trade unions. Following Perón's overthrow by rival military factions, she helped union leaders and sympathetic military officers to organise the 17 October 1945 demonstration which forced his reinstatement. Evita married Perón in the same month. As the first lady from 1946 onwards, she set up a major charity and social welfare fund, the *Fundación de Ayuda Social María Eva Duarte de Perón*. She campaigned for women's right to vote, which as a result of her efforts was obtained in September 1947. Her book *La Razón de mi Vida* (The Reason of my Life) was at one stage made obligatory reading in schools. Her humble origins helped explain her strong appeal to working-class Peronists and the enmity of the traditional Argentine upper classes. The General Confederation of Labour (CGT) and the wider Peronist movement led a campaign to nominate her as vice presidential candidate for the 1951 elections, but Evita refused on the grounds of growing illness. She died of cancer on 26 July 1952. Her embalmed body was installed in the CGT headquarters pending plans (never fulfilled) to build a major mausoleum. After the 1955 anti-Peronist coup, her body was secretly removed on the orders of the military regime, and was only returned to Argentina in 1975. Later leftist factions of the Peronist movement saw Evita Perón as an embodiment of the more revolutionary content of the Peronist ideology.

See also ***Descamisados***; **Montoneros; Perón, Gen. Juan Domingo; Peronism**.

Perón, Gen. Juan Domingo

1895–1974. Founder and leader of Argentina's Peronist movement. President 1946–55 and 1973–4, and key figure in national politics for almost four decades. After entering the Military College in 1911 he became professor of military history (1930–6), military attaché at the Argentine embassy in Chile, and member of an Argentine military mission to Italy. As a colonel, he joined the influential GOU army lodge and was a supporter of the 4 June 1943 military coup. As head of the newly-created Secretariat of Labour and Welfare he began building a personal following among labour unions. Perón coordinated rescue work in the San Juan earthquake of January 1944, where he met his future wife, Eva Duarte. He rose to become war minister and vice-president by July 1945. But his growing influence was opposed by rival military factions, who ordered his arrest in October 1945. A mass demonstration on 17 October forced the government to order his release and reinstatement, and to purge his opponents. He married Eva Duarte the same month and emerged as the official candidate for the February 1946 elections, winning with 56% of the vote.

Critics argue that Perón's rule was marked by moves towards a one-party state, a personality cult of Perón and Evita, and corruption. But it was also a period of import-substituting industrialisation, nationalisation of key industries, development of the welfare state, and income redistribution. Perón expounded the ideology of *justicialismo* (social justice) and a 'third way' between capitalism and socialism. The death of Evita, economic difficulties, and growing political opposition undermined his support in the years immediately prior to 1955. Perón faced army resentment over his personality cult and entered into a damaging conflict with the Catholic bishops, during which his supporters burned churches. A first military uprising in June 1955 was quelled after fighting which left an estimated 200 dead. The September 1955 military rebellion was successful, with Perón initiating an 18-year exile.

Based in Spain from 1960, he led the mass opposition to successive military regimes. He finally returned to Argentina on a short visit in November 1972 when Gen. Lanusse allowed the Peronists to participate in the electoral campaign. Although his own candidacy was banned, his representative Dr Cámpora won the elections. Cámpora resigned to permit Perón to stand in new elections in September 1973, which he won with a landslide 62% share of the vote. Perón took office in October 1973, but proved unable to stop the growing factional war between right and left wings of the movement. He died on 1 July 1974, leaving the presidency to his second wife, Isabel.

See also **Montoneros; Perón, Evita; Perón, Isabel; Peronism**.

Perón, Isabel (María Estela Martínez de Perón)

b. 1931. President of Argentina 1974–6. María Estela Martínez acquired the name Isabel on her confirmation and used it in her career as a dancer. According to several accounts, she first met Gen. Juan Perón in 1956, when she was a dancer in the Happyland night club in Panama. But in 1974 the official version maintained that they met in 1955 when she was a ballerina performing with her ballet troupe in Caracas. After their meeting, she became Gen. Perón's personal secretary, following him to Venezuela and the Dominican Republic before they finally settled in Madrid in 1960. They were married in 1961 (Perón's previous wife Evita had died in 1952). Isabel became Perón's political emissary, visiting Argentina in 1964 and 1965 – in the latter case to try and re-assert her husband's authority over the increasingly independent-minded Peronist union leaders. She accompanied her husband on his definitive return to Argentina in early 1973.

In mid-1973, after President Cámpora resigned to allow Perón to stand in new elections, Isabel was chosen as his running mate. The Perón–Perón ticket won the 23 September 1973 polls with a landslide 62% of the vote. As vice-president, Isabel visited Spain, Italy, and Switzerland in mid-1974; she returned only days before her husband's death on 1 July. Succeeding him as president, Isabel presided over a growing economic crisis and an intensifying internecine war within the Peronist movement. In November 1974 she declared a state of siege, allowing the military a free reign in combatting the guerrilla movements. Killings by the Triple-A death squad increased sharply – Isabel was believed to be under the influence of social welfare minister José López Rega, the right-wing *eminence grise* who controlled the death squads. She was forced to remove López Rega under trade union and army pressure in 1975, but by then, with the economy slipping into hyper-inflation and guerrilla actions steadily increasing, there was open speculation on the coming coup.

She was deposed by the armed forces on 24 March 1976, and held under house-arrest for the next five years before being released into exile in Spain. Although remaining the titular head of the Peronist movement, she refused to take part in party politics in the 1983 electoral campaign, returning to Argentina only briefly to attend the inauguration of Raúl Alfonsín as president.

See also **López Rega; Perón, Gen. Juan Domingo; Peronism**.

Peronism

An Argentine mass political movement founded and led by Gen. Juan Domingo Perón, centrally important to national politics from 1945 onwards. It is now also known as the Justicialist Party (*Partido Justicialista*/PJ). Variously described as populist, reformist, and fascist, the movement developed strong trade union support and defended the cause of social justice and a 'third way' between capitalism and socialism.

The date of the birth of Peronism as an organised movement is generally given as 17 October 1945, when a mass demonstration forced the reinstatement of the then Col. Perón, who had been removed from the military government as a result of a factional struggle. He went on to win the February 1946 elections and held the presidency in 1946–55. Perón was supported by dissident Radicals, trade union leaders, nationalists, Catholics, and some conservatives, whom he integrated into a single Peronist party. Appointments and party disputes were all resolved by Perón personally – a doctrine eventually known as *verticalismo*, or obedience to the leader. Peronist rule was characterised by industrialisation, redistribution of income, a personality cult of Perón and his wife Evita, domination of the media and education system by the ruling party and repression of political opponents. The General Confederation of Labour (CGT) strongly backed the government and was formally incorporated as one of the three branches of the Peronist movement (the other two were the male and female branches of the party).

After the 1955 coup which ousted Gen. Perón, the movement entered an 18-year period of political persecution and disenfranchisement. It nevertheless retained its strong popular base. From exile, Gen. Perón remained a key political actor in the 1960s and 1970s, using his followers to make the country ungovernable for a succession of anti-Peronist military regimes. but the movement also became more heterogeneous. On the right powerful trade union leaders often negotiated independently with the military. On the left, Gen. Perón encouraged 'special formations' involved in sabotage campaigns against successive military regimes; these were to develop into the Montoneros guerrilla movement which sought to give Peronism a specifically revolutionary and socialist content. After the military announced a return to democracy, the movement formed the Justicialist Liberation Front (FREJULI) coalition, whose presidential candidate, Héctor Cámpora, won the March 1973 elections. Cámpora then resigned to allow Gen. Perón himself to stand; the coalition won with 62% of the vote in September.

Peronism in power, however, was afflicted by violent factional struggles involving the Montoneros, the trade union leadership, and right-wing death squads allegedly organised by the social welfare minister, José López Rega. The clashes worsened after Gen. Perón's death in July 1974 and his replacement by his widow, Isabel Perón. It was against this background of factional warfare and growing economic chaos that a new military regime took power in March 1976 and inaugurated a period of repression. After the political collapse of the dictatorship in the wake of the Falklands/Malvinas war, the Peronists were defeated in the October 1983 elections by Dr Raúl Alfonsín of the Radicals – the first time they had lost free elections since their emergence as an organised political movement. This led to a new period of internal conflict, with a split between the old guard and the 'renovating wing'. Despite suffering a further loss of support in the 1985 congressional elections, in 1987 the party began a comeback, pushing the Radicals into second place in both the congressional and provincial contests. In July 1988 Carlos Menem, the governor of La Rioja, was elected in the party's first primaries as Peronism's presidential candidate for the 1989 elections.
See also **General Confederation of Labour; Justicialist Liberation Front; Montoneros; Perón, Evita; Perón, Gen. Juan Domingo; Perón, Isabel**.

Peronist Party: see **Peronism** (Argentina).

personalismo

The practice of basing a political movement, or even an entire political culture, around the personality of a charismatic leader, rather than around ideological or practical issues. Peronism in Argentina (centred on Juan Domingo Perón) and *'velasquismo'* in Ecuador (the movement of Jose María Velasco Ibarra) are prominent examples in South America. *'Torrijismo'* in Panama and *'duvalierisme'* in Haiti may be cited as recent examples elsewhere in the region.
See also ***continuismo***.

PERU, Republic of

Independence (from Spain): 1821 (declared); 1824 (Spanish forces defeated)
Capital: Lima
Area: 1,280,219 sq km
Population (1987): 20.73m (68.3% urban)
Pop. growth rate (1980): 2.6%
Pop. density: 16.19/sq km
Infant mortality (1980–5): 98.6 per thousand
Life expectancy at birth (1980–6): 58.6

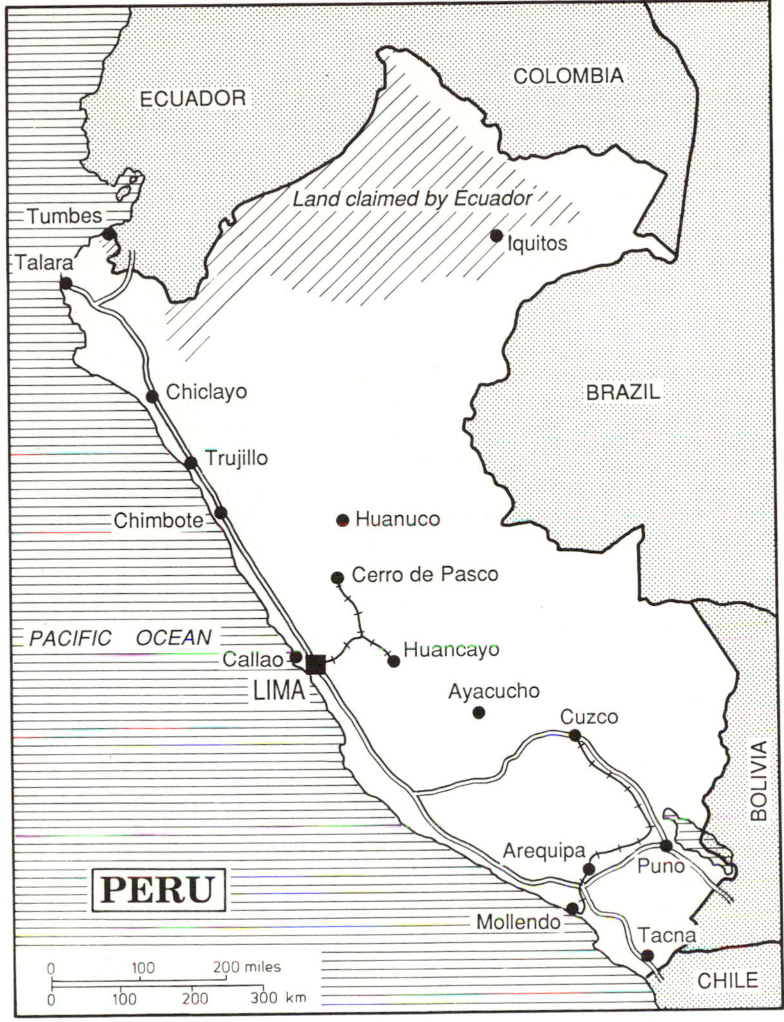

Literacy (1986): 86%
GDP per capita (1986e): US$1,250
Foreign debt per capita (1987e): US$780
Main exports (1985): oil (21.8%); lead and zinc (16%); copper (15.6%); silver (5%)

Political system

Constitution: 1980. *Head of state/government*: President Alan García Pérez (APRA) (1985–); elected to succeed Fernando Belaúnde Terry (AP) (1980–5). The bicameral Congress and the president are elected for five years by universal adult (18+) suffrage. The president must obtain at least 36% of the vote; a second round is held if this is not achieved. The 60-member Senate is mainly elected on a regional basis, but former elected presidents hold seats for life. The 180-member Chamber of Deputies is elected by proportional representation. The most recent elections were in April 1985.

Political organisations

Parties (seats in Senate/Chamber of Deputies): American Popular Revolutionary Alliance/APRA (32/107); United Left coalition/IU (15/48); Democratic Covergence/CD [alliance between Popular Christian Party/PPC and Hayista Base Movement/MBH] (7/12); Popular Action/AP (5/10); Nationalist Left/in (1/1). The remainder of Chamber of Deputies seats are held by two independents.

The following parties have no parliamentary representation: National Workers' and Peasants' Front (FNTC/FRENATRACA); Christian Democrat Party (PDC); Marxist Revolutionary Workers' Party–Socialist Workers' Party (PORM-PST); Workers' Revolutionary Party (PRT); Socialist Party of Peru (PSP); Odriísta National Union (UNO); Revolutionary Socialist Action (ASR); Communist Party of Peru-Red Flag (PCP–*Bandera Roja*); Movement of the Revolutionary Left (MIR); Revolutionary Vanguard; Peruvian Democratic Movement (MDP). Armed organisations: Shining Path; Unified Communist Committee–Marxist Leninist (CCUML); National Liberation Army (ELN); Túpac Amaru Revolutionary Movement (MRTA); Marxist-Leninist Nuclei; Puka Llakta; Victoria Navarro; Victoriano Espárraga Cumbi.

Main labour organisations (affiliation): Democratic Trade Union Front/FSD, comprising Workers' Central of the Peruvian Revolution/CTRP, General Confederation of Workers of Peru/CGTP (Communist Party), National Confederation of Workers/CNT (Popular Christian Party), and Confederation of Peruvian Workers/CTP (APRA); Inter-sectoral Confederation of State Workers/CITE; Federation of Peruvian Mineworkers/FNTMMP; Movement of Class Workers and Labourers/MTOC. *Main employers' organisations*: Confederation of Chambers of Commerce and Production of Peru; National Industrial Society (*Sociedad Nacional de Industrias*).

Peruvian Aprista Party (PAP): see **APRA**.

Peruvian Communist Party (*Partido Comunista Peruano*/PCP)
Founded as the Peruvian Socialist Party (PSP) in 1928 by José Carlos Mariátegui, the party acquired its present name in 1930 on joining the Third International. Under the leadership of Eudocio Ravines it sought to acquire a working-class base, but was hampered by the growth of the populist APRA and by the strength of anarchist/libertarian socialist traditions among organised labour. In the aftermath of an abortive attempt at insurrection, in 1930 the party was banned and spent many years in clandestinity. Although still banned in 1939, it backed winning presidential candidate Manuel Prado, who eased restrictions on its operations. In

1945 the PCP joined APRA in a Democratic Front backing the presidency of José Luis Bustamante y Rivera, but Bustamante was overthrown three years later by Gen. Odría and the party was again proscribed.

As part of an international movement, the PCP was constitutionally forbidden to participate in politics, but it was nonetheless allowed to stand in the 1956 and 1962 elections. In the former it backed Belaúnde (who lost), on the grounds that he represented the 'national bourgeoisie'; while in 1962 it put forward its own candidate, obtaining less than 1% of the vote. Traditionally the party has been strongest in the south, as well as in industrial areas of central Peru. It was weakened by the growth in the 1960s of Castroite and Maoist groups. The Sino-Soviet split resulted in the formation in 1963 of the pro-Chinese PCP-Red Flag (*Bandera Roja*), which took with it most of the young communists and several regional committees (including Ayacucho).

Led by lawyer Saturnino Paredes and organised around the *Bandera Roja* newspaper, the PCP-BR favours armed struggle but has no military wing. It adopted a pro-Albanian position, and itself suffered a split in the late 1960s, with pro-Chinese dissidents (initially known as the National Coordinating Committee/CNC) forming the Red Nation (*Patria Roja*) group. Another split in 1974 produced the Marxist-Leninist Nuclei.

In 1968, the PCP backed the military reformism of Gen. Velasco Alvarado and gained ground in the trade union movement, in particular in the CPUSTAL affiliate, the General Confederation of Peruvian Workers (CGTP), re-established in 1968. This gives it the most important working-class base of all left-wing parties. Since 1979 it has been known as the PCP-'*Unidad*' ('Unity', after the party weekly) to distinguish it from the many other communist groups. In the early 1980s it suffered another split, with the formation by its most pro-Soviet faction of the PCP-*Mayoria* ('Majority') in response to the party's drift towards a less clearly aligned stance. Since 1980 it has belonged to the United Left (IU) coalition.

See also **Shining Path; United Left** (Peru).

Peruvian Democratic Movement (MDP): see **APRA**.

Pétkoff, Luben: see **Generation of 1958** (Venezuela).

Pétkoff, Teodoro: see **Generation of 1958** (Venezuela).

Phillips, Patricio: see **National Party** (Chile).

Pineiros, Gen. Luis: see **Vargas Pazzos rebellion**.

Piñerua, Luis: see **Herrera Campins Luis**.

Pinochet Ugarte, Gen. Augusto José Ramón

b. 1915. President of Chile by decree, 1973– . Born in Valparaíso, the eldest son of a dock clerk. Twice rejected by the military academy on grounds of poor physique, he eventually graduated with a commission in 1936. As a cadet he had attempted unsuccessfully to study law. His early tasks included command of a detention centre for communists, and he was briefly involved with freemasonry as a young officer. After working as an instructor at the military academy he received further training at the Army War College (1949–52), after which he became a staff officer. As a major in 1953, Pinochet was assigned to the Rancagua Regiment in the northern port of Arica. In 1954 he was a teacher at the Army War College, after which he was sent as military attaché to Ecuador (where he organised the army staff college) and, in 1956, to the USA. In 1961 he was appointed commander of the 7th Infantry Regiment ('Esmeralda') in Antofagasta. In 1964 he returned to the Army War College as assistant director and professor of geopolitics and geography. One of his several books on these subjects was made a school text. He also wrote a study of the nineteenth-century War of the Pacific.

He rose to the rank of colonel in 1966. Having attended training courses in the Panama Canal Zone (US Southern Command) in 1965 and 1968, he toured the USA at the invitation of the US government in the latter year. As commander of the Buín Artillery Regiment, he helped put down the *tancazo* coup attempt against the Allende government in June 1973. Mistakenly considered to be a 'constitutionalist', Pinochet was appointed armed forces chief-of-staff, and then, in August 1973, commander-in-chief of the armed forces and a member of the cabinet. His predecessor, the loyalist Gen. Carlos Prats, had been forced out by his subordinates, who were plotting a coup. This finally took place on 11 September 1973, whereupon Pinochet took charge of the four-man junta which assumed legislative and executive functions.

His forces are conservatively estimated to have killed over 11,000 opponents in his first year in power. On the economic front he implemented extreme monetarist policies under advice from 'Chicago school' economists, resulting in an acute concentration of wealth. His aims included the depoliticisation of labour, decentralising and rolling back state control, privatising services and permanently excluding the left from Chilean politics. In 1978 a plot by junta member Gen. Gustavo Leigh to oust Pinochet was discovered, and Leigh was retired as head of the air force. Pinochet reformed the constitution in 1980 after seven years of de facto rule, introducing, among other things, a ban on Marxist political parties. The reform was submitted on 11 September 1980 to a referendum which was widely condemned as fraudulent, due to the government monopoly on information and the lack of either an electoral register or independent verification, as well as other flaws, but which resulted in a significant political victory for Pinochet.

On 5 October 1988 another plebiscite was due to be held, this time on the question of Pinochet's candidacy for the next 'presidential term'. If he were to win a simple majority he would rule until 1996/7. Pinochet was slightly wounded in a September 1986 assassination attempt by Manuel Rodríguez Patriotic Front guerrillas in which five bodyguards died. He later hinted that he thought the US Central Intelligence Agency might have been involved. The general's increasing isolation was marked in 1986–7 by the move into opposition of sectors of the right, including formerly unconditional supporters of the government and by discrepancies within the armed forces over his continuing in power beyond 1989. Even the United States, which had played an important role in the 1973 coup, indicated that it would like him to step down.

See also **Allende Gossens; Chicago Boys; Letelier case; Popular Unity**.

Pizarro Leongómez, Carlos: see **M–19**.

Plan Vert (Green Plan)

An ambitious, government-aided scheme to develop sparsely-populated French Guiana by large-scale immigration from France. Launched in 1975 by French overseas territories minister Olivier Stirn, the plan aroused much enthusiasm and thousands applied to be settlers. However, it soon ran out of steam, due to lack of money, poor organisation, and opposition from the local Guianese. Only a hundred or so settlers ever reached Guiana.

P

Plaza Lasso, Galo

1906–87. President of Ecuador 1948–52; secretary general of the OAS 1968–75. Born in Quito, the son of former President Leonidas Plaza Gutiérrez (1901–5 and 1912–16). Educated at the University of Maryland and the University of California. Defence minister (1938) and ambassador to the USA (1944–6). A wealthy landowner, Galo Plaza gave much of his land to his tenants and made efficient use of the remainder, unlike many Ecuadorean landlords.

Elected president in 1948 as the candidate of the National Civic-Democratic Movement (MCDN), an *ad hoc* grouping of independent Liberals, Plaza was the first president since the mid-1920s to be fairly elected and to serve out his term. In office, he reformed the public administration and won international respect for his struggle to extend political freedom and improve living standards. His presidency was regarded as an era of stability and progress, though many of his projects were not implemented due to lack of funds and he faced a series of poor harvests, as well as a severe earthquake in 1949. Agricultural production was stimulated, particularly in hitherto isolated parts of the coast.

In 1960 he was the unsuccessful presidential candidate of the National Democratic Front (FDN), a coalition of Radical Liberals (PL), Socialists (PSE), and independent Liberals. After the resignation of the military junta in 1966, he proposed Clemente Yeroví as provisional president. From 1968 to 1975 he served as secretary general of the Organisation of American States, having previously acted as UN observer or mediator in the Lebanon (1958), Congo (1960), and Cyprus (1964–6). In 1979 he and Yeroví, concerned at right-wing calls for a constituent assembly, set up a committee to defend the re-establishment of democracy according to the official timetable. President Osvaldo Hurtado (1981–4) often consulted him whilst in office, but he was very critical of the monetarist economic policies of Hurtado's successor, León Febres Cordero, and talked just before his death of returning to politics. Twelve days before he died he helped mediate in the release of President Febres, who was kidnapped by air force commandos.

Political Committee for the Coordination of Mobilisation (CPCM): see **Popular Democratic Movement**.

Politico-Military Organisation (*Organización Político-Militar*/OPM)
A Paraguayan guerrilla organisation which was discovered and broken up by the regime of Gen. Alfredo Stroessner in April–May 1976. A police attack on OPM headquarters led to an intense firefight, in which some 30 guerrillas and five policemen were killed. Subsequently some 1,500 people, mainly peasants and students, were arrested in a police mopping-up operation. According to the government version, the OPM was formed by radical Catholic students and was linked to the Argentine People's Revolutionary Army (ERP) guerrillas. Seven Jesuit priests were subsequently expelled from the country on charges of 'spreading communist propaganda'. The OPM was also known as the 1 March Organisation (*Organización Primero de Marzo*).
See also **People's Revolutionary Army; Stroessner**.

Polk, James K.: see **Monroe doctrine**.

POLOP (Workers' Politics): see **guerrilla movements** (Brazil).

Ponce Enríquez, Camilo: see **Conservative Party** (Ecuador); **Social Christian Party** (Ecuador).

Ponte Rodríguez, Capt. Manuel: see **FLN/FALN**.

Pope John XXIII: see **liberation theology**.

Pope John Paul II: see **Latin American Bishops' Council**.

Pope Paul VI: see **Latin American Bishops' Council; Medellín**.

Popular Action (*Acción Popular*/AP)
A Peruvian political party, founded in 1956 on the basis of the electoral machine created to back the candidacy of Fernando Belaúnde Terry in that year's presidential elections. Belaúnde came second, but the AP movement already existed in embryo as an alliance of upper-middle class and technocratic elements with a certain popular following, attracted by proposals including oil nationalisation and land reform within a mixed economy. It suffered an almost immediate split, when the Progressive Social Movement (MSP) broke away in 1956. In 1962 Belaúnde again stood, losing by a very narrow margin (less than 1%) to the APRA candidate. He claimed fraud and called on his contacts among the armed forces hierarchy to intervene: in July 1962 a junta took over and eventually called fresh elections for 1963. After the military had moved against left-wing parties, Belaúnde, this time in alliance with the Christian Democrats (PDC), beat his APRA rival.

In power the party was pragmatic and technocratic, favouring mild reforms and major public works projects financed from abroad. Its base has traditionally been in Lima and in the undeveloped, Quechua-speaking south. It has suffered from being largely a vehicle for Belaúnde, in that its parliamentary representation has been weaker than its presidential vote. At various times it has been allied, officially or unofficially, not only with the PDC but also with the Communists (PCP) and MSP. In 1968 Belaúnde was overthrown in a military coup led by Gen. Velasco Alvarado, and the party split in two, with a small minority faction supporting the armed forces. The pro-Belaúnde wing was outlawed, and although he was allowed back in 1976, the party refused to participate in the 1978 constituent assembly elections.

In 1980 Belaúnde was re-elected president on the AP ticket, serving out his term to 1985. The AP platform by now was moderate conservative, and it governed with the support of the right-wing Popular Christian Party (PPC) up to 1984. A combination of a disastrous economic performance and the activities of the Shining Path guerrillas helped bring about a dramatic defeat for the party in the 1985 elections, in which its vote slumped from the 45% it received in 1980 to under 6% in the presidential poll and its seats in the Chamber of Deputies were reduced to ten.
See also **Belaúnde Terry; Democratic Front**.

Popular Action Front (FRAP): see **Popular Front**.

Popular Alliance: see **Conservative Party** (Ecuador); **Social Christian Party** (Ecuador).

Popular Assembly: see **COB; Torres González.**

popularazo, el

Widespread student protests and street clashes in Venezuela in October and November 1960, during the presidency of Rómulo Betancourt. The protests began after the government ordered the arrest of some members of the Movement of the Revolutionary Left (MIR), on charges of inciting subversion through the party journal *Izquierda*. The education minister ordered the closure of secondary schools; in response university students went on strike and higher education was also closed down. As demonstrations spread to Caracas, Coro, Maracaibo, and other areas, unidentified armed men attacked print works used by opposition publications. In early November pro-government trade unions organised counter-demonstrations. On 21 November 1960 the rival groups marked Students' Day in different parts of Caracas. Street fighting soon broke out and intensified over the following days until on 28 November President Betancourt ordered the suspension of constitutional guarantees. Ciudad Universitaria – protected by university autonomy regulations – was surrounded and isolated by troops. Leftist papers were closed down and Communist Party (PCV) and MIR offices placed under surveillance. In the two-month period 19 people died, 300 were injured, and many police stations were attacked and cars and buses burnt.
See also **Betancourt; FLN/FALN**.

Popular Christian Party (PPC): see **Democratic Convergence**.

popular Church: see **Medellín**.

Popular Colorado Movement (*Movimiento Popular Colorado*/MOPOCO)
A dissident faction of the Paraguayan Colorado Party, opposed to Gen. Alfredo Stroessner. When the state of siege was lifted briefly in April 1959, clashes between police and protesting students quickly broke out. The lower house of Congress passed a resolution condemning police brutality. Gen. Stroessner reacted by re-imposing the state of siege and sending the army in to occupy Asunción. About 400 Colorados opposed to Stroessner were imprisoned or sent into exile, where they formed the *Movimiento Popular Colorado* (known by its acronym MOPOCO), initially under the leadership of Epifanio Méndez Fleitas, who had himself been forced into exile three years earlier in 1956.

p

In 1973 a minority of MOPOCO, seeking re-accommodation with the Colorado leadership in Paraguay, broke ranks. The majority remained committed to coordinated action with other opposition parties, and in 1979 joined the *Acuerdo Nacional* coalition. In December 1983 the government announced that MOPOCO leaders, most of whom had by then been in exile for 24 years, were free to return to Paraguay. The change in policy was attributed to pressure by the new Argentine civilian government for democratisation – but those MOPOCO leaders who returned to Asunción were subject to tight surveillance and harassment.
See also **National Accord; Colorado Party** (Paraguay); **Stroessner**.

Popular Democracy (*Democracia Popular*/DP)
An Ecuadorean Christian Democrat party, founded in 1978 as the result of a merger between the Christian Democratic Party (PDC) and the progressive wing of the Conservative Party under Julio César Trujillo. The merged group was known as Popular Democracy–Christian Democrat Union (DP-UDC). Christian Democrat leader Osvaldo Hurtado Larrea was adopted as running mate of Jaime Roldós (CFP) in the 1978–9 elections, the first after seven years of military rule, and their campaign was successful. After the death of Roldós in 1981, Hurtado became president. In the 1984 elections the DP share of congressional seats fell from five to three, but it recovered to seven in 1988. Its presidential candidate in 1988, Jamil Mahuad, obtained around 10% of the vote, and in the second round the DP backed the winning candidate, Rodrigo Borja. It allied itself with Borja's ID party in Congress and was given a cabinet post (the industry portfolio).
See also **Hurtado Larrea; Progressive Front**.

Popular Democratic Coalition (CPD): see **Hurtado Larrea**.

Popular Democratic Movement (*Movimiento Democrático Popular*/MDP)
A Chilean opposition coalition, founded in September 1983 after its member parties were excluded from the Democratic Alliance (AD). Banned by the military government on 1 February 1985, the MDP is dominated by the Communist Party (PCCh). Other members are: the Socialist Party of Chile (comprising the PS-Almeyda, the PS–24th

Congress; and the PS-CNR (National Regional Coordinating Group)); the Movement of the Revolutionary Left (MIR); and the United Popular Action Movement–Worker Peasant tendency (MAPU-OC). All remain banned under the 1987 Law of Political Parties, but the MDP is strong in the shanty towns, among students and in some trade unions.

At a National Assembly in 1984 the MDP put forward proposals for an 'advanced democracy'. It was the major force (with the Socialist Bloc and trade unions) behind the national strikes of October 1984, September 1985, and July 1986. Many of its leaders have been harassed and imprisoned: MDP president Dr Manuel Almeyda was jailed for two months and past general secretary Jaime Isunza was exiled in 1984. The MDP as a movement decided not to sign the National Agreement for a Transition to Full Democracy drafted by the AD and others in August 1985, both because of reservations over its content and because it had been excluded from preliminary discussions, though some member parties were less categorical. It has been rebuffed by the AD over its calls for a broad front, though the two have worked together on some mass protests. In March 1986 they established the Political Committee for the Coordination of Mobilisation (CPCM) to plan protest strategy, a move denounced by the right, which saw it as a de facto Christian Democrat–Communist pact. They also both backed the National Civic Assembly and its '*Demanda de Chile*', although disputes between the two major parties later undermined the Assembly. The MDP amended its position in mid-1986, indicating that it would be prepared to accept a military-backed transition to democracy if Gen. Pinochet resigned as president. Despite this, the Christian Democrats (PDC) continued to rule out a formal alliance with the MDP, while the divisions emerged within the latter over the PDC's 'free elections' campaign. Some saw this as legitimising the Pinochet constitution, which the MDP insists must be annulled.

See also **Communist Party of Chile; Democratic Alliance; National Agreement on a Transition to Full Democracy; United Left** (Chile).

Popular Front (*Frente Popular*)

A broad anti-fascist front in Chile, founded in 1936 on the initiative of the Communist Party (PCCh). The Socialists (PS) opposed an alliance with the bourgeois Radical Party (PR), but in March 1937 they gave in. Other members were the Radical Socialist Party (PSR) and the Confederation of Workers of Chile, formed in December 1937, which represented workers of all political persuasions except anarcho-syndicalists. The Front became one of the country's most powerful political forces and its candidate, Pedro Aguirre Cerda (PR), won the presidency in 1938. The most lasting achievement of the Popular Front government was the creation of the State Development Agency (CORFO), set up to promote industrialisation and funded by a tax on copper exports. Aided by protectionist policies, manufacturing grew rapidly under the Front and succeeding PR governments. The PS, which suffered a decline as a result of its membership of the Front, withdrew by 1941, followed by the PCCh, and the Front was dissolved that year after the death of Aguirre. But despite

rivalry in subsequent years between the PS and the PCCh, their alliance was renewed in the 1950s and 1960s, as the People's Front and then the Popular Action Front (FRAP). The latter was the precursor of the Popular Unity (UP) coalition of 1970–3, in which the PR also participated.
See also **member parties**.

Popular Liberation Army (ELP) (Colombia): see **People's Liberation Army**.

Popular Movement for National Liberation (MPLN): see **Democratic and Popular Union**.

Popular National Vanguard (VNP): see **Communist Party of Chile**.

Popular Party (PP): see **Neves**.

Popular Republican Union (UPR): see **Concentration of Popular Forces**.

Popular Revolutionary Alliance (APR): see **Intransigent Party**.

Popular Revolutionary Vanguard (VPR): see **guerrilla movements** (Brazil).

Popular Socialist Party (PSP) (Chile): see **Ibáñez del Campo**.

Popular Socialist Union (USOPO): see **Democratic Alliance**.

Popular Union: see **Venezuelan Communist Party**.

populism
A term used in the Latin American context to describe mass popular movements involving a multi-class alliance, based on an emotive call (e.g. nationalism, social justice), and often organised around a single charismatic leader. The exact definition of the concept remains the subject of academic debate. At times it is used to refer specifically to the attempt by intellectuals to work with the rural poor (a kind of 'back to the land' movement, sometimes echoed in the work of radical Catholic groups). But the most common usage is in the context of urban politics. Perhaps the most mentioned examples of populist movements are those led by Gen. Juan Domingo Perón in Argentina (Peronism) and Getulio Vargas in Brazil (*Trabalhismo*), both of which, in different ways, sought to introduce the demands and aspirations of the urban working classes and sectors of the rural poor to the political system. There have been many other movements and leaders which can be described as wholly or partly populist – they include Víctor Raúl Haya de la Torre's APRA in Peru, and Assad Bucaram's Concentration of Popular Forces (CFP) in Ecuador.
See also **Concentration of Popular Forces; Haya de la Torre; Perón; Peronism; *Trabalhismo*; Vargas**.

***Por la Patria*:** see **Blanco Party; Ferreira Aldunate**.

Port of Spain protocol: see **Essequibo dispute**.

Poveda Burbano, Adm. Alfredo: see **military governments (Ecuador/1961–79).**

Prado, Manuel: see **APRA**.

Prats, Gen. Carlos: see **Fatherland and Freedom**.

Prestes, Julio: see **Vargas**.

Prestes, Luis Carlos: see **Brazilian Communist Party; Communism; Long March; Marighela**.

Proceso

The name used by officers in Uruguay to describe the military movement which took power in 1973 and ruled the country until 1985. The *Proceso* shared many characteristics with other contemporary military regimes. Its leaders saw themselves as stepping in to 'save' the country from communist infiltration and the depredations of corrupt politicians. In the Uruguayan case, the politicisation of the armed forces was accelerated by their involvement in the counter-insurgency struggle against the MLN-Tupamaros guerrillas. In the process of fighting the guerrillas the military became aware of the ease with which they could take power; at the same time the officers picked up evidence on corrupt politicians from guerrillas they had interrogated and used the information to attack the existing civilian political system.

Military thinking evolved in a sometimes ambiguous fashion. In February 1973, for example, the armed forces presented President Juan María Bordaberry with a 16-point ultimatum, which led to the installation of a national security council (COSENA) with effective powers to veto decisions taken by the president and his ministers. Points 4 and 7 of the ultimatum, however, referred to the need for land reform and spoke of the army's refusal to be used by employers as a tool against their workers. This led to hopes within the PCU and other sectors of the Uruguayan left that there might be a faction of reformist or *peruanista* (after the post-1968 miltary government in Peru) officers making itself felt. In the event, however, the officers who closed down Congress and banned political and trade union activity in June 1973 could by no means be described as reformist. Although Bordaberry had allied himself to them and stayed on as president, it was the military who established a tight control on the country. Their rule was characterised by extreme and systematic repression and monetarist economic policy which favoured the rich at the expense of the working classes and much of the middle classes. Torture was used systematically and the number of political prisoners rose to over 5,000, considered at the time to be one of the highest proportions in the world, relative to total population.

In 1976 Bordaberry fell out with the top generals, who disagreed with his plans for a neo-fascist constitution and the total elimination of all political parties. Although committed to purging the traditional political parties, the military would not countenance doing away with them entirely. Bordaberry was sacked and replaced by civilian figureheads (first

Alberto Demicheli, then Aparicio Méndez) with no real power of their own. Through a series of institutional acts the regime deprived thousands of people of their political rights and set up a Council of State, composed of appointed members, to play the role of a weak legislative power. In November 1980 a draconian new constitution, which would have institutionalised the role of the armed forces as controllers of the political system, was defeated in a referendum. This opposition victory heralded the beginning of the end of the *Proceso*. The next year Gen. Gregorio Alvarez, one of the more ambitious officers, took over the presidency, though he was carefully watched by his colleagues, unwilling to end the tradition of collegiate leadership. After internal party elections in 1982 and under increasing popular pressure, the armed forces began to negotiate the terms of their withdrawal to barracks. Elections were held in November 1984, and a civilian government took over in March 1985; military efforts to impose a new constitution on the incoming civilians failed.

See also ***Club Naval*** **Pact; referendum of 1980**.

Process of National Reorganisation (*Proceso de Reorganización Nacional*/PRN)

The title taken by the Argentine military regime established after the 24 March 1976 coup, and which lasted to 1983. Power was vested in a junta of three commanders (one from each force). Congress was closed and political and trade union activity was banned. The PRN was characterised by the 'dirty war' against guerrilla movements and widespread human rights violations, described by critics as a form of state terrorism. The victims of political violence were estimated at over 30,000. Repression was directed at all forms of opposition, and continued until well after the guerrillas no longer posed a military threat. Economy minister José Martínez de Hoz, in office during the 1976–81 period, cut wage levels, removed controls on the financial sector, cut import tariffs, and generally sought the elimination of 'inefficient' industries and a return to specialisation in areas of comparative advantage such as agriculture and livestock. The policy of high interest rates and an overvalued peso led to industrial recession and the expansion of speculative financial activity. The foreign debt was multiplied by a factor of five in 1976–83 (from US$8.3bn to US$43.6bn) while the economy remained stagnant. Foreign policy was marked by growing tension with Chile over the Beagle Channel dispute, which took both countries to the brink of war in 1978–9.

The PRN's first president, Gen. Jorge Rafael Videla, was replaced by Gen. Roberto Viola on 29 March 1981. But the financial crisis, together with growing inter-force rivalries, led to the removal of Viola on 22 December 1981, and his replacement by Gen. Leopoldo Galtieri. Galtieri sought to reverse the growing political isolation of the regime by ordering the occupation of the Falklands/Malvinas islands. But defeat by Britain in the South Atlantic War led, in the short term, to the removal of Galtieri (16 June 1982) and, in the longer term, to the collapse of the entire PRN regime. Gen. Reynaldo Bignone, the last PRN president,

was appointed on 1 July 1982 and called elections for 30 October 1983, handing power to the new constitutional president, Raúl Alfonsín, on 10 December of the same year.
See also **Beagle Channel dispute; dirty war; Galtieri; Martínez de Hoz; South Atlantic War; Videla; Viola**.

Progressive Front (*Frente Progresista*/FP)
In Ecuador, a loose, legislative alliance of left-wing and centre-left parties (also known as the Democratic Progressive Front, or Progressive Bloc) opposed to the 1984–8 Febres Cordero government. The FP began in 1984 as a 37-seat bloc in the 71-member Congress, but defections gave the government an effective majority within a year. In the June 1986 mid-term elections, however, the FP regained its majority. The Front's most important member was the Democratic Left (ID); other member parties were Popular Democracy (DP), the Socialist Party (PSE), the Roldosista Party (PRE), the Popular Democratic Movement (MPD), the Broad Left Front (FADI), People, Change and Democracy (PCD) and (at the outset) the Democrat Party (PD). Attempts to convert the FP from a purely tactical alliance into a united electoral front did not prosper, and member parties presented alternative slates for the 1988 elections.
See also **Broad Left Front; Democratic Left; Ecuadorean Socialist Party; Popular Democracy**.

Progressive Reform Party (*Vooruitstrevende Hervormings Partij*/VHP)
A conservative Surinamese political party largely representing the East Indian community. Founded in 1949 by Jaggernath Lachmon as the United Hindustani Party, it became the Vatan Hitkarie Party in 1967 and adopted its present name in 1973. Lachmon formed an alliance with the country's other major party, the National Party of Suriname/NPS, in 1953, and the two governed as a coalition between 1958 and 1967, when the alliance ended. The party initially opposed plans in 1974–5 for independence from the Netherlands, but later accepted them. The VHP was banned, along with all other parties, after the 1980 military coup. It resumed activities when the ban was lifted in 1985 and joined the NPS and Suriname's third main party, the KTPI, in a Front for Democracy and Development. The VHP won 16 seats in the November 1987 elections to become the largest party in parliament, which elected party member Ramsewak Shankar as president of the republic in January 1988. The VHP formed a coalition goverment with the two other Front parties later that month.
See also **Lachmon**.

Progressive Social Movement (MSP): see **Popular Action**.

Propaganda Due
The name of a secret Italian Masonic lodge whose members traded in political influence and financial favours. The lodge had important Latin American connections. P–2 came to light in March 1981 when police raided the office of its Grand Master, Licio Gelli, and discovered a list of

962 members including Italian cabinet ministers, members of parliament, military officers, diplomats, bankers, the heads of the two intelligence services, and many others. The lodge also had prominent political and military members in Latin American countries, particularly Argentina, Brazil, and Venezuela. The P–2 scandal led to the fall of the Christian Democratic government of Arnaldo Forlani and long-running parliamentary investigations into what was called a 'parallel structure of power'. Gelli himself escaped to Switzerland, was arrested, bribed his way out, and took refuge in Latin America. After four years on the run he surrendered to the Swiss authorities in September 1987. A shadowy figure, he had many contacts in Argentina and Uruguay. In Uruguay Gelli owned a villa and worked through Umberto Ortolani, a financier who owned the Bafisud bank; Gelli had good relations with the army commander in 1981, Gen. Luis Queirolo.

In the case of Argentina P–2 had had a long involvement: in November 1972 Gelli personally chartered the aeroplane which took Gen. Juan Perón back to Buenos Aires, in return for which he was made commercial counsellor at the Argentine Embassy in Rome and given an Argentine passport. After the 1976 military coup against the Peronists, however, Gelli maintained excellent relations with the military regime, particularly through Adm. Eduardo Massera, one-time junta member and navy commander, and also a P–2 member. According to press reports, Gelli tried to obtain additional Exocet missiles for the Argentine navy during the 1982 South Atlantic War with Britain, using the Banco Andino of Lima. The bank was a subsidiary of Banco Ambrosiano, the Italian bank run by another P–2 member, Roberto Calvi. Calvi was found dead, hanging under Blackfriars Bridge in London in June 1982, only days after the end of hostilities in the South Atlantic. No definitive explanation for his death (whether it was suicide or murder was one point at issue) has been established, although the theories range from his involvement in the attempt to supply Exocets, through to in-fighting within P–2 over the collapse of Banco Ambrosiano and even to his involvement with Vatican finances.

See also **López Rega; South Atlantic War**.

Puebla: see **Medellín**.

***Puka Llacta*:** see **Shining Path**.

Pulacayo, Thesis of (*Tesis de Pulacayo*)

The core of the political programme of the Bolivian miners' union (the FSTMB), approved at an extraordinary congress in November 1946 held in the southern mining settlement of Pulacayo. Drafted by the POR (Revolutionary Workers' Party) it sought to apply a Trotskyist analysis to Bolivian trade union objectives and theoretically committed the FSTMB to the abolition of capitalism and the establishment of the dictatorship of the proletariat. This radical stance, to which even members of the Revolutionary Nationalist Movement (MNR) paid lip-service,

remained a key feature of the miners' struggle – and hence of Bolivian politics – up to the 1980s.
See also **Revolutionary Nationalist Movement**.

Punta del Este, Charter of: see **Alliance for Progress**.

Punto Fijo

A crucial Venezuelan political agreement reached between Democratic Action (AD), COPEI, and the Democratic Republican Union (URD) after the fall of the Marcos Pérez Jiménez dictatorship, to guarantee the stability of the new democracy. The pact was signed on 31 October 1958 at *Punto Fijo*, Rafael Caldera's house. Apart from Caldera for COPEI the signatories included Rómulo Betancourt for AD and Jovito Villalba for the URD. Also present were representatives of the business group Fedecámaras, the CSUN trade union group, student representatives of the *Federación de Centros Universitarios*, and the *Junta Patriótica*. Although the three parties recognised that efforts to agree on a candidate of national unity for the impending presidential elections had failed, they undertook to keep the political contest within certain acceptable limits, ruling out personal attacks or inter-party violence. The signatories also committed themselves to defend the elected government against any coup attempt.

Under the terms of *Punto Fijo*, independently of whoever became president for the 1959–64 term, all parties were to be represented in the cabinet, and each promised not to seek hegemony. The sum of votes for the three parties in the elections of 7 December 1958 were to be considered 'an affirmation of popular will in favour of the constitution and the consolidation of the rule of law'. Historically, *Punto Fijo* is credited with terminating the cycle of military coups in Venezuela and establishing the 'rules of the game' for a functioning democracy.
See also **Betancourt; Caldera; *Junta Patriótica***.

'*punto final*' law: see **due obedience**.

py nandí

Peasant supporters of the Colorado Party in Paraguay, at times organised into militias. The name comes from Guaraní and can be translated literally as 'the barefoot ones'. *Py nandí* militias – some 15,000 strong – played a crucial role in support of the government in the 1947 civil war. Some Colorado militants at the time, such as Edgar Ynsfran, praised the violence of the *py nandí*, a 'barbarism' which he said was an indication of the party's vitality: 'a sign that Coloradoism is a true movement of the people, not just a clique of café society intellectuals'. Under the rule of Gen. Alfredo Stroessner after 1954, the *py nandí* formed a network of surveillance and political intelligence.

In August 1973, at a time when Gen. Stroessner was facing criticism within the army, the *py nandí* were instrumental in the success of a mass pro-Stroessner rally in Asunción. The existence of the *py nandí* has also been credited as one of the factors behind the failure of the guerrillas in 1959 and 1960. While the Cuban peasantry had supported the guerrilla

movement, in Paraguay it was often the *py nandí* who reported their movements to the army.
See also **Colorado Party** (Paraguay).

Quadros, Jânio da Silva

1917– . Elected president of Brazil in 1961, but resigned after only seven months in office. Born in Mato Grosso do Sûl, he studied law, and in 1947 was elected councillor (*vereador*) in São Paulo for the Christian Democratic Party. He was elected São Paulo state deputy in 1950, mayor in 1953, and governor in 1954. His rapid political rise was achieved despite frequent changes of party affiliation. Quadros' presidential campaign was formally launched in 1959 by the *Partido Trabalhista Nacional* and other small parties, but he later received the backing of the conservative Nationalist Democratic Union (UDN). Quadros won the elections with 48% of the vote; he was the first president to be sworn in in the new federal capital of Brasília (on 31 January 1961).

In office he pursued an orthodox, conservative economic policy, but coupled this with a non-aligned foreign policy tailored to appeal to domestic nationalists. He launched anti-corruption measures, but his individualistic, autocratic style led to increasing political difficulties. The conservatives were angered by the re-establishment of diplomatic links with the Soviet Union, and the refusal to follow the US lead in isolating revolutionary Cuba.

Opposition came to a head after Quadros bestowed the Order of the Cruzeiro do Sûl (Brazil's highest honour) on Che Guevara in August 1961. Carlos Lacerda, who had been the main supporter of Quadros within the UDN, but had later become a sworn enemy, accused the president of planning a coup to give himself absolute powers. In a surprise move Quadros responded to the crisis by resigning on 25 August 1961 and leaving immediately for Europe. Returning to the country in 1962 he unsuccessfully stood for election as governor of São Paulo. Following the 1964 military coup, Quadros' political rights were suspended. He returned to political life in 1978. In November 1985 he won the elections for mayor of São Paulo.
See also **Lacerda; Nationalist Democratic Union**.

Queirolo, Gen. Luis: see ***Propaganda Due***.

'*quemados*' case

The name given in Chile to the case of two teenagers whom soldiers set on fire after dousing them with an inflammable liquid (*quemados* = 'burned ones'). The incident occurred on 2 July 1986, during a two-day general strike. The victims were Carmen Quintana, 18, and Rodrigo Rojas, 19. Rojas, who died a few days later, had returned in May 1986 from exile in Washington DC, and his US connections helped give the case international notoriety. His funeral was attended by the US ambassador. When Pope John Paul II visited Chile in 1987 he met Carmen Quintana, who had been permanently scarred by her burns. Under pressure, the military government questioned 25 soldiers and arrested a lieutenant (Pedro Fernández) on charges of manslaughter and negligence.These were later scaled down to 'unnecessary violence' and Fernández was released on bail. A colonel involved was given early retirement in early 1987 for having failed to inform his superiors of the incident.

Quintana, Carmen: see ***'quemados'* case**.

q

Quintín Lame Movement (*Movimiento Quintín Lame*)
A small, indigenous-based armed movement in Colombia, founded in 1984 and active in Cauca province. Named after an indian leader, Manuel Quintín Lame (d. 1967), it focuses on the issue of land. Since 1985 it has belonged to the National Guerrilla Coordinating Group.
See also **National Guerrilla Coordinating Group**.

Quiroga Santa Cruz, Marcelo: see **Socialist Party-One**.

Radical Alfarist Front (*Frente Radical Alfarista*/FRA)

An Ecuadorean party, founded by Abdón Calderón Muñoz after his expulsion from the Liberal Party in 1972. The party came fifth, with 10% of the vote, in the first round presidential elections of 1978, when Calderón was its candidate. His policies included the expulsion from Ecuador of the IMF and the Inter–American Development Bank (IDB). However, Calderón was assassinated in late 1978 and the leadership of the party was taken over by his daughter, economist Cecilia Calderón. The FRA was barred from the 1979 elections after losing its legal status because it had not presented candidates in sufficient provinces, but this was restored after President Roldós (whom it had backed) took power. Roldós named Cecilia Calderón to the constitutional tribunal (TGC), but she resigned over differences with the government.

The FRA won five seats in 1984 and initially participated in the opposition bloc. In mid-1985 it switched its support to the government of León Febres Cordero, but it withdrew from the governing coalition in early 1986 and (with the CFP) was the biggest loser in the mid-term elections of that year, which reduced its seats to three. These were cut to two in 1988.

radical Church (Brazil)

After the 1964 military coup, important sectors of the Brazilian Catholic Church underwent a process of radicalisation. Although conservative Catholics had figured prominently in the pre-coup agitation against President João Goulart and the Church had blessed the military takeover, not all the clergy welcomed the new regime; some sectors such as the Catholic Youth and the Basic Education Movement (MEB) in the north-east distanced themselves from it. From the late 1960s through to the early 1980s the bulk of the Church moved into the opposition camp.

Changing attitudes were accelerated by the Latin American Episcopal Conference at Medellín, Colombia, in 1968, which aligned the Church with the continent's poor and oppressed and was also a landmark in the development of liberation theology. The 1969 murder of a priest associated with the social work of Dom Helder Cámara, Archbishop of Recife and Olinda (and himself a former conservative who became highly critical of the regime) underlined the growing tension in Church–State relations.

Many more committed priests were to die in subsequent years, mainly at the hands of gunmen in the pay of landowners in rural areas.

The progressive wing of the Church developed the basic Christian communities (CEBs), a grass-roots movement which linked both religious and socio-political activism, and which grew to a membership of about 4m. Individual bishops became strongly critical of government policies and of the social cost of the 'economic miracle'. Cardinal Paulo Evaristo Arns in São Paulo fostered a local and international network of human rights groups. In Amazonia Dom Pedro Casaldáliga defended peasants' land rights; and many others became involved in social and political action. The National Bishops' Conference (CNBB), dominated by the progressives, took an outspoken stand on issues such as torture and the need for land reform. The Church was at the forefront of the struggle for re-democratisation, and after the return to civilian rule in March 1985, the CNBB continued to stress the need for far-reaching social reforms to help the country's poor.
See also **liberation theology; Medellín**.

Radical Democracy Party: see **Radical Party** (Chile).

Radical Liberal Party (PLR) (Ecuador): see **Democratic Left (ID); National Reconstruction Front**.

Radical Liberal Party (Paraguay) (*Partido Liberal Radical*/PLR)
The PLR became the mainstream of the Paraguayan Liberals, after a minority faction split away in 1961 under the name of Liberal Party (*Partido Liberal*/PL). Granted legal recognition by the regime of Gen. Alfredo Stroessner, it participated in elections in 1967 (to a constituent assembly), 1968, and 1973. The party was led by reformist liberals in 1975–7, but the conservatives regained control after a series of court cases. The party then came to be considered part of the token opposition to the Stroessner regime. It took part in further elections in 1978. In 1983 its presidential candidate, Dr Enzo Doldán, obtained 5.7% of the vote. With 13 deputies and six senators, the PLR was the second largest bloc in Congress, after the ruling Colorado Party.
See also **Authentic Radical Liberal Party; Liberals** (Paraguay); **Stroessner**.

Radical Party (Argentina) (*Unión Cívica Radical*/UCR)
One of the two political movements which dominated Argentina in the twentieth century. The party emerged in 1890 when dissidents split away from the *Unión Cívica* to lead an unsuccesful uprising against President Miguel Juárez Celman. There was another attempted uprising in 1905. The UCR established a policy of boycotting all elections until the government agreed to introduce universal franchise and eliminate corrupt electoral practices. Its main demands were met in 1912 with the promulgation of the Sáenz Peña law, which established universal male suffrage. The party lifted the boycott, and subsequently won the Santa Fé and Buenos Aires province elections. In 1916 the UCR candidate, Hipólito Yrigoyen, won the presidential elections, inaugurating an uninterrupted period of

UCR rule until 1930. Yrigoyen's first term in office in 1916–22 established his credentials as a charismatic leader of the new middle classes.

In 1922–8 the presidency was held by Marcelo T. de Alvear, leader of what became known as the UCR's 'anti-personalist' faction, which on some issues came close to the Conservatives. Yrigoyen was re-elected in 1928, but encountered growing political and economic difficulties, and was deposed in 1930 in a coup led by Gen. José Félix Uriburu. The UCR was banned from participating in elections until 1946 when it formed part of the unsuccessful anti-Peronist *Unión Democrática* alliance, together with Communists, Socialists, and Progressive Democrats. After the elections, those who favoured a common front against the Peronists – known as *unionistas* – lost control of the party to the *intransigentes*, who believed that the UCR should stand on its own. A representative of this sector, Dr Ricardo Balbín, stood unsuccessfully against Gen. Juan Domingo Perón in the 1951 elections.

After the 1955 coup against Gen. Perón, tensions within different sectors of the party over policy towards the Peronists grew. The 1956 party convention elected Dr Arturo Frondizi, a supporter of an understanding with the Peronists, as its presidential candidate. This led Dr Balbín and other sectors to break away and form the People's Radical Party (*UCR del Pueblo /UCRP)*. Frondizi's wing, which took the name Intransigent Radical Party (*UCR Intransigente*/UCRI), won the 1958 elections with Peronist support. After the 1962 military coup against Frondizi, Dr Arturo Illia of the UCRP won the July 1963 elections. A new crisis within the defeated UCRI led to a split between Frondizi, who set up a party eventually known as the Movement for Integration and Development (*Movimiento de Integración y Desarrollo*/MID), and Oscar Alende, who created the Instransigent Party (*Partido Intransigente*/PI). After the 1966 coup against Illia, the mainstream of the Radicals, under the leadership of Balbín's *Línea Nacional* faction, again adopted the title of UCR

In the 1973 elections Balbín stood twice for the presidency, and was defeated both times by the Peronists. During the Process of National Reorganisation military regime in 1976–83, the UCR was in opposition and joined the *Multipartidaria* coalition. The presidential nomination in 1983 was won by Dr Raúl Alfonsín of the *Renovación y Cambio* (Renewal and Change) faction of the party. Alfonsín's victory in the 30 October 1983 poll was the first time that the UCR had defeated the Peronists in free elections.

See also **Alfonsín; Infamous Decade; Illia; Intransigent Party; Movement for Integration and Development; Yrigoyen**.

Radical Party (Chile) (*Partido Radical*/PR)

A Chilean party, founded in 1861 as a breakaway from the Liberals (PL) and affiliated since the late 1960s to the Socialist International (SI). It gradually evolved from laissez-faire liberalism towards a collectivist approach, acquiring a substantial base in the growing middle class, and by the 1930s was Chile's biggest party. Its breakthrough came when the

PR's Pedro Aguirre Cerda was elected president at the head of the Popular Front coalition in 1938. As a party containing many private capitalists, the PR steered the Front away from state ownership of industry towards a state-protected but privately run economy. After the break-up of the Front in 1941 the Radicals continued to hold power until 1952, a period in which they accounted for an average 20–25% of the vote. Their period in government saw the strengthening of the labour movement and a major programme of import substitution. However, the party was weakened by internal divisions, with two factions breaking away in the 1940s and 1950s, and it did not again hold power in its own right, though it joined Alessandri's National Party cabinet in the early 1960's.

In 1969 the minority right wing formed the Radical Democracy Party (PDR) which backed Alessandri, while the PR itself went on to join the Popular Unity (UP) coalition headed by Salvador Allende which won the 1970 elections. In 1970 the Radicals took 13% of the vote, but this was almost halved by the time of the 1973 coup which ousted the UP. By this stage the PR was effectively split into three separate parties, with opponents of changes to its constitution having formed the Radical Left Party (PIR), which went into opposition. These splits were exacerbated by the problems of repression and exile. The wing of the party led by Enrique Silva Cimma joined the Democratic Alliance and advocates European-style social democracy, while the PR in exile (headed by Anselmo Sule and, latterly, by Fernando Luengo and Hugo Miranda) favoured the Communist-led Popular Democratic Movement (MDP) and became a member of the United Left in 1987. A tendency headed by Aníbal Palma favoured an alliance with the Socialist Bloc. The influence of the Sule wing was initially heightened by its control of international funds, especially from the SI, but since July 1986 Silva Cimma, rather than Sule, has been an SI vice president, and since the mid-87 split in the PR the Silva Cimma wing has been the one recognised by the International.

See also **Democratic Alliance; Popular Front; Popular Unity; Socialist International; United Left** (Chile).

Radical Socialist Party (PRS): see **Socialist Party of Chile**.

Rally for the Republic (RPR): see **Brune**.

Rangel, Domingo Alberto: see **guerrilla insurgency** (Venezuela); **Movement of the Revolutionary Left** (Venezuela).

Rangel, José Vicente: see **Generation of 1958** (Venezuela); **Movement towards Socialism; *Nueva Alternativa***.

raza cósmica*:** see ***indigenismo.

Real, Juan José: see **Latin American Integration Association**.

Rebel APRA: see **APRA**.

Recabarren, Luis Emilio: see **Communism; Communist Party of Chile**.

referendum of 1980 (Uruguay)
The constitutional referendum of 30 November 1980 was called by the military regime in Uruguay in an attempt to institutionalise the armed forces', control of the political system. The proposed new constitution gave the executive wide-ranging powers and the military a right of veto over elected governments. Plans were under way for presidential elections after the Referendum, with only one candidate – almost certainly a retired military officer – to stand; only after the first five-year presidential term were the traditional political parties to be allowed to field candidates. The winning party in elections was to be assigned an automatic majority in parliament.

The opposition parties were given little chance to campaign for a 'no' vote in the referendum. All leftist parties remained banned and many political tendencies within the traditional parties were also persecuted. The campaign for a 'yes' vote dominated the officially controlled media and the opposition was restricted to indoor meetings under heavy secret police surveillance. Yet despite this the referendum resulted in an overwhelming defeat for the proposed constitutional changes, by 58% to 42% . The success of the 'no' vote – and the apparent decision by the regime not to use fraud – took many observers by surprise, particularly as in Chile only three months earlier a similar authoritarian constitution had been successfully put to a plebiscite. It was a severe blow for the Uruguayan dictatorship, in many ways the beginning of a process which was eventually to lead to elections in November 1984 and the return of civilian rule in March 1985.
See also ***Proceso***.

Reid, Ptolemy: see **Hoyte**.

Renovation and Change Movement: see **Alfonsín**.

Republican Right (DR): see **Democratic Alliance**.

Resck, Luis Alfonso: see **Christian Democrat Party** (Paraguay).

Restrepo, Luis Alberto: see **Workers' Self-Defence Movement**.

***Revolución Argentina*:** see **Argentine Revolution**.

Revolution (Bolivian): see **Revolutionary Nationalist Movement**.

Revolution in Liberty: see **Frei Montalva**; **Christian Democrat Party** (Chile).

Revolution of 1958 (Venezuela)
The combined military rebellion and popular uprising of January 1958 which overthrew the dictatorship of Gen. Marcos Pérez Jiménez. Pérez Jiménez had tried to prolong his rule by holding a referendum in December 1957 in which the authorities claimed an 85% approval rate,

but the results were clearly fraudulent. On 1 January 1958 there was a revolt at an army base in Caracas, led by Col. Hugo Trejo, and at Maracay air base, led by Col. Jesús María Castro León. Jets flew over Caracas, but the risings were put down. Navy officers also expressed their discontent with the regime. Rioting broke out in Caracas on 14 January; the opposition *Junta Patriótica* called a general strike starting on 21 January, and there were widespread protests by university students. On 21 and 22 January there was heavy street fighting between protestors and the police. In the early hours of the 23rd Peréz Jiménez fled the country. The power vacuum was filled by a civilian military junta. Crowds took the headquarters of *Seguridad Nacional*, the secret police, by force, and burnt them down; there were also attacks on the residences of Pérez Jiménez and other top officials in the dictatorship, and on the offices of *El Heraldo*, a pro-regime newspaper. Contemporary accounts put the number of dead at between 300 and 500 during the fighting, with the injured in the thousands.

r

The Revolution of 1958 is widely considered the starting point for modern Venezuelan democracy, as it inaugurated a long period of relatively stable democratic rule, based on the *Punto Fijo* accord between the main political parties of the time. More immediately, it helped shape a new radical generation of politicians, many of whom were to join the guerrilla struggle in the early 1960s.

See also **Generation of 1958** (Venezuela); **Pérez Jiménez; *Punto Fijo***.

Revolutionary Action Group (GAR): see ***Nueva Alternativa***.

Revolutionary Alliance of the Left (ARDI): see **Democratic Action**.

Revolutionary Anti-imperialist Front: see **Revolutionary Party of the Nationalist Left**.

Revolutionary Armed Forces of Colombia (*Fuerzas Armadas Revolucionarias de Colombia*/FARC)

A guerrilla movement founded in 1964 (though not formally until April 1966) by 46 men, led by Manuel Marulanda Vélez (*'Tirofijo'*), Jacobo Arenas, and Jaime Caracas, in response to the Colombian army's invasion of the 'independent republics' of Marquetalia and El Chocó. In January 1966 the orthodox Communist Party (PCC), four of whose central committee were among the guerrilla leadership, adopted it and gave it its present name at the 10th PCC Congress. The PCC continued to maintain officially that a revolutionary situation did not exist in the country, and this ambivalence has persisted ever since. In 1967 the FARC tried and failed to unite with the pro-Cuban National Liberation Army (ELN). FARC strategy was to avoid a war of position and 'liberated zones' and to organise support throughout the country for an insurrection.

Today the movement claims to have around 5,000 combatants, organised into 27 'fronts'. The FARC has attempted to negotiate with successive governments. President Alfonso López Michelsen (1974–8) sought a peace treaty but was thwarted by the military. Under President Turbay Ayala (1978–82) a top-level commission was formed, but its demand that the guerrillas lay down their arms in exchange for an amnesty was rejected. In June 1983 joint military operations with the M–19 guerrilla movement began. Agreement on an alliance with M–19 and the National Liberation Army (ELN) followed in November 1983. On 28 March 1984 the FARC and a minor allied group, Workers' Self-Defence (ADO), signed a ceasefire agreement with the government of Belisario Betancur. The agreement, which did not require it to lay down arms, came into effect at the end of May. (A breakaway group, the Ricardo Franco Front, continued the struggle.) A truce was signed in December 1984, and this was followed by the integration of the movement into civilian politics with the formation of the Patriotic Union (UP).

The government committed itself to a series of political, social, and economic reforms, including agrarian reform, the direct election of mayors and equality for parties other than the Liberals and Conservatives, on whose implementation depended the final peace treaty, due to be signed in December 1985. This proved over-ambitious, and the truce was later extended indefinitely. The FARC abandoned plans to campaign openly for the 1986 elections, because of a large number of assassinations of UP and FARC members, but in early 1986 it offered to dismantle its military apparatus and become a party. In early 1987 there were signs of a widening gap between the FARC and the UP, with the former calling for a 'broad national coalition government', while the latter sought ties with parties to its right and insisted its only relation to the FARC was as a way back into civilian politics for ex-guerrillas. The killing by FARC members of 27 soldiers in an ambush in June 1987 brought the truce close to collapse, but neither side formally declared it at an end. The FARC called for urgent talks with the government, but rejected a demand to lay down its arms. In October 1987 the FARC was party to the launch of the Simón Bolívar Guerrilla Coordinating Group, an attempt to unite all Colombian guerrilla organisations, though it continued formally to honour the ceasefire.

See also **Communist Party of Colombia; Marquetalia; National Guerrilla Coordinating Group; Patriotic Union**.

Revolutionary Christian Democrat Party (PDCR): see **Christian Democrat Party** (Bolivia); **Movement of the Revolutionary Left** (Bolivia).

Revolutionary Communist Party (PCR): see **United Left** (Peru).

Revolutionary Labour Movement (MLR): see ***velasquismo*** (Peru).

Revolutionary Left Front (FIR): see **Blanco; Movement of the Revolutionary Left** (Peru).

Revolutionary Legion: see ***tenentes***.

Revolutionary Movement of the Christian Left (MRIC): see **Broad Left Front**.

Revolutionary Nationalist Movement (*Movimiento Nacionalista Revolucionario*/MNR)

A Bolivian political party, founded in 1941 by university lecturers and journalists, veterans of the Chaco War, who represented various different political traditions. Many had been supporters of Lt Col. Germán Busch, who had ousted Col. David Toro's regime in 1937 and ruled as an elected president from 1938 until his death in 1939. Its principal leaders were Hernán Siles Zuazo (formerly of the Beta Gama leftist group), Víctor Paz Estenssoro (an independent), and Carlos Montenegro (formerly linked with fascist groups). Paz became the leader and Siles his deputy. Their initial influences were the Peruvian APRA party and European fascism, which led them to back the Axis powers in World War II. But the MNR's post-war programme stressed the removal of the 'feudal' oligarchy, agrarian reform, and the nationalisation of mines and foreign trade. Another leader, Wálter Guevara, emphasised an alliance between workers, peasants, and the middle class.

The party played a major role in the 1943 military uprising and obtained many seats in the 1944 Congress. Between 1943 and 1944 it was in government under President Villarroel, and developed strong links with the unions, particularly the mineworkers. Paz became minister of finance. After the overthrow of Villarroel many MNR leaders were killed or exiled and it was not until 1949 that it stood again in congressional elections. Its success caused it to seek control of the government by force, but this failed. In 1951 it was cheated of electoral victory and a military junta took over, but in April 1952 it was able to take power with the assistance of the police, as well as that of the miners, who staged an armed revolt.

The MNR became the most powerful party in Bolivian history, but internal divisions grew as the left wing (*sector de izquierda*) successfully pushed through nationalisation of mines and agrarian reform, but then saw the government impose a US-designed economic 'stabilisation plan'. In 1956 Siles Zuazo was elected to succeed Paz. The right wing, led by Guevara, broke away in 1959 to form the Authentic Revolutionary Party (PRA) after he was denied the presidential candidacy in favour of a second term for Paz Estenssoro and the vice presidency for Juan Lechín Oquendo, Trotskyist leader of the tin miners. The left wing under Lechín broke away prior to the 1964 elections to become the Revolutionary Party of the Nationalist Left (PRIN), feeling that the revolution had been slowed unacceptably. The MNR won comfortably in 1964, but was overthrown by the army (under Paz's Vice president, Gen. René Barrientos) six months later. For the next 15 years it lacked clear leadership and organisation. Paz himself spent seven years in exile in Peru, while the party was divided into four main factions.

In 1971 the MNR backed a right-wing coup by Gen. Hugo Bánzer and became part of the government. Siles Zuazo then split away (in 1972) to join the Left MNR (*MNR de Izquierda*/MNRI, founded in 1970). This party (now very weak and renamed the Democratic Left/ID) is today a social democratic ally of the Communists (PCB) and the parliamentary left, and calls itself 'revolutionary and anti-imperialist'. In 1974 the MNR was expelled from government by the armed forces. When the military regime called elections in 1978, the MNRI led a new left-wing coalition (the Democratic and Popular Union/UDP), while Paz's renamed Historic MNR (*MNR-Histórico*/MNR-H) stood alone. In both the 1979 and 1980 elections Paz came second to Siles, but no one candidate obtained an absolute majority and the military intervened on both occasions. Siles eventually became president in 1982, after the armed forces had ruled for two years, when the 1980 election results were ratified, but in the course of his presidency not only the UDP but the MNRI itself became fragmented. By 1985 it was split three ways, with a right wing under Federico Alvarez Plata wanting rapprochement with the MNR-H and a left wing anxious for talks with the unions. Paz and the MNR-H were victors in 1985, despite obtaining fewer votes than ex-President Bánzer, due to broader support in Congress. The MNR-H was revealed as, if anything, further to the right than the avowedly right-wing ADN of Bánzer himself. By the time of the 1988 municipal elections it was clear that Paz's party was well behind both the ADN and the Movement of the Revolutionary Left (MIR) in terms of popularity.

Most other factions of the MNR which have emerged as independent forces have little support. They include the MNR-U (led by Guillermo Bedregal), the AFIN-MNR (Roberto Jordán Pando), and the MNRI–1 (a breakaway from the MNRI). However, the Vanguard MNR (MNR-VR), led by Carlos Serrate Reich, won almost as many seats (six) in 1985 as the MNRI, becoming the fifth largest parliamentary party. The MNR–H chose Gonzalo Sánchez de Lozada as its presidential candidate for 1989.

See also **Guevara Arce; Lechín Oquendo; Paz Estenssoro; Siles Zuazo**.

Revolutionary Party of Bolivian Workers (PRTB): see **Democratic and Popular Union.**

Revolutionary Party of the Nationalist Left (*Partido Revolucionario de la Izquierda Nacionalista*/PRIN)

Founded in Bolivia in 1964. Formerly the left-wing faction (*Sector de Izquierda*) of the Revolutionary Nationalist Movement (MNR), it split off in 1963 under tin miners' leader Juan Lechín Oquendo, partly in protest at MNR leader Víctor Paz Estenssoro's decision to go for a third term of office as president, but mostly over the MNR's anti-labour policies and slow pace of reform.

The PRIN's outlook is left nationalist, rather than explicitly socialist and its structure and ideology have never been firm. Even so, it has been influential in the union movement as a result of Lechín's personal standing. Having abstained in the 1964 elections, it initially backed Gen. Barrientos' military takeover of that year, as part of the People's Revolutionary Committee, but it was soon disillusioned. In Barrientos' 1966 elections it joined the People's Democratic Committee (CODEP) with the Trotskyist POR, the Maoists, the MNR left, and independents, but the Front won no seats. It took part with most of the left in the brief Popular Assembly under Gen. Torres in 1970 and in the short-lived Revolutionary Anti-imperialist Front (FRA) against Gen. Bánzer in the early 1970s. In 1978, as part of the Left Revolutionary Front (FRI) with the PCML, PRTB, and VCPOR, it backed peasant leader Casiano Amurrio for the presidency. In 1979, as part of the UDP coalition, it backed the candidacy of Hernán Siles Zuazo of the Left MNR (MNR-I). Lechín stood for the presidency on the PRIN ticket in 1980, but withdrew in favour of the UDP. In 1985 the PRIN joined the United People Front (FPU) behind the candidacy of Antonio Arañíbar Quiroga. See also **Lechín Oquendo**.

Revolutionary Socialist Party (PSR) (Colombia): see **Colombian Communist Party**.

Revolutionary Socialist Party (PSR) (Peru): see **Movement of the Revolutionary Left** (Peru); **Túpac Amaru Revolutionary Movement; United Left** (Peru); ***velasquismo*** (Peru).

Revolutionary Vanguard (VR): see **United Left** (Peru).

Revolutionary Workers' Party (Bolivia): see **Pulacayo, Thesis of**.

r

Revolutionary Workers' Party (Colombia): see **National Guerrilla Coordinating Group**.

Revolutionary Workers' Party – People's Revolutionary Army
(*Partido Revolucionario de los Trabajadores – Ejército Revolucionario del Pueblo*/PRT-ERP)
An Argentine leftist movement influenced by Trotskyism and Guevarism. The ERP became one of the two main guerrilla organisations in the country in the 1970s, but suffered military defeat after the counter-insurgency onslaught by the Process of National Reorganisation government in 1976–9. The PRT, the political wing, predated the ERP and followed a Marxist-internationalist line; it was affiliated to the Fourth International (Unified Secretariat) until June 1973. At the PRT's 5th Congress in July 1970 a decision was taken to form the ERP as an armed wing. The ERP began a campaign of attacks on the army during military rule. But unlike the Montoneros it regarded Peronism as a bourgeois movement. In the 1973 elections the ERP called for abstention and announced its decision to intensify the guerrilla war. A minority decided to support Peronist candidates, breaking away to form ERP–22 August.

Under the administrations of Gen. Juan Domingo Perón and Isabel Perón in 1973–6 the ERP stepped up its military activity; operations included the attack on the *Azul* army garrison in January 1974, development of a rural guerrilla *foco* in impoverished Tucumán province, and an attack on the Monte Chingolo barracks (in a joint operation with Montoneros). After the 1976 coup the movement was defeated during the prolonged 'dirty war'; the top leadership, including Roberto Santucho, was killed.
See also **dirty war; *foquismo*; Montoneros; Process of National Reorganisation; Trotskyism**.

Revolutionary Workers' Party (POR and PST) (Peru): see **Blanco**.

Reyes, Simón: see **Communist Party of Bolivia**.

Ribeiro, Darcy: see **Democratic Labour Party**.

Ricardo Franco Front: see **National Guerrilla Coordinating Group; Revolutionary Armed Forces of Colombia**.

Rincón Quiñones, Gen.: see **National Liberation Army** (Colombia).

Rio de Janeiro Protocol: see **border dispute** (Peru/Ecuador).

Ríos, Juan Antonio: see **Frei Montalva; Socialist Party of Chile**.

Ríos Gamara, Jorge: see **Guevara Arze**.

Rio Treaty (Inter-American Treaty on Reciprocal Assistance)
A regional security pact signed in Rio de Janeiro, Brazil, in 1947. Also known by its Spanish acronym, TIAR. Signatories (the US and most Latin American nations) agree to assist one another in the event of armed aggression within the hemisphere, and to consult one another in the event of armed aggression outside the hemisphere or of other types of aggression within it. The central principle of the treaty is that 'an armed attack by any State against an American State shall be considered as an attack against all', a principle enunciated in the Rio declaration of 1942 and embodied in the Act of Chapultepec in 1945. Signatories also pledge not to resort to war, and to submit disputes for peaceful settlement within the organisation before resorting to the United Nations.

The decision-making body for treaty purposes is the Meeting of Consultation of foreign ministers of the Organisation of American States (OAS), though provisional decisions can be taken by the OAS Permanent Council. A two-thirds vote by ministers is binding on members. Sanctions contemplated by the treaty include diplomatic, economic, and military measures. A protocol to the treaty was agreed in 1975 against US objections, though it has yet to be ratified. This would recognise 'ideological pluralism' and make the lifting of sanctions more straightforward. The treaty has been invoked on a score of occasions since its introduction, most of them involving situations in the Caribbean basin.
See also **Organisation of American States**.

Rivadeneira, Ricardo: see **Party of National Renovation**.

Roca-Runciman Pact: see **Infamous Decade**.

Rodney, Walter
b. 1942. Guyanese historian and politician, murdered in 1980. Author of *A History of the Guyanese Working People* (1980). After studying at the University of the West Indies (UWI) in Jamaica and at London University, Walter Rodney taught at a Tanzanian university from 1966, returning to teach African history at UWI in 1968. When, after a trip abroad, he was barred from re-entering Jamaica in October that year, 'black power' demonstrations erupted in Kingston, triggering others elsewhere in the region and marking a watershed in Anglo-Caribbean consciousness.

Rodney's book *Groundings with My Brothers* (1969) was one of the main inspirations of the 'black power' and 'new left' nationalist movements which sprang up in the region at the time.

He returned to his job in Tanzania, wrote *How Europe Underdeveloped Africa* (1972), and went back to Guyana in 1974 to take up a job at the university. However, the job was withdrawn under government pressure. Rodney then became the informal leader of the leftist Working People's Alliance, which aimed to break the racial mould of Guyanese politics. He was killed in Georgetown on 13 June 1980 by a bomb widely believed to have been planted by individuals linked with the government of President Forbes Burnham.
See also **Working People's Alliance**.

Rodríguez, Gen. Leonidas: see ***velasquismo*** (Peru).

Rodríguez Grez, Dr Pablo: see **Fatherland and Freedom**.

Rodríguez Lara, Gen.: see **Concentration of Popular Forces; military governments (Ecuador/1961–79)**.

r

Rojas de Moreno Díaz, María Eugenia: see **ANAPO**; **Rojas Pinilla**.

Rojas, Rodrigo: see **'*quemados*' case**.

Rojas Pinilla, Gen. Gustavo

1900–75. De facto ruler of Colombia 1953–7. Trained at the National Military Academy, Bogotá. Commander of the 3rd Brigade, Cali, during the '*Bogotazo*' and the beginning of the '*violencia*' period. Member of the Inter-American Defense Board. Commander-in-chief of the armed forces and minister of communications, 1952.

Rojas deposed the unpopular Conservative (PC) President Laureano Gómez on 13 June 1953 and appointed a cabinet composed almost entirely of Gómez's moderate opponents within the party. He immediately announced an amnesty for the Communist and Liberal guerrillas, many of whom took advantage of it, but he failed to end the *violencia*. He sought to implement authoritarian reforms, using Peronist-style tactics, including the creation of a 'third party' (described as 'Christian and Bolivarist') and the wooing of organised labour. These moves soon united Liberals and Conservatives against him, along with the Catholic Church and the business community. After he had secured a constitutional amendment permitting him a second term, and made it clear he would not tolerate a free election, he was persuaded in 1957 by the heads of the armed forces to go into exile on the grounds that he had no support in the country.

Rojas was replaced by a provisional military junta which then gave way to a 'national unity' government comprising five Liberals and five Conservatives. Later, he was convicted of abuses of power by a national tribunal, but he returned to politics with the formation in 1960 of the Popular National Alliance (ANAPO). As ANAPO candidate for presidency he came close to winning the 1970 election; according to his supporters, he was only deprived of victory by fraud. After his death in

1975, his daughter, María Eugenia Rojas de Moreno Díaz, assumed his political mantle.
See also **ANAPO; *Bogotazo*; 19 April Movement; *violencia, la*.**

Roldós Aguilera, Jaime

1940–81. President of Ecuador 1979–81. Elected with a personal landslide majority (over 62% of the vote) in April 1979 as the first civilian president of Ecuador for nine years and the youngest in Latin America. Roldós, who campaigned as the 'president of the poor', had originally been put forward as a stand-in by his wife's ambitious uncle, Assad Bucaram, an outspoken populist opponent of the military regime who had been prevented from standing, ostensibly on the grounds of his Lebanese parentage. Roldós, a lawyer from Guayaquil, thus became the candidate of Bucaram's Concentration of Popular Forces (CFP) party, but even before his inauguration major differences between the two had become apparent. Bucaram, in alliance with the right, became president of Congress and led a congressional spoiling operation against reformist legislation proposed by Roldós. The president was forced to forge a new majority in Congress, based mainly on the Popular Democracy (DP) and Democratic Left (ID) parties, and he was assisted when ID's Raúl Baca Carbo replaced Bucaram as president of the legislature in 1980.

Frustrated domestically, Roldós was active abroad, restoring relations with Cuba and cultivating Nicaragua and the Salvadorean left-wing opposition, to the annoyance of Washington. Relations with Peru deteriorated, however, and border clashes took place during his presidency. Declining oil revenues forced public spending cuts and the postponement of reforms, and austerity measures led to some violence on the streets as the labour movement protested. Roldós died in a plane crash on 24 May 1981, along with his defence minister and both their wives. This was officially attributed to mechanical failure, despite allegations of US Central Intelligence Agency involvement by some supporters. Vice-president Osvaldo Hurtado served out the remainder of his term (to 1984), while León Roldós Aguilera, the late president's brother, was elected to the vice presidency.
See also **Bucaram; Concentration of Popular Forces; Hurtado Larrea**.

Roldós Aguilera, León: see **Ecuadorean Roldosista Party; Roldós Aguilera**.

Roopnaraine, Rupert: see **Working People's Alliance**.

Roosevelt Corollary: see **Monroe doctrine**.

Roosevelt, Franklin Delano: see **dollar diplomacy; good neighbour policy; Monroe doctrine**.

Roosevelt, Theodore: see **Monroe doctrine**.

Rucci, José: see **Montoneros**.

Rotela, José: see **guerrilla invasions** (Paraguay).

S

Sáenz Peña, Roque: see **Yrigoyen**.

Saguier, Abdón: see **Authentic Radical Liberal Party**.

Sajón, Edgardo: see **Lanusse**.

Salgado, Plinio: see **Integralism**.

salida al mar (**'access to the sea'**)
Only two countries in the Americas, Bolivia and Paraguay, have no sea coast. Paraguay has access to the Atlantic Ocean via the Paraguay and Paraná rivers, but Bolivia has been without access to the Pacific Ocean since the 1879–84 War of the Pacific, which it fought in alliance with Peru against Chile. In the course of the war, the Chileans annexed the coastal territory belonging to Bolivia, including the port of Antofagasta, though they later built the Arica–La Paz railway in partial compensation. Peru also lost territory, and Bolivian attempts to regain ocean access have been hampered by the 1929 Treaty of Ancón between Peru and Chile, under which no territory formerly belonging to Peru may be ceded to a third country without Peruvian permission. Bolivia also failed to win full access to the Pacific via the Paraguay river after the Chaco War of the early 1930s.

Relations with Chile remain strained as a result of the problem, which has often been used by Bolivian governments to stir up nationalist sentiment. In 1962 Bolivia broke diplomatic relations after accusing Chile of reducing the flow of the Lauca river into Bolivia; and ties were not restored until 1975. Top-level contacts took place in the 1970s between the military regimes of Gen. Bánzer in Bolivia and Gen. Pinochet in Chile, but the 1975 Chilean proposals for a solution (which did not meet with instant Peruvian approval) eventually proved unacceptable to Bolivia. They included the condition that Bolivia relinquish an equal area of territory in exchange for an 8-mile wide corridor to the sea along the Peruvian border. Relations deteriorated again and were broken by the Bolivians on 17 March 1978. A Peruvian proposal in that year for a coastal area governed by all three countries was rejected by Chile and Bolivia.

In 1979 the Organisation of American States resolved to back the Bolivian claim. President Paz Estenssoro sought new talks with Chile in early 1986, but met with opposition at home. The two sides eventually

met, at foreign minister level, in Uruguay in April 1987, where Bolivia proposed that Chile cede either a 2,800 km corridor to the Pacific or a 1,200 km enclave on the coast. Compensation was offered in the form of natural gas and other goods. The Chilean government said it would study the proposal, but nothing came of it. Later that year Bolivia withdrew its consul from Santiago and said it would 'never again' negotiate with Pinochet.
See also **Chaco War**.

salida electoral

Literally, 'electoral way out', a phrase frequently used towards the end of military regimes, when those in power begin to plan elections. Contemporary Latin American history has been rich in different types of *salidas*.

At one extreme are those where an incumbent military regime, either because it has failed, or is politically exhausted, or because from the start it sought a purely transitional or caretaker role, allows impartial elections and the unconditional transfer of power to the winner. More frequently, the outgoing regime seeks to influence the choice of its successor, either by subtle methods, such as fine-tuning electoral regulations to favour particular parties, or by crude ones, such as banning and persecuting candidates and parties it dislikes. Many *salidas* have taken place in two stages, with the first involving the drafting of a new constitution by a constituent assembly. Where military regimes have been involved in human rights violations and political violence, officers have sought to place limits on possible prosecutions under a future civilian administration. There have also been attempts to preserve for the armed forces a special advisory role, often going as far as a power of veto over the elected government in areas such as national security.

At the other extreme the *salida* is one in name only, a way of prolonging military rule under a new cloak of respectability. Typical examples of this are the holding of 'elections' with a single candidate, and referendums or plebiscites where the questions are posed in such a way as to elicit exactly the answer the regime is seeking. In these cases the exercise has more to do with improving a regime's image than with any real democratisation.

San Andrés dispute

Sovereignty over the Caribbean islands of San Andrés and Providencia (with their associated islets, or cays, of Roncador, Quitasueño, and Serrana) is disputed by Colombia and Nicaragua. A 1928 treaty (known alternatively as the Esguerra-Bárcenas, Bárcenas Meneses-Esguerra or Guerra-Meneses Treaty) in which Nicaragua ceded the islands to Colombia was declared null and void by the Nicaraguan government on 4 February 1980 on the grounds that the islands were in its territorial waters (extended to 200 miles in December 1979) and that the treaty had been signed under US pressure by a 'traitorous' regime in Managua (US troops occupied Nicaragua at the treaty date). Colombia, which bases its claim on an order of the Spanish Crown of 1803, then recalled its ambassador. Panama (which also has a dormant claim to the islands) offered to mediate. Under the same treaty, Colombia had renounced its claim to the Miskito coast of Nicaragua and the offshore Mangle islands.

The San Andrés archipelago lies about 180 km from the Nicaraguan coast and 480 km from Colombia. It holds Colombia's most important tourist complex and the San Andrés free port. The possible presence of oil in the surrounding waters complicates the issue. A 1972 treaty (Sánchez-Vásquez Carrizosa or Vázquez Sakio) between Washington and Bogotá granted US recognition of Colombian sovereignty and returned a number of islets which had been under US occupation. Nicaragua requested in 1979 that the treaty should not be ratified by Washington, but despite this the US Senate ratified it on 31 July 1981. In March 1980 Colombia took the dispute to the UN Law of the Sea conference, but in May 1980 Nicaragua and Colombia agreed to indefinite bilateral talks on the issue. Further friction was evidenced in 1986, when Nicaragua again insisted on its claim and Colombia despatched warships to the islands. In August that year Honduras renounced its own claim to many of the smaller cays in a treaty with Colombia.

Sánchez-Vásquez Carrizosa Treaty: see **San Andrés dispute**.

saneamento

A word often used by Brazilian military officers to denote a 'cleansing' or purging of the political system. This was a favourite concept employed by the generals who led the 1964 coup and who argued that civilian politics had suffered a process of degeneration, corruption, and infiltration by subversive forces such as Communism. It was only through a period of necessarily authoritarian military rule that the body politic could be restored to health, the argument went.
See also **Coup of 1964** (Brazil); **National Security doctrine**.

Sanguinetti, Julio María

b. 1936. President of Uruguay 1985– . A lawyer and journalist, he became a member of the Colorado Party and was elected to the Chamber of Deputies, where he held a seat continuously between 1962 and 1973. He served under the Colorado presidency of Jorge Pacheco Areco, and his successor Juan María Bordaberry, first as minister of labour and industry (1969–72) and then as minister of education and culture (1972–3). As education minister he faced widespread student protests and implemented the government 'intervention' of the education system, for which he earned the dislike of the Uruguayan left. He nevertheless refused to be associated with the military coup of 27 June 1973, remaining in opposition for the following 12 years, during part of which time he served as president of a UNESCO commission for the promotion of books in Latin America.

Sanguinetti participated in the opposition campaign against the military's constitutional proposals in the November 1980 referendum, and his sector of the Colorado Party emerged as the strongest after the November 1982 internal party elections. His weekly newspaper, *Correo de los Viernes*, was subject to censorship and at one stage one of his

personal assistants was kidnapped by the army. Nominated by the Colorados as their presidential candidate, Sanguinetti carried out a successful campaign, winning the 25 November 1984 polls with 39% of the vote and taking office on 1 March 1985. Sanguinetti's presidency was marked by a generally centre-right stance. At the outset Parliament voted an amnesty for left-wing political prisoners, which Sanguinetti supported, but the president was later at the forefront of efforts in 1986 to obtain an amnesty for military officers involved in human rights violations.
See also **Colorado Party** (Uruguay).

Santucho, Roberto: see **Revolutionary Workers' Party – People's Revolutionary Army**.

São Paulo revolt

An armed rebellion by the Brazilian state of São Paulo against the federal government of President Getúlio Vargas in July–October 1932. Resentment against Vargas had been growing since his 1930 assumption of power, with the *paulistas* suspecting him of dictatorial ambitions. São Paulo coffee and industrial interests were concerned at the influence of the radical *tenentes* on Vargas. The conflict was accentuated by the presidential appointment of a *tenente* north-easterner, João Alberto Lins de Barros, as governor, instead of a leader of the São Paulo Democratic Party as had been previously promised. Although the *paulistas* succeeded in forcing João Alberto's resignation in July 1931, they were still unable to have their way in the naming of a successor.

The initial São Paulo rebel plan had been for a political coup, rather than a military rising, against Vargas and the *tenentes*, counting on support from other states such as Rio Grande do Sûl and Minas Gerais. But premature defiance by one member of the conspiracy, Mato Grosso army commander Gen. Bertoldo Klinger, forced São Paulo to launch the rebellion early. The other states failed to deliver the promised support, and the federal army remained loyal to Vargas. São Paulo's own army, the *Força Publica*, fought a defensive trench warfare around the state's frontiers, but was outgunned and outnumbered by the federal army, making an eventual admission of defeat unavoidable. São Paulo's upper classes and industrialists had been the most enthusiastic supporters of the state's defiance, but working-class leaders were more indifferent as to the outcome. The defeat of São Paulo has been interpreted as a sign of the shift in the balance of power, away from state-level groups and regional interests, and towards the emerging federal state structure and national interests.
See also ***tenentes***; **Vargas**.

São Paulo Socialist Party: see ***tenentes***.

Saravia, Aparicio: see **Blanco Party** (Uruguay).

Sarney, José

b. 1930. Brazilian poet, politician, and president, 1985– ; the first civilian to take office after the end of the 1964–85 military regime. Born in

S

Maranhão, one of 14 children, he was baptised José Ribamar Costa, but took the name of José Sarney in honour of his father, Sarney Araujo Costa. He worked as a journalist in Maranhão and became an assistant to the state governor in 1950. The first of a series of poetry and prose works by Sarney was published in 1952. As a member of the conservative Nationalist Democratic Union (UDN) party he was elected state representative in 1956 and subsequently re-elected in 1958 and 1962. He was a member of the younger, modernising tendency within the UDN, known as the *Bossa Nova*. He supported the 1964 military coup against João Goulart and was elected governor of Maranhão for 1965–70 (before the military regime banned direct gubernatorial elections in 1966). He then joined the newly created pro-government party ARENA.

Following the 1979 political reforms, Sarney became president of the PSD, the successor to ARENA. But when in mid-1974 the majority of the party threw its support behind the controversial Paulo Maluf in the presidential race, Sarney aligned himself with the dissident faction which broke away to form the Liberal Front (PFL). As part of the negotiations by which the PFL joined the Democratic Alliance composed of the PMDB and other groups supporting the opposition candidate Tancredo Neves, Sarney was awarded the vice-presidential nomination. While his sympathies remained largely with the PFL, the arrangement involved him formally joining the PMDB, the third party in his political career. The Neves–Sarney ticket was victorious in the indirect presidential elections in January 1985. But Tancredo Neves fell ill only hours before the inauguration ceremony on 15 March 1985 and Sarney took office as acting president. On the death of Neves in April, Sarney was confirmed in the presidency.

Although many questioned his ability to carry out a job which had come to him by chance, and his past links with the disgraced military regime were a liability, Sarney managed in his first two years in office to hold together the broad coalition originally formed around Tancredo Neves. His February 1986 anti-inflationary Cruzado Plan, a price and wage freeze coupled with the introduction of a new currency of the same name was initially highly popular. Low inflation and high economic growth during 1986 earned the president some of the highest popularity ratings registered in the country, although these later fell to the lowest ever recorded as the economic situation started deteriorating again in 1987. In September–October 1987 the PFL-PMDB coalition collapsed, and Sarney faced growing political difficulties.
See also **Brazilian Democratic Movement Party; Cruzado; Liberal Front Party; Neves**.

Savisky, Silvestre: see **Communist Party of Colombia**.

Schultz, George: see **Monroe doctrine**.

Second Independence Movement (MSI): see **Broad Left Front.**

Second Vatican Council: see **liberation theology**.

Sendero Luminoso: see **Shining Path.**

Sendic, Raúl

b. 1925. Founding member of Uruguay's National Liberation Movement – Tupamaros (*Movimiento Nacional de Liberación – Tupamaros*/MLN-T), the urban guerrilla movement active in the 1960s and early 1970s. Trained as a lawyer, he was initially involved with the Socialist Party and in helping to organise sugar cane workers in the northern department of Salto. He left the party in the early 1960s and began forming the nucleus of the MLN-T, committed to revolutionary armed struggle in reaction to what was regarded as the failure of the parliamentary left.

Sendic led the guerrilla movement through the upsurge in armed activities in the late 1960s, characterised by raids and kidnaps of diplomats and politicians. Imprisoned, he escaped in a daring jail break-out during this period. He was arrested again in a shoot-out in February 1972, during which he received serious gunshot wounds to his jaw and mouth. After the 1973 military coup Sendic was held with eight other MLN-T leaders as hostages, under army threat of execution if the guerrillas should resume their operations. He was tortured during his captivity, and his injuries were never given adequate medical attention. Constantly transferred between prisons and barracks, Sendic was given prolonged periods of solitary confinement, and at one stage he was held for six months in a disused well. He was released under the terms of the amnesty introduced by the new civilian government in March 1985. Sendic then called for peaceful political action by the MLN-T, in view of the changed political situation.

See also **National Liberation Movement – Tupamaros**.

Seregni, Gen. Líber

b. 1916. Senior Uruguayan army officer who after retiring became a leader of the Broad Front (*Frente Amplio*) left-wing coalition. Seregni had an outstanding military career, becoming commander of the 1st military region (which includes Montevideo) in 1968. Although a strong candidate for the post of commander-in-chief, Seregni asked for early retirement that same year in protest at President Jorge Pacheco Areco's policy of using the army, under state of siege regulations, to break up strikes. In 1971, following the formation of the *Frente Amplio* coalition, he agreed to stand as its presidential candidate. In the November 1971 elections Seregni received 18% of the vote – a record percentage for any leftist candidate.

Following the 27 June 1973 military coup, Seregni joined demonstrations in support of the two-week long general strike called to oppose it. He was arrested and freed in 1974; but new charges were brought and he was arrested again in 1976. The charges included 'conspiring against the constitution'; he was also demoted by an army honour tribunal. Eventually sentenced to 14 years' imprisonment, Seregni was released in March 1984 as the military regime prepared to allow elections. Although himself banned from standing in the elections in November that year, he played a crucial role in negotiations with the outgoing regime (leading to

the *Club Naval* Pact) and in campaigning for the *Frente Amplio*, whose candidate, Juan José Crottogini, received 20% of the vote. After the return of civilian rule in March 1985, the status of retired general was restored to Seregni by an army tribunal. He remained one of the country's key political leaders.
See also **Broad Front; *Club Naval* Pact**.

Serrate Reich, Carlos: see **Revolutionary Nationalist Movement**.

Shankar, Ramsewak
b. 1937. President of Suriname 1988– . An agronomist, Shankar was minister of justice and then agriculture between 1969 and 1971, when he became director of the country's biggest rice farm, the state-run operation at Wageningen. He helped negotiate the 1975 independence aid package with the Dutch. He left government service for the private sector after the 1980 military coup and headed a Dutch-owned insurance company. In 1985, he became an adviser to the agriculture ministry. He joined the Progressive Reform Party (VHP) in 1987 and was unanimously elected president of the republic by parliament in January 1988.

Shining Path (*Sendero Luminoso*/SL)
A Peruvian Maoist guerrilla movement, which split off in 1970 from the country's pro-Albanian communist party, Red Flag (*Bandera Roja*). Its leader is Abimael Guzmán (aka Comrade/President Gonzalo). *Sendero's* full name is the Communist Party of Peru – for the Shining Path of José Carlos Mariátegui. (Mariátegui (1895–1930) was the founder of Peruvian communism: he favoured a return to the Inca system of cooperative agriculture.) The party spent years selecting recruits and preparing its strategy before launching its armed struggle in July 1980, having gone underground in 1977. Guzmán was professor of philosophy and personnel director at San Cristóbal de Huamanga University in Ayacucho and at the centre of a radical circle known as the Revolutionary Student Front for the Shining Path of Mariátegui. SL believes in 'prolonged popular war' (which could last 50 years) in which the cities will be surrounded from the countryside. It believes the indians should once more rule Peru, and is closest to the traditional Maoism of the 'Gang of Four' (though it derides all foreign communist governments). Its original base was in Ayacucho department, but as this has been saturated militarily it has increasingly carried out attacks in Lima and elsewhere. Its influence is spreading in universities, trade unions, and left-wing parties. It also has bases in the central jungles. A semi-autonomous 'Annihilation Squad' (*Escuadrón de Aniquilamiento*) also operates in the capital. In February 1982, SL freed 360 prisoners from jail in Ayacucho. In 1983 it formed the People's Revolutionary Army (estimated strength: 2,000–3,000), backed by both rural militia and urban cells.

SL's operations include sabotage, kidnapping, and the murder of local officials and members of the security forces. Suspected informers are often mutilated and sometimes killed, and government counter-insurgency forces have responded with great brutality. Alleged SL massacres have sometimes been shown to be the work of these forces. Of some 15,000 deaths attributed to this struggle up to mid-1988, most are said by human rights organisations to be the work of security forces. In June 1986 troops and police killed some 250 SL prisoners after crushing mutinies in three Lima gaols.

SL has absorbed several small groups, including: the Communist Proletarian Revolutionary Vanguard (VRPC or *Huaccaycholo*); the *Victoria Navarro* and *Victoriano Esparraga Cumbi* groups of the Movement of the Revolutionary Left (MIR); a faction of *Puka Llacta* (meaning 'Red Land' in Quechua, a splinter from the *Patria Roja* communist party) with support in the mining region of La Oroya/Cerro de Pasco; the Marxist-Leninist Nuclei, another *Patria Roja* splinter; some members of a revived National Liberation Army (ELN); and the rump of the Lima-based Marxist-Leninist Revolutionary Vanguard (VRPM). Some sections of the CCP peasant organisation and the teachers' union SUTEP are also said to back it. Although SL is usually said to have no foreign links, it did affiliate in April 1984 with the Revolutionary Internationalist Movement in London (a Trotskyist group led mainly by Iranian radicals).

In June 1988, Shining Path's second-in-command, Osman Morote, was captured and put on trial.

See also **Lurigancho massacre; Uchurracay incident**.

Siles Salinas, Luis Adolfo: see **Christian Democrat Party** (Bolivia).

S

Siles Zuazo, Hernán

b. 1914. President of Bolivia 1956–60 and 1982–5. Born in La Paz, the son of President Hernando Siles (1926–30). Nicknamed '*el conejo*' (the rabbit) because of his appearance. Decorated during the 1930s Chaco War. Educated at the Universidad Mayor de San Andrés (law degree 1939). Congressional deputy, 1940–6. Hernán Siles was, with Víctor Paz Estenssoro and Wálter Guevara Arce, one of the three major figures who founded the Revolutionary Nationalist Movement (MNR). He was exiled with Paz in 1946, and went on to lead the three-day insurrection in April 1952 which brought the MNR to power and became known as the Bolivian revolution. When it succeeded he was sworn in as interim president until Paz returned from exile.

From 1952 to 1956 he served as vice president to Paz, and was himself elected president in 1956. His first term of office, though presented as a continuation of the revolution, in fact saw the beginnings of its reversal, due in large measure to a serious economic crisis and the opportunity this presented for the US and the IMF to take charge of the economy. Wages were frozen, government expenditure severely cut back, and food subsidies removed (under a 'stabilisation plan'). When miners went on strike in protest, Siles staged a hunger strike, a tactic he was to make use of several times in his career. Within the MNR he substituted bureaucracy for internal democracy and centralised the hitherto diffuse power structure, thus helping to split the party into rival factions. By 1964 he was openly opposed to Paz, whom he termed a 'counter-revolutionary'. After calling for the replacement of Paz with a military committee, Siles was expelled from the MNR in 1964. He was exiled to Paraguay from September–November that year, from where he encouraged the coup against Paz by his vice president, Gen. René Barrientos. However, he subsequently sought asylum in the Uruguayan embassy (July 1965), and was exiled (in Santiago de Chile, 1966–73, and then in Argentina), during the military regimes which followed. Unlike Paz, he was firmly opposed to the Bánzer regime (1971–8) from the beginning. During this period he joined the Left MNR (MNRI), which became the focus of the reformist Popular and Democratic Union (UDP) coalition until the end of 1984.

Between 1978 and 1980 he won three consecutive elections at the head of the UDP, but not until 1982 did the military allow him to take power. Once more his term of office was a period of acute economic crisis and conflict with organised labour. Mineral prices fell as extraction costs rose, and with communists in the government the banks proved unwilling to bargain when Bolivia proposed limiting its debt repayments (standing at almost 60% of export earnings). Floods wiped out a large part of the country's agriculture, and the only boom area was the illegal cocaine trade. By 1985 inflation had reached around 20,000%. The unions, led by the COB, called for revolutionary measures, but although Siles gave in to pressure on wages and did not repress the labour movement, he refrained from radical policies. By late 1984 he was totally isolated, the UDP coalition having been reduced to a rump of the MNRI. He had little choice but to acquiesce in the so-called 'church coup' (*golpe eclesiástico*) when the bishops proposed cutting short his term by a year and holding elections in July 1985. In a poll criticised on all sides for irregularities, Siles' MNRI slumped to only eight congressional seats.
See also **Democratic and Popular Union; Revolutionary Nationalist Movement**.

Silva Cimma, Enrique: see **Radical Party** (Chile).

Simón Bolívar Guerrilla Coordinating Group: see **National Guerrilla Coordinating Group**.

SINAMOS: see ***velasquismo*** **(Peru)**.

Sitges Declaration: see **Gómez, Laureano**.

62 Organisations: see **General Confederation of Labour**.

'slow coup': see *autogolpe*.

Soares, Airton: see **Workers' Party.**

Social Christian Conservative Party (PCSC): see **Christian Democrat Party** (Chile).

Social Christian Party (PSC): see **Christian Democrat Party** (Bolivia).

Social Christian Party (Ecuador) (*Partido Social Cristiano*/PSC)
Founded in 1951 as the Social Christian Movement (MSC) around Camilo

Ponce Enríquez, who became president in 1956. Its outlook is virtually identical to that of the Conservatives (PC), with whom it has often been formally allied, and a brief (1964–6) change of name to the Christian Democrat Party aroused protests from the international Christian Democrat movement. Opposition to the military junta from 1963 to 1966 had gained it fresh prestige among coastal voters, later the key stronghold for President Febres. As the 'Popular Alliance' (with the PC) it unsuccessfully put forward Ponce for the presidency in 1968.

The PSC managed to maintain a public profile during the 1972–9 military regime, which it also opposed. The death of Ponce Enríquez in 1976 left it adrift for a time, and its candidate for the presidency in 1979, Sixto Durán Ballén, lost to Jaime Roldós. Its fortunes revived in 1984 when PSC candidate León Febres Cordero won the presidency with the backing of the right-wing parties in the National Reconstruction Front. Although the PSC itself won only nine out of 71 seats in Congress, this was increased to 15 in the June 1986 mid-term poll. In 1988 the PSC fared badly, however. Its presidential candidate, Sixto Durán, came third, with under 13%, and it won only eight seats.
See also **Febres Cordero Rivadeneiro; National Reconstruction Front**.

Social Christian Party (PSC) **(Venezuela):** see **COPEI**.

Social Conservative Party (*Partido Social Conservador*/PSC)
Founded in Colombia in the 1840s as the Conservative Party (PC) by future President Mariano Ospina Rodríguez, a leading member of the Popular Societies opposed to the Liberal-led Democratic Societies. Pro-Church traditional landowners or monopoly capitalists were its original leaders. Its guiding principles were order and authority and it ensured a central place for the Catholic Church in the 1886 constitution. Its differences with the Liberal Party (PL) gradually became blurred, despite armed conflicts at the turn of the century (1895, and the 1899–1902 War of the Thousand Days) as both came to see class interests as paramount.

The PC dominated Colombian politics for the first three decades of the twentieth century, until a combination of internal dissent and popular protest at political and economic repression brought the PL to power in 1930. A Falangist right-wing under Laureano Gómez took control of the party in the 1930s and won the presidency in 1946 (Ospina Pérez) and 1950 (Gómez himself). PC attacks on the Liberals in this period provided the initial impetus for the 'violence' (*la violencia*) which escalated after the popular uprising of 1948 (the *Bogotazo*) was brutally put down by the government, backed by traditional PL leaders. Gómez's attempt to establish a corporativist state was foiled by an army coup led by Gen. Rojas Pinilla, whose ambition of creating a 'third force' to rival the traditional parties led the PC and the PL to forge a pact leading to the National Front agreement (1958–74) under which they alternated in power.

The modern PC is less ideological, although its main base still lies in the rural areas. From the 1950s onwards it was divided into two main wings, one led by Alvaro Gómez Hurtado (son of the former president) and the other (the 'Unionists' or 'Ospinists'), by Mariano Ospina Pérez. The Gómez faction was the more doctrinaire and right-wing of the two. In the 1970s the more moderate (*'Ospino-Pastranista'*) faction was led by ex-President Misael Pastrana and the widow of Mariano Ospina. The two came together in 1982 to back the first post-National Front PC presidential candidate, Belisario Betancur, whose moderate campaign had failed by only 150,000 votes in 1978 against the PL's Julio César Turbay, but who won convincingly against a divided PL in 1982.

In 1986, however, the withdrawal from the campaign of PL dissident Luis Carlos Galán, helped ensure a PL victory over the unpopular right-wing Conservative Alvaro Gómez Hurtado. Offered token ministerial posts, the PC initially broke a 28-year tradition by declining, though it insisted on the maintenance of the bipartisan system for some other posts and after a few months of ineffectual opposition began to demand cabinet representation. The introduction of direct elections for mayors in 1988 was expected to work heavily against it in municipal politics, but in practice it won almost as many towns as the PL, due to splits in the ranks of the latter. The party adopted its present name in July 1987.

See also **Betancur Cuartas; *Bogotazo*; Liberal Party** (Colombia); **National Front; *violencia, la*.**

Social Democratic Party (Brazil) (*Partido Social Democrático*/PSD) Created by President Getúlio Vargas, the PSD played an important role in Brazilian politics for the two decades before its disappearance in 1965. Vargas prepared for the 1945 elections by creating two political groupings: the PTB, which was based on the working class and the government-controlled trade union movement, and the PSD, based on middle classes and the government-controlled state governors and federal bureaucracy. Vargas was forced to resign before the elections and was unable to maintain complete control of the PSD. He publicly supported the party's candidate, Gen. Eurico Dutra, only four days before the vote, and although this was perhaps crucial in helping him gain victory with 56%, once in office Dutra was able to take an independent line.

During the Dutra presidency the PSD moved steadily to the right, cooperating with the conservative Nationalist Democratic Union (UDN) and supporting the government's moves against the Communist Party. In 1950 Vargas mounted a successful presidential campaign at the head of the PTB, beating the PSD candidate. But the party once again carried a presidential candidate to victory in 1955 with the election of Juscelino Kubitschek. The process of import-substituting industrialisation and capitalist development under Kubitschek was enthusiastically supported by the emerging business interests within the PSD. The party lost power in 1960, however, and suffered internal tensions between those who wanted to make alliances to the right (with the UDN and other forces around President Jânio Quadros) and those who wanted to move to the left (with the PTB). When João Goulart reached the presidency in 1961, the old PTB–PSD alliance was temporarily re-formed. But many PSD members had second thoughts when Goulart started

spelling out his agenda for reform. Many PSD members of congress ended up supporting the 1964 coup. But the PSD ceased to exist in November 1965 when Institutional Act 2 abolished all political parties then in operation. Most congressmen who had been PSD members then joined the Nationalist Renovating Alliance (ARENA), the new pro-government party.
See also **Kubitschek; National Democratic Union; Nationalist Renovating Alliance; Vargas**.

Social Democrat Party (PSD) (Chile): see **Democratic Alliance**.

Socialist Bloc (*Bloque Socialista*)
A Chilean opposition coalition, founded in September 1983 (although it was not fully functional until March 1984) as the successor to the Socialist Convergence (*Convergencia Socialista*, f. 1980) group. Members were the Socialist Party-Briones; the Socialist Party-Mandujano; the United Popular Action Movement (MAPU); and the Christian Left (IC). Some member parties were close to one or other of the rival fronts, and only MAPU consistently upheld the role of the Bloc as such.

The Bloc aimed to embrace the full range of socialist and 'popular Christian' tendencies. Its programme was summed up as: (i) strengthening popular organisations and civil disobedience; (ii) unifying all (non-communist) socialist forces; and (iii) moving directly to democracy without preconditions. It sought – unsuccessfully – to play a pivotal role between the two major opposition fronts, the Democratic Alliance (AD) and the Popular Democratic Movement (MDP). In 1984 it failed to achieve its goal of forging a Constitutional Pact to unite all three. Right-wing parties opposed the involvement of the MDP, and the latter was also critical of the Pact's alleged lack of a specific strategy for the removal of the military government. By 1986 the socialist Bloc had folded, and in 1987 most member parties joined members of the MDP in a new alliance, the United Left (IU).
See also **member parties; Democratic Alliance; Popular Democratic Movement; United Left** (Chile).

Socialist Christian Movement (MSC): see **Conservative Party** (Ecuador).

Socialist Convergence: see **Socialist Bloc**.

Socialist Homeland Movement (MPS): see ***Nueva Alternativa***.

Socialist (Second) International
The world social democrat organisation, founded in 1864 and currently (1987) representing 82 political parties and organisations worldwide. The SI's origins are in late nineteenth- and early twentieth-century European politics and its formal involvement with Latin America dates from the 1976 Geneva Congress, at which it took the decision to broaden its scope beyond Europe. It has placed stress on arms control and disarmament, North-South dialogue, the democratisation of Latin America, and mediation in regional conflicts.

Member parties in South America (* indicates consultative member) are: the Radical Party (PR/Chile); the Peruvian Aprista Party (APRA*); Democratic Action (AD/Venezuela); the People's Electoral Movement (MEP/Venezuela*); Movement of the Revolutionary Left (MIR/Bolivia*); the Democratic Left (ID/Ecuador); the Revolutionary Febrerista Party (PRF/Paraguay); the Democratic Labour Party (PDT/Brazil*); and the Working People's Alliance (WPA/Guyana*). Carlos Andrés Pérez, former president of Venezuela, is a vice president of the SI, as are Rodrigo Borja, president of Ecuador, and Enrique Silva Cimma of the Chilean Radicals. The supreme decision-making bodies of the organisation are the triennial congress and the council (including all member parties and organisations) which meets twice a year. There is also a Regional Committee for Latin America and the Caribbean (SICLAC) and a special committee on Chile. In June 1986 the congress met for the first time in Latin America when Lima, Peru, was the host city.

Socialist Party (Argentina): see **Argentine Communist Party**.

Socialist Party (Bolivia) (*Partido Socialista*/PS)
A name originally used by a short-lived party of the 1920s and revived in 1970 by a group led by Mario Miranda Pacheco and Marcelo Quiroga Santa Cruz. The new PS – a fusion of the Workers' Revolutionary Action Front (FARO), Quiroga's National Union of the Revolutionary Left (UNIR), and the rump of the National Liberation Front (FLIN) – stated that it was independent of the then government of Gen. J. J. Torres, despite the latter's leftist stance. The PS was Marxist, but non-aligned internationally and with a loose structure and ideology, though it had a certain amount of labour support. Quiroga's wing split away at the end of the Bánzer period, taking the name PS-One (PS–1), while the centrist wing, led by Guillermo Aponte, backed the UDP coalition of Hernán Siles Zuazo and became the less significant Socialist Party-Aponte (PSA). See also **Socialist Party-One**.

Socialist Party-One (Bolivia) (*Partido Socialista-Uno*/PS–1)
Founded in March 1979 by Marcelo Quiroga Santa Cruz (1931–80), who disagreed with the decision by the PS to join the UDP coalition of Hernán Siles Zuazo. Quiroga was a highly popular figure who, as oil minister under Gen. Ovando in 1969, had nationalised Gulf Oil's monopoly holdings in Bolivia. An independently-minded Marxist, he was a former member of the Revolutionary Party of the National Left (PRIN) and had several times been jailed. Quiroga's best showing in the presidential polls was 8% in 1980. As a congressman for Cochabamba, Quiroga then initiated a parliamentary inquiry into former dictator Hugo Bánzer's abuse of power. When the García Meza coup took place in July 1980, Quiroga was kidnapped, tortured, and murdered.

The PS–1 won five seats in Congress in 1985, and is now known as the PS–1 (Marcelo Quiroga), to distinguish it from a splinter group under Wálter Vázquez. It adopted a stance of clear opposition to the economic

and social policies of the Paz government, and by January 1987 claimed to be second in the opinion polls, ahead of the MIR.
See also **Socialist Party** (Bolivia).

Socialist Party of Chile (*Partido Socialista*/PS)

Founded in 1933 after the fusion of several small parties, the most important of which was New Public Action (NAP), led by Col. Marmaduke Grove, who had briefly headed the 1932 Socialist Republic. It had a strong trade union presence, represented by the National Confederation of Legal Trade Unions (CNSL) and later by some illegal unions associated with the Communist Left (*Izquierda Comunista*), which in 1937 merged with the PS. The party was fervently opposed to the government of Arturo Alessandri (who had beaten Grove in the presidential election): it formed an alliance with the Communist Left, the Democratic Party, and the Radical Socialists (PRS) which was later (1936) broadened to include Communists (PCCh) and Radicals (PR) and renamed the Popular Front.

Grove's nomination as Front candidate in 1938 was blocked by the PCCh. Tension between the PS and the PCCh has been a constant feature of Chilean politics, and has helped bring about many splits in the PS. The Socialists left the Popular Front in the mid-1940s over Communist support for the Axis powers in World War II. The party at that time adopted a Peronist line, but later became Titoist and then supported Peking in the Sino-Soviet split. After withdrawing from the Front it voted in Congress to ban the PCCh. It returned to government under the PR's Juan Antonio Ríos, but another split came in 1943 when Grove led a breakaway faction wishing to support Ríos and discuss a merger with the PCCh. He returned to the PS in 1946/7 when his faction merged with the PCCh. In the 1946 elections the PS came fourth after a split in the Confederation of Chilean Workers left it isolated. In 1948 two PS deputies who had voted for the ban on Communists (*'Ley Maldita'*) were expelled from the party and formed the Socialist Party of Chile (*PS de Chile*/PSCh). The opposite wing became the Popular Socialist Party (*PS Popular*/PSP), committed to a Marxist-Leninist line. The former joined the government of González Videla (1946–52). In 1952 the bulk of the PSP backed former dictator Carlos Ibáñez, and subsequently joined his government. The faction led by Dr Salvador Allende opposed Ibáñez, and was backed by the PSCh and the Communists. Both PSP and the PSCh later joined the Popular Action Front (FRAP) and in 1957 they merged again as the Socialist Party of Chile.

At its 1967 Chillán congress the party officially declared itself Marxist-Leninist and for the first time entertained the idea of armed struggle; however, the validity of these decisions was in later years hotly debated. Allende was the FRAP candidate in 1958 and 1964, coming second both times. In 1970, as the candidate of Popular Unity (UP) – an expanded FRAP – he finally won. PS standing was at its high point by 1971, when it won a much higher portion of the overall UP vote (22.8%) than did the Communists. Internal strains remained, however, with the party leadership under secretary general Carlos Altamirano taking a much more radical stance than the government, including support for land and factory seizures. As a large, open party with no history of clandestine organisation, the PS was badly hit by the repression which followed the 1973 coup, with many leaders, jailed, exiled, or killed.

The splits continued, both in exile and at home, and by 1987 two major and several minor factions were operating. The principal split was between the Núñez and Almeyda socialists. The Núñez (formerly Briones) faction, founded in 1983, favours a national united opposition, including the Christian Democrats (PDC), and opposes armed struggle. Led first by Carlos Briones, the successor to Altamirano, and latterly by Ricardo Núñez, it is influenced by European socialist parties and is a member of the Socialist Bloc. (Until 1987 it was also a member of the Democratic Alliance.) It signed the 1985 National Agreement and opted not to join the United Left in 1987. The party led by Dr Clodomiro Almeyda (foreign minister under Allende), which formally emerged in 1979, when Almeyda split with Altamirano, and is closely linked to the PCCh, became a member of the Popular Democratic Movement. It cautiously welcomed but refused to sign the National Agreement. In April 1987 the Almeyda party announced its unification with the two other PS factions in the MDP, the PS (24th Congress) and the PS-National Regional Coordinator/CNR. These two had previously (April 1986) formed the *PS-Unitario*, a name retained by the rank and file despite the subsequent fusion, out of which emerged the Socialist Party of Chile, a founder member of the United Left (IU).

The three groups which came together support 'all forms of struggle' against the Pinochet regime, so long as they are associated with mass political work. The faction led by Manuel Mandujano is a 1984 splinter from the PS-Briones, with similar policies but favouring closer relations with left-wing factions. It is a member of the Socialist Bloc and a signatory of the National Agreement. The Historic Socialist Party, a PS-Mandujano splinter which claims to be the political heir of Allende, is a member of the IU. Preliminary talks were due to be held in late 1987 leading to a 'Socialist Unity' convention in early 1988.

A 'Socialist Party' which sought registration under the new party law in 1987 was reported to be the creation of the intelligence service, the CNI.

See also **Allende Gossens; Communist Party of Chile; Democratic Alliance; National Agreement; Party for Democracy; Popular Democratic Movement; Popular Unity; Socialist Bloc; United Left** (Chile).

Socialist Republic

A twelve-day Chilean government in 1932, headed by Col. Marmaduke Grove, after one of a succession of coups following the break-up of the Ibáñez dictatorship. Its importance, out of proportion to its brevity, was due to its direct role in the founding of the Socialist Party and its legislation, which – unrepealed – would 40 years later provide the Popular Unity (UP) government with most of the powers it needed to take over

industries. The Republic, which had Communist support though its policies were not full-blown socialism, also encouraged the belief, for the first time, that the working class could take state power. Chile was returned to civilian rule by presidential elections held in the same year and won by Arturo Alessandri.
See also **Popular Unity; Socialist Party of Chile.**

Socialist Workers' Party (POS): see **Communism; Communist Party of Chile**.

Socialist Workers' Party (PST): see **Socialist Party of Chile**.

Socialist Workers' Party (PST): see **Communist Party of Colombia; Democratic Left Unity**.

Society for the Defence of Tradition, Family and Property (TFP): see ***Gremialismo***.

Sole Revolutionary Party (*Partido Unico de la Revolución*): see **Peronism**.

Sophia Declaration: see **People's National Congress**.

South Atlantic War

Armed conflict between Argentina and Britain over the Falkland/Malvinas islands in April–June 1982. Following UN Resolution 2065 of 1965, calling for negotiations on the sovereignty dispute, bilateral talks had led to some economic cooperation, but no resolution of the underlying disagreement over the islands. Tensions rose in 1982 after a deadlock in negotiations and conflict over the presence of Argentine scrap merchants on South Georgia. The Argentine president, Gen. Leopoldo Galtieri, ordered a full-scale military occupation of the islands on 2 April 1982, securing the surrender of the small British garrison. Britain broke diplomatic relations; the UN Security Council approved Resolution 502, calling for the immediate withdrawal of troops and a peaceful settlement of the sovereignty dispute.

The British Prime Minister, Margaret Thatcher, ordered the dispatch of a naval task force to recover the islands, announcing a 200-mile exclusion zone around them. The US Secretary of State, Alexander Haig, began a 'shuttle diplomacy' effort to mediate, but no mutually acceptable formula was found. On 25 April British forces landed and recovered South Georgia, defeating the Argentine garrison under the command of navy Lt Alfredo Astiz. The *ARA Belgrano* was torpedoed and sunk outside the exclusion zone by a British submarine on 2 May; there was heavy loss of life. *HMS Sheffield* was hit and destroyed by an Exocet missile two days later. Military operations intensified, with the loss of aircraft on both sides. Britain rejected the latest Argentine proposals for a negotiated settlement on 19 May. The burnt remains of a British Sea King helicopter were discovered in Chile, raising speculation over discreet Chilean support for the task force. British troops landed in force at San Carlos on 21 May, establishing a bridgehead. In heavy Argentine air raids on disembarking forces, *HMS Ardent* was sunk, and one destroyer and three frigates damaged. *HMS Coventry* and *Atlantic Conveyor* were sunk on 25 May. British land forces captured Goose Green and Port Darwin after heavy fighting, and substantial casualties, on 29 May. The British troop carriers *Sir Galahad* and *Sir Tristram* were bombed in Fox Bay on 8 June; there was heavy loss of life. But British forces initiated the final offensive on Port Stanley (which had been renamed Puerto Argentino by the occupying forces), securing the surrender and capture of the entire Argentine garrison on 14 June 1982.

The surrender led to a major political crisis in Argentina. Gen. Galtieri was deposed on 16 June and the regime was forced to promise elections. The navy and the air force withdrew from the ruling junta. The war dead totalled approximately 250 Britons and 1,000 Argentines. After the return to civilian rule in Argentina in 1983, top military officials who ordered the occupation of the islands were placed on trial facing charges over their conduct of the war. In May 1986 the Supreme Tribunal of the Armed Forces sentenced Gen. Galtieri to 12 years' imprisonment for his part in the war. Adm. Jorge Anaya and Brig. Basilio Lami Dozo, the other two members of the ruling junta at the time of the war, were sentenced to 14 and eight years' imprisonment respectively. A further 13 defendants were acquitted.

See also **Falklands/Malvinas; Galtieri; Process of National Reorganisation**.

Spartacus Revolutionary Movement (MRE): see **Movement of the Revolutionary Left** (Bolivia).

state of siege

The constitutions of most countries in the region have provisions for a declaration of a state of siege, under which a number of citizens' constitutional guarantees are suspended (such as the right not to be detained without trial, the right of freedom of expression, to public gatherings, etc.) and the executive is granted special emergency powers. In some countries the state of siege exists alongside a less drastic state of emergency; in others the exceptional measures go under a different name (such as 'urgent security measures', 'suspension of guarantees', etc.). In most cases they allow the authorities to impose a curfew and stringent censorship. During civilian rule, presidents usually have to seek congressional approval for the imposition of the exceptional measures, which if granted have a limited duration (often 30 or 90 days) and must be put to the vote again. Most constitutions allow the imposition of the state of siege in cases of external military threat or internal commotion. In practice, however, exceptional measures have almost always been imposed in response to domestic public disorders of the kind posed by mass demonstrations or guerrilla movements.

Some authoritarian governments have found the state of siege necessary on a virtually continual basis. In Paraguay a state of siege was in effect in Asunción, the capital, for 40 years virtually without interruption in 1947–87. Following the outbreak of *la violencia* in Colombia in

1948, state of siege measures were in place there for most of the following 10 years, and again were frequently imposed into the 1970s and 1980s. See also ***violencia, la***.

Stroessner, Gen. Alfredo

b. 1912. Long-serving Paraguayan military ruler; president of the country since 1954. Stroessner was the son of a German immigrant who had established a brewery in the country. He entered the Military College in 1929 and fought in the Chaco War, earning distinction as the commander of an artillery section and promotion to the rank of lieutenant. He rose to the rank of captain in 1936 and major in 1940; he also underwent an artillery training course in Brazil. After attending the Superior War College in 1943–5, Stroessner was given the command of the General Bróguez artillery regiment and promoted to lieutenant-colonel. In the 1947 civil war he commanded government forces in the crucial battles against the rebels. In the series of coups and counter-coups that followed, he managed to align himself with the winners in each successive confrontation. After promotion to brigadier-general in 1949, he helped bring Dr Federico Chávez to the presidency in 1950, and was rewarded with a series of further promotions, culminating with the posts of head of the first military region and finally overall commander of the armed forces. It was in this capacity that Stroessner deposed Chávez in a violent coup on 5 May 1954. He had himself nominated presidential candidate for the Colorado Party, and was elected unopposed on 11 July that year.

S

Once in office (from 15 August 1954) Stroessner began to consolidate his position, with successive purges of rival factions and personalities within both the Colorado Party and the army. He built up a repressive police state, systematically crushing all forms of opposition, including a general strike in 1958, ill-fated attempts to start guerrilla campaigns in 1958–60, and an assassination plot in 1974. Stroessner's regime was marked by extreme anti-Communism. There were systematic human rights violations, including a number of cases of death by torture. At the same time, however, the regime kept up with the outward forms of democracy, passing legislation through a pliant Congress in which a token opposition presence was maintained. Stroessner was re-elected in 1958 (unopposed), and again in 1963 (with token opposition from the Liberals). In 1967 a constituent assembly removed the ban on the president standing for re-election for another consecutive term. Stroessner therefore ran again in 1968, winning with a claimed 70% of the vote; three opposition parties were allowed to campaign for congressional seats. In 1973 Stroessner was again re-elected, this time with a claimed 80% of the vote.

In 1977 a new constitutional amendment was approved, lifting all limits on the number of consecutive terms in office Stroessner could serve. In the 1978 election Stroessner won with a claimed 90% of the vote, a percentage which was again claimed in 1983. The opposition parties have repeatedly described these elections as fraudulent. A rather uncharismatic figure, prone to dull speeches, Stroessner was nevertheless noted for his

meticulous attention to detail, his organisational skills, and his ability to work long hours. Already the longest-serving ruler in Latin America, in 1988 he was again re-elected, for an eighth term in office, with a claimed 89% of the vote.
See also **Colorado Party** (Paraguay).

Sule, Anselmo: see **Radical Party** (Chile).

Superior War School (*Escola Superior de Guerra*/ESG)
A Brazilian higher military training institute founded in 1949; it was identified with a specific 'model' of economic development and political organisation for the country, which the 1964–85 military regime sought to implement. During the first 20 years of its existence, about 2,000 students took the ESG's special one-year course. At the time of the 1964 coup, two-thirds of the generals on active duty were ESG graduates; many influential civilians also took the ESG's courses. ESG teachers stressed the link between national security and development. The threat to national security, both internally and externally, was identified as communism. The emphasis was on strategic planning, geopolitics, and the importance of Brazil for the defence of the West. But while the ESG was clearly linked to US Cold War concerns, it also served to express some of the nationalist and independent thinking of the officer corps inherited from *tenentismo*. Another feature was the insistence on the importance of the centralised state to mobilise the national development effort. The civilian economists associated with the ESG held that in any conflict between economic growth and distribution, priority should be given to growth.
See also **Authoritarian Nationalist; Coup of 1964** (Brazil); **National Security Doctrine; *tenentes*.**

Supreme Court incident (Bogotá): see **Betancur Cuartas. M–19**

SURINAME, Republic of
Capital: Paramaribo
Independence (from the Netherlands): 1975
Area: 163,820 sq km
Population (1987): 357,000 (64.7% urban)
Pop. growth rate (1980–5): 1.1%
Pop. density: 2.5/sq km
Infant mortality (1984): 27.6 per thousand
Life expectancy at birth (1980–5): 68.
Literacy (1984): 84%
GDP per capita (1987): US$3,257
Foreign debt per capita (1987e): US$200
Main exports: bauxite, alumina, and aluminium.

Political system

Constitution: 1987, returning the country to civilian government in January 1988 after eight years of military rule. *President*: Ramsewak Shankar (1988–). *Vice president, prime minister:* Henck Arron (1988–).

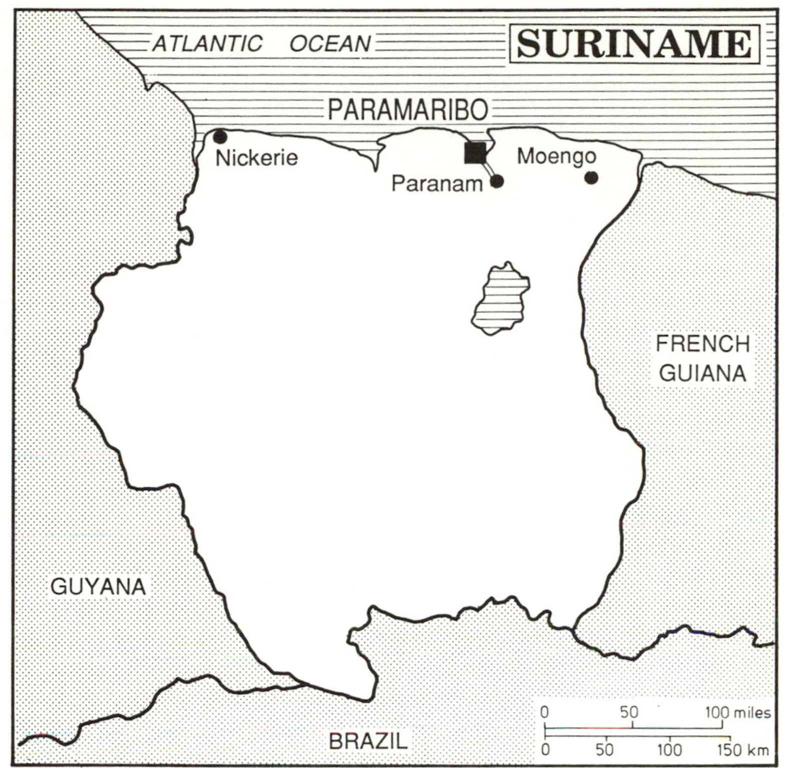

A 51-member parliament is elected for five years and chooses by a two-thirds majority an executive president of the republic, who also serves for five years. An advisory council of state with all major interest groups represented, including the army, has much influence. The army, led by Col. Desi Bouterse, retains constitutional powers, notably to 'guarantee conditions' for a return to a 'democratic and morally just society'. *Last elections*: November 1987.

Political organisations

Party activity was re-authorised by the military in 1985 after being officially banned since the 1980 military coup. The Netherlands had cut off aid in December 1982 in protest against the army's execution of 15 opposition figures and said it would not restore it until the return of democracy. The resulting severe economic pressure – and from mid–1986 a foreign-backed rebel movement in eastern Suriname led by a former soldier, Ronnie Brunswijk – persuaded the regime to have dealings with the political parties again

Political Parties (seats in parliament) (leaders): progressive Reform Party/VHP (16) (Jaggernath Lachmon), f. 1949; National Party of Suriname/NPS (14) (Henck Arron), f. 1946; Party of National Unity and Harmony/KTPI (10) (Willy Soemita), f. 1947; Pendawalima (4) (Marsha Jamin), f. 1980; Progressive Workers' and Farmers' Party/PALU (4) (Iwan Krolis) f. 1975; National Democratic Party/NDP (3) (Jules Wijdenbosch), f. 1987. *Parties with no elected representatives*: Suriname Labour Party/SPA (Fred Derby), f. 1987; Party for the Development of Suriname/PPRS (René Kaiman), f. 1987.

Trade unions (and leaders): Moederbond/General Trade Union Confederation/AVVS (Fred van Russel), f. 1952; Centrale 47/C–47 (Fred Derby), f. 1970; Union of Civil Servants' Organisations/CLO (Hendrik Sylvester), f. 1971; Progressive Employees' Organisation/PWO (Ramon Cruden), f. 1948; Ravaksur (Fred Derby), f. 1987. *Employers' organisations*: Suriname Trade and Industry Association/VSB; Suriname Manufacturers' Association/ASFA.

T

Tachira group: see **Gómez, Gen. Juan Vicente.**

Tacnazo

A military uprising in Chile in October 1969, led by the commander of the First Army Division in Antofagasta, Roberto Viaux. Grievances over pay and conditions stemming from President Eduardo Frei's cuts in the military budget were the main cause. Viaux had been campaigning for higher pay and interpreted an order that he retire from active service as a response to this. He flew to Santiago and headed a revolt from the headquarters of the Tacna Motorised Artillery Regiment. Frei foresaw a possible coup d'etat, although Viaux stressed that it was an internal military affair. Although he received messages of support from several garrisons, his move was unsuccessful. Both the defence minister and the commander-in-chief of the armed forces were dismissed and the government promised action on the budget demands.
See also **Frei Montalva**.

Taft, William Howard: see **dollar diplomacy**.

***tancazo*:** see **Fatherland and Freedom; Pinochet Ugarte**.

Tantaleán, Gen. Javier: see ***velasquismo*** (Peru).

Tarigo, Enrique: see **Colorado Party** (Uruguay).

Távora, Juárez: see **Long March**.

Teeté Liberal Party (PLT): see **Liberal Party** (Paraguay).

tenentes

Young Brazilian military officers who were critical of the elitist upper class control of the federal government, and the dominance of rich states such as São Paulo and Minas Gerais, during the Old Republic. The *tenentes* resented the excessive power of the coffee-growing oligarchy. In July 1922 the *tenentes* led a revolt at Copacabana fort barracks, Rio de Janeiro. The uprising was provoked by alleged insults to army honour in a conflict between states over the presidential succession. The rising was quelled after two days, but the martyrdom of its leaders was to provide a powerful myth for the *tenente* movement. There were new uprisings in São Paulo and Rio Grande do Sûl in July and October 1924. Both were defeated (in São Paulo, after rebels held the city for a month) and the survivors marched to Paraná, where they began the Long March under leaders such as Luis Carlos Prestes and Miguel Costa. The *tenente* leaders formed part of the Liberal Alliance which backed Getúlio Vargas in his accession to the presidency in 1930. They opposed a return to the old system of 'oligarchic' state control, and insisted on a process of 'cleansing' (*saneamento*) before new elections could he held.

Many *tenente* leaders were active in the formation of the Revolutionary Legion, later to become the National Revolutionary Party, which mixed radicalism on land reform with nationalism and authoritarian/fascist overtones. But the Legion was short-lived, fading as a political force by late 1931. *Tenente* leaders fought for Vargas against the São Paulo revolt in 1932. The movement was divided over participation in the May 1933 constituent assembly elections which followed São Paulo's surrender. Some *tenente* leaders made efforts to create workers' parties: the most important was Miguel Costa's São Paulo Socialist Party.
See also **Long March; Vargas**.

Terán, Sgt Mario: see **Guevara de la Serna**.

terceristas: see **Christian Democrat Party** (Chile); **Christian Left**.

Terra, Dr Gabriel

1873–1942. President of Uruguay 1931–8. A Colorado Party leader who had moved to the right, Terra assumed dictatorial powers in 1933 in an '*autogolpe*' (literally, 'a coup against oneself') in which Congress was closed down. This interruption in democratic rule – the first important breakdown in the political system established at the beginning of the century – was associated with the international recession. Terra moved quickly to help landowning groups by devaluing the peso and establishing rigorous controls on the labour movement. Terra's *golpe malo* ('bad coup') was followed in 1942 by a *golpe bueno* ('good coup') by his successor, Gen. Alfredo Baldomir, which re-established full democratic freedoms.

Thatcher, Margaret: see **South Atlantic War**.

Thieme, Walter Roberto: see **Fatherland and Freedom**.

'third force': see **Christian Democrat Party** (Chile); **Christian Left**.

'third way': see **Christian Democracy; Peronism**.

Tiradentes Revolutionary Movement (MRT): see **guerrilla movements** (Brazil).

'Tirofijo': see **Communist Party of Colombia; Marquetalia; Revolutionary Armed Forces of Colombia**.

Tlatelolco Treaty

The treaty establishing a nuclear-free zone in Latin America, more formally known as the Treaty for the Prohibition of Nuclear Weapons in

Latin America, which was signed in the Tlatelolco district of Mexico City on 14 February 1967. The treaty invoked the need for world disarmament and noted that 'the existence of nuclear weapons in any country of Latin America would make it a target for possible nuclear attacks and would inevitably set off . . . a ruinous race in nuclear weapons . . .' It commits the signatories to developing nuclear energy for purely peaceful purposes. The treaty bans the 'testing, use, manufacture, production, or acquisition by any means whatsoever of any nuclear weapons'; there is also a ban on the deployment or storage of nuclear weapons in Latin America by the signatories or by third parties.

The treaty established a special agency for verifying its implementation, the Organisation for the Prohibition of Nuclear Weapons in Latin America (OPANAL). Despite the ban on nuclear weapons the treaty specifically permits what are described as 'explosions of nuclear devices for peaceful purposes'. Additional Protocol I of the treaty seeks to make its provisions binding on extra-regional powers who are responsible, *de facto* or *de jure*, for territories within Latin America. Additional Protocol II commits extra-regional signatories not to use or threaten to use nuclear weapons against Latin American countries.

Cuba was the only country within the region which refused to sign the Tlatelolco Treaty, in protest at the maintenance of US bases with nuclear weapons in Guantánamo, Puerto Rico, and the American Virgin Islands. Argentina signed but did not ratify the treaty, arguing that some of its clauses were commercially discriminatory, allowing the preservation of an exclusive 'nuclear club' and accepting restrictions on developing countries' access to nuclear technology. Brazil expressed similar reservations when it ratified the treaty in January 1968. The USA signed Additional Protocol II, but with important reservations: that it did not consider itself impeded by the treaty from transporting nuclear weapons by air or sea through the non-nuclear zone; and that, while it would not threaten to use nuclear weapons against Latin American countries, that guarantee would lapse should any Latin American state, with the help of another nuclear power, launch an armed attack on the United States.

Toledo Plata, Carlos: see **M–19**.

Tómic, Radomiro: see **Christian Democrat Party** (Chile).

Topberaad (Supreme Council): see **Arron.**

Toranzo Montero, Gen. Federico: see ***Azules* and *Colorados*.**

Toro, Col. David: see **Revolutionary Nationalist Movement**.

Torrelio Villa, Gen. Celso: see **Bolivian governments post-Bánzer**.

Torres González, Gen. Juan José

1921–1976. President of Bolivia from October 1970 to August 1971. Born in Cochabamba of humble origins. Educated at the Military College. Promoted to captain in 1952 and colonel in 1954. Commander of the Oruro garrison in the early 1960s. For a time a member of the Bolivian

Socialist Falange (FSB). Served as ambassador to Uruguay and as minister of labour. Chief-of-staff of the armed forces (1967) during the government of Gen. Barrientos. During the Ovando government (1969–70) Torres successfully performed the task of expropriating Gulf Oil, which controlled 90% of Bolivia's gas. The office of commander-in-chief of the armed forces, which he occupied under Ovando, was abolished in 1970.

Army commander Gen. Rogelio Miranda was Torres' immediate replacement, under a system whereby overall command rotated among the different branches. Miranda, a right-winger, overthrew Ovando in October 1970, but Torres staged an immediate counter-coup, assisted by a general strike call from the union confederation COB, which he then invited to participate in government. This request was turned down, although the COB offered 'militant support' for Torres' aims of increasing state control of the economy and restricting foreign capital. He promised to arm the workers if the armed forces turned against them, a pledge he never fulfilled but which angered the right. An attempt by Cols Bánzer Súarez and Edmundo Valencia to overthrow him in January 1971 was foiled by union mobilisation. Worried by the expropriation of a US-owned mine, Washington moved to destabilise the Torres government by blocking loans and forcing down the price of tin. Under further pressure from the mass movement, Torres closed down a US-backed union organisation and expelled the Peace Corps. In June 1970 the left and the unions set up the Popular Assembly, an 'organ of workers' and popular power' independent of the government. Thoroughly alarmed, the right, led by Col. Bánzer who had returned from enforced exile, moved to overthrow Torres in August 1971, supported by the US, Brazil, and Argentina. Torres was forced into exile and later joined parties of the left in the Anti-imperialist Revolutionary Front (FRA). He was assassinated in June 1976 in Buenos Aires.
See also **Bánzer Suárez**.

Torres Restrepo, Camilo

1929–66. Colombian priest, sociologist, and revolutionary. Born in Bogotá, son of an affluent pediatrician and of the daughter of one of the most prominent Colombian families. Educated at the German School (Bogotá), the National University, and a diocesan seminary. Ordained in 1954, after which he went to the University of Louvain, Belgium, to study sociology. Obtained a master's degree, then became vice rector of the Latin American College seminary, returning to Colombia in 1958 to research for a doctorate (written but never defended) on socioeconomic conditions in Bogotá. Chaplain and lecturer at the *Universidad Nacional* (1959–62), where he co-founded the sociology faculty. Elected rector by the students in 1962, whereupon the official rector closed the university and Torres was ordered by the Archbishop of Bogotá to resign as chaplain and teacher. He became dean of the Institute of Social Administration at the Higher School of Public Administration, and thus a member of the governing board of the agrarian reform institute, INCORA.

In 1965 Torres founded the People's United Front (*Frente Unido del Pueblo*) political movement in an attempt to bring together opposition groups on the left. Its platform was said by the archbishop to contain 'points . . . irreconcilable with the doctrine of the Church' and Torres asked to be laicised. This took place on 26 June 1965. He then sought to organise *Frente* cells all over the country, and was jailed at least twice by the police. The *Frente*, which espoused the violent overthrow of the existing order, fell apart through internal dissension and Torres joined the National Liberation Army (ELN) guerrilla group in October 1965, enrolling as an ordinary combatant. After issuing a declaration 'from the mountains' in January 1966, explaining his decision, he was killed on 15 February in a clash with soldiers in Santander department and buried secretly by the army.
See also **liberation theology; National Liberation Army** (Colombia).

Townley, Michael: see **Letelier case**.

Tównsend, Andrés: see **APRA; Democratic Convergence**.

Trabalhismo

A Brazilian political movement set in motion by President Getúlio Vargas in the 1940s, based on the development of trade unionism within a corporatist framework, closely linked to, and controlled by the state. Since the creation of the *Estado Nôvo* in 1937 the government had been building up a centrally-controlled union movement and developing a paternalist concern for the social wellbeing of the workers. In a number of speeches the president stressed the importance of emancipating the working classes while at the same time rejecting the notion of class struggle and emphasising a conservative view of social harmony. After the appointment of Alexandre Marcondes Filho as labour minister in 1941, a new Labour Code was drawn up, with further provisions being made for 'model restaurants' and 'factory schools'. Some of these developments paralleled those in Argentina, where in 1943 Col. Perón had become secretary for labour and was also developing the political potential of the union movement.

In 1945 Vargas set about creating two political parties – one, the *Partido Trabalhista Brasileiro* (PTB), was to represent the proletariat and be based on the labour machine created by Marcondes Filho, while the other, the *Partido Social Democrático* (PSD) was to represent the middle classes. Vargas was removed from the presidency later that year, but the PTB survived and provided the vehicle for his comeback to win the 1950 presidential elections, in a campaign in which the appeal to the working class figured prominently. In his last period in office (1950–4) Vargas removed restrictions on trade union activity imposed by his predecessor and made efforts to increase the minimum wage. The greater freedom led to an upsurge of labour militancy, including important strikes in São Paulo in 1953, which saw the beginnings of more independent union leadership emerging alongside the *pelego*, or government-controlled, bureaucracy. The appointment of João Goulart as labour minister in the same year led to a storm of conservative protest. Goulart proposed a 100% minimum wage increase, implemented in February 1954.

Following the August 1954 crisis culminating in Vargas' suicide, Goulart effectively inherited the role of PTB leader. When he became president in 1961 the conservative opposition was ready to accuse him of seeking to impose a left-wing 'trade union republic' in the country. In fact, while Goulart was ready to work with the Communist Party (PCB) inside the labour movement, he was also trying to maintain the PTB's own influence. The union movement sought to defend Goulart's reform programme, increasingly under attack from the right, but was in the end unable to halt the process leading the 1964 coup and the persecution of PTB members including the dissolution of the party in 1965.

After the relaxation of military rule in the late 1970s the *Trabalhista* tradition broke into at least three main strands. Many members of Congress whose origins lay with the PTB had been absorbed into the single opposition party under military rule, the MDB (later re-named PMDB). Others organised around Leonel Brizola, Goulart's brother-in-law and governor of Rio Grande do Sûl in the early 1960s. But after a court case in 1980 Brizola and his supporters were denied the right to use the old party name, opting instead for *Partido Democrático Trabalhista* (PDT). A smaller group, led by Ivete Cue de Vargas, the former president's niece, retained the PTB name.

See also **Brazilian Democratic Movement; Brizola; Goulart; Peronism; Vargas**.

t

Trade Union Confederation of Bolivian Rural Workers (CSUTCB): see **COB**.

tradicionalistas see **Colorado Party** (Paraguay).

Trejo, Col. Hugo: see **Revolution of 1958** (Venezuela).

trienio

The three year period in Venezuelan history (1945–8) when power was in the hands of a revolutionary military junta and the *Acción Democrática* (AD) party. The 18 October 1945 coup against the government of Gen. Isaías Medina Angarita was led by young military officers, who installed AD's Rómulo Betancourt in the presidency. A seven-man Revolutionary Junta was created, consisting of five civilians (the President and Raúl Leoni, Gonzalo Barrios, Luis Beltrán Prieto, and Edmundo Fernández) and two military officers (Carlos Delgado Chalbaud and Mario Ricardo Vargas Cárdenas). The junta enjoyed widespread popular support for its programme of structural reforms, including the promise of full democracy, land reform, and the expansion of public health, housing, and education. Members of the former regimes were put on trial on charges of corruption and illegal enrichment. In November 1945 the most senior of these former officials, including former Presidents Eleázar López Contreras and Isaías Medina Angarita, were sent into exile.

Elections to a constituent assembly were held on 27 October 1946, with AD winning 78% of the vote, followed by COPEI (founded less

than a year earlier) with 13.2%, the Democratic Republican Union (URD) with 4.2% and the Communists (PCV) with 3.6%. The resulting new constitution, promulgated on 5 July 1947, established universal secret voting for the presidency, federal and state legislatures, and the municipalities. The exclusion of illiterates was lifted and the voting age was fixed at 18. General elections under the terms of the new constitution were held on 6 January 1948, and were won by Rómulo Gallegos of AD with 73% (second place was taken by Rafael Caldera of COPEI with 22%). Gallegos took office on 15 February, promising respect for democracy and peaceful coexistence (while declaring himself an anti-communist he insisted that the PCV would not be persecuted if it acted within the law). His government was nevertheless considered weak, and became a victim to growing conspiracies within the armed forces; Gallegos was deposed and arrested in the military coup of 24 November 1948, which inaugurated the 10-year dictatorship of Gen. Marcos Pérez Jiménez.
See also **Democratic Action; Gallegos**.

Triple A: see **death squad**.

Trotskyism

Latin America has played an important role in the development of the Trotskyist 4th International (f. 1938), but as in other parts of the world, the FI and its splinter groups have remained for the most part politically marginal, although they have made an intellectual contribution (e.g. to 'dependency' theory and the debate on relations of production in rural areas). The Trotskyists have historically been most active in Guatemala, Brazil, Peru, Argentina (the intellectual headquarters), and Bolivia, where the Revolutionary Workers' Party (POR) was prominent in the 1950s 'revolution'. In 1953, the split in the FI was reproduced in Latin America, with the Latin American Bureau of the FI under Juan Posadas following the majority line of Michel Raptis ('Pablo') and the Latin American Secretariat of Orthodox Trotskyism (SLATO, whose most prominent figure was Nahuel Moreno) backing the International Committee. A few minor organisations in Latin America remained with the IC after the reunification of the FI in 1963. Posadas led a further split in 1965, but the 'Posadist' tendency was moribund by the 1970s.

An orthodox Trotskyist, peasant-based guerrilla movement, under Hugo Blanco and others, was active in Peru in the early 1960s, but it was not until 1969 (at its 9th Congress) that the FI formally embraced armed struggle in Latin America as 'the only realistic perspective'. This line was later abandoned, but not before the People's Revolutionary Army (ERP) of Argentina had made a serious attempt to put it into practice. The Argentine Socialist Workers' Party (PST) rejected the line and developed a large working-class base, becoming for a time perhaps the biggest Trotskyist group in the world. The 'Committee for the Reconstruction of the 4th International' (to which several Latin American organisations belonged) was highly critical of guerrilla 'adventurism'. In 1979 the issue of Nicaragua, and the role of the Argentine/Colombian-led 'Simón Bolívar' brigade there, brought another serious split, with the bulk of Latin American Trotskyists joining what became the International Committee of the 4th International (which broke up in 1981). Electorally, the major (if short-lived) success in Latin America was the largely Trotskyist FOCEP front in Peru, which won 12% of the vote in 1978.

Curently active Trotskyist parties in South America include: the Movement towards Socialism (MAS, Argentina); the Workers' Party (PO, Argentina); the Marxist-Leninist Communist Workers' Party (POCML, Argentina); the Workers' Revolutionary Party–People's Revolutionary Army (PRT-ERP, Argentina); the Workers' Revolutionary Party (POR, Bolivia); POR-*Combate* (Bolivia); the Posadist Trotskyist POR (PORTP, Bolivia); POR-United (POR-U, Bolivia); Freedom and Struggle (Libelu, Brazil); the Worker–Peasant–Student Popular Front (FOCEP, Peru); the Marxist Revolutionary Workers' Party-Socialist Workers' Party (PORM-PST, Peru); the Workers' Revolutionary Party (PRT, Peru); the Trotskyist Revolutionary Workers' Party (PORT, Uruguay); the Workers' Revolutionary Party (PRT, Uruguay); and the Socialist League (*Liga Socialista*, Venezuela).

See also **Blanco; Communism; Pulacayo, Thesis of; Revolutionary Workers' Party–People's Revolutionary Army**.

truce (Colombia 1982): see **Betancur Cuartas**

Trujillo, Julio César: see **Popular Democracy.**

Trujillo, Rafael: see **Betancourt doctrine**.

t

Túpac Amaru Revolutionary Movement (*Movimiento Revolucionario Túpac Amaru*/MRTA)

A Peruvian Marxist guerrilla organisation, founded in 1983 by Luis Varese Scotto, formerly of the Revolutionary Socialist Party (PSR). Effectively the armed wing of Varese's PSR-Marxist-Leninist/MIR *El Militante* group, it went into action (with the seizure of a radio station) in June 1984. It is named after an eighteenth-century indian rebel leader executed by the Spaniards. Of an estimated 200 militants, the majority were in Lima and Huancayo, with smaller groups in Arequipa, Chiclayo, Chimbote, and Trujillo. (A Cuzco group was broken up in November 1984.) It should not be confused with the Túpac Amaru group which was apparently absorbed by the Shining Path (*Sendero Luminoso*) guerrilla organisation. The MRTA, which has no connection with *Sendero*, joined the America Battalion set up by the Colombian M–19 movement in early 1986. A truce which it had declared after the inauguration of Alan García's government in 1985 was lifted on 6 November that year, and in August it declared that it would target the government, which was 'the enemy of the people'. In January 1987 it announced that it was joining forces with the MIR, which had been inactive for some time. Later that year it launched a rural offensive which led to the militarisation of part of San Martín department. It has clashed with Shining Path, especially in the Upper Huallaga Valley.

See also **America Battalion; Movement of the Revolutionary Left** (Peru); **Shining Path**.

Túpaj Katari Indian Movement (*Movimiento Indio Túpaj Katari*/MITKA)
A Bolivian indigenous movement, founded in the early 1970s as MINK'A, a group of indian activists led by Julio Tumiri Apaza. It took its name from the leader of a 1781 rebellion against Spanish and Creole rule. Based among the peasant communities of the *altiplano*, MINK'A sought to publicise the oppression of the indians and raise their political awareness. By 1975 it had become a political party, MITKA, whose policies involved a return to communal forms of production and the re-establishment of indigenous languages. It split in two after the end of the *banzerato*, with one section, under Constantino Lima, urging violence and indian separatism. The main group presented a candidate for the presidency in 1978 and 1979, and although it won less than 30,000 votes, these alone were seen as an indication of increasing politicisation among the peasantry.
See also **Túpac Amaru Revolutionary Movement**.

Túpaj Katari Peasant Movement: see **Bolivian Socialist Falange.**

Tupamaros: see **National Liberation Movement–Tupamaros (MLN–T).**

Turbay, Gabriel: see **Liberal Party** (Colombia).

Turbay Ayala, Dr Julio César
b. 1916. President of Colombia 1978–82. Journalist, politician, and diplomat. University education in Bogotá and Caracas. Honorary law degree, University of Cauca, 1957. Liberal Party (PL) member of the lower chamber of Congress under several administrations (1943–53); elected president of the chamber. Member of the senate (1962–70). Minister of mines and energy, 1957–8. President of the Liberal Party (PL) 1958–63. Delegate to the UN 1958–61 and 1967–9. Vice president (*primer designado*) of Colombia 1967–9 under President Lleras Restrepo. Ambassador to the UK, 1970. Ambassador to the US, 1974. Turbay's power and influence was (and is) based on control of the party 'machine', rather than on popularity or powers of oratory.

Turbay won a narrow victory in 1978, when two-thirds of the electorate abstained, and was thus unable to form a government entirely from his own party as he had promised. An electoral reform law introduced in 1979 preserved the principle of parity between Liberals and Conservatives (PC) established under the National Front agreement, and extended it into the upper echelons of the judiciary, though this was eventually ruled unconstitutional by the Supreme Court. The exclusion of non-*turbayista* Liberals from the party leadership led to the unification of various opposition tendencies within the party, and Turbay's government effectively became an alliance between his own PL faction and the two factions of the PC. It was also heavily influenced by the armed forces. On taking office as president, Turbay had immediately introduced a draconian Security Statute (*Estatuto de Seguridad*), ostensibly to combat common crimes such as kidnapping but whose provisions were widely seen (even by members of the Supreme Court) as an attack on civil liberties. (In

July 1985, three years after the end of his presidency, the country's highest court, the Council of State, condemned Turbay and his defence minister for tolerating institutionalised torture.)

On the economic front, Turbay faced declining coffee revenues and a sharp increase in the foreign debt. Business groups criticised the government for restricting credit and for allowing unfair competition from imported goods, as well as for the highest inflation figures in ten years. A massive 'National Integration Plan' (PIN), based largely on foreign loans, was the centrepiece of Turbay's economic strategy, but this too was ruled unconstitutional in 1981.

Foreign policy moved to the right, as was especially evident in a bitter fight with Cuba over a seat on the UN Security Council (Mexico was eventually chosen as a compromise), and alleged Cuban involvement with Colombian guerrillas, which in 1981 was the reason given for breaking relations with Havana. Turbay won favour at home, however, for the peaceful end to the 1980 Dominican Republic embassy siege involving M–19. He offered two limited amnesties to the guerrillas (in 1981 and 1982) but these were turned down, and although a Peace Commission under ex-president Lleras Restrepo made headway, Turbay would not accept their proposals. Just before leaving office, however, he lifted the state of siege which had been in force for six years.
See also **Liberal Party** (Colombia); **M–19; National Front**.

25 February Movement/*Stanvaste* (VFB): see **Bouterse, Col. Desi**.

26 March Movement: see **Broad Front** (***Frente Amplio***).

Ubaldini, Saúl

b. 1938. Argentine trade union leader who rose to prominence in the 1980s, becoming the general secretary of the General Confederation of Labour (CGT). The son of a waiter, he worked first in a meat-packing plant and later in the beer industry. His union activism led quickly to a full-time job as an official in the beer workers' union. In 1980, after negotiations between the leader of the engineering workers' union (UOM), Lorenzo Miguel, and other officials, Ubaldini was appointed general secretary of the CGT-Brazil, the name then taken by the more hard-line sector of the divided union movement. He rapidly made a name for himself as a fiery orator, leading the resurgence of union activity and struggle against the military government.

Although leaders from powerful unions like Miguel sought to control Ubaldini, a man from the relatively lightweight beer workers' union, he rapidly established his own independent appeal to the rank and file. Following his prominent role in the strikes against the dictatorship, and after the return of civilian rule in 1983, Ubaldini was made one of the four general secretaries of a re-unified CGT. As a result of a new reorganisation, he then became the CGT's single general secretary. Although he had not identified himself with any of the different tendencies inside the labour movement, preferring to play the role of mediator between them, by 1985/6 it was possible to identify a *ubaldinista* tendency of union officials. Ubaldini was one of the driving forces behind the CGT's policy of regular general strikes to mark its opposition to the Alfonsín government's economic policies.
See also **General Confederation of Labour; Peronism**.

Uchurracay incident

On 26 January 1983 eight Peruvian journalists and their guide were battered to death with stones and axes in the Andean settlement of Uchurracay. Their naked bodies were then buried in shallow graves, and were discovered by a security forces patrol two days later. The journalists, seven of whom worked for opposition papers, had been investigating the war between the guerrillas of the Shining Path (*Sendero Luminoso*) group and the Peruvian security forces. They were in Uchurracay because the commander of the military zone had told them the villagers had recently killed seven *senderistas*. A three-man commission under novelist Mario

Vargas Llosa, appointed by the government of President Belaúnde, reached the 'absolute conviction' that they had been killed by villagers who had mistaken them for guerrillas. It also stated that the villagers' belief that they were authorised by the security forces to kill *senderistas* was crucial to their action. Despite charges laid against 17 villagers, obstruction by the security forces and the refusal of the government to transfer the trial to Lima prevented their being tried. Crucial witnesses disappeared or were killed in later attacks, attributed to *Sendero*, which resulted in the abandonment of the village. A judge later found flaws in the commission's report and blamed the military for the deaths, but he was removed from the case.
See also **Lurigancho massacre; Shining Path**.

UDELPA: see **Aramburu**.

Ulloa, Manuel: see **Dynamo, The**.

***Unidad y Reforma*:** see **Colorado Party** (Uruguay).

Unified Marxist-Leninist Committee *(CCU-ML)*: see **Movement of the Revolutionary Left** (Peru).

Unified National Trade Union Committee (CSUN): see **Confederation of Venezuelan Workers**.

***Unión Cívica*:** see ***Club Naval* Pact**.

Union of the Argentine People (UDELPA): see **Aramburu**

Union of the Democratic Centre (*Unión del Centro Democrático*/UCD)

A conservative Argentine political party created in the early 1980s by Alvaro Alsogaray. The UCD emerged from a coalition of eight smaller parties, all loosely identified with the political 'centre' – the self-description favoured by the Argentine civilian right. In the October 1983 elections the UCD obtained two seats in the Chamber of Deputies. Under Alsogaray the party expressed strong support for a free market economy, attacking what it described as the bloated public sector and the distortions in the Argentine economy created by the populist policies of Peronist and Radical Party (UCR) administrations. In the September 1987 congressional elections the UCD increased its representation in the Chamber of Deputies to six seats.
See also **Conservatives** (Argentina).

Unión para Avanzar (UPA): see **Venezuelan Communist Party** .

Union Steadfastness (*Constancia Gremial*): see ***Nueva Alternativa***.

Unitary Vanguard (VU): see **Movement of the Revolutionary Left** (Venezuela); **Movement towards Socialism**; ***Nueva Alternativa***; **Venezuelan Communist Party**.

United Conservative Party (PCU): see **National Party** (Chile).

United Force (UF): see **Burnham**.

United Hindustani Party (UHP): see **Lachmon**.

United Left (Chile) (*Izquierda Unida*)
A coalition launched by seven political parties and movements on 26 June 1987. Founder members were: the Socialist Party of Chile (PSCh); the Historical Socialist Party; the Communist Party (PCCh); the Christian Left (IC); the United Popular Action Movement (MAPU); the left of the Radical Party (PR), and the Movement of the Revolutionary Left (MIR). The IU superseded the Popular Democratic Movement (MDP), whose members it included along with members of the Socialist Bloc. Its stated aim is to 'put an end to [Gen. Augusto] Pinochet's regime'. Unlike the Communist-dominated MDP, the IU was built around the Socialists, and was therefore seen as more likely to be able to forge a pact with the Democratic Alliance, headed by the Christian Democrats (PDC). Clodomiro Almeyda of the PSCh was appointed to chair its governing committee, which called on the PDC to join the coalition. Differences emerged between the PCCh and other members, partly over moves by the latter to encourage voter registration.
See also **member parties; Popular Democratic Movement; Socialist Bloc**.

United Left (Peru) (*Izquierda Unida*/IU)
A left-wing political front, founded in 1980, in response to the left's poor electoral showing that year. Its founding members were three parties – the 'Unity' Communist Party (PCP-U), the Revolutionary Communist Party (PCR), and the Revolutionary Socialist Party (PSR, *velasquista*) – and a loose coalition, the Popular Democratic Unity front (UDP, comprising the Movement of the Revolutionary Left (MIR) and the Revolutionary Vanguard (VR). They were joined by the National Union of the Revolutionary Left (UNIR, comprising the Communist Party–Red Nation (PCP-PR), the MIR-Peru and the National Liberation Front (FLN)), the Worker, Peasant, Student Popular Front (FOCEP, Trotskyist), and the more recently formed Unified Mariateguista Party (PUM, a fusion of 10 left-wing parties). The National Integration Party (PADIN) joined in 1985.

In the December 1980 municipal elections IU came second in Lima and won six departmental capitals, including Arequipa. In the 1983 municipal polls it won 29% of the vote. IU president, labour lawyer and independent Marxist, Alfonso Barrantes, was elected mayor of Lima. The front remained plagued by internal divisions and the lack of an independent secretariat, but in 1985 it nonetheless polled 21% of the general election votes, winning 48 seats in the lower house and 15 in the Senate. Barrantes came second in the presidential race and opted not to force a run-off. Its platform included a 'people's survival programme' to improve living standards, paid for in part by debt repudiation and the removal of tax exemptions for foreign oil companies. It also planned to nationalise the country's leading bank and main copper producer. IU was divided on how to react to the Alan García presidency, with Barrantes (a former member of APRA) arguing for 'realism' against the demands of the left of the coalition for a clearer form of opposition. The main division was between the 'Unity' Communists and the left, led by the PUM.

In the November 1986 municipal polls IU lost several of the cities it had controlled, including Lima, where Barrantes was ousted as mayor. In May 1987 Barrantes resigned from the leadership, citing a 'defamation campaign' against him within the coalition. He was sharply criticised by the PCP, which had swung against him. By this stage IU was already referring to APRA as 'bourgeois' and 'pro-imperialist', but although it conceded the legitimacy of armed struggle in some circumstances it also condemned the Shining Path guerrillas.

United Left Front (FUI): see **Movement of the Revolutionary Left** (Peru).

United Liberal Party (PLU): see **Liberals** (Paraguay).

United National Liberation Front (FULNA): see **guerrilla invasions** (Paraguay).

United People Front: see **Communist Party of Bolivia; Revolutionary Party of the Nationalist Left**.

United People's Front (FPU): see **Movement of the Revolutionary Left** (Bolivia).

United Revolutionary Action Front (FUAR): see **Gaitán**.

United Workers' Front (FUT): see **Communist Party of Ecuador**.

Unzaga de la Vega, Oscar: see **Bolivian Socialist Falange**.

Uribe, Alvaro: see **Liberal Revolutionary Movement**.

Uriburu, Gen. José Felix: see **Infamous Decade**; **Radical Party** (Argentina); **Yrigoyen**.

URUGUAY, Oriental Republic of

Independence (from Spain and from the rival claims of the United Provinces, Argentina and Brazil): 1825
Capital: Montevideo
Area: 176,215 sq km
Population (1987): 3.06m (85% urban)
Population growth rate (1980–5): 0.5%
Pop. density: 17/sq km
Infant mortality (1980–5): 37.6 per thousand
Life expectancy at birth (1980–5): 70.3
Literacy (1983): 96.3
GDP per capita (1987e): US$2,733
Foreign debt per capita (1987e): US$1,324
Main commodity exports (% of total 1985 exports): wool (19.2%), meat (13%), hides (14%)

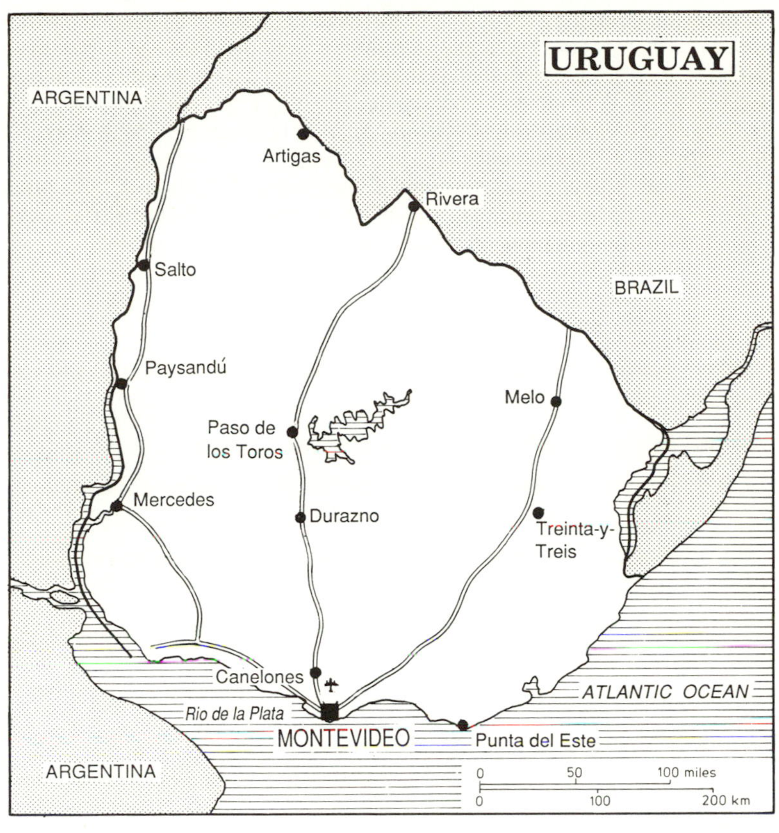

U

Political system

Constitution: 1967. *Head of state/government:* President Julio María Sanguinetti (Colorado party) (1985–); elected on restoration of democratic rule, to succeed Gen. Gregorio Alvarez (1981–5). Elections to the presidency and to the two chambers of Congress are held every five years. The president is elected under the double simultaneous vote system (*Ley de Lemas*). The Chamber of Representatives has 99 members, elected by proportional representation; there must be at least two from each department. The Senate has 60 members, also elected on the basis of proportional representation.

Political organisations

Parties (seats in Senate/Chamber of Representatives): Colorado Party (13/41); Blanco (National) Party (11/35); Broad Front/FA (6/21); Civic Union/UC (-/2). The FA is a multi-party coalition, whose main members include the Communist Party/PCU, Socialist Party/PSU; Christian Democratic Party/PDC, Party for the Government of the People/PGP,

Groups for Unifying Action/GAU, and the 26 March Movement. *Parties without congressional representation:* Movement for National Liberation-Tupamaros/MLN-T; Socialist Convergence/CS; Revolutionary Communist Party/PCR; Laborista Party/PL; Patriotic Union/UP; Workers' Revolutionary Party/PRT; Workers' Party/PT; Party for the Victory of the People/PVP.

Main labour organisation: National Convention of Workers/CNT. *Main employers' organisations:* Uruguayan Chamber of Industries/CIU; *Federación Rural*; Union of Uruguayan Exporters/UEU.

V

Valdovinos, Arnaldo: see **guerrilla invasions** (Paraguay).

Valencia, Col. Edmundo: see **Torres González.**

Valencia, Luis Emiro: see **Gaitán.**

Valverde Barbery, Carlos: see **Bolivian Socialist Falange**.

van der Schroeff, G. J. C.: see **National Party of Suriname**.

Vandor, Augusto: see **General Confederation of Labour Peronism**.

***Vanguardia Febrerista*:** see ***Febreristas*; guerrilla invasions** (Paraguay).

VAR-Palmares (Armed Revolutionary Vanguard): see **guerrilla movements** (Brazil).

Varese Scotto, Luis: see **Túpac Amaru Revolutionary Movement**.

Vargas, Dr Getúlio Dorneles

1883–1954. President of Brazil 1930–45 and 1950–4. A key figure in the development of the modern Brazilian state, Vargas was a populist leader who held the presidency both as the head of the authoritarian *Estado Nôvo* and later as a constitutional ruler. Born in Rio Grande do Sûl, he entered the army at 16 and left at 20 to study law. He was influenced by the Rio Grande do Sûl tradition of centralised, authoritarian government. Elected deputy, Rio Grande do Sûl legislature, 1909. Deputy, federal congress, 1923. Minister of finance, then governor, Rio Grande do Sûl, 1928. He formed the Liberal Alliance to contest the March 1930 presidential elections, but was defeated by the official candidate, Julio Prestes. Against a background of widespread opposition to Prestes, Vargas led an armed uprising on 3 October 1930; the military took power to avert a civil war, but then appointed Vargas head of a provisional government.

In office Vargas faced growing tension between the liberals demanding elections and the restoration of the influence of the traditionally powerful economic groups, and *tenente* reformism. But he began building up a political machine based on the federal government, resisting challenges from the states such as the 1932 São Paulo revolt, and the later threat from Minas Gerais (the *caso mineiro* of 1933). Elections to a constituent assembly in May 1933 showed the continuing influence of the state-level political machines, but the assembly confirmed Vargas as president and widened central government powers. Facing new challenges by state politicians preparing for presidential elections, due in 1938, Vargas and his military allies planned a pre-emptive coup to retain power. Invoking the communist threat, the federal army seized the weapons of state forces. Vargas established dictatorial control on 10 November 1937, closing Congress, banning political parties and ushering in the corporatist *Estado Nôvo*. While the period was characterised by the repression of the opposition, after 1942, coinciding with the government's alignment with the allies in World War II, Vargas began developing programmes aimed at improving working-class living standards (the beginning of *Trabalhismo*). Faced by growing pressure for a return to democracy Vargas promised elections and a new political system in which *Trabalhismo* was to play a role. By 1945 the Communist Party (PCB) had decided to support Vargas, while the conservative opposition formed the Nationalist Democratic Union (UDN) alliance. The government organised two political parties: the Brazilian Trabalhista Party (PTB), based on labour unions, and the Social Democratic Party (PSD) based on the government-appointed state authorities. The policies of the PTB and popular agitation for Vargas to stand for re-election worried the UDN, military officers, and the United States. An army ultimatum forced his removal on 31 October 1945.

Despite his fall from power, Vargas retained influence through the PTB–PSD political machines. His support was important for the victory of PSD candidate Eurico Gaspar Dutra in the December 1945 elections. Vargas was elected senator for São Paulo and then stood as presidential candidate for the PTB, winning the October 1950 elections with 49% of the vote. He took office in January 1951, appointing a multi-party ministerial team. Vargas adopted a moderate nationalist stance on profit remittances by foreign companies and local control of the oil industry. He sought increases in real wages. But a strike wave early in 1953, together with growing inflation and balance of payments difficulties, led to a growing opposition movement which, under the influence of the Cold War, considered Vargas to be soft on Communism. The appointment of João Goulart as labour minister further angered the right. In April 1954 Vargas announced a 100% minimum wage increase, as recommended by Goulart. In August of the same year members of the presidential bodyguard attempt to assassinate Carlos Lacerda, the government's most vocal critic, but failed, killing an air force officer in the process. While Vargas was not involved, the subsequent uproar helped tip military opinion against the president. Senior officers called for Vargas' resignation; when it became clear that a proposed 'leave of absence' would be permanent, Vargas committed suicide by shooting himself on 23 August 1954.

See also **Goulart; Lacerda; Social Democratic Party** (Brazil); ***tenentes*; *Trabalhismo***.

Vargas Cárdenas, Mario Ricardo: see ***trienio***.

Vargas Llosa, Mario: see **Democratic Front; Uchurracay incident**.

Vargas Pazzos rebellion
A serious challenge to the government of León Febres Cordero in Ecuador began on 7 March 1986 when the head of the air force and acting armed forces chief-of-staff, Lt Gen. Frank Vargas Pazzos, 51, refused to acept his dismissal by the defence minister, Gen. Luis Pineiros. Vargas had accused the minister and the head of the army, Gen. Manuel Albuja, of corruption and of planning a dictatorship. He seized the air base at Manta, where he held out temporarily before surrendering in exchange for trial by a special board of senior officers. Two days later he seized the *Mariscal Sucre* air base in Quito, claiming that the government had not honoured the bargain. His calls for the armed forces and people to join him in forming a military–civilian government went largely unheeded, and amid a state of emergency troops stormed the base and arrested Vargas. Pineiros and Albuja both resigned, and a congressional committee recommended the latter's prosecution for 'illicit enrichment'.

In November 1986, Vargas expressed from jail his wish to stand for president in the 1988 elections on the ticket of any centrist or left-wing party. On 16 January 1987 air force paratroops loyal to the general kidnapped Febres, his defence minister, and others at the Taura air base after a congressional pardon for Vargas had been vetoed by the president. In exchange for his release 11 hours later, Febres granted the pardon, but despite an agreement not to take reprisals against the troops, allowed them to be put on trial in March by military courts (58 were eventually jailed for up to 16 years). Vargas, still facing possible trial for his own alleged corruption, went into hiding, but offered to give himself up in exchange for their release. Febres' own party, the PSC, paid a US$37,000 bail to enable the general to appear in public and he stood in the 1988 elections as the presidential candidate of a left-wing (APRE/Socialist Party) coalition, coming fourth with around 10%.
See also **Febres Cordero**.

Vargas Peña, Benjamín: see **guerrilla invasions** (Paraguay).

Vásquez, Wálter: see **Socialist Party-One.**

Vásquez Castaño, Fabio: see **National Liberation Army** (Colombia).

Vatan Hitkarie Party (VHP): see **Lachmon**.

Vatican II: see **liberation theology**.

Vega Uribe, Gen. Miguel: see **Betancur Cuartas**.

Végh Villegas, Alejandro: see **Chicago Boys**.

Velasco Alvarado, Gen. Juan
1910–77. President of Peru 1968–75. Born in Castilla, Piura, into a working-class family. As a teenager, Alvarado travelled to Lima as a stowaway on a ship, with the intention of entering the officers' academy. Instead, he had to join as a recruit and was trained at the NCOs' school of the Chorrillos academy (1929). He then won a place at the *Escuela*

Militar through a national examination and graduated top of his class in 1934. Later he undertook further training at the *Escuela Superior de Guerra* (1945–6) and at Ft Gulick, Panama Canal Zone, becoming the Peruvian army's youngest brigadier-general for decades in 1959. Subsequent posts included Commander of the 2nd Light Infantry Division (Lima, 1960–2). Velasco was then sent as military attaché to France (1962–4), where he became an admirer of Gen. Charles De Gaulle. On his return he became chief-of-staff of the 1st military region (Piura), then inspector-general of the army in 1965, at which point he was promoted to division general. After serving as a delegate to the Inter-American Defense Board (Washington DC), he became chief of the army general staff (1965–7). As army commander and acting chair of the joint armed forces command from 1967, he led a military coup against the widely discredited government of President Belaúnde on 3 October 1968, and became president of the Revolutionary Government of the Armed Forces.

Leading a strong, radical military regime from 1968 to 1975, Velasco introduced a series of major socio-economic reforms, including agrarian reform and worker participation in industrial management. He confronted the US over a number of issues, including the nationalisation of assets belonging to a subsidiary of Standard Oil and resumption of relations with Cuba. The US military mission was asked to leave Peru. He retired from the army in 1969. From 1973 to 1977 he fought a losing battle against illness. Circulatory problems cost him his right leg early in 1973. On 29 August 1975, when terminally ill, he was forced to hand over power to right-winger Gen. Francisco Morales Bermúdez. He died in Lima on Christmas Eve, 1977.

See also **Belaúnde Terry; Morales Bermúdez**.

Velasco Ibarra, José María

1893–1979. President of Ecuador, 1934–5; 1944–7; 1952–6; 1960–1; 1968–72. Educated at the *Universidad Central* (Quito) and the Sorbonne. Professor of law, writer, noted orator, and mason. First elected president in 1934 in a relatively honest election, but dissolved Congress after failing to gain support for his economic programme. He resigned when threatened with a military coup in 1935. His second attempt, in 1940, was unsuccessful, after the election was allegedly rigged by supporters of the winner, Carlos Arroyo; whereupon Velasco became the leader of the existing opposition forces. In 1944 he was placed in power by military decree upon the overthrow of Arroyo, with the support of the largely left-wing Ecuadorean Democratic Alliance (ADE), an *ad hoc* group including Socialists, Communists, Conservatives, and dissident Liberals. He claimed to belong to the liberal/left tradition, but his ideology was ill-defined and populist. Perhaps its most consistent thread was independence in foreign policy: Velasco opposed the expulsion of the Castro regime from the OAS, for example, and maintained close links with the USSR and communist China. He had widespread support among the mass of the electorate.

In office he ruled as a conservative and an authoritarian, suspending the 1945 constitution which restricted the power of the executive. With the aid of the Conservatives, he promulgated a new constitution in 1946, but he was deposed and sent into exile in the following year by the armed forces after he had alienated all the parties which had formerly supported him. However, he was elected again in 1952 with the backing of a new anti-conservative coalition, comprising his own National Velasquista Federation (FNV), the Concentration of Popular Forces (CFP), the Ecuadorean Nationalist Revolutionary Action (ARNE), and independent Liberals. He managed to complete his term, which was noted for a lack of government unity, further unconstitutional measures, and (once more) the alienation of his supporters. During this period the long-standing border dispute with Peru again came to a head.

Velasco won a fourth term in 1960, defeating ex-President Galo Plaza, only to repeat the former pattern, having various members of Congress arrested, 'reorganising' parliament to his own liking, and dismissing his vice president. Deposed once more in November 1961 (this time by the air force), he was succeeded by vice president Carlos Julio Arosemena Monroy. After returning from exile in Argentina in March 1968, he stood again in the 1968 elections, alleging during the campaign that his opponent, Camilo Ponce, had reached a secret agreement with the interim president that their parties would henceforth alternate in power. Velasco won, and began a term of office which was again to end in de facto rule. Social unrest had mounted to a critical level by 1970, and in June that year, after a week of student riots, Velasco suspended the constitution, closed down Congress and the Supreme Court, and occupied the universities with tanks. Widespread arrests followed, and he ruled by decree, with military support, until 15 February 1972, when – apparently because he was preparing for free elections – he was overthrown in a military coup and exiled to Panama. He died in 1979.

See also ***velasquismo* (Ecuador)**.

V

velasquismo (Ecuador)

A populist political movement associated with five-times President José María Velasco Ibarra. Its origins lie in the National Workers' Compact (*Compactación Obrera Nacional*), founded to fight the 1932 elections, the first free poll in almost 40 years, but whose victory was not recognised by Congress. Velasco's parliamentary opposition forced a fresh election and he became president. His support came consistently from the poorest in society, particularly in the coastal cities, but never from organised trade unionism as such. During his later presidencies, the agro-exporting oligarchy also backed him, taking many senior posts in the running of the economy. His most fervent opponents were the trade unions and the student movement.

The National Velasquista Federation (*Federación Nacional Velasquista*/FNV) was founded in 1952 (though not legally constituted until 1968) as an electoral vehicle for Velasco, who had by now served a second presidential term (1944–7) and been an unsuccessful candidate in 1940. Velasco won again in 1952, backed not only by the FNV but also by the Concentration of Popular Forces (CFP), the Ecuadorean Nationalist Revolutionary Action (ARNE), and independent Liberals. He was also elected in 1960 and 1968 as FNV candidate. On the latter occasion the FNV (which barely existed outside election periods) created a Velasquista Popular Front Movement (MFPV) which attracted multi-party support. The party itself had no ideological content beyond support for its *caudillo*, who generally claimed to be centre-left while in opposition but switched to conservatism once elected.

In 1977 Velasco shifted his allegiance to his nephew's Ecuadorean Democratic Action (ADE) party, and in March 1979 he died. The FNV barely survived. It became the National Velasquista Party (PNV) in 1979 and won one congressional seat, which it subsequently lost.
See also **Velasco Ibarra**.

velasquismo (Peru)

A radical, reformist political current associated with the policies and practices of Gen. Juan Velasco Alvarado (president, 1968–75). Velasco's attempts while in power to create a political movement in support of his government were unsuccessful. He sought to by-pass existing parties and form mass organisations, but these were usually taken over by the left and subsequently closed down by the government. In 1970 the regime established the short-lived Committees for the Defence of the Revolution (CDRs); and in 1971 it set up SINAMOS (the National System for the Support of Social Mobilisation), under Gen. Leónidas Rodríguez, a key left-wing associate of Velasco in the 1968 coup. SINAMOS tried, with limited success, to mobilise support among the peasantry and in the shanty towns, but among the labour unions it was outflanked by corporatists in the government who set up their own confederation, the CTRP. This was largely a paper organisation, backed by the Revolutionary Labour Movement (MLR), a vehicle for fisheries minister Gen. Javier Tantaleán which relied heavily on bribery and violence.

When Velasco was about to be ousted by Gen. Francisco Morales Bermúdez, Tantaleán sought to convert the MLR into the mass party of the Peruvian revolution, while Rodríguez and others wanted an organisation based on SINAMOS-sponsored groups, including the peasant confederation, the CNA. But *velasquismo* was soon to become a minority current. The reformers, including Rodríguez, were forced out in October 1975 and formed the Revolutionary Socialist Party (PSR), which staged an abortive coup in July 1976. Rodríguez was exiled from 1977 to 1978, but after his return the PSR won six out of 100 seats in the 1978 constituent assembly. He stood unsuccessfully for the presidency in 1980 on the Union of the Left (UI) ticket, comprising the PSR and the Communists (PCP-U), and the party remains a member of the expanded IU.
See also **Velasco Alvarado**.

Velasquista Popular Front Movement (MFPV): see ***velasquismo*** (Ecuador).

VENEZUELA, Republic of

Independence (from Spain): 1811 (declared); 1821 (Spanish forces defeated): (from Gran Colombia) 1830
Capital: Caracas
Area: 898,805 sq km
Population (1987): 18.27m (78.5% urban)
Pop. growth rate (1980–5): 2.9%
Pop. density: 19.3/sq km
Infant mortality (1980–5) 38.7 per thousand
Life expectancy at birth (1980–5): 69
Literacy (1984): 85.9%
GDP per capita (1987e): US$4,107
Foreign debt per capita (1987e): US$1,779
Principal export commodity (% of total 1985 exports): oil (90%)

Political system

Constitution: 1961. *Head of state/government:* President Jaime Lusinchi (AD) (1984–); elected to succeed Luis Herrera Campins (COPEI) (1979–84). The bicameral Congress, the president, and state and municipal legislative assemblies are elected every five years. Two senators are elected for every state and two for the federal district; some are also elected on the principle of minority representation. In addition, former

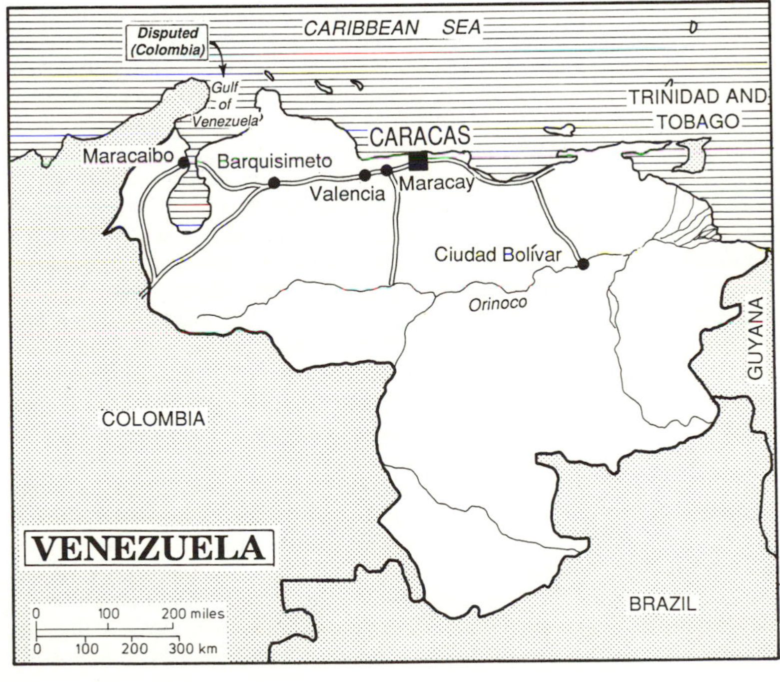

V

presidents are made senators for life. One deputy is elected for every 50,000 inhabitants, with a minimum of two for every state and one for the federal district. The most recent general elections were held in December 1983.

Political organisations

Parties (seats in Senate/Chamber of Deputies): Democratic Action/AD (27/109); Social Christian Party/COPEI (16/60); Movement towards Socialism/MAS (2/10); Democratic Republican Union/URD (2/8); National Opinion/OPINA (-/3); Movement of the Revolutionary Left/MIR (-/2); Communist Party/PCV (-/2); National Integration Movement/MIN (-/1); New Alternative/NA (-/1). *The following parties have no congressional representation:* People's Electoral Movement/MEP; Movement of National Integration/MIN; Socialist League/LS; Party of the Venezuelan Revolution/PRV; New Generation/NG; and National Rescue/RN.

Main labour organisation; Confederation of Venezuelan Workers/CTV. *Main employers' organisation:* Venezuelan Federation of Chambers and Associations of Commerce and Production/ FEDECAMARAS.

Venezuelan Communist Party (*Partido Comunista Venezolano*/PCV)

One of the first Marxist organisations in Venezuela was the *Partido Revolucionario Venezolano* (PRV), set up in 1926; the core membership of the PRV went on to found the *Partido Comunista Venezolano* in 1936. For its first 11 years the party operated in clandestinity, although during the presidency of Gen. Isaías Medina Angarita (1941–5) the government was well disposed towards it. In the September 1944 municipal elections the ruling *Partido Democrático Venezolano* (PDV) called on its members to vote for candidates of the *Unión Popular*, the PCV's legal front, in certain areas. The move was a local reflection of the alliance between the USSR, USA, and UK in the Second World War. The PCV was not legalised, however, until the 1945 coup by military officers and members of AD. It presented candidates in the October 1946 elections to a constituent assembly, winning two out of the 160 available seats and receiving a total of 50,000 votes or 3.6%. In the December 1947 presidential elections the PCV candidate Gustavo Machado came third. Following the installation of a new military regime in 1948, the PCV was again banned in May 1950, and its members suffered intense persecution during the dictatorship of Gen. Marcos Pérez Jiménez.

In January 1958, following the popular uprising which forced Pérez Jiménez to flee the country, the PCV was again made legal. In the December 1958 elections it supported Adm. Wolfgang Larrázabal (also backed by URD) who came second. The party obtained 6.2% of the congressional vote. In May 1962, under the Rómulo Betancourt presidency, the PCV was again banned, on the grounds that it was taking part in guerrilla activities against the government. In 1967 the PCV leadership decided to abandon armed struggle in favour of the creation of 'a broad popular movement for progressive democratic change'. At the same time the leadership expelled Douglas Bravo, a former member of the political bureau and the party's best known guerrilla commander, for refusing to accept the decision to lay down arms. In 1969 the PCV regained its legal status; in the December 1968 elections it had gained five deputies, standing in the name of *Unión para Avanzar* (UPA), a legal PCV front. As a result of the 1968 invasion of Czechosovakia and an internal polemic on the form of socialism to be established, an important group left the PCV in January 1971 to form the MAS. After the 1973 elections the number of PCV deputies fell to only two.

In November 1974 another group of dissidents, which had been demanding the 'democratisation' of the party, left to form a new group, *Vanguardia Unitaria* (Unity Vanguard). In 1978 the PCV presidential candidate received less than 1% of the vote; in the 1983 elections the party supported the *Nueva Alternativa* candidate, José Vicente Rangel, and again won two seats in the Chamber of Deputies.
See also **Bravo; Movement towards Socialism**.

Venezuelan Democratic Party (PDV): see **Venezuelan Communist Party**.

Venezuelan Revolutionary Organisation (ORVE): see **Democratic Action**.

Venezuelan Revolutionary Party (PRV): see **Venezuelan Communist Party**.

verticalismo: see **Peronism**.

Viaux, Roberto: see ***Tacnazo***.

Vicentistas: see **Gómez, Gen. Juan Vicente**.

Vidal, Paulo: see **Lula (Luis Inácio da Silva)**.

Videla, Gen. Jorge Rafael

b. 1925. Leader of the 1976 military coup in Argentina and president, 1976–81, during the period of violent repression known as the 'dirty war'. Promoted to general in 1971, he was chief of army general staff in 1973–5 and army commander in 1975–8. Videla was known to favour a major military onslaught against the guerrilla groups and other forms of opposition. He planned the coup against the administration of President Isabel Perón with care, taking power on 24 March 1976.

The new government, which took the name Process of National Reorganisation (PRN), sought to eliminate all opposition, reorganise the economy, and perpetuate military rule. The armed guerrilla organisations were defeated in a campaign of terror. Although Videla publicly expressed support for human rights he was later shown to have been fully responsible for the working of the repressive system. In 1978 Videla retired from active service, and therefore was made to leave the ruling junta. However, under the terms of an inter-force agreement he stayed on as president (subordinate to the junta) until early 1981.

After the return to civilian rule, when charges were brought against him for human rights violations, Gen. Videla refused to accept the authority of the civilian courts and continued to justify his role. In December 1985 the Federal Appeals Court found him guilty of involvement in 66 counts of murder and 93 of torture, among other crimes. He was stripped of military rank and sentenced to life imprisonment.
See also **dirty war; Massera; Process of National Reorganisation; Viola**.

Vieira, Gilberto: see **Communist Party of Colombia**.

Vildoso Calderón, Gen. Guido: see **Bolivian governments post-Bánzer**.

Villalba, Jóvito: see **Democratic Republican Union; Generation of 1928** (Venezuela); ***Punto Fijo***.

Villanueva, Armando: see **APRA**.

Villarroel, President Gualberto: see **Revolutionary Nationalist Movement**.

Viola, Gen. Roberto

b. 1924. Argentine army general prominent in the Process of National Reorganisation (PRN) military regime who became president in 1981. Promoted to general in 1971, Viola ascended to head of the 2nd Army Corps, 1975 and commander of the army and member of the ruling military junta in 1978–9. During the first period of the PRN he was a leader of the dominant military faction, known as the 'two Vs line' (after Gens Videla and Viola). Viola used his influence to support Videla against navy and air force criticism and from challenges from within the army. In September 1979 he quelled an ultra-right revolt in Córdoba led by Gen. Luciano Benjamín Menéndez. Viola supported 'dirty war' tactics against the guerrilla movements and the wider opposition.

Appointed to succeed Videla in April 1981, despite the misgivings of the other forces represented the junta, he sought a partial political liberalisation. But the new president fell victim to a growing economic crisis, factional in-fighting, and a destabilisation campaign led by the ambitious new army commander, Gen. Leopoldo Galtieri. Ill-health was cited by the junta as the reason for Viola's removal in December 1981, after less than nine months in office. But he later insisted he had been removed for essentially political reasons. After the return to civilian rule in 1983, Viola was placed on trial on human rights charges by the administration of Dr Raúl Alfonsín. In December 1985 he was found guilty and sentenced to 17 years' imprisonment.
See also **dirty war; Galtieri; Process of National Reorganisation; Videla**.

violencia, la ('the violence')

A period of bloody civil strife in Colombia, roughly from 1948 to 1958, which is estimated to have cost up to 200,000 lives in the first five years and a further 100,000 between 1953 and 1958. Although the symptoms were evident several years earlier, the assassination of reformist Liberal Party (PL) leader Jorge Eliécer Gaitán in 1948, together with the days of rioting which followed, is normally regarded as the trigger.

The violence took the form, superficially, of a rural civil war between supporters of the PL and those of the Conservative Party (PC). Large landowners used this as a cover to carry out large-scale evictions and killings of peasants, while bandits also took advantage of the chaos. Tens of thousands fled to city slums to escape. In power from 1949 to 1953 was President Laureano Gómez of the PC, an admirer of Hitler and Mussolini, who introduced a state of siege and systematically purged PL members from public life. Gómez was eventually overthrown in a military coup by Gen. Gustavo Rojas Pinilla, under whom the rate of killing subsided somewhat. The trauma of these years of sectarian strife, and the hostility of both the PC and the PL to Gen. Rojas, brought the two parties together, and after the fall of Rojas in 1957 they agreed on a 16-year period of power-sharing, known as the National Front.

See also ***Bogotazo;*** **Gaitán; Gómez, Laureano; National Front; Rojas Pinilla**.

Violeteros: see **Dynamo, The**.

War of the Pacific: see **Chaco War**.

War of the 1000 Days: see **Social Conservative Party**.

Workers' Federation of Chile (FOCh): see **Communist Party of Chile**.

Workers' Party (*Partido dos Trabalhadores*/PT)
A Brazilian left-wing labour party which emerged from the growing independent trade union movement in the late 1970s in the industrial districts of São Paulo (particularly in the factories of the 'ABC' neighbourhoods). The new unionism was characterised by a series of pathbreaking strikes led by Luis Inácio da Silva (Lula) in the engineering industry. Lula, the president of the metalworkers' federation, founded the PT in 1980 along with others such as Airton Soares and Jaco Bitar. Many of the party's leaders could trace their political roots back to the old Brazilian Trabalhista Party (PTB) under President Vargas. In 1981 ten PT leaders including Lula were sentenced to 2–3½ years in prison on charges of incitement to murder. The charges arose from speeches they had made at the funeral of a peasant leader shot by opponents of land reform. The authorities had claimed that the speeches were instrumental in a later revenge killing by peasants. Lula and four other co-defendants were acquitted in 1984. Although the PT does not describe itself as socialist or revolutionary, it does call for 'a society without exploiters and exploited'. The party is closely linked to the CUT (*Central Unica dos Trabalhadores*), a confederation of independent trade unions. See also **Lula (Luis Inâcio da Silva)**.

Workers' Politics (POLOP): see **guerrilla movements** (Brazil).

Workers' Revolutionary Action Front (FARO): see **Socialist Party** (Bolivia).

Workers' Self-Defence (ADO): see **Revolutionary Armed Forces of Colombia**.

Workers' Self-defence Movement (*Movimiento de Autodefensa Obrera*/MAO)
A Colombian armed left-wing movement which emerged publicly in September 1978, with a communique claiming responsibility for the

assassination (by the '14 September Commando') of former interior minister Rafael Pardo Buelvas. During Pardo's term of office more than a dozen (12–18) people had been killed by the security forces in response to the 14 September 1977 general strike. Two Jesuit priests, Jorge Arango and Luis Alberto Restrepo, spent six months in jail in 1979 accused of involvement in the murder, but were acquitted. MAO's leaders included: Armando López Suárez ('Coleta'), Oscar Mateus Puerto, Hector Fabio Abadía Rey, and Juan Bautista González. In late 1978 the organisation staged brief occupations of several Bogotá radio stations. Many leading members (including López and Mateus) were arrested in early 1979 and 1980, and eight received lengthy jail sentences for the Pardo murder. The organisation was again active by mid-1981 and rejected the government's November 1982 amnesty, but observed a ceasefire from 1 September 1984. Its current leader is Adelaida Abadía Rey.

Workers' Vanguard (VO): see **Democratic and Popular Union**.

Working People's Alliance (WPA)
A Guyanese opposition party. Founded in 1974 by several left-wing groups aiming to transcend the country's traditional politico-racial divisions, the WPA declared itself a political party in 1979. It was informally led by historian Walter Rodney until his assassination in June 1980, and thereafter by Rupert Roopnaraine and Eusi Kwayana. The party decided to take part in electoral politics after Burnham's death in August 1985, and Kwayana won its first parliamentary seat in the 1985 elections. See also **Rodney**.

World Confederation of Labour (WCL): see **CLAT**.

World Federation of Trade Unions (WFTU): see **CPUSTAL**.

Yeroví, Clemente: see **military governments (Ecuador/1961–79); Plaza Lasso.**

Ynsfran, Edgar: see ***py nandí.***

Yrigoyen, Hipólito

1851–1933. Founding member of Argentina's Radical Party (UCR), and president 1916–22 and 1928–30. Yrigoyen is regarded as the country's first twentieth-century mass political leader. In his early career he worked as a school teacher, lawyer, and police official. He campaigned against the Conservatives' use of electoral fraud to maintain the landowning oligarchy's control of the government. Yrigoyen developed the UCR's tactic of electoral abstention in protest of these unfair practices. In 1905 he led an unsuccessful uprising against the government. But he was subsequently able to persuade a new conservative president, Roque Sáenz Peña, of the need for electoral reform. The result was the 1912 Sáenz Peña law which provided for universal, compulsory, and secret male franchise. As a result of the law, the UCR won important provincial elections and then, with Yrigoyen as its candidate won the presidential elections of 1916.

His first presidency, in 1916–22, was marked by economic growth, due to the high prices obtained for Argentine exports during World War I. The development of the oil industry was begun, and a state-owned oil company, *Yacimientos Petrolíferos Fiscales* (YPF) was set up. But the administration was also marked by a crack-down on labour unrest, particularly during the 1919 *Semana Trágica* ('Tragic Week'), in which striking workers were repressed. A reform of higher education established university autonomy and gave students representation on governing bodies. In 1922 Yrigoyen was succeeded by Marcelo T. de Alvear who, although also a UCR member, was more conservative. Yrigoyen was again elected president in 1928, but faced growing economic difficulties in the context of the Great Depression. These played an important part in the 6 September 1930 coup against him by Gen. José Felix Uriburu. See also **Infamous Decade; Radical Party** (Argentina).

Z

Zumarán, Alberto: see **Blanco Party**.

List of entries by country

Argentina

Alfonsín, Dr Raúl
Angeloz, Eduardo César
Aramburu, Gen. Pedro Eugenio
ARGENTINA, Republic of
Argentine Communist Party
Argentine Revolution
Army–Union Pact
Austral
Azules and *Colorados*
Cámpora, Dr Héctor José
Conservatives
Cordobazo
descamisados
due obedience
Frondizi, Dr Arturo
Galtieri, Gen. Leopoldo Fortunato
General Confederation of Labour
The Hour of the People
Illia, Dr Arturo Umberto
Infamous Decade
Intransigent Party
Justicialist Liberation Front (FREJULI)
Lanusse, Gen. Alejandro Agustín
Liberals
Martínez de Hoz, José
Massera, Adm. Emilio
Menem, Carlos Saúl
Montoneros
Mothers of the Plaza de Mayo
Movement of Integration and Development (MID)
Onganía, Gen. Juan Carlos
Perón, Evita
Perón, Gen. Juan Domingo
Perón, Isabel
Peronism
Process of National Reorganisation (PRN)
Radical Party (UCR)
Revolutionary Workers' Party–People's Revolutionary Army (PRT-ERP)
Ubaldini, Saúl
Union of the Democratic Centre (UCD)
Videla, Gen. Jorge Rafael
Viola, Gen. Roberto
Yrigoyen, Gen. Hipólito

Bolivia

Bánzer Suárez, Gen. Hugo
BOLIVIA, Republic of
Bolivian Communist Party
Bolivian governments post-Bánzer
Bolivian Socialist Falange (FSB)
Christian Democrat Party (PDC)
COB
Democratic and Popular Union (UDP)
Guevara Arze, Wálter
Lechín Oquendo, Juan
Movement of the Revolutionary Left (MIR)
Nationalist Democratic Action (ADN)
National Liberation Army (ELN)
Party of the Revolutionary Left (PIR)
Paz Estenssoro, Víctor
Pulacayo, Thesis of

Revolutionary Nationalist Movement (MNR)
Revolutionary Party of the Nationalist Left (PRIN)
Siles Zuazo, Hernán
Socialist Party (PS)
Socialist Party–One (PS–1)
Torres González, Gen. Juan José
Túpaj Katari Indian Movement (MITKA)

Brazil

Action for National Liberation (ALN)
amnesty (1979)
Authoritarian Nationalists
BRAZIL, Federative Republic of
Brazilian Communist Party (PCB)
Brazilian Democratic Movement (MDB)
Brazilian Democratic Movement Party (PMDB)
Brazilian Economic Miracle
Brazilian Expeditionary Force (FEB)
Brizola, Leonel de Moura
cassações
Castello Branco, Gen. Humberto de Alençar
Communist Party of Brazil (PC do B)
coronelismo
Costa e Silva, Gen. Arthur da
Coup of 1964
Cruzado
Democratic Labour Party (PDT)
Democratic Social Party (PDS)
diretas já
distensão
Dutra, Gen. Eurico Gaspar
Estado Nôvo
Figueiredo, Gen. João Baptista de Oliveira
Garrastazu Medici, Gen. Emilio
Geisel, Gen. Ernesto
Goulart, João Belchior Marques
guerrilla movements
Guimarães, Ulysses
Institutional Acts
Integralism
Kubitschek de Oliveira, Juscelino
Lacerda, Carlos
Liberal Front Party (PFL)
Long March
Lula (Luis Inâcio da Silva)
Marighela, Carlos
MR–8
Nationalist Democratic Union (UDN)
National Renovating Alliance (ARENA)
Neves, Dr Tancredo Almeida
Old Republic
Peasant Leagues
pelegos
Quadros, Jânio da Silva
radical Church
saneamento
São Paulo revolt
Sarney, José
Social Democratic Party (PSD)
Superior War School
tenentes
Trabalhismo
Vargas, Dr Getulio Dorneles
Workers' Party (PT)

Chile

Alessandri Rodríguez, Jorge
Allende Gossens, Dr Salvador
CHILE, Republic of
Christian Democrat Party (PDC)
Christian Left (IC)
Corvalán Lepe
Democratic Alliance (AD)
Fatherland and Freedom
Frei Montalva, Eduardo
Gremialismo
Ibáñez del Campo, Col. Carlos
Letelier case
Manuel Rodríguez Patriotic Front (FPMR)
MAPU
momio
Movement of the Revolutionary Left (MIR)

National Agreement for a Transition to Full Democracy
National Civic Assembly
National Party (PN)
Party for Democracy
Party of National Renovation (PARENA)
Pinochet Ugarte, Gen. Augusto José Ramón
Popular Democratic Movement (MDP)
Popular Front
'*quemados*' case
Radical Party (PR)
Socialist Bloc
Socialist Party
Socialist Republic
Tacnazo
United Left (IU)

Colombia

ANAPO
Barco Vargas, Virgilio
Betancur Cuartas, Belisario
Bogotazo
COLOMBIA, Republic of
Communist Party of Colombia (PCC)
Communist Party of Colombia–Marxist–Leninist (PCC-ML)
Democratic Left Unity (UDI)
Gaitán, Jorge Eliécer
Gómez, Laureano
Independent and Revolutionary Workers' Movement (MOIR)
Liberal Party (PL)
Liberal Revolutionary Movement (MRL)
López Michelsen, Alfonso
M–19
Marquetalia
Movement of Workers, Students and Peasants (MOEC)
National Front
National Guerrilla Coordinating Body (CNG)
National Latin Movement (MLN)
National Liberation Army (ELN)
New Liberalism
Patriotic Union (UP)
People's Liberation Army (EPL)
Quintín Lame Movement
Revolutionary Armed Forces of Colombia (FARC)
Rojas Pinilla, Gen. Gustavo
Social Conservative Party (PSC)
Torres Restrepo, Camilo
Turbay Ayala, Dr Julio César
la violencia
Workers' Self-defence Movement (MAO)

Ecuador

Alfaro Lives!
Borja Cevallos, Rodrigo
Broad Left Front (FADI)
Bucaram, Assad
Communist Party of Ecuador (PCE)
Concentration of Popular Forces (CFP)
Conservative Party
Democratic Left (ID)
ECUADOR, Republic of
Ecuadorean Socialist Party (PSE)
Febres Cordero Rivadeneiro, León
Free Nation Montoneras
Hurtado Larrea, Dr Osvaldo
National Reconstruction Front (FRN)
Plaza Lasso, Galo
Popular Democracy (DP)
Progressive Front (FP)
Radical Alfarist Front (FRA)
Roldós Aguilera, Jaime
Social Christian Party (PSC)
Vargas Pazzos rebellion
Velasco Ibarra, José María
velasquismo

French Guiana

Bertrand, Léon
Castor, Elie
FRENCH GUIANA/GUYANE

Holder, Gérard
Plan Vert

Guyana

Burnham, Forbes
Green, Hamilton
GUYANA, Republic of
Hoyte, Desmond
Jagan, Cheddi
People's National Congress (PNC)
People's Progressive Party (PPP)
Rodney, Walter
Working People's Alliance (WPA)

Paraguay

Authentic Radical Liberal Party (PLRA)
Christian Democrat Party (PDC)
Colorado Party (ANR)
Febreristas
Franco, Col. Rafael
guerrilla invasions
Laíno, Dr Domingo
Liberal Party (PL)
Liberals
Morínigo, Gen. Higinio
National Accord
PARAGUAY, Republic of
Paraguayan Civil War
Paraguayan Communist Party
Politico-Military Organisation (OPM)
Popular Colorado Movement (MOPOCO)
py nandí
Radical Liberal Party (PLR)
Stroessner, Gen. Alfredo

Peru

APRA
Belaúnde Terry, Fernando
Blanco, Hugo
búfalo
Christian Democrat Party (PDC)
Democratic Convergence (CODE)
Democratic Front
Dynamo, The
García Pérez, Alán
Haya de la Torre, Víctor Raúl
Lurigancho massacre
Morales Bermúdez Cerruti, Gen. Francisco
Movement of the Revolutionary Left (MIR)
PERU, Republic of
Peruvian Communist Party (PCP)
Popular Action (AP)
Shining Path
Túpac Amaru Revolutionary Movement (MRTA)
Uchurracay incident
United Left (IU)
Velasco Alvarado, Gen. Juan
velasquismo

South America

abertura
Alliance for Progress
Amazon Pact
America Battalion
American Institute for Free Labor Development (AIFLD)
Andean Pact
Antarctic Treaty
Beagle Channel dispute
border dispute (Peru/Ecuador)
cacique
caudillo, caudillismo
Chaco War
Chicago Boys
cholo
Christian Democracy
CLAT
Communism
continuismo
CPUSTAL
cuartelazo
death squad
desaparecidos
dirty war
dollar diplomacy
Economic Commission for Latin America and the Caribbean (ECLAC)

Essequibo dispute
Falklands/Malvinas
foquismo
gamonal
good neighbour policy
gorilas
Gremialismo
Guevara da la Serna, Dr Ernesto Che
Gulf of Venezuela dispute
indigenismo
Inter-American Defense Board
Inter-American Development Bank
junta
ladino
latifundio
Latin American Bishops' Council (CELAM)
Latin American Economic System (SELA)
Latin American Energy Organisation (OLADE)
Latin American Integration Association (LAIA)
liberation theology
Lima Group
Medellín
Monroe doctrine
National Security doctrine
Non-Aligned Movement
ORIT
Organisation of American States (OAS)
personalismo
populism
Propaganda Due
Rio Treaty
salida al mar
salida electoral
San Andrés dispute
Socialist (2nd) International
South Atlantic War
state of siege
Tlatelolco Treaty
Trotskyism

Suriname

Arron, Henck
Bouterse, Col. Desi
Jungle Commando/Suriname National Liberation Army (SNLA)
Lachmon, Jaggernath
National Party of Suriname
Progressive Reform Party
Shankar, Ramsewak
SURINAME, Republic of

Uruguay

Alvarez, Gen. Gregorio
amnesty (1985, 1986)
autogolpe
Batllismo
Blanco Party
Bordaberry, Juan María
Broad Front
Club Naval Pact
collegiate executive
Colorado Party
Communist Party
coparticipación
Ferreira Aldunate, Wilson
Ley de Lemas
National Liberation Movement – Tupamaros
Pacheco Areco, Jorge
Proceso
Referendum of 1980
Sanguinetti, Julio María
Sendic, Raúl
Seregni, Gen. Líber
Terra, Dr Gabriel
URUGUAY, Oriental Republic of

Venezuela

Betancourt, Rómulo
Betancourt doctrine
Bravo, Douglas
Caldera, Rafael
Confederation of Venezuelan Workers (CTV)
COPEI
Delgado Chalbaud, Col. Carlos

Democratic Action (AD)
Democratic Republican Union (URD)
FLN/FALN
Gallegos, Rómulo
Generation of 1928
Generation of 1958
Gómez, Gen. Juan Vicente
guerrilla insurgency
Herrera Campins, Luis
Junta Patriótica
Leoni, Raúl
López Contreras, Gen. Eleázar
Lusinchi, Dr Jaime
Medina Angarita, Gen. Isaias
Movement of the Revolutionary Left (MIR)
Movement towards Socialism (MAS)
Nixon's visit
Nueva Alternativa
oil nationalisation
People's Electoral Movement (MEP)
Pérez, Carlos Andrés
Pérez Jiménez, Gen Marcos
el popularazo
Punto Fijo
Revolution of 1958
trienio
Unified Centre of Venezuelan Workers (CUTV)
VENEZUELA, Republic of
Venezuelan Communist Party